The Essential
Air Fryer Cookbook

Ultimate Air Fryer Recipes for Busy Beginners | Healthy and Delicious Homemade

Meals for Friends and Family | Incl. Meat Poultry Vegetable Desserts & More

Delois Townsend

© Copyright 2023 – All rights reserved.

The content contained within this book may not be reproduced, duplicated or transmitted without direct written permission from the author or the publisher.

Under no circumstances will any blame or legal responsibility be held against the publisher, or author, for any damages, reparation, or monetary loss due to the information contained within this book, either directly or indirectly.

Legal Notice:

This book is copyright protected. It is only for personal use. You cannot amend, distribute, sell, use, quote or paraphrase any part, or the content within this book, without the consent of the author or publisher.

Disclaimer Notice:

Please note the information contained within this document is for educational and entertainment purposes only. All effort has been executed to present accurate, up to date, reliable, complete information. No warranties of any kind are declared or implied. Readers acknowledge that the author is not engaged in the rendering of legal, financial, medical or professional advice. The content within this book has been derived from various sources. Please consult a licensed professional before attempting any techniques outlined in this book.

By reading this document, the reader agrees that under no circumstances is the author responsible for any losses, direct or indirect, that are incurred as a result of the use of the information contained within this document, including, but not limited to, errors, omissions, or inaccuracies.

Contents

1   Contents

1   Introduction

4   4 Weeks Meal Plan

6   Chapter 1 Breakfast Recipes

18   Chapter 2 Snacks and Appetizers Recipes

28   Chapter 3 Vegetables and Sides Recipes

40   Chapter 4 Fish and Seafood Recipes

52   Chapter 5 Poultry Mains Recipes

67   Chapter 6 Beef, Pork, and Lamb Recipes

80   Chapter 7 Dessert Recipes

90   Conclusion

91   Appendix 1 Measurement Conversion Chart

92   Appendix 2 Air Fryer Cooking Chart

93   Appendix 3 Recipes Index

Introduction

Welcome to the wonderful world of air fryer cooking!

An air fryer is a brilliant appliance – it allows you to cook delicious and healthy food without using a lot of oil or fat. People are busy and have no time for cooking delicious and healthy for their families. The air fryer makes your life easier and gives you mouthwatering and healthy food in very little time.

In this cookbook, you will find recipes that can be used with any brand and model of an air fryer. It is an efficient appliance and creates yummy and crispy food. The air fryer has seven cooking programs: Air crisp, Air fry, Air roast, Air broil, Reheat, Bake, Dehydrate, etc. The benefit of an air fryer cooking appliance is that it has a large capacity to cook food. You didn't need to cook food in batches.

The cleaning method of this kitchen appliance is pretty simple. It comes with useful accessories such as an air fryer basket, dehydrating tray, reversible rack, etc. With these cooking programs, you can cook delicious and crispy food on any occasion. Let's start air frying!

What Is an Air Fryer?

An air fryer is the best kitchen appliance that fits nicely on your kitchen countertop. The air fryer has seven useful cooking programs: Air crisp, Air fry, Air roast, Air broil, Reheat, Bake, Dehydrate, etc. It has user-friendly operating buttons: temperature arrows, time arrows, start/stop buttons, and power buttons. The air fryer comes with useful accessories such as a reversible rack, air fryer basket, dehydrating rack, etc. You can prepare food in very little time. This cooking appliance has a simple cleaning process. You can adjust the temperature and cooking time. Place food in the air fryer basket and insert it in the unit. Prepare any food such as poultry, beef, lamb, vegetable, pork, dessert, snacks, and breakfast meals. Choose your favorite recipe and start cooking with your favorite cooking function.

Benefits of Using Air Fryer

The benefits of using an air fryer are followings:

Cooking in Less Fat: or Oil:
Everyone wants to eat healthy food. The air fryer cooking appliance is the best choice for cooking healthy food. It can cook food in little-to-no oil and still enjoy satisfying and delicious food.

Easy and Versatile:
The process of using an air fryer is simple. The air fryer is a versatile cooking appliance. It has a user-friendly operating button. It is safe to use.

Time-saving Appliance:
An air fryer cooking appliance is a perfect way to cook food in very little time. Now, you don't need to cook for a lot of time. Air frying is the fastest cooking method to cook food faster.

Safe to Use:
Air frying is the safest cooking appliance in the world because there is no risk of the splatter of hot oil on your face. Place food in the basket and cover with a lid. Adjust temperature and cooking time.

Seven Cooking Programs in One Pot:
The air fryer has seven cooking programs: Air crisp, Air fry, Air roast, Air broil, Reheat, Bake, Dehydrate, etc. You didn't need to purchase an oven for baking, a dehydrator for dehydrating, and a broiler for broiling foods. You will get all the useful cooking functions in one pot.

Simple Cleaning Process:
Air frying has a simple cleaning process. Remove accessories from the main unit and rinse with soapy and warm water. Wipe the main unit with a soft cloth.

User-friendly Operating Buttons:
The air fryer has user-friendly operating buttons. The display shows a message on the screen. It will guide you while cooking. The cooking time will show on the screen. The power button is used to turn on/off the device.

Before First Use

Remove the main unit from the packaging. Remove all accessories from the package and rinse the ceramic-coated basket with warm and soapy water. Then, rinse and dry thoroughly. When all parts get dried, return to the main unit. Don't put the main unit in the dishwasher.

Step-By-Step Air Frying:
The air fryer has a simple method to use. Here, step-by-step method of using an air fryer:
Select Recipe:

I added air frying recipes in my cookbook. Pick up a recipe that you want to cook in your air fryer. You will find breakfast, dinner, lunch, snacks, and dessert recipes. Read the recipe two times before cooking.

Prepare the Air Fryer Unit:
Plug in the air fryer appliance in the outlet. Some recipes call for air fryer baskets, reversible racks, and dehydrate racks. For baking recipes, you should use muffins or cake pans. Insert the air fryer basket in the main unit.

Prepare the Ingredients:
Gather all ingredients according to the recipe instructions. When prepared, place ingredients in the air fryer basket, cake pan, rack, or pans. Then insert it in the main unit.

Use parchment baking paper or spray with oil to prevent food from sticking. Don't overfill the ingredients in the basket. Place all food ingredients in the basket. You didn't need to cook food in batches.

Adjust the Temperature and Time:

Adjust the cooking temperature and cooking time according to the recipe instructions. Most air fryers preset functions that make it easy to set according to each recipe.

Check Food During Cooking:

Many air fryer recipes need to check the food while it's cooking. Open the lid of the unit. Remove the air fryer basket. Flip the food and return the basket to the unit. The cooking time will resume while flipping the food.

Helpful Tips

For tender and browning food, make sure that the ingredients are arranged in one layer at the bottom of the basket.

Temperature and cooking time can be adjusted at any time during cooking. Press time and temperature arrows to adjust the cooking temperature and cooking time.

When cooking time is selected, press the start/stop button to start cooking immediately.

For perfect results, remove food immediately after the cooking time is complete to prevent overcooking.

The main unit will take three minutes for preheating.

Turn the cooking function to broiler and crisp the food to make the food crispy.

For perfect results with potatoes and vegetables, use 1 tbsp. of oil. Add more oil if desired.

Cleaning and Maintenance of Air Fryer

The unit should be cleaned after every use thoroughly.

Unplug the unit from the outlet before cleaning.

Remove all accessories from the main unit.

To clean the main unit and control panel, wipe them with a clean and moist cloth.

Place reversible rack, dehydrating rack, and air fryer basket in the dishwasher. Rinse them with warm and soapy water.

If food is stuck in the basket or rack, place it in the warm and soapy water overnight. The next day, rinse under clean water.

When all parts get dried, return to the main unit.

4-Week Diet Plan

Week 1

Day 1:
Breakfast: Creamy Broccoli Casserole
Lunch: Cheese Cauliflower Tots
Snack: Bacon Pickle Spear Rolls
Dinner: Pork Tenderloin with Bell Pepper
Dessert: Creamy Cheesecake Bites

Day 2:
Breakfast: Olives and Eggs Medley
Lunch: Beans and Sweet Potato Boats
Snack: Zucchini Chips with Cheese
Dinner: Awesome Duck with Potato Rösti
Dessert: Plum Almond Cake

Day 3:
Breakfast: Coconut Muffins with Cinnamon
Lunch: Herbed Potatoes Medley
Snack: Pickles with Egg Wash
Dinner: Fish Mania with Mustard
Dessert: Delicious Walnut Bars

Day 4:
Breakfast: Tomatoes Hash with Cheddar Cheese
Lunch: Turmeric Tofu Cubes
Snack: Coconut Granola with Almond
Dinner: Pork Meatloaf with Onion
Dessert: Vinegar Cake

Day 5:
Breakfast: Spinach Bacon Spread
Lunch: Turmeric Cauliflower Patties
Snack: Yogurt Bread
Dinner: Delectable Beef with Kale Pieces
Dessert: Almond Pudding

Day 6:
Breakfast: Coconut Veggie and Eggs Bake
Lunch: Tasty Sweet Potato Wedges
Snack: Parmesan Cauliflower Dip
Dinner: Typical Cod Nuggets
Dessert: Blackberries Cake

Day 7:
Breakfast: Simple Tomato Cheese Sandwich
Lunch: Herbed Mushroom Pilau
Snack: Garlic Mushroom Bites
Dinner: Creamy Turkey Sausage Cups
Dessert: Chia Cinnamon Pudding

Week 2

Day 1:
Breakfast: Mozzarella Eggs with Basil Pesto
Lunch: Creamy Garlic Bread
Snack: Air Fried Pork with Fennel
Dinner: Basic BBQ Chicken
Dessert: Divine Apple Pie

Day 2:
Breakfast: Classical Eggs Ramekins
Lunch: Pungent Mushroom Pizza
Snack: Roasted Nut Mixture
Dinner: Lemon Salmon Fillet
Dessert: Enticing Ricotta Cheese Cake

Day 3:
Breakfast: Enticing Scotch Eggs
Lunch: Garlicky Mushrooms with Parsley
Snack: Asparagus Pork Fries
Dinner: Spiced Rib Eye Steak
Dessert: Moist Cinnamon Muffins

Day 4:
Breakfast: Cheese Taquitos with Cilantro
Lunch: Creamy Cauliflower Puree
Snack: Juicy Beef Meatballs
Dinner: Grilled Curried Chicken Wings
Dessert: Vanilla Spread

Day 5:
Breakfast: Bacon Wrapped Eggs
Lunch: Crispy Spiced Asparagus
Snack: Air Fried Cheese Sticks
Dinner: Glazed Meatloaf
Dessert: Zucchini Bars with Cream Cheese

Day 6:
Breakfast: Zucchini Mix
Lunch: Lemon Cabbage with Cilantro
Snack: Delectable Fish Nuggets
Dinner: Savory Breaded Shrimp
Dessert: Yummy Apple Chips

Day 7:
Breakfast: Mushrooms Spread
Lunch: Parmesan Zucchini Gratin
Snack: Cinnamon Almonds
Dinner: Simple Lemon Chicken Thighs
Dessert: Cheese Cake with Strawberries

Week 3

Day 1:

Breakfast: Shrimp Rice Frittata
Lunch: Fried Brussel Sprouts
Snack: Smoked Almonds
Dinner: Breaded Salmon Patties
Dessert: Blueberry Vanilla Muffins

Day 2:

Breakfast: Cheddar Hash Brown
Lunch: Roasted Garlic Head
Snack: Cheesy Brussels sprouts
Dinner: Paprika Pork Chops
Dessert: Chocolate Lava Cake

Day 3:

Breakfast: Stuffed Poblanos
Lunch: Air Fried Artichokes
Snack: Chicken Bowls with Berries
Dinner: Spiced Lamb Kebabs
Dessert: Vanilla Pineapple Cinnamon Treat

Day 4:

Breakfast: Monkey Bread with Cinnamon
Lunch: Broccoli Salad
Snack: Easy-to-make Cheese Rounds
Dinner: Classical Greek Keftedes
Dessert: Almond Pecan Muffins

Day 5:

Breakfast: Raspberries Cinnamon Oatmeal
Lunch: Kale Olives Salad
Snack: Chicken Bites with Coconut
Dinner: Salmon Fillets
Dessert: Chocolate Peanut Butter Mug Cake

Day 6:

Breakfast: Tasty Spinach Frittata
Lunch: Air-Fried Eggplant
Snack: Air Fried Shrimp & Bacon
Dinner: Flank Steaks with Capers
Dessert: Lemon Creamy Muffins

Day 7:

Breakfast: Flavorful Cheesy Frittata
Lunch: Broccoli and Asparagus
Snack: Parmesan Steak Nuggets
Dinner: Mayo Shrimp
Dessert: Scones with Cream Cheese

Week 4

Day 1:

Breakfast: Simple Cherry Tarts
Lunch: Olives, Green beans and Bacon
Snack: Delicious Mushroom Pizzas
Dinner: Honey Turkey Tenderloin
Dessert: Cinnamon Butter Muffins

Day 2:

Breakfast: Creamy Eggs and Leeks
Lunch: Cajun Peppers
Snack: Coated Cauliflower
Dinner: Lemon Jumbo Scallops
Dessert: Spiced Apple Chips

Day 3:

Breakfast: Strawberries Coconut Oatmeal
Lunch: Mozzarella Spinach Mash
Snack: Pork Rinds with Keto Tomato Sauce
Dinner: Pork Chops with Soy Sauce
Dessert: Pumpkin Almond Flour Muffins

Day 4:

Breakfast: Tomatoes Chard Salad
Lunch: Creamy Cilantro Peppers Mix
Snack: Mouthwatering Squash Bites
Dinner: Old Bay Cod Fish Fillets
Dessert: Chocolate Banana Brownie

Day 5:

Breakfast: Canadian Bacon English Muffin
Lunch: Flavorful Radish Salad
Snack: Bacon with Chocolate Coating
Dinner: Crunchy Chicken Bites
Dessert: Almond Cherry Bars

Day 6:

Breakfast: Seasoned Cheese Sticks
Lunch: Coconut Brussels Sprouts
Snack: Enticing Jalapeno Poppers
Dinner: Spiced Pork Chops
Dessert: Fluffy Cocoa Cupcakes

Day 7:

Breakfast: Banana Cinnamon Bread
Lunch: Zucchini and Potato Polenta
Snack: Mild Shishito Peppers
Dinner: Garlic Beef Cubes
Dessert: Butter Cheesecake

Chapter 1 Breakfast Recipes

Zucchini Fritters	7	Dijon Chicken	12
Yogurt Eggs with Chives	7	Fish Tacos	12
Scrambled Eggs with Spinach	7	Chicken Vegetable Omelet	12
Creamy Broccoli Omelet	7	Herbed Potatoes with Bacon	13
Cheddar Bacon Frittata	7	Zucchini Mix	13
Banana-Pecan French Toast	7	Hard-Boiled Eggs	13
Mozzarella Eggs with Basil Pesto	7	Mushroom Salad	13
Coconut Veggie and Eggs Bake	7	Scrambled Eggs	13
Creamy Baked Sausage	8	Morning Frittata	13
Paprika Zucchini Spread	8	Strawberries Coconut Oatmeal	13
Creamy Broccoli Casserole	8	Asparagus Arugula Salad	13
Yummy Bagel Breakfast	8	Raspberries Bowls	13
Kale and Eggplant Omelet	8	Squash Fritters	13
Crispy Fish Sticks	8	Mushrooms Spread	14
Turkey Casserole with Cheddar Cheese	8	Tuna Onions Salad	14
Simple Tomato Cheese Sandwich	8	Cinnamon Pudding	14
Hot Egg Cups	9	Tomatoes Chard Salad	14
Sausage and Potato Frittata	9	Egg Cheese Roll Ups	14
Baked Eggs with Mascarpone	9	Ham Egg Cups	14
Olives and Eggs Medley	9	Olives Kale Salad	14
Fried Bacon with Pork Rinds	9	Raspberries Cinnamon Oatmeal	14
Simple Eggplant Spread	9	Scotch Eggs	14
Baked Eggs	9	Simple Strawberry Toast	15
Flavorful Cheesy Frittata	9	Stuffed Poblanos	15
Classical Eggs Ramekins	9	Sweet-Potato Chips	15
Mozzarella Chicken and Pork Muffins	10	Quiche Cups	15
Herbed Omelet	10	Ham Omelet	15
Coconut Muffins with Cinnamon	10	Canadian Bacon English Muffin	15
Creamy Broccoli Florets with Eggs	10	Asparagus Egg Strata	15
Simple Cherry Tarts	10	Shrimp Rice Frittata	15
Baked Parmesan Eggs with Kielbasa	10	Monkey Bread with Cinnamon	16
Cinnamon French Toast	10	Ham Cup	16
Tomatoes Hash with Cheddar Cheese	10	Seasoned Cheese Sticks	16
Avocado Parsley Omelet	11	Onion Omelet	16
Egg Peppers Cups	11	Shirred Eggs	16
Enticing Scotch Eggs	11	Cheddar Hash Brown	16
Bacon Muffins	11	Sunflower Bread	16
Classical French Frittata	11	Pesto Gnocchi	16
Spinach Bacon Spread	11	Avocado Cabbage Salad	16
Tasty Spinach Frittata	11	Banana Cinnamon Bread	17
Mozzarella Rolls	11	Creamy Bread	17
Parmesan Spinach Muffins	11	Broccoli Quiche	17
Grilled Butter Sandwich	12	Walnut Banana Bread	17
Cheese Taquitos with Cilantro	12	Walnut Zucchini Bread	17
Garlic Chicken Strips	12	Chocolate Bread	17
Creamy Eggs and Leeks	12	Cauliflower Rice	17
Cheddar Peppers	12		
Bacon Wrapped Eggs	12		

Zucchini Fritters

Prep Time: 10 minutes | Cook time: 8 minutes | Serves: 4

2 zucchinis, grated
3 tablespoons almond flour
1 medium egg, beaten
¼ teaspoon salt
¼ teaspoon ground black pepper
¼ teaspoon minced garlic
1 tablespoon spring onions, chopped
¼ teaspoon chili flakes

1. In a bowl, add the grated zucchinis and the almond flour. 2. Then place in the salt, ground black pepper, minced garlic, chili flakes, green peas, and egg. 3. Using a fork stir together the ingredients until homogenous. 4. Before cooking, heat your air fryer to 365 degrees F/ 185 degrees C. 5. To make the fritters, put the mixture on the baking paper with a spoon. 6. Transfer into the preheated air fryer and cook for 8 minutes. Halfway through cooking, flip the fritters to the other side. 7. Serve.
Per serving: Calories: 64; Fat: 3.8g; Sodium: 175mg; Total Carbs: 4g; Net Carbs: 2g; Fiber: 1.7g; Sugars: 1.8g; Protein: 3.8g

Yogurt Eggs with Chives

Prep Time: 5 minutes | Cook time: 20 minutes | Serves: 4

Cooking spray
Salt and black pepper to the taste
1 ½ cups Greek yogurt
4 eggs, whisked
1 tablespoon chives, chopped
1 tablespoon cilantro, chopped

1. Mix the Greek yogurt, eggs, chives, salt, and black pepper in a bowl, and whisk well. Using the cooking spray, grease a suitable pan that fits the air fryer. 2. Pour in the egg mixture evenly on the pan. 3. Transfer the pan to the air fryer and cook inside at 360 degrees F/ 180 degrees C for 20 minutes. When cooked, divide the omelet and serve on plates. 4. Enjoy your breakfast!
Per serving: Calories: 101; Fat: 5.4g; Sodium: 78mg; Total Carbs: 2g; Net Carbs: 0.5g; Fiber: 0g; Sugars: 2.4g; Protein: 10.6g

Scrambled Eggs with Spinach

Prep Time: 5 minutes | Cook time: 20 minutes | Serves: 4

1 tablespoon olive oil
½ teaspoon smoked paprika
12 eggs, whisked
3 cups baby spinach
Salt and black pepper to the taste

1. Mix together smoked paprika, eggs, spinach, salt, and pepper in a bowl until whisk well. 2. Grease a suitable pan that fits in your air fryer. 3. Transfer inside the air fryer and preheat your air fryer to 360 degrees F/ 180 degrees C. 4. When it has preheated, mix the spinach mix and eggs in the pan. 5. Close the air fryer and cook for 20 minutes. 6. Serve on plates.
Per serving: Calories: 225; Fat: 16.7g; Sodium: 203mg; Total Carbs: 2g; Net Carbs: 0.5g; Fiber: 0.6g; Sugars: 1.1g; Protein: 17.3g

Creamy Broccoli Omelet

Prep Time: 10 minutes | Cook time: 14 minutes | Serves: 4

4 eggs, beaten
1 tablespoon cream cheese
½ teaspoon chili flakes
½ cup broccoli florets, chopped
¼ teaspoon salt
¼ cup heavy cream
¼ teaspoon white pepper
Cooking spray

1. In a large bowl, place the beaten eggs, salt, white pepper, and chili flakes. 2. With a hand whisker, stir together until the salt is dissolved. 3. Place the heavy cream and cream cheese in the bowl and again stir until homogenous. 4. Then add the broccoli florets. 5. Before cooking, heat your air fryer to 375 degrees F/ 190 degrees C. 6. Using cooking spray, spray the air fryer basket from inside. 7. Pour in the egg liquid and cook in the air fryer for 14 minutes.
Per serving: Calories: 102; Fat: 8.1g; Sodium: 223mg; Total Carbs: 1.5g; Net Carbs: 1g; Fiber: 0.3g; Sugars: 0.6g; Protein: 6.2g

Cheddar Bacon Frittata

Prep Time: 8-10 minutes | Cook time: 15 minutes | Serves: 2

¼ cup green bell pepper, seeded and chopped
1 tablespoon olive oil
¼ cup spinach, chopped
2 bacon slices, chopped
4-6 cherry tomatoes, make halves
3 large eggs
¼ cup cheddar cheese, shredded

1. On a flat kitchen surface, plug your air fryer and turn it on. 2. Preheat your air fryer for about 4-5 minutes to 360 degrees F/ 180 degrees C. 3. Gently coat your air frying basket with cooking oil or spray. 4. In a medium sized bowl, mix the tomatoes, bell pepper, and bacon thoroughly. 5. Place into the basket. 6. Transfer the basket in the air fryer. Let it cook for the next 8 minutes. 7. Mix thoroughly the spinach, cheese, and eggs in a medium sized bowl. 8. Remove the basket; Mix them together and cook for 8 more minutes. 9. Serve warm!
Per serving: Calories: 377; Fat: 27.6g; Sodium: 647mg; Total Carbs: 11g; Net Carbs: 6.7g; Fiber: 3.2g; Sugars: 7.9g; Protein: 22.4g

Banana-Pecan French Toast

Prep Time: 15 minutes | Cook time: 10 minutes | Serves: 8

8 slices of whole-grain bread
¾ cup of any milk you like
1 sliced banana
1 cup of rolled oats
1 cup of pecan, chopped
2 tablespoons of ground flax seeds
1 teaspoon of cinnamon

1. At 350 degrees F/ 175 degrees C, preheat your air fryer. 2. Mix nuts, cinnamon, oats, and flax seeds into a food processor and pulse until crumbly. 3. Pour milk into a deep and wide bowl. 4. Soak 1–2 pieces of bread for almost 15-30 seconds per side. 5. Transfer the soaked bread pieces to the oats mixture and cover with it from per side. 6. Set the prepared soak bread slices into the air fryer basket in 1 layer. 7. Cook them at 350 degrees F/ 175 degrees C for 3 minutes, flip, and continue cooking for 3 more minutes. 8. Repeat the same steps with the remaining bread slices. 9. Serve with maple syrup and banana slices. 10. Enjoy your Banana-Nut French Toast!
Per serving: Calories: 206; Fat: 5.2g; Sodium: 192mg; Total Carbs: 31g; Net Carbs: 15g; Fiber: 5.5g; Sugars: 6.1g; Protein: 8.5g

Mozzarella Eggs with Basil Pesto

Prep Time: 5 minutes | Cook time: 20 minutes | Serves: 4

2 tablespoons butter, melted
6 teaspoons basil pesto
1 cup mozzarella cheese, grated
6 eggs, whisked
1 tablespoons basil, chopped
A pinch of salt and black pepper

1. Before cooking, heat your air fryer to 360 degrees F/ 180 degrees C. 2. Mix the basil pesto, mozzarella cheese, the whisked egg, basil, salt, and black pepper together in a bowl. Whisk. 3. Drizzle the baking pan with butter and then add the mixture. 4. Cook in your air fryer at 360 degrees F/ 180 degrees C for 20 minutes. 5. When the cooking time is up, transfer from the air fryer and serve on plates. 6. Enjoy your breakfast.
Per serving: Calories: 166; Fat: 13.6g; Sodium: 176mg; Total Carbs: 0.8g; Net Carbs: 1g; Fiber: 0g; Sugars: 0.5g; Protein: 10.4g

Coconut Veggie and Eggs Bake

Prep Time: 5 minutes | Cook time: 30 minutes | Serves: 6

Cooking spray
2 cups green and red bell pepper, chopped
2 spring onions, chopped
1 teaspoon thyme, chopped
Salt and black pepper to the taste
1 cup coconut cream
4 eggs, whisked
1 cup cheddar cheese, grated

1. Place all the ingredients except the cooking spray and cheese in a mixing bowl and mix up to combine. 2. Using the cooking spray to grease a suitable pan. 3. Pour the eggs mixture and bell peppers evenly on your pan. 4. Sprinkle the top with the cheese. 5. Transfer the pan inside your air fryer and close the air fryer. 6. Cook the coconut veggie and eggs bake at 350 degrees F/ 175 degrees C for 30 minutes. 7. When cooked, transfer onto plates and serve for breakfast.
Per serving: Calories: 212; Fat: 18.7g; Sodium: 165mg; Total Carbs: 3g; Net Carbs: 1g; Fiber: 1.1g; Sugars: 1.8g; Protein: 9.4g

Creamy Baked Sausage

Prep Time: 15 minutes | Cook time: 23 minutes | Serves: 6

2 jalapeno peppers, sliced
7 ounces ground sausages
1 teaspoon dill seeds
3 ounces Colby Jack Cheese, shredded

4 eggs, beaten
1 tablespoon cream cheese
½ teaspoon salt
1 teaspoon butter, softened
1 teaspoon olive oil

1. Before cooking, heat your skillet and then pour the olive oil inside the skillet. 2. Place salt and ground sausage in the skillet and cook for 5 to 8 minutes on medium heat. 3. During cooking, stir the mixture from time to time. 4. At the same time, heat your air fryer ahead of time to 400 degrees F/ 205 degrees C. 5. Using softened butter, grease your air fryer basket. 6. Transfer the cooked sausage inside the greased basket and flatten the mixture. 7. Sprinkle the sliced jalapeno pepper on the top of the mixture. 8. Then add shredded cheese. 9. In a second bowl, beat the eggs together and mix together with cream cheese. 10. Pour the egg-cheese mixture over the sausage mixture. 11. Sprinkle with dill seeds. 12. Cook the egg-cheese mixture in your air fryer at 400 degrees F/ 205 degrees C for 16 minutes. 13. If prefer a crunchy crust, cook for a few more minutes.
Per serving: Calories: 230; Fat: 18.9g; Sodium: 705mg; Total Carbs: 1g; Net Carbs: 0g; Fiber: 0.3g; Sugars: 0.4g; Protein 13.4g

Paprika Zucchini Spread

Prep Time: 5 minutes | Cook time: 15 minutes | Serves: 4

4 zucchinis, roughly chopped
1 tablespoon sweet paprika

Salt and black pepper to the taste
1 tablespoon butter, melted

1. Using butter, brush the bottom of a suitable baking pan. 2. Then add the rest ingredients in the baking pan. 3. Cook in your air fryer at 360 degrees F/ 180 degrees C for 15 minutes. 4. Transfer the cooked mixture to a blender and pulse well. 5. Serve into bowls and enjoy your breakfast.
Per serving: Calories: 62; Fat: 3.5g; Sodium: 41mg; Total Carbs: 7.5g; Net Carbs: 2.5g; Fiber: 2.8g; Sugars: 3.6g; Protein: 2.7g

Creamy Broccoli Casserole

Prep Time: 5 minutes | Cook time: 25 minutes | Serves: 4

1 broccoli head, florets separated and roughly chopped
2 ounces cheddar cheese, grated
4 eggs, whisked

1 cup almond milk
2 teaspoons cilantro, chopped
Salt and black pepper to the taste

1. Mix milk, chopped cilantro, salt, pepper, and whisked eggs together. 2. Dip the chopped broccoli in the egg mixture and spread in the air fryer pan and sprinkle with the cheddar cheese. 3. Cook in your air fryer at 350 degrees F/ 175 degrees C for 25 minutes. 4. When it has cooked, transfer from the air fryer and serve in plates. 5. Enjoy your breakfast.
Per serving: Calories: 266; Fat: 23.5g; Sodium: 166mg; Total Carbs: 5g; Net Carbs: 2g; Fiber: 1.9g; Sugars: 2.8g; Protein: 11.1g

Yummy Bagel Breakfast

Prep Time: 8-10 minutes | Cook time: 6 minutes | Serves: 5-6

2 bagels, make halves

4 teaspoons butter

1. On a flat kitchen surface, plug your air fryer and turn it on. 2. Preheat your air fryer for about 4-5 minutes to 370 degrees F/ 185 degrees C. 3. Gently coat your air frying basket with cooking oil or spray. 4. Place the bagels to the basket. 5. Transfer the basket in the air fryer. Let it cook for the next 3 minutes. 6. Remove the basket; spread the butter over the bagels and cook for 3 more minutes. 7. Serve warm!
Per serving: Calories: 112; Fat: 3.1g; Sodium: 175mg; Total Carbs: 17g; Net Carbs: 8g; Fiber: 0.8g; Sugars: 1.8g; Protein: 3.5g

Kale and Eggplant Omelet

Prep Time: 10 minutes | Cook time: 20 minutes | Serves: 4

1 eggplant, cubed
4 eggs, whisked
2 teaspoons cilantro, chopped

Salt and black pepper to the taste
½ teaspoon Italian seasoning
Cooking spray

½ cup kale, chopped
2 tablespoons cheddar, grated

2 tablespoons fresh basil, chopped

1. Place all the ingredients except the cooking spray in a bowl. 2. Using the cooking spray, coat a suitable pan. 3. Pour in the eggs mix and spread to cook evenly. 4. Put the pan inside your air fryer and cook at 370 degrees F/ 185 degrees C for 20 minutes. 5. When cooked, serve on plates. 6. Enjoy your breakfast!
Per serving: Calories: 105; Fat: 5.2g; Sodium: 89mg; Total Carbs: 8.1g; Net Carbs: 1g; Fiber: 4.2g; Sugars: 3.9g; Protein: 7.8g

Crispy Fish Sticks

Prep Time: 15 minutes | Cook time: 10 minutes | Serves: 4

8 ounces cod fillet
1 egg, beaten
¼ cup coconut flour
¼ teaspoon ground coriander
¼ teaspoon ground paprika
¼ teaspoon ground cumin

¼ teaspoon Pink salt
⅓ cup coconut flakes
1 tablespoon mascarpone
1 teaspoon heavy cream
Cooking spray

1. Roughly chop the cod fillet. Then transfer into a blender. 2. Place in coconut flour, paprika, cumin, egg, salt, and ground coriander. Then mix the mixture together until smooth. 3. Then place the mixture into a bowl. 4. Place the fish mixture onto lined parchment paper and then shape into flat square. 5. Cut the square into sticks. 6. Whisk mascarpone and heavy cream together in a separate bowl. 7. Sprinkle the fish sticks with the mascarpone mixture and coat with coconut flakes. 8. At 400 degrees F/ 205 degrees C, heat your air fryer in advance. 9. Using cooking spray, spray the air fryer basket. 10. Place the fish sticks evenly inside the air fryer basket. 11. Cook the fish sticks in the preheated air fryer for 10 minutes. 12. Halfway through cooking, flip the fish sticks to the other side. 13. When cooked, remove from the air fryer and serve with your favorite dip.
Per serving: Calories: 295; Fat: 5.4g; Sodium: 456mg; Total Carbs: 40g; Net Carbs: 21g; Fiber: 3.1g; Sugars: 0.5g; Protein: 22.2g

Turkey Casserole with Cheddar Cheese

Prep Time: 5 minutes | Cook time: 25 minutes | Serves: 4

4 turkey breast, skinless, boneless, cut into strips and browned
2 teaspoons olive oil
2 cups almond milk

2 cups cheddar cheese, shredded
2 eggs, whisked
Salt and black pepper to the taste
1 tablespoon chives, chopped

1. Mix the milk, cheese, pepper, salt, chives, and the eggs in a mixing bowl. 2. Gently grease a baking pan that fits in your air fryer. 3. Before cooking, heat your air fryer with the baking pan to 330 degrees F/ 165 degrees C. 4. Add the turkey pieces onto the baking pan. Spread flat on the baking pan. 5. Pour in the egg mixture and toss for a while. 6. Cook in the preheated air fryer for 25 minutes. 7. Serve immediately and enjoy your breakfast.
Per serving: Calories: 577; Fat: 52.2g; Sodium: 613mg; Total Carbs: 8.5g; Net Carbs: 1g; Fiber: 2.8g; Sugars: 5.2g; Protein: 23.2g

Simple Tomato Cheese Sandwich

Prep Time: 8-10 minutes | Cook time: 6 minutes | Serves: 2

8 tomato slices
4 bread slices
2 Swiss cheese slices

Black pepper and salt as needed
4 teaspoons margarine

1. On a flat kitchen surface, plug your air fryer and turn it on. 2. Preheat your air fryer for about 4-5 minutes to 355 degrees F/ 180 degrees C. 3. Gently coat an air frying basket with cooking oil or spray. 4. In the basket, place one cheese slice over one bread slice. 5. Then add 2 tomato slices on top. Sprinkle with salt and pepper. Top with another bread slice. 6. Insert the basket inside the air fryer. Let it cook for about 5 minutes. 7. Remove the basket; spread 2 teaspoons of margarine on both sides of each sandwich. Cook for about one more minute. 8. Serve warm!
Per serving: Calories: 116; Fat: 8g; Sodium: 134mg; Total Carbs: 6.5g; Net Carbs: 1g; Fiber: 0.6g; Sugars: 1.4g; Protein: 4.8g

Hot Egg Cups

Prep Time: 10 minutes | Cook time: 3 minutes | Serves: 6

6 eggs, beaten
2 jalapenos, sliced
2 ounces' bacon, chopped, cooked

½ teaspoon salt
½ teaspoon chili powder
Cooking spray

1. Spray cooking spray onto the inside of the silicone egg molds. 2. Mix up sliced jalapeno, bacon, beaten eggs, chili powder, and salt in the mixing bowl. 3. Gently whisk together the liquid and pour into the egg molds. 4. Before cooking, heat your air fryer to 400 degrees F/ 205 degrees C. 5. Place the egg cups inside the air fryer and close the air fryer. 6. Cook in your air fryer for 3 minutes. 7. Then cool the cooked cups for 2-3 minutes. 8. Remove from the silicone molds and serve.
Per serving: Calories: 99; Fat: 7.1g; Sodium: 404mg; Total Carbs: 0.8g; Net Carbs: 0g; Fiber: 0.2g; Sugars: 0.5g; Protein: 8g

Sausage and Potato Frittata

Prep Time: 8-10 minutes | Cook time: 10 minutes | Serves: 2

½ cup frozen corn
1 large potato, boiled, peeled, and cubed
3 jumbo eggs
1 tablespoon olive oil
½ of chorizo sausage, sliced

2 tablespoons feta cheese, crumbled
1 tablespoon fresh parsley, chopped
Pepper and salt as needed

1. On a flat kitchen surface, plug your air fryer and turn it on. 2. Preheat your air fryer for about 4-5 minutes to 355 degrees F/ 180 degrees C. 3. Gently coat your air frying basket with cooking oil or spray. Place the potato, sausage, and corn in the air fryer and cook till golden brown for 5-6 minutes. 4. Whisk in salt, pepper, and eggs in a medium sized bowl. 5. Toss the sausage mixture with the egg mixture. 6. Sprinkle with parsley and cheese. Continue cooking for 5 minutes. 7. Remove the sausage and potato frittata from the air fryer and serve warm.
Per serving: Calories: 366; Fat: 17.1g; Sodium: 239mg; Total Carbs: 40.5g; Net Carbs: 0g; Fiber: 5.2g; Sugars: 3.6g; Protein: 15.3g

Baked Eggs with Mascarpone

Prep Time: 10 minutes | Cook time: 3 minutes | Serves: 2

2 eggs
1 teaspoon mascarpone
¼ teaspoon ground nutmeg
¼ teaspoon dried basil
¼ teaspoon dried oregano

¼ teaspoon dried cilantro
¼ teaspoon ground turmeric
¼ teaspoon onion powder
¼ teaspoon salt

1. In a mixing bowl, whisk in the eggs. 2. Stir with mascarpone until homogenous. 3. Then add all spices and gently mix up the liquid. 4. Pour the liquid into the silicone egg molds. 5. Place on the air fryer basket. 6. Cook the baked eggs with mascarpone in your air fryer at 400 degrees F/ 205 degrees C for 3 minutes.
Per serving: Calories: 72; Fat: 4.9g; Sodium: 355mg; Total Carbs: 1g; Net Carbs: 0g; Fiber: 0.2g; Sugars: 0.6g; Protein: 5.9g

Olives and Eggs Medley

Prep Time: 5 minutes | Cook time: 20 minutes | Serves: 4

2 cups black olives, pitted and chopped
4 eggs, whisked
¼ teaspoon sweet paprika

1 tablespoon cilantro, chopped
½ cup cheddar, shredded
A pinch of salt and black pepper
Cooking spray

1. Add the olives into the beaten egg in a bowl and mix together all the ingredients except the cooking spray. 2. At 350 degrees F/ 175 degrees C, heat your air fryer in advance. 3. Grease your baking pan with the cooking spray. 4. Pour the olive-egg mixture evenly in the pan. 5. Transfer the pan inside your air fryer and cook for 20 minutes. 6. Serve the medley on plates. Enjoy your breakfast.
Per serving: Calories: 165; Fat: 12.6g; Sodium: 734mg; Total Carbs: 4g; Net Carbs: 2g; Fiber: 2.2g; Sugars: 0.4g; Protein: 9.6g

Fried Bacon with Pork Rinds

Prep Time: 10 minutes | Cook time: 12 minutes | Serves: 4

10 ounces bacon
3 ounces pork rinds
2 eggs, beaten

½ teaspoon salt
½ teaspoon ground black pepper
Cooking spray

1. Before cooking, heat your air fryer to 395 degrees F/ 200 degrees C. 2. Spritz the cooking spray over an air fryer basket. 3. While the air fryer is preheating, cut the bacon into 4 cubes and season with salt and ground black pepper. 4. Then dip the bacon in the beaten egg and coat in the pork rinds. 5. Transfer to the greased basket. 6. Cook the fried bacon with pork rinds in the air fryer for 12 minutes and flip to the other side halfway through cooking. Cook for one or a few more minutes if necessary until it is light brown. 7. When cooked, transfer from the air fryer and serve.
Per serving: Calories: 411; Fat: 29.6g; Sodium: 1829mg; Total Carbs: 1g; Net Carbs: 0g; Fiber: 0.1g; Sugars: 0.2g; Protein: 34.1g

Simple Eggplant Spread

Prep Time: 5 minutes | Cook time: 20 minutes | Serves: 4

3 eggplants
Salt and black pepper, to taste
2 tablespoons chives, chopped

2 tablespoons olive oil
2 teaspoons sweet paprika

1. In the air fryer basket, place the eggplants. 2. Cook in your air fryer at 380 degrees F/ 195 degrees C for 20 minutes. 3. Then peel the eggplants. Place the peeled eggplants in a blender. 4. Add the remaining ingredients in the blender. 5. When it had pulsed well, remove from the blender and serve in bowls. 6. Enjoy your breakfast.
Per serving: Calories: 166; Fat: 7.9g; Sodium: 9mg; Total Carbs: 24g; Net Carbs: 13.5g; Fiber: 15g; Sugars: 12.5g; Protein: 4.2g

Baked Eggs

Prep Time: 10 minutes | Cook time: 10 minutes | Serves: 3

3 eggs
½ teaspoon ground turmeric
¼ teaspoon salt

3 bacon slices
1 teaspoon butter, melted

1. Using the ½ teaspoon of melted butter, grease the silicone muffin molds. 2. Place the bacon slices on the molds, shaped into circles. 3. Before cooking, heat your air fryer to 400 degrees F/ 205 degrees C. 4. Cook the bacon inside the preheated air fryer for 7 minutes. 5. When cooked, with the remaining butter brush the center of the muffins. 6. Then crack in eggs in every bacon circles. 7. To season, sprinkle with ground turmeric and salt. 8. Cook again in your air fryer for 3 minutes or more.
Per serving: Calories: 178; Fat: 13.6g; Sodium: 703mg; Total Carbs: 0.9g; Net Carbs: 0g; Fiber: 0.1g; Sugars: 0.4g; Protein: 12.6g

Flavorful Cheesy Frittata

Prep Time: 10 minutes | Cook time: 20 minutes | Serves: 6

1 cup almond milk
Cooking spray
9 ounces cream cheese, soft
1 cup cheddar cheese, shredded

6 spring onions, chopped
Salt and black pepper to the taste
6 eggs, whisked

1. Grease the baking pan with cooking spray. 2. At 350 degrees F/ 175 degrees C, heat your air fryer in advance. 3. Mix together eggs with the rest ingredients. 4. Pour them together into the baking pan and cook in your air fryer for 20 minutes. 5. When cooked, remove from the air fryer and serve on plates.
Per serving: Calories: 303; Fat: 26g; Sodium: 330mg; Total Carbs: 4g; Net Carbs: 2g; Fiber: 0.4g; Sugars: 1.9g; Protein: 13.9g

Classical Eggs Ramekins

Prep Time: 5 minutes | Cook time: 6 minutes | Serves: 5

5 eggs
1 teaspoon coconut oil, melted

¼ teaspoon ground black pepper

1. Using coconut oil, grease the ramekins and whisk in eggs. 2. Sprinkle on the top with ground black pepper. 3. Then place in your air fryer and cook at 355 degrees F/ 180 degrees C for 6 minutes.
Per serving: Calories: 89; Fat: 6.6g; Sodium: 77mg; Total Carbs: 0.5g; Net Carbs: 0g; Fiber: 0g; Sugars: 0.4g; Protein: 6.9g

Mozzarella Chicken and Pork Muffins

Prep Time: 10 minutes | Cook time: 10 minutes | Serves: 6

1 cup ground chicken
1 cup ground pork
½ cup Mozzarella, shredded
1 teaspoon dried oregano
½ teaspoon salt
1 teaspoon ground paprika

½ teaspoon white pepper
1 tablespoon ghee, melted
1 teaspoon dried dill
2 tablespoons almond flour
1 egg, beaten

1. Mix together ground pork, ground chicken, salt, ground paprika, dried dill, white pepper, egg, dried oregano, and almond flour in a medium bowl until homogenous. Then add half the Mozzarella and using a spoon gently mix up the mixture. 2. Then brush the silicone muffin molds with melted ghee. 3. Place the meat mixture inside the molds, using a spoon to flatten. 4. Sprinkle the top with the remaining Mozzarella. 5. Before cooking, heat your air fryer to 375 degrees F/ 190 degrees C. 6. Place the muffin molds on the rack of your air fryer. Cook the mozzarella chicken and pork muffins in the air fryer for 10 minutes. 7. Serve the muffins at room temperature.
Per serving: Calories: 176; Fat: 8.2g; Sodium: 271mg; Total Carbs: 1g; Net Carbs: 0g; Fiber: 0.6g; Sugars: 0.1g; Protein: 23.5g

Herbed Omelet

Prep Time: 5 minutes | Cook time: 20 minutes | Serves: 4

10 eggs, whisked
½ cup cheddar, shredded
2 tablespoons parsley, chopped
2 tablespoons chives, chopped

2 tablespoons basil, chopped
Cooking spray
Salt and black pepper to the taste

1. Mix all ingredients except the cheese and the cooking spray together in a bowl until whisked well. 2. Before cooking, heat your air fryer to 350 degrees F/ 175 degrees C. 3. Grease the baking pan with cooking spray. 4. Pour the egg mixture inside the pan. 5. Cook in your air fryer for 20 minutes. 6. Serve on plates.
Per serving: Calories: 183; Fat: 12g; Sodium: 242mg; Total Carbs: 1g; Net Carbs: 0g; Fiber: 0.1g; Sugars: 1g; Protein: 17.4g

Coconut Muffins with Cinnamon

Prep Time: 10 minutes | Cook time: 10 minutes | Serves: 2

⅓ cup almond flour
2 tablespoons Erythritol
¼ teaspoon baking powder
1 teaspoon apple cider vinegar

1 tablespoon coconut milk
1 tablespoon coconut oil, softened
1 teaspoon ground cinnamon
Cooking spray

1. Place Erythritol, ground cinnamon, baking powder, and almond flour in a mixing bowl. Mix up. 2. Pour in coconut oil, coconut milk, and apple cider vinegar. 3. Stir the mixture until well combines. 4. Using cooking spray, grease the muffin molds. 5. Scoop the muffin batter in the muffin molds. 6. Using a spatula to spray every muffin. 7. Before cooking, heat the air fryer to 365 degrees F/ 185 degrees C. 8. Transfer the rack inside your air fryer. 9. Place the muffins onto the rack and cook them for 10 minutes at 365 degrees F/ 185 degrees C. 10. When cooked, transfer to another rack to cool. 11. Remove from the molds and serve.
Per serving: Calories: 108; Fat: 10.8g; Sodium: 4mg; Total Carbs: 2g; Net Carbs: 0.5g; Fiber: 1.3g; Sugars: 0.3g; Protein: 1.2g

Creamy Broccoli Florets with Eggs

Prep Time: 10 minutes | Cook time: 20 minutes | Serves: 2

3 eggs
2 tablespoons cream
2 tablespoons parmesan cheese or cheddar cheese, grated
salt to taste

black pepper to taste
½ cup broccoli small florets
½ cup bell pepper cut into small pieces

1. Using cooking spray, grease a baking pan that fits in your air fryer. 2. Place the broccoli florets and bell pepper inside the pan and cook in your air fryer for 7 minutes at 360 degrees F/ 180 degrees C. 3. While preheating, beat the eggs in a bowl. Add cream and stir together. 4. To season, add salt and pepper. 5. When cooked, toss the broccoli florets with the mixture and then pour the egg mixture on the top. 6. Cook again for 10 minutes. 7. Top with cheese and rest for 3 minutes. 8. Enjoy your meal!
Per serving: Calories: 202; Fat: 13.3g; Sodium: 435mg; Total Carbs: 4g; Net Carbs: 2g; Fiber: 0.4g; Sugars: 2.3g; Protein: 17.7g

Simple Cherry Tarts

Prep Time: 15 minutes | Cook time: 10 minutes | Serves: 6

For the tarts:
2 refrigerated piecrusts
⅓ cup cherry preserves
1 teaspoon cornstarch
Cooking oil

For the frosting:
½ cup vanilla yogurt
1 ounce cream cheese
1 teaspoon stevia
Rainbow sprinkles

1. Place the piecrusts on a flat surface. Make use of a knife or pizza cutter, cut each piecrust into 3 rectangles, for 6 in total. I discard the unused dough left from slicing the edges. 2. In a suitable bowl, combine the preserves and cornstarch. Mix well. 3. Scoop 1 tablespoon of the preserve mixture onto the top ½ of each piece of piecrust. 4. Fold the bottom of each piece up to close the tart. 5. Press along the edges of each tart to seal using the back of a fork. 6. Sprinkle the breakfast tarts with cooking oil and place them in the air fryer. 7. Cook for almost 10 minutes 8. Allow the breakfast tarts to cool fully before removing from the air fryer. 9. To make the frosting: 10. In a suitable bowl, mix the yogurt, cream cheese, and stevia. Mix well. 11. Spread the breakfast tarts with frosting and top with sprinkles, and serve.
Per serving: Calories: 96; Fat: 2g; Sodium: 66mg; Total Carbs: 17.5g; Net Carbs: 1g; Fiber: 0.4g; Sugars: 10.1g; Protein: 1.8g

Baked Parmesan Eggs with Kielbasa

Prep Time: 10 minutes | Cook time: 8 minutes | Serves: 4

4 eggs
1 tablespoon heavy cream
1 ounce Parmesan, grated

1 teaspoon dried parsley
3 ounces kielbasa, chopped
1 teaspoon coconut oil

1. Add the coconut oil in a suitable baking pan and melt it in your air fryer at 385 degrees F/ 195 degrees C for about 2 to 3 minutes. 2. At the same time in a mixing bowl, whisk the eggs and add heavy cream and the dried parsley. 3. Whisk them together. 4. Add the chopped kielbasa in the melted coconut oil. 5. Cook at 385 degrees F/ 195 degrees C for 4 minutes. 6. When cooked, add Parmesan and the whisked egg mixture and use a fork to stir them together. 7. Cook for 4 or more minutes, halfway through cooking scramble the mixture.
Per serving: Calories: 157; Fat: 12.2g; Sodium: 384mg; Total Carbs: 1g; Net Carbs: 0g; Fiber: 0g; Sugars: 0.3g; Protein: 10.7g

Cinnamon French Toast

Prep Time: 12 minutes | Cook time: 9 minutes | Serves: 2

⅓ cup almond flour
1 egg, beaten
¼ teaspoon baking powder
2 teaspoons Erythritol

¼ teaspoon vanilla extract
1 teaspoon cream cheese
¼ teaspoon ground cinnamon
1 teaspoon ghee, melted

1. Mix up baking powder, ground cinnamon, and almond flour in a mixing bowl. 2. Add in vanilla extract, cream cheese, egg, and ghee and stir together with a fork until smooth. 3. Place baking paper on the bottom of the mugs. 4. Add in almond flour mixture and use a fork to flatten well. 5. Before cooking, heat your air fryer to 255 degrees F/ 125 degrees C. 6. Transfer the mugs with toasts inside your air fryer basket. 7. Cook in your air fryer for 9 minutes. 8. When cooked, cool for a while. To serve, sprinkle Erythritol on the toasts.
Per serving: Calories: 171; Fat: 13.8g; Sodium: 43mg; Total Carbs: 4g; Net Carbs: 2g; Fiber: 2.2g; Sugars: 0.3g; Protein: 6.9g

Tomatoes Hash with Cheddar Cheese

Prep Time: 5 minutes | Cook time: 25 minutes | Serves: 4

2 tablespoons olive oil
1-pound tomatoes, chopped
½ pound cheddar, shredded

1½ tablespoons chives, chopped
Salt and black pepper to the taste
6 eggs, whisked

1. Gently grease a baking pan that fits in your air fryer with oil. 2. Before cooking, heat your air fryer with the baking pan to 350 degrees F/ 175 degrees C. 3. Add the whisked eggs, salt, chopped tomatoes, and pepper in the baking pan and whisk to combine well. 4. Top the mixture with the shredded cheddar cheese. 5. Sprinkle over with the chopped chives. 6. Cook in the preheated air fryer at 350 degrees F/ 175 degrees C for 25 minutes. 7. When cooked, remove from the air fryer. 8. Serve on plates and enjoy your breakfast.
Per serving: Calories: 274; Fat: 17.8g; Sodium: 445mg; Total Carbs: 6g; Net Carbs: 2.5g; Fiber: 1.5g; Sugars: 3.9g; Protein: 23.3g

Avocado Parsley Omelet

Prep Time: 5 minutes | Cook time: 15 minutes | Serves: 4

4 eggs, whisked
1 tablespoon parsley, chopped
½ teaspoon cheddar cheese, shredded

1 avocado, peeled, pitted and cubed
Cooking spray

1. Mix the whisked eggs, chopped parsley, shredded cheddar cheese, and avocado cubes together in a bowl. 2. Grease a suitable baking pan with cooking spray. 3. Pour the egg mixture into the baking pan and spread. 4. Insert the baking pan inside your air fryer and cook at 370 degrees F/ 185 degrees C for 15 minutes. 5. When cooked, serve warm.
Per serving: Calories: 167; Fat: 14.3g; Sodium: 67mg; Total Carbs: 4g; Net Carbs: 2g; Fiber: 3.4g; Sugars: 0.6g; Protein: 6.6g

Egg Peppers Cups

Prep Time: 10 minutes | Cook time: 12 minutes | Serves: 12

6 green bell peppers
12 eggs

½ teaspoon ground black pepper
½ teaspoon chili flakes

1. Before cooking, heat your air fryer to 395 degrees F/ 200 degrees C. 2. While preheating, cut the green bell peppers into halves and remove the seeds. 3. In the bell pepper halves, whisk the eggs. 4. Sprinkle the top with chili flakes and ground black pepper. 5. Arrange evenly the bell pepper halves onto a suitable baking pan. 6. Cook the egg pepper cups in the preheated air fryer for 4 minutes. (2 to 3 halves per batch)
Per serving: Calories: 164; Fat: 9.1g; Sodium: 126mg; Total Carbs: 9g; Net Carbs: 4.3g; Fiber: 1.7g; Sugars: 6.7g; Protein: 12.3g

Enticing Scotch Eggs

Prep Time: 15 minutes | Cook time: 13 minutes | Serves: 4

4 medium eggs, hard-boiled, peeled
9 ounces ground beef
1 teaspoon garlic powder
¼ teaspoon cayenne pepper

1 ounce coconut flakes
¼ teaspoon curry powder
1 egg, beaten
1 tablespoon almond flour
Cooking spray

1. Combine garlic powder and ground beef together in a mixing bowl. 2. Then add almond flour, curry powder, and cayenne pepper and stir until homogenous. 3. Wrap the peeled eggs in the beef mixture. 4. Shape them into meatballs. 5. And coat each ball with a beaten egg. Sprinkle with coconut flakes. 6. At 400 degrees F/ 205 degrees C, heat your air fryer in advance. 7. Using cooking spray, spray the air fryer basket. Then place the scotch eggs inside. 8. Close your air fryer and cook for about 13 minutes. 9. Flip the eggs on another side halfway cooking for 7 minutes.
Per serving: Calories: 301; Fat: 17.9g; Sodium: 160mg; Total Carbs: 4g; Net Carbs: 2g; Fiber: 1.5g; Sugars: 1.4g; Protein: 30g

Bacon Muffins

Prep Time: 15 minutes | Cook time: 15 minutes | Serves: 8

6 large eggs
3 slices of cooked and chopped bacon
½ cup of chopped green and red bell pepper
½ cup of shredded cheddar cheese

¼ cup of shredded mozzarella cheese
¼ cup of chopped fresh spinach
¼ cup of chopped onions
2 tablespoons milk
Black pepper and salt, to taste

1. Put eggs, milk, black pepper, and salt into a suitable mixing bowl. 2. Whisk it until well combined. 3. Add in chopped bell peppers, spinach, black peppers, onions, ½ of shredded cheeses, and crumbled bacon. Mix it well. 4. First, place the silicone cups in the air fryer, then pour the egg mixture into them and add the remaining cheeses. 5. At 300 degrees F/ 150 degrees C, preheat your Air fryer. 6. Cook the prepared egg muffins for almost 12–15 minutes. 7. Serve warm and enjoy your Egg Muffins with Bacon!
Per serving: Calories: 127; Fat: 9.3g; Sodium: 269mg; Total Carbs: 1g; Net Carbs: 0g; Fiber: 0.1g; Sugars: 0.7g; Protein: 9.6g

Classical French Frittata

Prep Time: 10 minutes | Cook time: 18 minutes | Serves: 3

3 eggs

1 tablespoon heavy cream

1 teaspoon Herbs de Provence
1 teaspoon almond butter, softened

2 ounces Provolone cheese, grated

1. Before cooking, heat your air fryer to 365 degrees F/ 185 degrees C. 2. Whisk the 3 eggs together in a medium bowl and then add the heavy cream. Whisk again with a hand whisker until smooth. 3. Then add herbs de Provence and the grated cheese. 4. Gently stir the egg mixture. 5. Using almond butter, grease the baking pan. 6. Then pour the egg mixture evenly on the baking pan. 7. Cook in the preheated air fryer for 18 minutes. 8. When it has preheated, cool to room temperature, and slice and serve.
Per serving: Calories: 179; Fat: 14.3g; Sodium: 229mg; Total Carbs: 1.9g; Net Carbs: 1g; Fiber: 0.5g; Sugars: 0.7g; Protein: 11.6g

Spinach Bacon Spread

Prep Time: 5 minutes | Cook time: 10 minutes | Serves: 4

2 tablespoons coconut cream
3 cups spinach leaves
2 tablespoons cilantro

2 tablespoons bacon, cooked and crumbled
Salt and black pepper to the taste

1. Combine coconut cream, spinach leaves, salt, and black pepper in a suitable baking pan. 2. Transfer the baking pan into your air fryer and cook at 360 degrees F/ 180 degrees C for 10 minutes. 3. When cooked, transfer to a blender and pulse well. 4. To serve, sprinkle the bacon on the top of the mixture.
Per serving: Calories: 74; Fat: 5.9g; Sodium: 239mg; Total Carbs: 1g; Net Carbs: 0g; Fiber: 0.7g; Sugars: 0.3g; Protein: 4.3g

Tasty Spinach Frittata

Prep Time: 5 minutes | Cook time: 20 minutes | Serves: 4

1 tablespoon chives, chopped
1 eggplant, cubed
8 ounces spinach, torn

Cooking spray
6 eggs, whisked
Salt and black pepper to the taste

1. Mix the chopped chives, cubed eggs, spinach, whisked eggs, salt, and black pepper together in a bowl. 2. Grease a suitable baking pan with the cooking spray. 3. Pour the egg mixture onto the baking pan and spread. 4. Cook in your air fryer at 380 degrees F/ 195 degrees C for 20 minutes. 5. When the cooking time is up, serve on plates. 6. Enjoy your breakfast.
Per serving: Calories: 138; Fat: 7.1g; Sodium: 140mg; Total Carbs: 9.3g; Net Carbs: 1g; Fiber: 5.3g; Sugars: 4.2g; Protein: 11.1g

Mozzarella Rolls

Prep Time: 15 minutes | Cook time: 6 minutes | Serves: 6

6 wonton wrappers
1 tablespoon keto tomato sauce
½ cup Mozzarella, shredded

1 ounce pepperoni, chopped
1 egg, beaten
Cooking spray

1. Before cooking, heat your air fryer to 400 degrees F/ 205 degrees C. 2. Spritz the cooking spray over an air fryer basket with cooking spray. 3. Mix the pepperoni, shredded Mozzarella cheese, and tomato sauce in a big bowl until homogenous. 4. Separate the mixture onto wonton wraps. 5. Roll the wraps into sticks. 6. Use the beaten eggs to brush the sticks. 7. Arrange evenly on the air fryer basket and cook in your air fryer for 6 minutes and flip the sticks halfway through cooking.
Per serving: Calories: 137; Fat: 3.7g; Sodium: 354mg; Total Carbs: 19g; Net Carbs: 6.7g; Fiber: 0.7g; Sugars: 0.4g; Protein: 5.8g

Parmesan Spinach Muffins

Prep Time: 5 minutes | Cook time: 15 minutes | Serves: 4

2 eggs, whisked
Cooking spray
1 and ½ cups coconut milk
3 ounces almond flour

1 tablespoon baking powder
4 ounces baby spinach, chopped
2 ounces parmesan cheese, grated

1. Grease the muffin molds with cooking spray. 2. Mix the whisked eggs, coconut milk, baking powder, baby spinach, parmesan cheese, and almond flour together in a mixing bowl. 3. Transfer onto the greased molds. 4. Cook in your air fryer at 380 degrees F/ 195 degrees C for 15 minutes. 5. When the cooking time is up, serve on plates. 6. Enjoy your breakfast.
Per serving: Calories: 124; Fat: 9g; Sodium: 189mg; Total Carbs: 4g; Net Carbs: 2g; Fiber: 1.1g; Sugars: 0.3g; Protein: 9g

Grilled Butter Sandwich

Prep Time: 15 minutes | Cook time: 10 minutes | Serves: 1

2 slices of bread
3 slices of any cheese
1 tablespoon of melted butter

1. At 350 degrees F/ 175 degrees C, preheat your air fryer. 2. Spread the melted butter over 1 side of each piece of bread. 3. Arrange the cheese slices over the bread and make a sandwich. 4. Put it in the air fryer and fry at 350 degrees F/ 175 degrees C for almost 10 minutes almost. 5. Serve warm and enjoy your Grilled Butter Sandwich! 6. Sandwich Fillings: Spread some pesto inside the sandwich and use just mozzarella cheese. 7. Put cooked bacon and use only cheddar cheese. 8. Add some fresh spinach with Swiss cheese inside the sandwich.
Per serving: Calories: 488; Fat: 40g; Sodium: 726mg; Total Carbs: 10.2g; Net Carbs: 0g; Fiber: 0.4g; Sugars: 1.2g; Protein: 22.4g

Cheese Taquitos with Cilantro

Prep Time: 15 minutes | Cook time: 10 minutes | Serves: 3

3 white corn tortillas
3 teaspoons of roasted green chilies
1 teaspoon of crumbled cheese
3 cheese sticks
1 tablespoon of cilantro
1 teaspoon of olive oil

1. At 400 degrees F/ 205 degrees C, preheat your air fryer. 2. Lightly grease corn tortillas with olive oil on per side. 3. Cut a small pocket at the center of cheese sticks and put chilies in the pockets. 4. Put the stuffed cheese on the tortillas and roll them up. 5. Put them in the preheated air fryer, seam side down. 6. Cook the tortillas at 400 degrees F/ 205 degrees C for 7–10 minutes. 7. Top with cilantro and crumbled cheese. 8. Serve warm and enjoy your Cheesy Taquitos!
Per serving: Calories: 209; Fat: 10.5g; Sodium: 336mg; Total Carbs: 22g; Net Carbs: 10g; Fiber: 2.5g; Sugars: 0.2g; Protein: 5.6g

Garlic Chicken Strips

Prep Time: 15 minutes | Cook time: 11 minutes | Serves: 4

1 teaspoon garlic powder
1 pound chicken fillet
½ teaspoon salt
½ teaspoon black pepper

1. Prepare all the recipe ingredients. Cut the chicken fillet into strips. 2. Sprinkle the chicken fillets with salt, black pepper, and garlic. 3. At 365 degrees F/ 185 degrees C, preheat your air fryer. 4. Place the butter in the air fryer tray and add the chicken strips. 5. Cook the chicken strips for 6-min. 6. Turn the chicken strips to the other side and cook them for almost an additional 5 minutes. 7. Serve warm
Per serving: Calories: 218; Fat: 8.4g; Sodium: 389mg; Total Carbs: 0.7g; Net Carbs: 1g; Fiber: 0.1g; Sugars: 0.2g; Protein: 33g

Creamy Eggs and Leeks

Prep Time: 5 minutes | Cook time: 7 minutes | Serves: 2

2 leeks, chopped
4 eggs, whisked
¼ cup Cheddar cheese, shredded
½ cup Mozzarella cheese, shredded
1 teaspoon avocado oil

1. Before cooking, heat your air fryer to 400 degrees F/ 205 degrees C. 2. Using avocado oil, grease your air fryer basket. 3. Combine the whisked eggs with the remaining ingredients. 4. Cook in your air fryer for 7 minutes. 5. When they are cooked, remove from the air fryer and serve warm.
Per serving: Calories: 260; Fat: 15.3g; Sodium: 271mg; Total Carbs: 13g; Net Carbs: 7g; Fiber: 1.7g; Sugars: 4.2g; Protein: 18g

Cheddar Peppers

Prep Time: 5 minutes | Cook time: 20 minutes | Serves: 4

½ cup cheddar cheese, shredded
2 tablespoons chives, chopped
A pinch of salt and black pepper
¼ cup coconut cream
1 cup red bell peppers, chopped
Cooking spray

1. Grease a suitable baking pan with cooking spray. 2. Mix shredded cheddar cheese, chopped chives, salt, black pepper, coconut cream, and the chopped red bell peppers in a medium bowl. 3. Pour the mixture in the greased pan. 4. Cook in your air fryer at 360 degrees F/ 180 degrees C for 20 minutes. 5. When the cooking time is up, serve warm

on plates.
Per serving: Calories: 101; Fat: 8.4g; Sodium: 91mg; Total Carbs: 3.4g; Net Carbs: 1g; Fiber: 0.8g; Sugars: 2.1g; Protein: 4.2g

Bacon Wrapped Eggs

Prep Time: 15 minutes | Cook time: 5 minutes | Serves: 2

2 eggs, hard-boiled, peeled
4 bacon slices
½ teaspoon avocado oil
1 teaspoon mustard

1. Before cooking, heat your air fryer to 400 degrees F/ 205 degrees C. 2. Using avocado oil, grease your air fryer basket. 3. Then line the bacon slices inside. 4. Cook the bacon slices 2 minutes per side. 5. When cooked, cool to room temperature and wrap the eggs with bacon slices, two bacon slices for one egg. 6. Then secure the eggs with toothpicks. 7. Transfer onto the air fryer basket and cook in your air fryer at 400 degrees F/ 205 degrees C for 1 minute.
Per serving: Calories: 278; Fat: 20.9g; Sodium: 940m; Total Carbs 1g; Net Carbs: 0g; Fiber: 0.3g; Sugars: 0.5g; Protein: 20g

Dijon Chicken

Prep Time: 10 minutes | Cook Time: 25 minutes | Servings: 2

2 chicken breasts, boneless
1 tbsp. Dijon mustard
2 tbsp. mayonnaise
¼ cup almonds
Black pepper, to taste
Salt, to taste

1. Add almond into the food processor and process until ground. 2. Transfer almonds on a plate and set aside. 3. Mix mustard and mayonnaise, and then spread over chicken. 4. Coat chicken with almond and place into the "Air Fryer Basket" and air-fry the chicken and the almond at 350 degrees F/ 175 degrees C for about 25 minutes. 5. When done, serve and enjoy.
Per serving: Calories 409; Fat 22g; Total Carbs 6 g; Sugar 1.5 g; Net Carbs 2g; Protein 45 g; Fiber 1 g

Fish Tacos

Prep Time: 10 minutes | Cook Time: 15 minutes | Servings: 2

4 big tortillas
1 red bell pepper, chopped
1 yellow onion, chopped
1 cup corn
4 boneless white fish fillets,
½ cup salsa
A handful mixed romaine lettuce
4 tbsp. parmesan, grated

1. Place the fish fillets in your "Air Fryer Basket" and Air Fry them at 350 degrees F/ 175 degrees C for 6 minutes. 2. Meanwhile, heat up a suitable over medium-high heat 3. Add onion, bell pepper, and corn, stir for 1-2 minutes. 4. Spread the tortillas on a working surface. 5. Divide fish fillets, salsa, mixed vegies and mixed greens and parmesan on each tortilla. 6. Roll your tortillas, place them in the air fryer and Air Fry at 350 degrees F/ 175 degrees C for about 6 minutes more. 7. Divide fish tacos on plates. 8. Serve and enjoy.
Per serving: Calories: 217; Fat: 9.2g; Total Carbs 1.7g; Net Carbs 1.2g; Protein: 29.8g; Fiber: 0.4g; Sugar: 0.3g

Chicken Vegetable Omelet

Prep Time: 10 minutes | Cook Time: 12 minutes | Servings: 2

1 tsp. butter
1 small yellow onion, chopped
½ jalapeño pepper, seeded and chopped
3 eggs
Salt and ground black pepper, as required
¼ cup cooked chicken, shredded

1. In a frying pan, melt the butter over medium heat; add the onion and cook for 4-5 minutes; add the jalapeño pepper and cook for 1 minute. 2. Remove the pan from the heat and then set aside to cool slightly. Meanwhile, in a suitable bowl, add the eggs, salt, and black pepper and beat well. 3. Mix up the onion mixture and chicken until well-combined. Place the chicken mixture into a small baking pan. 4. Arrange pan over the "Wire Rack" and insert in the air fryer. 5. Air Fry the food at 355 degrees F/ 180 degrees C for 6 minutes. 6. Cut the omelet into 2 portions and serve hot.
Per serving: Calories 153; Fat 9.1 g; Net Carbs 3.4 g; Fiber 6 g; Total Carbs 4 g; Fiber: 0.9 g; Protein 13.8 g

Herbed Potatoes with Bacon

Prep Time: 10 minutes | Cook Time: 20 minutes | Servings: 2

4 potatoes, peeled and cut into medium cubes
6 garlic cloves, minced
4 bacon slices, chopped

2 rosemary springs, chopped
1 tbsp. olive oil
Salt and black pepper to the taste
2 eggs, whisked

1. In your "Air Fryer Basket", mix up the oil, potatoes, garlic, bacon, rosemary, salt, pepper, and eggs. 2. Cook them together at 400 degrees F/ 205 degrees C for 20 minutes on Air Fry mode. 3. When cooked, divide everything on plates and serve for breakfast. Enjoy!
Per serving: Calories: 164; Fat: 7.9g; Total Carbs 2g; Net Carbs 2g; Protein: 19.2g; Fiber: 0.1g; Sugar: 0g

Zucchini Mix

Prep Time: 10 minutes | Cook Time: 35 minutes | Servings: 2

1 lb. zucchini, sliced
1 tbsp. parsley, chopped
1 yellow squash, halved, deseeded, and chopped

1 tbsp. olive oil
Black pepper, to taste
Salt, to taste

1. Mix up all of the recipe ingredients in a large bowl. 2. Transfer the mixture into the "Air Fryer Basket" and Air Fry at 400 degrees F/ 205 degrees C for 35 minutes. 3. Serve and enjoy.
Per serving: Calories 249 Fat 3 g; Total Carbs 4 g; Sugar 2 g; Net Carbs 5g; Protein 1.5 g; Fiber: 0 g

Hard-Boiled Eggs

Prep Time: 8 minutes | Cook time: 16 minutes | Serves: 2

4 eggs

¼ teaspoon salt

1. Cook the eggs in your air fryer at 250 degrees F/ 120 degrees C for 16 minutes. 2. When the cooking time is up, cool the eggs in ice water. 3. Then peel the eggs and cut them into halve. 4. Season the egg halves with salt and serve.
Per serving: Calories: 126; Fat: 8.8g; Sodium: 414mg; Total Carbs: 0.7g; Net Carbs: 0g; Fiber: 0g; Sugars: 0.7g; Protein: 11.1g

Mushroom Salad

Prep Time: 10 minutes | Cook Time: 15 minutes | Servings: 2

10 mushrooms, halved
1 tbsp. fresh parsley, chopped
1 tbsp. olive oil
1 tbsp. mozzarella cheese, grated

1 tbsp. cheddar cheese, grated
1 tbsp. dried mix herbs
Black pepper, to taste
Salt, to taste

1. Add all the recipe ingredients into the bowl and toss well. 2. Transfer bowl mixture into the air fryer baking dish. 3. Place this dish in the air fryer and cook the food at 380 degrees F/ 195 degrees C on Air Fry mode for 15 minutes. 4. Serve and enjoy.
Per serving: Calories 90 Fat 7 g; Total Carbs 2 g; Sugar 1 g; Net Carbs 6g; Protein 5 g; Fiber: 7 g

Scrambled Eggs

Prep Time: 5 minutes | Cook Time:10 minutes | Servings: 2

4 large eggs.
½ cup shredded sharp Cheddar

cheese.
2 tbsps. unsalted butter; melted.

1. Crack eggs into 2-cup round baking dish and whisk. 2. Place the dish into the Air Fryer Basket. 3. Adjust the temperature to 400 degrees F/ 205 degrees C and set the timer for 10 minutes. 4. After 5 minutes of cooking time, stir the eggs and add the butter and cheese. 5. Let cook 3 more minutes and stir again. 6. Allow eggs to finish cooking an additional 2 minutes or remove if they are to your desired liking. 7. Use a fork to fluff. Serve warm.
Per serving: Calories: 228; Fat: 14.2g; Total Carbs 3.6g; Net Carbs 2g; Protein: 22.6g; Fiber: 1.1g; Sugar: 1.7g

Morning Frittata

Prep Time: 5 minutes | Cook Time: 15 minutes | Servings: 6

1 fennel bulb; shredded
6 eggs; whisked
2 tsp. cilantro; chopped.
1 tsp. sweet paprika

Cooking spray
Black pepper, to taste
Salt, to taste

1. In a suitable bowl, and mix all the recipe ingredients except the cooking spray and stir well. 2. Grease a baking pan with the cooking spray, then pour the frittata mix and spread well 3. Arrange this pan to the Air Fryer and cook at 370 degrees F/ 185 degrees C on Air Fry mode for15 minutes. 4. When cooked, divide the food between plates and serve them for breakfast.
Per serving: Calories: 201; Fat: 9.9g; Total Carbs 3g; Net Carbs 2g; Protein: 24.6g; Fiber: 0.7g; Sugar: 1.4g

Strawberries Coconut Oatmeal

Prep Time: 5 minutes | Cook Time: 15 minutes | Servings: 4

½ cup coconut; shredded
¼ cup strawberries
2 cups coconut milk

¼ tsp. vanilla extract
2 tsp. stevia
Cooking spray

1. Grease the "Air Fryer Basket" with the cooking spray, then add all of the recipe ingredients inside and toss 2. Cook the mixture at 365 degrees F/ 185 degrees C on Air Fry mode for 15 minutes. 3. When cooked, divide into bowls and serve for breakfast.
Per serving: Calories: 198; Fat: 9g; Total Carbs 2.2g; Net Carbs 2g; Protein: 26g; Fiber: 0.2g; Sugar: 0.1g

Asparagus Arugula Salad

Prep Time: 5 minutes | Cook Time: 10 minutes | Servings: 4

1 cup baby arugula
1 bunch asparagus; trimmed
1 tbsp. balsamic vinegar

1 tbsp. cheddar cheese; grated
A pinch of salt and black pepper
Cooking spray

1. Put the asparagus in your "Air Fryer Basket", grease the asparagus with some cooking spray, season with black pepper and salt and Air Fry at 360 degrees F/ 180 degrees C for 10 minutes. 2. In a bowl, mix the asparagus with the arugula and the vinegar, divide between plates after tossing well and serve hot with cheese sprinkled on top
Per serving: Calories: 283; Fat: 16.5g; Total Carbs 7g; Net Carbs 3g; Protein: 27.4g; Fiber: 1.8g; Sugar: 2g

Raspberries Bowls

Prep Time: 5 minutes | Cook Time: 12 minutes | Servings: 2

1 cup raspberries
2 tbsp. butter

2 tbsp. lemon juice
1 tsp. cinnamon powder

1. In the Air Fryer Basket, mix all the recipe ingredients and then cover. 2. Cook the mixture at 350 degrees F/ 175 degrees C on Air Fry mode for 12 minutes. 3. When cooked, divide into bowls and serve for breakfast
Per serving: Calories 208 Fat 6g; Fiber: 9g; Total Carbs 14g; Net Carbs 2g; Protein 3g; Sugar 1g; fiber 2g

Squash Fritters

Prep Time: 15 minutes | Cook Time: 8 minutes | Servings: 4

2 cups cooked spaghetti squash
1 large egg
¼ cup blanched ground almond flour.
2 tbsp. unsalted butter; softened.

2 stalks green onion, sliced
½ tsp. garlic powder.
1 tsp. dried parsley.

1. Remove excess moisture from the squash with a cheesecloth or kitchen towel. 2. Mix all the recipe ingredients in a large bowl. Form into 4 patties from this mixture. 3. Cut a piece of parchment to fit your Air Fryer Basket. 4. Place each patty on the parchment and place into the "Air Fryer Basket" 5. Air Fry the patties at 400 degrees F/ 205 degrees C for 8 minutes, flipping halfway through. 6. Serve warm.
Per serving: Calories 131; Protein 3.8g; Fiber: 2.0g; Fat 10.1g; Total Carbs 7.1g; Sugar 1g; fiber 2g

Mushrooms Spread

Prep Time:5 minutes | Cook Time: 20 minutes | Servings: 4

¼ cup mozzarella; shredded
½ cup coconut cream
1 cup white mushrooms

A pinch of salt and black pepper
Cooking spray

1. Put the mushrooms in your "Air Fryer Basket", grease with some cooking spray. 2. Cook the mushrooms in the air fryer at 370 degrees F/ 185 degrees C on Air Fry mode for 20 minutes. 3. Transfer to a blender, add the remaining ingredients and pulse well, divide into bowls and serve as a spread.
Per serving: Calories 202 Fat 12g; Fiber: 2g; Total Carbs 5g; Net Carbs 6g; Protein 7g; Sugar 1g; fiber 2g

Tuna Onions Salad

Prep Time: 5 minutes | Cook Time: 15 minutes | Servings: 4

14 oz. canned tuna, drained and flaked
2 spring onions; chopped.

1 cup arugula
1 tbsp. olive oil
A pinch of salt and black pepper

1. At 360 degrees F/ 180 degrees C, preheat your air fryer. 2. In a bowl, mix up all of the recipe ingredients except the oil and the arugula. 3. Grease the cooking pan that fits your air fryer with oil. 4. Pour the tuna mix onto the cooking pan and then cook at 360 degrees F/ 180 degrees C on Air Fry mode for 15 minutes 5. In a salad bowl, combine the arugula with the tuna mix, toss and serve.
Per serving: Calories 212 Fat 8g; Fiber: 3g; Total Carbs 5g; Net Carbs 8g; Protein 8g; Sugar 1g; fiber 2g

Cinnamon Pudding

Prep Time: 5 minutes | Cook Time: 12 minutes | Servings: 2

4 eggs; whisked
4 tbsp. erythritol
2 tbsp. heavy cream

½ tsp. cinnamon powder
¼ tsp. allspice, ground
Cooking spray

1. In a suitable bowl, mix up all of the recipe ingredients except the cooking spray. 2. Grease a suitable ramekin with the cooking spray and then add the mixture into it. 3. Transfer the ramekin to the Air Fryer Basket and cook the food at 400 degrees F/ 205 degrees C on Air Fry mode for 12 minutes. 4. Divide into bowls and serve for breakfast.
Per serving: Calories 201 Fat 11g; Fiber: 2g; Total Carbs 4g; Net Carbs 5g; Protein 6g; Sugar 1g; fiber 2g

Tomatoes Chard Salad

Prep Time: 5 minutes | Cook Time: 15 minutes | Servings: 4

4 eggs, whisked
3 oz. Swiss chard; chopped.
1 cup tomatoes; cubed

1 tsp. olive oil
Salt and black pepper to taste.

1. In a bowl, mix the eggs with the rest of the ingredients except the oil. 2. Grease a suitable cooking pan with the oil, pour the swish chard mix and Air Fry at 360 degrees F/ 180 degrees C for about 15 minutes. 3. Divide between plates and serve.
Per serving: Calories 202 Fat 14g; Fiber: 3g; Total Carbs 5g; Net Carbs 2g; Protein 12g; Sugar 1g; fiber 2g

Egg Cheese Roll Ups

Prep Time: 10 minutes | Cook Time: 25 minutes | Servings: 4

12 slices sugar-free bacon.
½ medium green bell pepper; seeded and chopped
6 large eggs.
¼ cup chopped onion

1 cup shredded sharp Cheddar cheese.
½ cup mild salsa, for dipping
2 tbsps. unsalted butter.

1. In your skillet, melt the butter over medium heat. 2. Toss in onion and pepper to and sauté for 3 minutes until the onions are translucent. 3. Beat eggs in a small bowl and pour over the vegies in the skillet, then scramble the eggs for 5 minutes. 4. On work surface, place 3 slices of bacon side by side, overlapping about ¼-inch. 5. Place ¼ cup scrambled eggs in a heap on the side closest to you and sprinkle ¼ cup cheese on top of the eggs. 6. Roll the bacon strips around the eggs and secure it with a toothpick. 7. Place each eggs roll into the "Air Fryer

Basket" 8. Select Air Fry mode, adjust the cooking temperature to 350 degrees F/ 175 degrees C and set the timer for 15 minutes. 9. Flip the rolls halfway through. 10. When fully cooked, the bacon shall be brown and crispy. 11. Serve immediately with salsa for dipping.
Per serving: Calories 460; Protein 28.2g; Fiber: 0.8g; Fat 31.7g; Total Carbs 6.1g; Sugar 1g; fiber 2g

Ham Egg Cups

Prep Time: 5 minutes | Cook Time: 12 minutes | Servings: 2

4 large eggs.
4 (1-oz.) slices deli ham
½ cup shredded medium Cheddar cheese.

¼ cup diced green bell pepper.
2 tbsp. diced red bell pepper.
2 tbsp. diced white onion.
2 tbsp. full-fat sour cream.

1. Place a slice of ham at the bottom of 4 suitable baking ramekins. 2. In a large bowl, crack the eggs and then whisk with sour cream; add the red pepper, green pepper, onion and stir well. 3. Pour the prepared egg mixture into ham-lined baking ramekins. Top with Cheddar. 4. Place cups into the Air Fryer Basket. 5. Select Air Fry mode, adjust the temperature to 320 degrees F/ 160 degrees C and set the timer for 12 minutes or cook the food until the tops are browned. 6. Serve warm.
Per serving: Calories 382; Protein 29.4g; Fiber: 1.4g; Fat 23.6g; Total Carbs 6.0g; Sugar 1g; fiber 2g

Olives Kale Salad

Prep Time:5 minutes | Cook Time: 20 minutes | Servings: 4

4 eggs; whisked
1 cup kale; chopped.
½ cup black olives, pitted and sliced

2 tbsp. cheddar; grated
Cooking spray
A pinch of salt and black pepper

1. In a bowl, mix the eggs with the rest of the ingredients except the cooking spray. 2. Take a pan that fits in your air fryer and grease it with the cooking spray, spread the olives mixture. 3. Put this pan into the air fryer and Air Fry the food at 360 degrees F/ 180 degrees C for 20 minutes. 4. Serve hot.
Per serving: Calories 220 Fat 13g; Fiber: 4g; Total Carbs 6g; Net Carbs 6g; Protein 12g; Sugar 1g; fiber 2g

Raspberries Cinnamon Oatmeal

Prep Time: 5 minutes | Cook Time:15 minutes | Servings: 4

1 ½ cups coconut; shredded
½ cups raspberries
2 cups almond milk
¼ tsp. nutmeg, ground

2 tsp. stevia
½ tsp. cinnamon powder
Cooking spray

1. Grease the "Air Fryer Basket" with some cooking spray and then mix up all of the recipe ingredients inside, cover and Air Fry at 360 degrees F/ 180 degrees C for 15 minutes. 2. Divide into bowls and serve.
Per serving: Calories 172 Fat 5g; Fiber: 2g; Total Carbs 4g; Net Carbs 6g; Protein 6g; Sugar 1g; fiber 2g

Scotch Eggs

Prep Time: 15 minutes | Cook Time: 15 minutes | Servings: 4

1-lb. ground breakfast sausage
3 tbsp. flour
4 hard-boiled eggs, peeled

1 egg
1 tbsp. water
¾ cup panko bread crumbs

1. In a suitable bowl, mix the sausage and 1 tablespoon of flour. 2. Form the prepared sausage mixture into 4 equal parts. 3. Place a hard-boiled egg in the center, then wrap the sausage around the egg, sealing completely. 4. Repeat with remaining sausage parts and hard-boiled eggs. 5. In a suitable bowl, whisk the egg and water until smooth. 6. Add the remaining flour and bread crumbs into separate bowls large enough to dredge the sausage-wrapped eggs. 7. Dredge the sausage-wrapped eggs in the flour, then in the whisked egg, and finally coat in the bread crumbs. 8. Arrange them in the Air Fryer Basket. Cook the food at 375 degrees F/ 190 degrees C on Air Fry mode for 20 minutes. 9. Flip them halfway through, or until the sausage is cooked to desired doneness. 10. Remove from the basket and serve on a plate.
Per serving: Calories 509; Fat 16g; Total Carbs 8g; Net Carbs 6g; Protein 24g; Sugar 16g; Fiber 8g

Simple Strawberry Toast

Prep Time: 8 minutes | Cook Time: 10 minutes | Servings: 4

4 slices bread, ½-inch thick
1 cup sliced strawberries
1 tsp. sugar
Cooking spray

1. Place the bread slices on a clean plate. 2. Arrange the bread slices (sprayed side down) in the Air Fryer Basket. 3. Evenly spread the strawberries onto them and then sprinkle with sugar. 4. Cook the food at 375 degrees F/ 190 degrees C on Air Fry mode for 8 minutes, or until the tops are covered with a beautiful glaze. 5. Remove from the basket and serve on a plate.
Per serving: Calories 375; Fat 22g; Total Carbs 2g; Net Carbs 8g; Protein 14g; Sugar 5g; Fiber 0g

Stuffed Poblanos

Prep Time: 10 minutes | Cook Time: 20 minutes | Servings: 4

½ lb. spicy ground pork breakfast sausage
4 large poblano peppers
4 large eggs.
½ cup full-fat sour cream.
4 oz. full-fat cream cheese, softened
¼ cup canned diced tomatoes and green chilies, drained
8 tbsp. shredded pepper jack cheese

1. In a suitable skillet, crumble and brown the ground sausage over medium heat. 2. Remove sausage and drain the fat from the pan. 3. Crack eggs into the pan, scramble and cook until no longer runny. 4. Place cooked sausage in a large bowl and fold in cream cheese. 5. Mix in diced tomatoes and chilies. Gently fold in eggs 6. Cut a 4"–5" slit in the top of each poblano, removing the seeds and white membrane with a small knife. 7. Separate the filling into 4 and spoon carefully into each pepper. 8. Top each with 2 tablespoons of pepper jack cheese. 9. Place the peppers into the Air Fryer Basket. 10. Select Air Fry mode, adjust the temperature to 350 degrees F/ 175 degrees C and set the timer for 15 minutes. 11. Serve immediately with the sour cream on the top.
Per serving: Calories 489; Protein 22.8g; Fiber: 3.8g; Fat 35.6g; Total Carbs 12.6g; Sugar 1g; fiber 2g

Sweet-Potato Chips

Prep Time: 7 minutes | Cook Time: 8 minutes | Servings: 7

1 small sweet potato, cut into ⅜-inch slices
2 tbsp. olive oil
Ground cinnamon

1. In a suitable bowl, toss the potato slices in olive oil. 2. Sprinkle with the cinnamon and mix well. 3. Spread potato slices in the Air Fryer Basket. 4. Cook the food at 375 degrees F/ 190 degrees C on Air Fry mode for 8 minutes, shaking the basket halfway through. 5. Remove from the basket and serve on a large dish lined with paper towels.
Per serving: Calories 385; Fat 18g; Total Carbs 5g; Net Carbs 2g; Protein 20g; Sugar 3g; Fiber 1g

Quiche Cups

Prep Time: 11 minutes | Cook Time: 15 minutes | Servings: 10

¼ lb. all-natural ground pork sausage
3 eggs
¾ cup milk
4 oz. sharp Cheddar cheese, grated
Cooking spray

1. On a clean work surface, slice the pork sausage into 2-ounce portions. 2. Shape each portion into a ball and gently flatten it with your palm. 3. Lay the patties in the "Air Fryer Basket" and cook them at 375 degrees F/ 190 degrees C on Air Fry mode for 6 minutes. 4. Flip the patties halfway through. 5. When cooked, Remove the patties from the basket and transfer them to a large dish lined with paper towels. 6. Crumble them into small pieces with a fork. Set aside. 7. Line 10 paper liner in each muffin cups and then lightly grease the muffin cups with some cooking spray. Arrange the muffin cups to the muffin pan. 8. Divide crumbled sausage equally among the ten muffin cups and sprinkle the tops with the cheese. 9. Arrange the muffin pan to the Air Fryer Basket. 10. Cook the food at 375 degrees F/ 190 degrees C for 8 minutes on Air Fry mode, until the tops are golden and a toothpick inserted in the middle comes out clean. 11. Remove from the basket and let cool for 5 minutes before serving.
Per serving: Calories 497; Fat 25g; Total Carbs 1g; Net Carbs 1g; Protein 28g; Sugar 5g; Fiber 4g

Ham Omelet

Prep Time: 10 minutes | Cook Time: 20 minutes | Servings: 6

¼ cup ham, diced
¼ cup green or red bell pepper, cored and chopped
¼ cup onion, chopped
1 tsp. butter
4 large eggs
2 tbsps. milk
⅛ tsp. salt
¾ cup sharp Cheddar cheese, grated

1. In a suitable bowl, whisk the eggs, milk, and salt until smooth and creamy. 2. Add the ham, bell pepper, onion, and butter into a 6×6×2-inch baking pan. 3. Arrange the pan to the Air Fryer Basket. 4. Cook the food at 375 degrees F/ 190 degrees C for 6 minutes on Air Fry mode. 5. Flip the food halfway through, or until the vegetables are soft; gently pour the milk mixture over the ham-vegetable mixture in the pan. 6. Resume cooking the food in your air fryer for 13 minutes more under the same mode. 7. Top it with the cheese and Air Fry for 1 minute more, or until the cheese is bubbly and melted. 8. Remove from the basket and cool for 5 minutes before serving.
Per serving: Calories 367; Fat 14g; Total Carbs 13g; Net Carbs 8g; Protein 18g; Sugar 2g; Fiber 2g

Canadian Bacon English Muffin

Prep Time: 5 minutes | Cook Time: 8 minutes | Servings: 4

4 English muffins
8 slices Canadian bacon
4 slices cheese
Cooking spray

1. Cut each English muffin in half on a clean work surface. 2. To assemble a sandwich, layer 2 slices of bacon and 1 cheese slice on the bottom of each muffin and put the other half of the bread on top. 3. Repeat with the remaining biscuits, bacon, and cheese slices. 4. Arrange the prepared sandwiches in the "Air Fryer Basket" and spritz with some cooking spray. 5. Cook the sandwiches at 375 degrees F/ 190 degrees C for 8 minutes on Air Fry mode, flipping halfway through. 6. Let them cool for 3 minutes before serving.
Per serving: Calories: 225; Fat: 10g; Total Carbs 5.2g; Net Carbs 1.2g; Protein: 26.5g; Fiber: 1.3g; Sugar: 0.9g

Asparagus Egg Strata

Prep Time: 15 minutes | Cook Time: 20 minutes | Servings: 4

6 asparagus spears, cut into 2-inch pieces
½ cup grated Havarti or Swiss cheese
4 eggs
2 slices whole-wheat bread, cut
into ½-inch cubes
3 tbsps. whole milk
2 tbsps. flat-leaf parsley, chopped
1 tbsp. water
Cooking spray

1. Place a 6×6×2-inch baking pan into the Air Fryer Basket. 2. Add 1 tablespoon of water, and asparagus spears into the baking pan. 3. Cook the asparagus spears at 325 degrees F/ 160 degrees C on Air Fry mode for 3 to 5 minutes. 4. Remove the asparagus spears from the baking pan. Drain and dry them thoroughly. 5. Place the asparagus spears and bread cubes in the pan, then spray with some cooking spray. Set aside. 6. Add the cheese, parsley, salt, and pepper. 7. Air Fry the food at 350 degrees F/ 175 degrees C for 11 to 14 minutes. 8. Remove the strata from the pan. 9. Let cool for 5 minutes before serving.
Per serving: Calories: 241; Fat: 12.5g; Total Carbs 4.7g; Net Carbs 2g; Protein: 24.6g; Fiber: 1.1g; Sugar: 1.8g

Shrimp Rice Frittata

Prep Time: 15 minutes | Cook Time: 18 minutes | Servings: 4

½ cup chopped shrimp, cooked
½ cup baby spinach
½ cup of rice, cooked
4 eggs
½ cup grated Monterey Jack
cheese
½ tsp. dried basil
Pinch salt
Cooking spray

1. Spritz a 6×6×2-inch baking pan with some cooking spray. 2. Mix the cooked shrimp, rice, and spinach in the pan until combine well. Then transfer the pan to the Air Fryer Basket. 3. Air Fry them at 325 degrees F/ 160 degrees C for 14 to 18 minutes. 4. Remove from the pan and cool for 3 minutes before cutting into wedges to serve.
Per serving: Calories: 235; Fat: 10.4g; Total Carbs 6g; Net Carbs 2g; Protein: 27.9g; Fiber: 1.3g; Sugar: 1.5g

Monkey Bread with Cinnamon

Prep Time: 5 minutes | Cook Time: 10 minutes | Servings: 4

1 can (8-oz.) refrigerated biscuits	½ tsp. cinnamon
3 tbsps. brown sugar	⅛ tsp. nutmeg
¼ cup white sugar	3 tbsps. unsalted butter, melted

1. Divide each biscuit into quarters on a clean work surface. 2. In a suitable mixing bowl, thoroughly mix up the brown and white sugar, nutmeg, and cinnamon. 3. Pour the melted butter into another suitable bowl. 4. Dip each biscuit in the melted butter, then in the sugar mixture to coat thoroughly. 5. Arrange the coated biscuits in a 6×6×2-inch baking pan and then transfer the pan to the Air Fryer Basket. 6. Air Fry the food in batches at 350 degrees F/ 175 degrees C for 6 to 9 minutes. 7. Transfer to a serving dish and cool for 5 minutes before serving.
Per serving: Calories: 243; Fat: 14.3g; Total Carbs 7g; Net Carbs 3g; Protein: 23.4g; Fiber: 2.1g; Sugar: 3.3g

Ham Cup

Prep Time: 10 minutes | Cook Time: 15 minutes | Servings: 18

5 whole eggs	1 ½ cups Swiss cheese
2 ¼ oz. Ham	¼ tsp. Salt
1 cup milk	¼ cup green onion
⅛ tsp. Pepper	½ tsp. Thyme

1. At 350 degrees F/ 175 degrees C, preheat your air fryer. 2. Beat Eggs into a suitable bowl. Add thyme onion, salt, Swiss cheese pepper, milk to the beaten eggs. 3. Prepare your baking forms for muffins and place ham slices in each baking form. 4. Cover the ham with egg mixture. 5. Transfer the forms to air fryer and cook for 15 minutes at 350 degrees F/ 175 degrees C on Bake mode.
Per serving: Calories 80 Fat 5 g; Net Carbs 5g; Protein 7 g; Total Carbs 0 g; Sugar 2g; Fiber: 2 g

Seasoned Cheese Sticks

Prep Time: 22 minutes | Cook Time: 7 minutes | Servings: 8

6 cheese sticks, snake-sized	¼ cup flour, whole wheat
¼ cup parmesan cheese, grated	¼ tbsp. rosemary, grounded
2 eggs	1 tbsp. garlic powder
1 tbsp. Italian seasoning	

1. Take cheese sticks and set aside. 2. Take a shallow bowl and beat eggs into it. 3. Mix cheese, flour, and seasonings in another bowl. 4. Roll the cheese sticks in the eggs and then in the batter. 5. Now do the process again till the sticks as well coated. 6. Place them in the Air Fryer Basket. 7. Air Fry them for 6-7 minutes at 370 degrees F/ 185 degrees C. 8. When done, serve and enjoy.
Per serving: Calories 50 Net Carbs 6g; Protein 3 g; Total Carbs 3 g; Fat 2 g; Sugar 2g; Fiber: 1.8 g

Onion Omelet

Prep Time: 5 minutes | Cook Time: 10 minutes | Servings: 2

2 eggs	¼ tsp. pepper
2 tbsp. grated cheddar cheese	1 tbsp. olive oil
1 tsp. soy sauce	
½ onion, sliced	

1. Whisk the eggs along with the pepper and soy sauce. 2. Add the oil, prepared egg mixture and the onion to a suitable cooking pan. 3. Air Fry the food at 350 degrees F/ 175 degrees C for 8 to 10 minutes. 4. Top with the grated cheddar cheese and enjoy.
Per serving: Calories 347 Fat 23.2 g; Net Carbs 3g; Protein 13.6 g; Total Carbs 6 g; Sugar 2g; Fiber: 1.2 g

Shirred Eggs

Prep Time: 6 minutes | Cook Time: 14 minutes | Servings: 2

2 tsp. butter, for greasing	¼ tsp. paprika
4 eggs, divided	¾ tsp. salt
2 tbsp. heavy cream	¼ tsp. pepper
4 slices ham	2 tsps. chopped chives
3 tbsp. parmesan cheese	

1. Grease a pie pan with the butter. 2. Place the ham slices on the pan. 3. Whisk one egg along with the salt, heavy cream, and pepper in a suitable bowl. 4. Pour the prepared mixture over the ham slices. 5.

Crack the other eggs over the ham. Sprinkle with parmesan cheese. 6. Air Fry the food at 360 degrees F/ 180 degrees C for 14 minutes. 7. Season with paprika, garnish with chives and serve with low carb bread.
Per serving: Calories 279; Fat 20 g; Net Carbs 2g; Protein 20.8 g; Total Carbs 1.8 g; Sugar 2g; Fiber: 0.2 g

Cheddar Hash Brown

Prep Time: 30 minutes | Cook Time: 20 minutes | Servings: 6

1½ lbs. hash browns	1 cup cheddar cheese; shredded
6 bacon slices; chopped.	1 cup almond milk
8 oz. cream cheese; softened	A drizzle of olive oil
1 yellow onion; chopped.	Salt and black pepper to taste
6 eggs	
6 spring onions; chopped.	

1. At 350 degrees F/ 175 degrees C, preheat your Air Fryer. 2. In a heatproof bowl, mix all other ingredients except the spring onions. 3. Transfer the bowl to the air fryer basket and cook the food at 350 degrees F/ 175 degrees C for 20 minutes on Air Fry mode. 4. Divide between plates, sprinkle the spring onions on top and serve.
Per serving: Calories: 202; Fat: 8.9g; Total Carbs 6.6g; Net Carbs 2g; Protein: 22.5g; Fiber: 0.6g; Sugar: 3.2g

Sunflower Bread

Prep Time: 15 minutes | Cook Time: 18 minutes | Servings: 4

⅔ cup whole-wheat flour	½ sachet instant yeast
⅔ cup plain flour	1 tsp. salt
⅓ cup sunflower seeds	⅔-1 cup lukewarm water

1. In a suitable bowl, mix up the flours, sunflower seeds, yeast, and salt. 2. Slowly, add in the water, stirring continuously until a soft dough ball forms. 3. Move the dough onto a lightly floured surface and knead for 5 minutes using your hands. 4. Make the dough into balls and place them into a bowl. 5. With a plastic wrap, cover the bowl and place at a warm place for 30 minutes. 6. Set the cooking temperature of air fryer to 390 degrees F/ 200 degrees C. Grease a suitable cake pan. 7. Coat the top of dough with water and place into the prepared cake pan. 8. Arrange the cake pan into an Air Fryer Basket. 9. Air Fry the food at 390 degrees F/ 200 degrees C for 18 minutes or until a toothpick is clean inserted from the center. 10. Remove from air fryer and place the pan onto a wire rack for 10-15 minutes. 11. Carefully, take out the bread from pan and put onto a wire rack until it is completely cool before slicing. 12. Cut the bread into desired size slices and serve.
Per serving: Calories 177g; Total Carbs 33g; Net Carbs 6g; Protein 5.5g; Fat 2.4g; Sugar 0.2g; Fiber 58g

Pesto Gnocchi

Prep Time: 15 minutes | Cook Time: 16 minutes | Servings: 4

1 jar (8-oz.) pesto	1 onion, chopped
⅓ cup Parmesan cheese, grated	3 cloves garlic, sliced
1 package (16-oz.) shelf-stable gnocchi	1 tbsp. olive oil

1. Mix the oil, onion, garlic, and gnocchi in a 6×6×2-inch baking pan. 2. Place the prepared pan into the Air Fryer Basket. 3. Air Fry the food at 400 degrees F/ 205 degrees C for 16 minutes. 4. Stir once halfway through cooking. 5. When done, transfer the gnocchi to a serving dish. 6. Sprinkle with the Parmesan cheese and pesto. 7. Stir well and serve warm.
Per serving: Calories: 229; Fat: 5.6g; Total Carbs: 4.7g; Net Carbs 2g; Protein: 38.4g; Fiber: 0.8g; Sugar: 1.6g

Avocado Cabbage Salad

Prep Time: 5 minutes | Cook Time: 15 minutes | Servings: 4

2 cups red cabbage, shredded	small avocado, peeled, pitted and sliced
A drizzle of olive oil	
1 red bell pepper, sliced	Salt and black pepper to the taste

1. Grease a suitable cooking pan with the oil. 2. Add all the recipe ingredients, toss, cover and Air Fry them at 400 degrees F/ 205 degrees C for 15 minutes in the air fryer. 3. Divide into bowls and serve cold for breakfast.
Per serving: Calories 209g; Total Carbs 4g; Net Carbs 2g; Protein 9; Fat 8g; Sugar 2g; Fiber 2g

Banana Cinnamon Bread

Prep Time: 10 minutes | Cook Time: 20 minutes | Servings: 8

1 ⅓ cups flour	1 tsp. salt
⅔ cup sugar	½ cup milk
1 tsp. baking soda	½ cup olive oil
1 tsp. baking powder	3 bananas, peeled and sliced
1 tsp. ground cinnamon	

1. Take a suitable bowl of a stand mixer and mix well all of the ingredients. 2. Grease a loaf pan. 3. Place the prepared mixture into the prepared pan. 4. Arrange the loaf pan into an Air Fryer Basket. 5. Air Fry the food at 330 degrees F/ 165 degrees C for 20 minutes or until a toothpick is clean inserted from the center. 6. Remove from air fryer and place the pan onto a wire rack for 10-15 minutes. 7. Carefully, take out the bread from pan and put onto a wire rack until it is completely cool before slicing. 8. Cut the bread into desired size slices and serve.
Per serving: Calories 295g; Total Carbs 44g; Net Carbs 5g; Protein 3.1g; Fat 13.3g; Sugar 22.8g; Fiber 5g

Creamy Bread

Prep Time: 20 minutes | Cook Time: 55 minutes | Servings: 12

1 cup milk	2 tbsps. milk powder
¾ cup whipping cream	1 tsp. salt
1 large egg	¼ cup fine sugar
4½ cups bread flour	3 tsps. dry yeast
½ cup all-purpose flour	

1. In the baking pan of a bread machine, place all the recipe ingredients in the order recommended by the manufacturer. 2. Place the baking pan in bread machine and close with the lid. 3. Select the Dough cycle and press Start button. 4. Once the cycle is completed, remove the paddles from bread machine but keep the dough inside for 45-50 minutes to proof. 5. Set the cooking temperature of air fryer to 375 degrees F/ 190 degrees C. Grease 2 loaf pans. 6. Remove the dough from pan and place onto a lightly floured surface. 7. Divide the dough into 4 equal-sized balls and then, roll each into a rectangle. 8. Tightly, roll each rectangle like a Swiss roll. 9. Place two rolls into each prepared loaf pan. 10. Set aside for 1 hour. 11. Arrange the loaf pans into the Air Fryer Basket. 12. Air Fry the food at 375 degrees F/ 190 degrees C for 50-55 minutes or until a toothpick inserted into the center comes out clean. 13. Remove the pans from air fryer and place onto a wire rack for 10-15 minutes. 14. Then, remove the bread rolls from pans and place onto a wire rack until they are completely cool before slicing. 15. Cut each roll into desired size slices and serve.
Per serving: Calories 215g; Total Carbs 36.9g; Net Carbs 8g; Protein 6.5g; Fat 3.1g; Sugar 5.2g; Fiber 18g

Broccoli Quiche

Prep Time: 20 minutes | Cook Time: 30 minutes | Servings: 2

4 eggs	¼ cup feta cheese, crumbled
1 cup whole milk	1 cup grated cheddar cheese
2 medium broccolis, cut into florets	Black pepper and salt, to taste
2 medium tomatoes, diced	1 tsp. Chopped parsley
4 medium carrots, diced	1 tsp. Dried thyme

1. Put the broccoli and carrots in a food steamer and cook until soft, about 10 minutes. 2. In a suitable bowl, crack in the eggs, add the parsley, salt, pepper, and thyme. 3. Using a whisk, beat the eggs while adding the milk gradually until a pale mixture is attained. 4. Once the broccoli and carrots are ready, strain them through a sieve and then set aside. 5. In a 3 x 3 cm quiche dish, add the broccoli and carrots. 6. Put the tomatoes, then the feta and cheddar cheese on top. 7. Pour the prepared egg mixture over the layering and top with the remaining cheddar cheese. 8. Place the dish in the air fryer and Air Fry the food at 350 degrees F/ 175 degrees C for 20 minutes.
Per serving: Calories 316 Fat 23.8 g; Net Carbs 6g; Protein 9.9 g; Total Carbs 5 g; Sugar 2g; Fiber: 1 g

Walnut Banana Bread

Prep Time: 15 minutes | Cook Time: 25 minutes | Servings: 10

1½ cups self-rising flour	⅔ cup plus ½ tbsp. caster sugar
¼ tsp. bicarbonate of soda	2 medium eggs
5 tbsp. plus 1 tsp. butter	3½ oz. walnuts, chopped

2 cups bananas, peeled and mashed

1. In a suitable bowl, mix the flour and bicarbonate of soda. 2. Add the butter, and sugar in another large bowl. Beat until pale and fluffy. 3. Put the eggs, one at a time along with a little flour and mix them well. 4. Stir in the remaining flour and walnuts. 5. Now, add the bananas and mix well. 6. Grease a loaf pan. 7. Place the prepared mixture evenly into the prepared pan. 8. Arrange the loaf pan into an Air Fryer Basket. 9. Air Fry the food for 10 minutes on 355 degrees F/ 180 degrees C, then cook for 15 minutes more at 340 degrees F/ 170 degrees C. 10. Once done, remove from air fryer and place the pan onto a wire rack for 10-15 minutes. 11. Carefully, take out the bread from pan and put onto a wire rack until it is completely cool before slicing. 12. Cut the bread into desired size slices and serve.
Per serving: Calories 337g; Total Carbs 44.5g; Net Carbs 6g; Protein 7.3g; Fat 16g; Sugar 21.6g; Fiber 1g

Walnut Zucchini Bread

Prep Time: 15 minutes | Cook Time: 20 minutes | Servings: 16

3 cups all-purpose flour	1 cup vegetable oil
1 tsp. baking powder	3 eggs
1 tsp. baking soda	3 tsps. vanilla extract
1 tbsp. ground cinnamon	2 cups zucchini, grated
1 tsp. salt	1 cup walnuts, chopped
2¼ cups white sugar	

1. Take a suitable bowl and mix the flour, baking powder, baking soda, cinnamon, and salt. 2. In another large bowl, add the sugar, oil, eggs, and vanilla extract. Beat well. 3. Then, add in the flour mixture and stir well. 4. Gently, fold in the zucchini and walnuts. 5. Grease and flour 2 suitable loaf pans. 6. Place the prepared mixture evenly into the prepared pans. 7. Arrange the loaf pans into an Air Fryer Basket. 8. Air Fry the food at 320 degrees F/ 160 degrees C for 20 minutes or until a toothpick is clean inserted from the center. 9. Remove the pans from Air Fryer and place onto a wire rack for 10-15 minutes. 10. Carefully, take out the bread from pans and put onto a wire rack until it is completely cool before slicing. 11. Cut the breads into desired size slices and serve.
Per serving: Calories 377g; Total Carbs 47.9g; Net Carbs 2g; Protein 5.5g; Fat 19.3g; Sugar 28.7g; Fiber 4g

Chocolate Bread

Prep Time: 15 minutes | Cook Time: 30 minutes | Servings: 8

¾ cup all-purpose flour	1 egg
¼ cup cocoa powder	⅓ cup unsweetened applesauce
¼ cup sugar	¼ cup plain Greek yogurt
½ tsp. baking soda	½ tsp. vanilla extract
½ tsp. baking powder	⅓ cup creamy peanut butter
⅛ tsp. salt	⅓ cup mini chocolate chips

1. In a suitable bowl, mix the flour, cocoa powder, sugar, baking soda, baking powder, and salt. 2. In another bowl, add the egg, applesauce, yogurt, and vanilla extract. Beat well. 3. Then add in the flour mixture and mix well. 4. Add the peanut butter and mix until smooth. 5. Gently, fold in the chocolate chips. 6. Grease a loaf pan. 7. Place the prepared mixture evenly into the prepared pan. 8. Arrange the loaf pan into an Air Fryer Basket. 9. Air Fry the mixture at 350 degrees F/ 175 degrees C for 30 minutes or until a toothpick is clean inserted from the center. 10. Remove from Air Fryer and place the pan onto a wire rack for 10-15 minutes. 11. Carefully, take out the bread from pan and put onto a wire rack until it is completely cool before slicing. 12. Cut the bread into desired size slices and serve.
Per serving: Calories 191g; Total Carbs 24.9g; Net Carbs 5g; Protein 6.1g; Fat 8.6g; Sugar 12.6g; Fiber 1g

Cauliflower Rice

Prep Time: 5 minutes | Cook Time: 15 minutes | Servings: 4

12 oz. cauliflower rice	2 tbsps. lime juice
3 tbsps. stevia	1 lb. fresh spinach, torn
2 tbsps. olive oil	1 red bell pepper, chopped

1. In a suitable cooking pan, add all of the ingredients and toss well. 2. Transfer the cooking pan to the air fryer. 3. Air Fry the food at 370 degrees F/ 185 degrees C for 15 minutes on Air Fry mode, shaking halfway. 4. When done, divide the food between plates and serve for breakfast.
Per serving: Calories 219g; Total Carbs 5g; Net Carbs 2g; Protein 7; Fat 14g; Sugar 2g; Fiber 3g

Chapter 2 Snacks and Appetizers Recipes

Tasty Shrimp Bacon Wraps 19

Mouthwatering Squash Bites 19

Mayo Tortellini 19

Potato Pastries 19

Squash Chips with Sauce 19

Air Fried Shrimp & Bacon 19

Duck Fillet Wraps 19

Bacon Pickle Spear Rolls 20

Olives Fritters with Zucchinis 20

Garlic Mushroom Bites 20

Pork Rinds with Keto Tomato Sauce 20

Easy-to-make Cheese Rounds 20

Cheese Sticks with Coconut 20

Avocado Balls 20

Fresh Shrimp Balls 20

Zucchini Chips with Cheese................................... 20

Salmon Bites with Coconut 20

Delicious Zucchini Crackers 21

Turmeric Chicken Cubes with Coriander 21

Eggplant Chips... 21

Beef Meatballs with Chives 21

Pickles with Egg Wash... 21

Bacon with Chocolate Coating............................... 21

Chicken Bites with Coconut 21

Delicious Mushroom Pizzas................................... 21

Coconut Granola with Almond............................... 21

Bacon Smokies with Tomato Sauce 22

Simple Pizza Bites 22

Air Fried Pork with Fennel 22

Crispy Paprika Chips 22

Mexican Beef Muffins with Tomato Sauce 22

Delectable Chaffles 22

Squash Chips with Parmesan 22

Simple Apple Chips 22

Yogurt Bread 22

Crispy Mustard Fried Leek 23

Coated Cauliflower 23

Crispy Kale Chips 23

Spicy Cocktail Wieners 23

Parmesan Cauliflower Dip 23

Parmesan Steak Nuggets 23

Sprouts Wraps Appetizer 23

Potatoes with Bacon... 23

Delectable Fish Nuggets 23

Zucchini with Parmesan Cheese 24

Chicken Bowls with Berries................................... 24

Crispy Cauliflower Florets 24

Roasted Nut Mixture 24

Enticing Jalapeno Poppers 24

Air-fried Sweet Potato Bites.................................. 24

Cinnamon Almonds 24

Cauliflower Bites 24

Caraway Bread 24

Cabbage Crackers 25

Broccoli Tots 25

Juicy Beef Meatballs 25

Bacon Poppers... 25

Lemon Tofu 25

BBQ Chicken Wings 25

Vegetable Kabobs 25

Shrimp Kabobs 25

Mild Shishito Peppers 25

Thai Chicken Wings... 25

Tofu Steaks 26

Air Fried Cheese Sticks 26

Broccoli Nuggets 26

Chicken Jalapeno Poppers 26

Artichoke Dip 26

Crab Mushrooms 26

Chicken Dip... 26

Smoked Almonds... 26

Parmesan Zucchini Bites 26

Broccoli Pop-corn 27

Rosemary Beans 27

Cheesy Brussels sprouts 27

Mushrooms with Sauce 27

Baguette Bread... 27

Cheese Artichoke Dip 27

Crusted Onion Rings 27

Asparagus Pork Fries 27

Pork Meatballs... 27

Tasty Shrimp Bacon Wraps

Prep Time: 8-10 minutes | Cook time: 8 minutes | Serves: 8-10

½ teaspoon red pepper flakes, crushed
1 tablespoon salt
1 teaspoon chili powder
1 ¼ pounds shrimp, peeled and deveined

1 teaspoon paprika
½ teaspoon black pepper, ground
1 tablespoon shallot powder
¼ teaspoon cumin powder
1 ¼ pounds thin bacon slices

1. Prepare your clean air fryer. 2. Preheat the air fryer for 4 to 5 minutes at 360 degrees F/ 180 degrees C. 3. Oil or spray the air-frying basket gently. 4. Mix the shrimp and seasoning in a medium-size bowl thoroughly, until they are coated well. 5. Use a slice of bacon to wrap around the shrimps and use a toothpick to secure them. Then place them in the refrigerator and cool for 30 minutes. 6. Add the shrimps to the basket and then put the basket in the air fryer. 7. Cook the shrimps for 8 minutes. 8. You can serve with cocktail sticks or your choice of dip (optional).
Per serving: Calories: 199; Fat: 4.9g; Sodium: 2178mg; Total Carbs: 3g; Net Carbs: 1g; Fiber: 0.6g; Sugars: 0.1g; Protein: 34.1g

Mouthwatering Squash Bites

Prep Time: 8-10 minutes | Cook time: 20 minutes | Serves: 5-6

1 ½ pounds winter squash, peeled and make chunks
¼ cup dark brown sugar
2 tablespoons sage, chopped
Zest of 1 small-sized lemon

2 tablespoons coconut oil, melted
A coarse pinch salt
A pinch pepper
⅛ teaspoon allspice, ground

1. Prepare your clean air fryer. 2. Preheat the air fryer for 4 to 5 minutes at 350 degrees F/ 175 degrees C. 3. Oil or spray the air-frying basket lightly. 4. In addition to the squash, mix the other ingredients thoroughly in a medium-size bowl. 5. Let the squash chunks be covered with the mixture. 6. Arrange the chunks to the air-frying basket and place the basket to the air fryer. Cook the food for 10 minutes. 7. When the time is up, increase temperature to 400 degrees F/ 205 degrees C and cook for 8 more minutes. 8. Once done, serve warm!
Per serving: Calories: 110; Fat: 4.7g; Sodium: 5mg; Total Carbs: 18g; Net Carbs: 9.5g; Fiber: 2g; Sugars: 5.9g; Protein: 1g

Mayo Tortellini

Prep Time: 10 minutes | Cook time: 10 minutes | Serves: 4-5

½ cup flour
½ teaspoon dried oregano
1 ½ cups breadcrumbs
¾ cup mayonnaise

2 tablespoons mustard
1 egg
2 tablespoons olive oil
2 cups cheese tortellini, frozen

1. Prepare your clean air fryer. 2. Preheat the air fryer for 4 to 5 minutes at 355 degrees F/ 180 degrees C. 3. Let the flour and oregano be combined in a bowl, and the breadcrumbs and olive oil be combined in another bowl. 4. Mix the mustard and mayonnaise in a bowl of medium size, and set aside. 5. Thoroughly whisk the egg in another same-sized bowl. 6. Add the tortellini to the egg mixture, then into the flour, then into the egg again. At last, add the breadcrumbs to coat well. 7. Arrange the basket in the air fryer with the prepared tortellini in it. Cook for 10 minutes until turn golden. 8. When done, serve with the mayonnaise.
Per serving: Calories: 558; Fat: 24.6g; Sodium: 666mg; Total Carbs: 70.8g; Net Carbs: 0g; Fiber: 2.5g; Sugars: 4.7g; Protein: 14.6g

Potato Pastries

Prep Time: 15 minutes | Cook time: 37 Minutes | Serves: 8

2 large potatoes, peeled
1 tablespoon olive oil
½ cup carrot, peeled and chopped
½ cup onion, chopped
2 garlic cloves, minced

1 tablespoon fresh ginger, minced
½ cup green peas, shelled
Salt and ground black pepper, as needed
3 puff pastry sheets

1. Boil water in a suitable pan, then put the potatoes and cook for about 15-20 minutes 2. Drain the potatoes well and then mash the potatoes. 3. Heat the oil over medium heat in a skillet, then add the carrot, onion, ginger, garlic and sauté for about 4-5 minutes. 4. Then drain all the fat from the skillet. 5. Stir in the mashed potatoes, peas, salt and black pepper. Continue to cook for about 1-2 minutes. 6. Remove the potato mixture from heat and set aside to cool completely. 7. After placing the puff pastry onto a smooth surface, cut each puff pastry sheet into four pieces and cut each piece into a round shape. 8. Add about 2 tablespoons of veggie filling over each pastry round. 9. Use your wet finger to moisten the edges. 10. To seal the filling, fold each pastry round in half. 11. Firmly press the edges with a fork. 12. Set the temperature setting to 390 degrees F/ 200 degrees C. 13. Arrange the pastries in the basket of your air fryer and air fry for about 5 minutes at 390 minutes. 14. Work in 2 batches. 15. Serve.
Per serving: Calories: 192; Fat: 8.7g; Sodium: 55mg; Total Carbs: 25.8g; Net Carbs: 11g; Fiber: 3.4g; Sugars: 2.4g; Protein: 3.6g

Squash Chips with Sauce

Prep Time: 15 minutes | Cook time: 25 minutes| Serves: 4

½ cup seasoned breadcrumbs
½ cup Parmesan cheese, grated
Sea salt, to taste
Ground black pepper, to taste
¼-teaspoon oregano
2 yellow squash, cut into slices
½ tablespoon grapeseed oil

Sauce:
½ cup Greek-style yogurt
1 tablespoon fresh cilantro, chopped
1 garlic clove, minced
Freshly ground black pepper, to your liking

1. Thoroughly combine the seasoned breadcrumbs, Parmesan, salt, black pepper, and oregano in a prepared shallow bowl. 2. Dip the yellow squash slices in the prepared batter and press to make it adhere. 3. Place the squash slices in the basket of your air fryer and brush them with grapeseed oil. 4. Cook at 400 degrees F/ 205 degrees C for 12 minutes. Shake the basket periodically to ensure even cooking. Work in batches. 5. Meanwhile, whisk the sauce ingredients; place in your refrigerator until ready to serve. 6. Enjoy!
Per serving: Calories: 117; Fat: 7.1g; Sodium: 120mg; Total Carbs: 8g; Net Carbs: 3.5g; Fiber: 1.3g; Sugars: 4.5g; Protein: 5g

Air Fried Shrimp & Bacon

Prep Time: 10 minutes | Cook time: 10 minutes | Serves: 4-6

16 ounces sliced bacon

20 ounces peeled shrimp, deveined

1. Prepare your clean air fryer. 2. Preheat the air fryer for 4 to 5 minutes at 390 degrees F/ 200 degrees C. 3. Make the shrimps under the bacon regularly. Put them in the refrigerator and cool for 15 to 20 minutes. 4. After that, take out the shrimps and place them in the air-frying basket. 5. Let the shrimps be cooked for 6 minutes in the air fryer. 6. Serve and enjoy!
Per serving: Calories: 482; Fat: 35.3g; Sodium: 1850mg; Total Carbs: 4.5g; Net Carbs: 0.5g; Fiber: 0.1g; Sugars: 0g; Protein: 34.4g

Duck Fillet Wraps

Prep Time: 15 minutes | Cook time: 6 minutes | Serves:6

1 pound duck fillet, boiled
1 tablespoon mascarpone
1 teaspoon chili flakes
1 teaspoon onion powder

6 wonton wraps
1 egg yolk, whisked
Cooking spray

1. Chop the boiled duck fillet and mix it up with mascarpone, onion powder and chili flakes. 2. After that, fill the wonton wraps with the duck mixture and roll them in the shape of pies. 3. Use the egg yolk to brush the duck pies. 4. Preheat the air fryer to 385F. 5. Put the duck pies in the air fryer and Spray the duck pies with the cooking spray after putting them on the cooking tray in the air fryer. 6. Cook the duck pies at 385 degrees F/ 195 degrees C for 6 minutes, flipping halfway through. 7. When done, serve and enjoy.
Per serving: Calories: 76; Fat: 2.3g; Sodium: 40mg; Total Carbs: 5g; Net Carbs: 1g; Fiber: 0.1g; Sugars: 0.3g; Protein: 8.9g

Bacon Pickle Spear Rolls

Prep Time: 5 minutes | Cook time: 20 minutes | Serves: 4

4 dill pickle spears, sliced in half   1 cup avocado mayonnaise
8 bacon slices, halved

1. Use a bacon slice to wrap a pickle spear. 2. Arrange the wraps in the basket of air fryer and cook them for 20 minutes at 400 degrees F/ 205 degrees C. 3. After dividing into bowls and serve as a snack with the mayonnaise.
Per serving: Calories: 213; Fat: 16g; Sodium: 1663mg; Total Carbs: 2g; Net Carbs: 0.5g; Fiber: 0.8g; Sugars: 0.7g; Protein: 14.3g

Olives Fritters with Zucchinis

Prep Time: 5 minutes | Cook time: 12 minutes | Serves: 6

Cooking spray   Salt and black pepper to the taste 3
½ cup parsley, chopped   spring onions, chopped
1 egg   ½ cup Kalamata olives, pitted and
½ cup almond flour   minced 3 zucchinis, grated

1. In addition to the cooking spray, thoroughly mix up the other ingredients in a bowl and then shape medium fritters. 2. Grease the fritters with cooking spray after placing them in the basket of your air fryer. 3. Cook for 12 minutes at 380 degrees F/ 195 degrees C, flipping halfway through. 4. Serve them as an appetizer.
Per serving: Calories: 59; Fat: 4.6g; Sodium: 167mg; Total Carbs: 2g; Net Carbs: 0.5g; Fiber: 1.2g; Sugars: 0.1g; Protein: 2.5g

Garlic Mushroom Bites

Prep Time: 5 minutes | Cook time: 12 minutes | Serves: 6

Salt and black pepper to the taste   1 tablespoons basil, minced
1 ¼ cups coconut flour   ½ pound mushrooms, minced
2 garlic clove, minced   1 egg, whisked

1. In addition to the cooking spray, thoroughly mix up other ingredients and shape medium balls out of this mix. 2. Arrange the balls in the basket of your air fryer and grease them with cooking spray. 3. Air fry at 350 degrees F/ 175 degrees C for 6 minutes on each side. 4. Serve as an appetizer.
Per serving: Calories: 90; Fat: 2.8g; Sodium: 19mg; Total Carbs: 12.5g; Net Carbs: 6g; Fiber: 6.6g; Sugars: 1.1g; Protein: 5.3g

Pork Rinds with Keto Tomato Sauce

Prep Time: 10 minutes | Cook time: 10 minutes | Serves:3

6 oz. pork skin   1 teaspoon olive oil
1 tablespoon keto tomato sauce

1. Chop the pork skin into the rinds. 2. Sprinkle the pork rinds with the sauce and olive oil. Mix up well. 3. Place the pork skin rinds in the air fryer basket and cook for 10 minutes at 400 degrees F/ 205 degrees C, flipping halfway through. 4. When done, serve and cook.
Per serving: Calories: 175; Fat: 10.5g; Sodium: 659mg; Total Carbs: 1g; Net Carbs: 0g; Fiber: 0.3g; Sugars: 0.7g; Protein: 17.4g

Easy-to-make Cheese Rounds

Prep Time: 10 minutes | Cook time: 6 minutes | Serves:4

1 cup Cheddar cheese, shredded

1. Preheat the air fryer to 400 degrees F/ 205 degrees C. 2. Prepare the air fryer basket by lining it with baking paper. 3. Sprinkle the cheese on the baking paper in the shape of small rounds. 4. Cook them for 6 minutes or until the cheese is melted and starts to be crispy. 5. Serve and enjoy!
Per serving: Calories: 114; Fat: 9.4g; Sodium: 175mg; Total Carbs: 0.4g; Net Carbs: 1g; Fiber: 0g; Sugars: 0.2g; Protein: 7g

Cheese Sticks with Coconut

Prep Time: 10 minutes | Cook time: 4 minutes | Serves:4

1 egg, beaten   6 oz. Provolone cheese
4 tablespoons coconut flakes   Cooking spray
1 teaspoon ground paprika

1. Cut the cheese into sticks. 2. Dip every cheese stick in the beaten egg. 3. After this, mix up coconut flakes and ground paprika. 4. Coat the cheese sticks in the coconut mixture. 5. Preheat the air fryer to degrees F/ 205 degrees C. Put the cheese sticks in the air fryer and spray them with cooking spray. 6. Cook the meal for 2 minutes from each side. 7. Cool them well before serving.
Per serving: Calories: 184; Fat: 14.2g; Sodium: 389mg; Total Carbs: 2g; Net Carbs: 0.5g; Fiber: 0.7g; Sugars: 0.7g; Protein: 12.5g

Avocado Balls

Prep Time: 5 minutes | Cook time: 5 minutes | Serves: 4

1 avocado, peeled, pitted and   1 tablespoon lime juice
mashed   2 tablespoons cilantro
¼ cup ghee, melted   A pinch of salt and black pepper
garlic cloves, minced 2 spring   4 bacon slices, cooked and crum-
onions, minced   bled cooking spray
1 chili pepper, chopped

1. In addition to the cooking spray, mix the other ingredients well in a bowl and shape medium balls out of this mix. 2. Grease the balls with cooking spray after placing them in the basket of your air fryer. 3. Cook the balls at 370 degrees F/ 185 degrees C for 5 minutes. 4. Serve as a snack.
Per serving: Calories: 319; Fat: 30.5g; Sodium: 443mg; Total Carbs: 5g; Net Carbs: 2g; Fiber: 3.5g; Sugars: 0.3g; Protein: 8.1g

Fresh Shrimp Balls

Prep Time: 5 minutes | Cook time: 15 minutes | Serves: 4

1 pound shrimp, peeled, deveined   ½ cup coconut flour
and minced   1 tablespoon avocado oil
1 egg, whisked   1 tablespoon cilantro, chopped
3 tablespoons coconut, shredded

1. In a bowl, mix shrimp, the whisked egg, shredded coconut, coconut oil, avocado oil, and cilantro well and shape the mixture into medium balls out of this mix. 2. Arrange the balls in your lined air fryer's basket. 3. Cook the balls at 350 degrees F/ 175 degrees C for 15 minutes. 4. When done, you can serve as an appetizer.
Per serving: Calories: 228; Fat: 6.2g; Sodium: 293mg; Total Carbs: 12g; Net Carbs: 7g; Fiber: 6.5g; Sugars: 0.3g; Protein: 29.4g

Zucchini Chips with Cheese

Prep Time: 10 minutes | Cook time: 13 minutes | Serves:8

2 zucchinis, thinly sliced   2 eggs, beaten
4 tablespoons almond flour   ½ teaspoon white pepper
2 oz. Parmesan   Cooking spray

1. Prepare your clean air fryer and preheat it to 355 degrees F/ 180 degrees C. 2. Thoroughly mix up almond flour, Parmesan and white pepper in a large bowl. 3. After that, dip the zucchini slices in the egg and coat in the almond flour mixture. 4. Place the prepared zucchini slices in the preheated air fryer and cook them for 10 minutes. 5. Flip the vegetables on another side and cook them for 3 minutes more or until crispy. 6. Serve and enjoy.
Per serving: Calories: 114; Fat: 7.1g; Sodium: 174mg; Total Carbs: 4.9g; Net Carbs: 1g; Fiber: 1.5g; Sugars: 1.9g; Protein: 9.3g

Salmon Bites with Coconut

Prep Time: 5 minutes | Cook time: 10 minutes | Serves: 12

2 avocados, peeled, pitted and   2 tablespoons coconut cream
mashed   1 teaspoon avocado oil
4 ounces smoked salmon, skinless,   1 teaspoon dill, chopped
boneless and chopped   A pinch of salt and black pepper

1. Mix the avocados, smoked salmon, coconut cream, avocado oil, the chopped dill, salt, and black pepper well in a clean bowl. 2. Shape medium balls out of this mix. 3. Place the balls in the basket of your air fryer. 4. Cook at 350 degrees F/ 175 degrees C for 10 minutes. 5. Serve as an appetizer.
Per serving: Calories: 171; Fat: 15.1g; Sodium: 383mg; Total Carbs: 6g; Net Carbs: 2.5g; Fiber: 4.6g; Sugars: 0.5g; Protein: 4.9g

Delicious Zucchini Crackers

Prep Time: 15 minutes | Cook time: 20 minutes | Serves:12

1 cup zucchini, grated
2 tablespoons flax meal
1 teaspoon salt
3 tablespoons almond flour
¼ teaspoon baking powder

¼ teaspoon chili flakes
1 tablespoon xanthan gum
1 tablespoon butter, softened
1 egg, beaten
Cooking spray

1. Squeeze the zucchini to remove the vegetable juice and transfer to a large bowl. 2. Thoroughly mix up the flax meal, salt, almond flour, baking powder, chili flakes and xanthan gum. 3. Add butter and egg. Knead the non- sticky dough. 4. Place the mixture on the baking paper and cover with another baking paper. 5. Roll up the dough into the flat square. 6. After this, remove the baking paper from the dough surface. 7. Cut it on medium size crackers. 8. Prepare the air fryer basket by lining it with baking paper, and then put the crackers inside it. 9. Spray them with cooking spray. Cook them for 20 minutes at 355 degrees F/ 180 degrees C. 10. Serve and enjoy.
Per serving: Calories: 62; Fat: 5.1g; Sodium: 209mg; Total Carbs: 2g; Net Carbs: 0.5g; Fiber: 1.2g; Sugars: 0.2g; Protein: 2.3g

Turmeric Chicken Cubes with Coriander

Prep Time: 10 minutes | Cook time: 12 minutes | Serves: 6

8 oz. chicken fillet
½ teaspoon ground black pepper
½ teaspoon ground turmeric
¼ teaspoon ground coriander

½ teaspoon ground paprika
3 egg whites, whisked
4 tablespoons almond flour
Cooking spray

1. Mix up ground black pepper, turmeric, coriander, and paprika well in a shallow bowl. 2. Chop the chicken fillet on the small cubes. 3. Sprinkle them with spice mixture. Stir well and add egg white. 4. Mix up the chicken and egg whites well. 5. After that, coat every chicken cube with the almond flour. 6. Preheat the air fryer to 375F. 7. Arrange the chicken cubes to the basket of your air fryer and gently spray with cooking spray. 8. Cook the chicken cubes for 7 minutes at 375 degrees F/ 190 degrees C, then shake the chicken popcorn well and cook it for 5 minutes more. 9. Once cooked, serve and enjoy!
Per serving: Calories: 110; Fat: 5.1g; Sodium: 51mg; Total Carbs: 1g; Net Carbs: 0g; Fiber: 0.7g; Sugars: 0.2g; Protein: 13.8g

Eggplant Chips

Prep Time: 10 minutes | Cook time: 25 minutes | Serves:4

1 eggplant, sliced
1 teaspoon garlic powder

1 tablespoon olive oil

1. Mix the garlic powder and olive oil well. 2. Brush every eggplant slice with a garlic powder mixture. 3. Place the eggplant slices in the cooking pan of your air fryer. Cook them for 15 minutes at 400 degrees F/ 205 degrees C. 4. When the time is up, flip the eggplant slices and cook the other side for 10 minutes. 5. Serve and enjoy!
Per serving: Calories: 61; Fat: 3.7g; Sodium: 2mg; Total Carbs: 7g; Net Carbs: 3g; Fiber: 4.1g; Sugars: 3.6g; Protein: 1.2g

Beef Meatballs with Chives

Prep Time: 5 minutes | Cook time: 20 minutes | Serves: 6

1 pound beef meat, ground
1 teaspoon onion powder
1 teaspoon garlic powder

A pinch of salt and black pepper
2 tablespoons chives, chopped
Cooking spray

1. In addition to the cooking spray, mix the other ingredients well in a bowl and shape medium meatballs out of this mix. 2. Place the balls in the basket of your air fryer and oil them. 3. Cook for 20 minutes at 360 degrees F/ 180 degrees C. 4. When done, serve as an appetizer.
Per serving: Calories: 167; Fat: 6.5g; Sodium: 73mg; Total Carbs: 0.7g; Net Carbs: 0g; Fiber: 0.1g; Sugars: 0.3g; Protein: 24.9g

Pickles with Egg Wash

Prep Time: 10 minutes | Cook time: 8 minutes | Serves:4

2 pickles, sliced
1 tablespoon dried dill

1 egg, beaten
2 tablespoons flax meal

1. Coat the sliced pickles with the egg, then sprinkle with the dried ill and flax meal. 2. Arrange the pickles to the basket of your air fryer and cook for 8 minutes at 400 degrees F/ 205 degrees C.
Per serving: Calories: 110; Fat: 5.1g; Sodium: 51mg; Total Carbs: 1.5g; Net Carbs: 1g; Fiber: 0.7g; Sugars: 0.2g; Protein: 13.8g

Bacon with Chocolate Coating

Prep Time: 5 minutes | Cook time: 10 minutes | Serves: 4

4 bacon slices, halved
1 cup dark chocolate, melted A

pinch of pink salt

1. Make each bacon slice be coated some chocolate and then sprinkle pink salt over them. 2. Arrange them in the cooking tray of your air fryer. 3. Cook at 350 degrees F/ 175 degrees C for 10 minutes. 4. When cooked, serve as a snack.
Per serving: Calories: 327; Fat: 20.4g; Sodium: 472mg; Total Carbs: 25g; Net Carbs: 16g; Fiber: 1.4g; Sugars: 21.6g; Protein: 10.3g

Chicken Bites with Coconut

Prep Time: 5 minutes | Cook time: 20 minutes | Serves: 4

2 teaspoons garlic powder
2 eggs
Salt and black pepper to the taste
¾ cup coconut flakes

Cooking spray
1 pound chicken breasts, skinless, boneless, and cubed

1. In a bowl, put the coconut in and mix the eggs with garlic powder, salt and pepper in a second one. 2. Dredge the chicken cubes in eggs and then in coconut. 3. Arrange all the prepared chicken cubes to the basket. 4. Grease with cooking spray and cook them at 370 degrees F/ 185 degrees C for 20 minutes. 5. When cooked, place the chicken bites on a platter and serve as an appetizer.
Per serving: Calories: 306; Fat: 15.8g; Sodium: 132mg; Total Carbs: 3.5g; Net Carbs: 0.5g; Fiber: 1.5g; Sugars: 1.4g; Protein: 36.3g

Delicious Mushroom Pizzas

Prep Time: 10 minutes | Cook time: 7 minutes | Serves:6

6 cremini mushroom caps
3 oz. Parmesan, grated
1 tablespoon olive oil

½ tomato, chopped
½ teaspoon dried basil
1 teaspoon ricotta cheese

1. Oil the mushroom caps and arrange them in the air fryer. 2. Sprinkle the mushroom caps with olive oil and put in the air fryer basket in one layer. 3. Cook them for 3 minutes at 400 degrees F/ 205 degrees C. 4. After this, mix up the ricotta cheese and tomato. 5. Fill the mushroom caps with tomato mixture. Then top them with parmesan and sprinkle with dried basil. 6. Cook the mushroom pizzas for 4 minutes at 400 degrees F/ 205 degrees C. 7. When done, serve and enjoy.
Per serving: Calories: 132; Fat: 8.2g; Sodium: 199mg; Total Carbs: 5g; Net Carbs: 2g; Fiber: 0.1g; Sugars: 1.7g; Protein: 10.1g

Coconut Granola with Almond

Prep Time: 10 minutes | Cook time: 12 minutes | Serves:4

1 teaspoon monk fruit
1 teaspoon almond butter
1 teaspoon coconut oil
2 tablespoons almonds, chopped
1 teaspoon pumpkin puree
½ teaspoon pumpkin pie spices

2 tablespoons coconut flakes
2 tablespoons pumpkin seeds, crushed
1 teaspoon hemp seeds
1 teaspoon flax seeds
Cooking spray

1. Mix up almond butter and coconut oil in a big bowl and then microwave the mixture until melted. 2. Continue to mix up the pumpkin spices, pumpkin seeds, monk fruit, coconut flakes, hemp seeds and flax seeds in another suitable bowl. 3. Add the pumpkin puree and melted coconut oil, then stir the mixture until homogenous. 4. Arrange the pumpkin mixture on the baking paper and make the shape of square, then cut the square on the serving bars and transfer in the air fryer. 5. Cook them for 12 minutes at 350 degrees F/ 175 degrees C. 6. Once done, serve and enjoy.
Per serving: Calories: 88; Fat: 7.9g; Sodium: 2mg; Total Carbs: 3g; Net Carbs: 1g; Fiber: 1.4g; Sugars: 0.6g; Protein: 2.8g

Bacon Smokies with Tomato Sauce

Prep Time: 15 minutes | Cook time: 10 minutes | Serves:10

12 oz. pork and beef smokies	1 teaspoon Erythritol
3 oz. bacon, sliced	1 teaspoon avocado oil
1 teaspoon keto tomato sauce	½ teaspoon cayenne pepper

1. Use the cayenne pepper and tomato sauce to sprinkle the smokies, then repeat the step with the Erythritol and olive oil. 2. After that, wrap every smokie in the bacon and use the toothpick to secure each roll. 3. Arrange the bacon smokies in the air fryer and cook for 10 minutes at 400 degrees F/ 205 degrees C. 4. During cooking, to avoid over cooking, shake them gently. 5. When done, serve and enjoy.
Per serving: Calories: 287; Fat: 24g; Sodium: 1036mg; Total Carbs: 2g; Net Carbs: 0.5g; Fiber: 0g; Sugars: 2.4g; Protein: 14g

Simple Pizza Bites

Prep Time: 15 minutes | Cook time: 3 minutes | Serves:10

10 Mozzarella cheese slices	10 pepperoni slices

1. Line the air fryer pan with baking paper and put Mozzarella cheese slices in it. 2. Cook them for 3 minutes at 400 degrees F/ 205 degrees C or until melted. Once cooked, remove the cheese from the air fryer and cool them to room temperature. 3. Put the pepperoni slices on the cheese and fold the cheese in the shape of turnovers. 4. Enjoy!
Per serving: Calories: 107; Fat: 7.4g; Sodium: 261mg; Total Carbs: 1g; Net Carbs: 0g; Fiber: 0g; Sugars: 0g; Protein: 9.3g

Air Fried Pork with Fennel

Prep Time: 10 minutes | Cook time: 25 minutes | Serves: 6

2 pounds pork belly, cut into strips	A pinch of salt and black pepper
2 tablespoons olive oil	A pinch of basil, dried
2 teaspoons fennel seeds	

1. Mix all the ingredients in a clean bowl. 2. Toss well and arrange the marinated pork strips to the basket of your air fryer. 3. Cook for 25 minutes at 425 degrees F/ 220 degrees C. 4. Before serving as a snack, divide into bowls.
Per serving: Calories: 122; Fat: 9.4g; Sodium: 281mg; Total Carbs: 0.4g; Net Carbs: 1g; Fiber: 0.3g; Sugars: 0g; Protein: 8.1g

Crispy Paprika Chips

Prep Time: 2 minutes | Cook time: 5 minutes | Serves: 4

8 ounces' cheddar cheese, shredded	1 teaspoon sweet paprika

1. Divide the cheese in small heaps in a suitable pan. 2. After sprinkling the paprika on top, arrange the cheeses to the air fryer and cook at 400 degrees F/ 205 degrees C for 5 minutes. 3. Cool the chips down before serving them.
Per serving: Calories: 139; Fat: 11.3g; Sodium: 211mg; Total Carbs: 0.7g; Net Carbs: 1g; Fiber: 0.2g; Sugars: 0.2g; Protein: 8.6g

Mexican Beef Muffins with Tomato Sauce

Prep Time: 10 minutes | Cook time: 15 minutes | Serves:4

1 cup ground beef	shredded
1 teaspoon taco seasonings	1 teaspoon tomato sauce
2 oz. Mexican blend cheese,	Cooking spray

1. Thoroughly mix up ground beef and taco seasonings in a mixing bowl. 2. Spray the muffin molds with cooking spray. 3. Transfer the ground beef mixture in the muffin molds. Place the cheese and tomato sauce on the top. 4. Transfer the muffin molds in the prepared air fryer and cook them for 15 minutes at 375 degrees F/ 190 degrees C. 5. When cooked, serve and enjoy.
Per serving: Calories: 202; Fat: 10.1g; Sodium: 232mg; Total Carbs: 0.7g; Net Carbs: 0g; Fiber: 0g; Sugars: 0.7g; Protein: 25.5g

Delectable Chaffles

Prep Time: 10 minutes | Cook time: 25 minutes | Serves:4

4 eggs, beaten	2 oz. bacon, chopped, cooked
1 cucumber, pickled, grated	½ teaspoon ground black pepper
2 oz. Cheddar cheese, shredded	Cooking spray
¼ teaspoon salt	

1. The chaffle batter should be cooked. 2. Spray the air fryer pan with cooking spray. 3. Mix up eggs, bacon, pickled cucumber, cheese, salt, and ground black pepper in a mixing bowl. Whisk the mixture gently. 4. Pour ¼ part of the liquid on the pan. 5. Arrange the pan to the air fryer and cook the chaffle for 6 minutes at 400 degrees F/ 205 degrees C. 6. When cooked, transfer the cooked chaffle in the plate. 7. Repeat the same steps with the remaining chaffle batter and you should get 4 chaffles. 8. Enjoy.
Per serving: Calories: 209; Fat: 15.1g; Sodium: 626mg; Total Carbs: 3g; Net Carbs: 1g; Fiber: 0.5g; Sugars: 1.7g; Protein: 14.8g

Squash Chips with Parmesan

Prep Time: 10 minutes | Cook time: 12 minutes | Serves 3

¾ pound butternut squash, cut into thin rounds	Ground black pepper, to taste
½ cup Parmesan cheese, grated	1 teaspoon butter
Sea salt, to taste	½ cup ketchup
	1 teaspoon Sriracha sauce

1. Stir the butternut squash with butter, Parmesan cheese, salt and black pepper. 2. Transfer the butternut squash rounds to the cooking basket of your air fryer. 3. Cook the butternut squash for 12 minutes at 400 degrees F/ 205 degrees C. 4. When cooking, shake the basket periodically to ensure even cooking. Work with batches. 5. Whisk the ketchup and siracha While the Parmesan squash chips are baking, set it aside. 6. When done, serve the Parmesan squash chips with Sriracha ketchup and enjoy!
Per serving: Calories: 116; Fat: 2.5g; Sodium: 503mg; Total Carbs: 23g; Net Carbs: 11g; Fiber: 2.4g; Sugars: 11.6g; Protein: 3.3g

Simple Apple Chips

Prep Time: 10 minutes | Cook time: 8 minutes | Serves: 3

3 medium apples, washed, cored, and thinly sliced	juice
Non-stick cooking spray	1 teaspoon cinnamon
½ cup freshly squeezed lemon	2 tablespoons avocado oil

1. Coat the apple slices with lemon juice and avocado oil lightly. 2. Arrange the apple slices to the air fryer and cook for 8 minutes at 200 degrees F/ 95 degrees C, turning once or twice during cooking to ensure even cooking. 3. Cooking in batches is suggested. 4. When done, take the apple slices out and serve, sprinkle with cinnamon and store them in an airtight container. 5. Enjoy!
Per serving: Calories: 140; Fat: 1.9g; Sodium: 11mg; Total Carbs: 32g; Net Carbs: 12g; Fiber: 6.4g; Sugars: 24.1g; Protein: 1.1g

Yogurt Bread

Prep Time: 20 minutes | Cook Time: 40 minutes | Servings: 10

1½ cups warm water, divided	3 cups all-purpose flour
1½ tsp. active dry yeast	1 cup plain Greek yogurt
1 tsp. sugar	2 tsps. kosher salt

1. Add ½ cup of the warm water, yeast and sugar in a stand mixer's bowl, fitted with the dough hook attachment and mix well. 2. Set aside for 5 minutes 3. Add the flour, yogurt, and salt and mix on medium-low speed until the dough comes together. 4. Then, mix on medium speed for 5 minutes 5. Place the dough into a bowl. 6. With a plastic wrap, cover the bowl and place in a warm place for 2-3 hours or until doubled in size. 7. Knead the dough into a smooth ball on a lightly floured surface. 8. Place the dough onto a greased baking paper-lined rack. 9. With a kitchen towel, cover the dough and let rest for 15 minutes 10. With a very sharp knife, cut a 4x½-inch deep cut down the center of the dough. 11. Cook the food at 325 degrees F/ 160 degrees C for 40 minutes on Roast mode. 12. Carefully, invert the bread onto wire rack to cool completely before slicing. 13. Cut the bread into desired-sized slices and serve.
Per serving: Calories 157; Total Carbs 31 g; Net Carbs 2g; Protein 5.5 g; Fat 5 g; Sugar 1.2 g; Fiber 1 g

Crispy Mustard Fried Leek

Prep Time: 15 minutes | Cook time: 10 minutes | Serves: 4

1 large-sized leek, cut into ½-inch wide rings	1 egg
Black pepper and salt, to taste	½ cup almond flour
1 teaspoon mustard	½ teaspoon baking powder
1 cup milk	½ cup pork rinds, crushed

1. Toss your leeks with black pepper and salt. 2. In a suitable mixing bowl, whisk the mustard, milk and egg until frothy and pale. 3. Now, combine almond flour and baking powder in another mixing bowl. In the third bowl, place the pork rinds. 4. Coat the leek slices with the almond meal mixture. 5. Dredge the floured leek slices into the milk/egg mixture, coating well. Finally, roll them over the pork rinds. 6. Air-fry for approximately 10 minutes at 370 degrees F/ 185 degrees C. Serve!
Per serving: Calories: 95; Fat: 4.9g; Sodium: 84mg; Total Carbs: 7g; Net Carbs: 3g; Fiber: 0.9g; Sugars: 3.8g; Protein: 5.8g

Coated Cauliflower

Prep Time: 10 minutes | Cook time: 30 Minutes | Serves: 2

½ lemon, juiced	½ teaspoon curry powder
1 head cauliflower	Sea salt to taste
½-tablespoon olive oil	Ground black pepper to taste

1. Cut out the leaves and core of the cauliflower and wash it. 2. Chop the processed cauliflower into equally-sized florets. 3. Mix together the fresh lemon juice and curry powder in a suitable bowl, then add in the cauliflower florets. 4. After sprinkling in the pepper and salt, mix again and coat the florets well. 5. Oil the cooking pan in your air fryer and then arrange the florets to it. 6. Cook the food for 20 minutes at 390 degrees F/ 200 degrees C. 7. Serve warm,
Per serving: Calories: 66; Fat: 3.8g; Sodium: 157mg; Total Carbs: 7g; Net Carbs: 3g; Fiber: 3.6g; Sugars: 3.2g; Protein: 2.8g

Crispy Kale Chips

Prep Time: 5 minutes | Cook Time: 5 minutes | Servings: 2

1 bunch of kale, remove stem and cut into pieces	1 tsp. olive oil
½ tsp. garlic powder	½ tsp. salt

1. Add all the recipe ingredients into the large bowl and toss well. 2. Transfer the kale mixture into the "Air Fryer Basket" and Air Fry for 3 minutes at 370 degrees F/ 185 degrees C. 3. When the time runs out, shake the basket well and Air Fry for 2 minutes more. 4. Serve and enjoy.
Per serving: Calories 37; Fat 1 g; Total Carbs 6 g; Sugar 1 g; Net Carbs 5g; Protein 3 g; Fiber 0 g

Spicy Cocktail Wieners

Prep Time: 10 minutes | Cook time: 15 Minutes | Serves: 4

1 lb. pork cocktail sausages	1 whole grain mustard
For the Sauce:	¼- ½ teaspoon balsamic vinegar
¼ cup mayonnaise	1 garlic clove, finely minced
¼ cup cream cheese	¼ teaspoon chili powder

1. Pork the sausages a few times with a fork, them place them on the cooking pan of your air fryer. 2. Cook the sausages at 390 degrees F/ 200 degrees C for 15 minutes; 3. After 8 minutes of cooking, turn the sausages over and resume cooking. 4. Check for doneness and take the sausages out of the machine. 5. At the same time, thoroughly combine all the ingredients for the sauce. 6. Serve with warm sausages and enjoy!
Per serving: Calories: 149; Fat: 12.8g; Sodium: 226mg; Total Carbs: 5.5g; Net Carbs: 1g; Fiber: 0.2g; Sugars: 1.1g; Protein: 3.6g

Parmesan Cauliflower Dip

Prep Time: 15 minutes | Cook time: 45 minutes | Serves: 10

1 cauliflower head, cut into florets	1 teaspoon Worcestershire sauce
1 ½ cups parmesan cheese, shredded	½ cup sour cream
2 tablespoons green onions, chopped	¾ cup mayonnaise
2 garlic clove	8 ounces cream cheese, softened
	2 tablespoons olive oil

1. Toss cauliflower florets with olive oil. 2. Add cauliflower florets into the air fryer basket and cook at almost 390 degrees F/ 200 degrees C for 20-25 minutes. 3. Add cooked cauliflower, 1 cup of parmesan cheese, cream cheese, green onion, garlic, Worcestershire sauce, sour cream, and mayonnaise into the food processor and process until smooth. 4. Transfer cauliflower mixture into the 7-inch dish and top with remaining parmesan cheese. 5. Place dish in air fryer basket and Cook at almost 360 degrees F/ 180 degrees C for almost 10-15 minutes. 6. Serve and enjoy.
Per serving: Calories: 194; Fat: 17.1g; Sodium: 251mg; Total Carbs: 7.2g; Net Carbs: 1g; Fiber: 0.7g; Sugars: 2g; Protein: 4.2g

Parmesan Steak Nuggets

Prep Time: 15 minutes | Cook time: 18 minutes | Serves: 4

1 pound beef steak, cut into chunks	½ cup pork rind, crushed
1 large egg, lightly beaten	½ cup parmesan cheese, grated
	½ teaspoon salt

1. Add egg in a suitable bowl. 2. In a suitable bowl, mix pork rind, cheese, and salt. 3. Dip each steak chunk in egg then coat with pork rind mixture and place on a plate. 4. Place in refrigerator for 30 minutes. 5. Grease its air fryer basket with cooking spray. 6. At 400 degrees F/ 205 degrees C, preheat your air fryer. 7. Place steak nuggets in air fryer basket and cook for almost 15-18 minutes or until cooked. 8. Serve and enjoy.
Per serving: Calories: 306; Fat: 13.4g; Sodium: 612mg; Total Carbs: 0.9g; Net Carbs: 1g; Fiber: 0g; Sugars: 0.1g; Protein: 43.9g

Sprouts Wraps Appetizer

Prep Time: 5 minutes | Cook time: 20 minutes | Serves: 12

12 bacon strips	A drizzle of olive oil
12 Brussels sprouts	

1. Use a bacon strip to wrap each Brussels. 2. Brush the wraps with olive oil before arranging them to the air fryer basket. 3. Cook the wraps for 20 minutes at 350 degrees F/ 175 degrees C. 4. When done, serve as an appetizer.
Per serving: Calories: 108; Fat: 9.1g; Sodium: 305mg; Total Carbs: 1g; Net Carbs: 0g; Fiber: 0.7g; Sugars: 0.4g; Protein: 4.7g

Potatoes with Bacon

Prep Time: 5 minutes | Cook time: 30 minutes | Serves: 4

4 potatoes, scrubbed, halved, cut lengthwise	Salt and black pepper to taste
1 tbsp. olive oil	4 oz. bacon, chopped

1. Brush the potatoes with olive oil and season with salt and pepper. 2. Transfer the seasoned potatoes to the cooking basket and arrange it to your air fryer. 3. Cook them at 390 degrees F/ 200 degrees C for 30 minutes, flipping and topping with bacon halfway through the cooking time. 4. When done, serve and enjoy.
Per serving: Calories: 330; Fat: 15.6g; Sodium: 668mg; Total Carbs: 33.9g; Net Carbs: 10g; Fiber: 5.1g; Sugars: 2.5g; Protein: 14.1g

Delectable Fish Nuggets

Prep Time: 10 minutes | Cook time: 10 Minutes | Serves: 4

1 cup all-purpose flour	1 lb. cod, cut into 1x2½-inch strips
2 eggs	Pinch of salt
¾ cup breadcrumbs	1 tablespoon olive oil

1. At 380 degrees F/ 195 degrees C, heat your air fryer in advance and grease an Air fryer basket. 2. In a shallow dish, place the dish, and whisk the eggs in another dish. 3. In the third shallow dish, mix up the breadcrumbs, salt and oil. 4. Let the fish strips be coated evenly in flour and dip in the egg. 5. Roll into the breadcrumbs evenly and arrange the nuggets in the basket of your air fryer. 6. Cook for about 10 minutes at 380 degrees F/ 195 degrees C. 7. When the time is up, dish out to serve warm.
Per serving: Calories: 344; Fat: 4.6g; Sodium: 307mg; Total Carbs: 38.6g; Net Carbs: 9g; Fiber: 1.8g; Sugars: 1.5g; Protein: 34.6g

Zucchini with Parmesan Cheese

Prep Time: 10 minutes | Cook time: 30 Minutes | Serves: 6

6 medium zucchini, cut into sticks
6 tablespoons Parmesan cheese, grated
4 egg whites, beaten
½-teaspoon garlic powder
1 cup bread crumbs
Pepper to taste
Salt to taste

1. At 400 degrees F/ 205 degrees C, heat your air fryer in advance. 2. Mix up the beaten egg whites with some salt and pepper in a suitable bowl. 3. In another bowl, add the garlic powder, bread crumbs, and Parmesan cheese and combine well. 4. Before rolling in the bread crumbs, dredge each zucchini stick in the egg whites. 5. Place the coated zucchini in the basket of your air fryer and for 20 minutes at 400 degrees F/ 205 degrees C.
Per serving: Calories: 130; Fat: 2.3g; Sodium: 217mg; Total Carbs: 20g; Net Carbs: 11g; Fiber: 3g; Sugars: 4.7g; Protein 8.7g

Chicken Bowls with Berries

Prep Time: 15 minutes | Cook time: 20 minutes | Serves: 2

1 chicken breast, skinless, boneless and cut into strips
2 cups baby spinach
1 cup blueberries
6 strawberries, chopped
½ cup walnuts, chopped
2 tablespoons balsamic vinegar
1 tablespoon olive oil
2 tablespoons feta cheese, crumbled

1. Oil the cooking pan that fits your air fryer and heat it up over medium heat, then add the meat and cook for 5 minutes or until browned. 2. After that, in addition to the spinach, add the rest of the ingredients and toss. 3. Arrange the mixture to the air fryer and cook at 370 degrees F/ 185 degrees C for 15 minutes. When the time is up, add the spinach, toss and cook for another 5 minutes. 4. Divide into bowls and serve.
Per serving: Calories: 384; Fat: 28.2g; Sodium: 103mg; Total Carbs: 17.7g; Net Carbs: 5g; Fiber: 5.3g; Sugars: 9.7g; Protein: 20.4g

Crispy Cauliflower Florets

Prep Time: 8 minutes | Cook time: 20 minutes | Serves: 2

3 cups cauliflower florets
½ teaspoon sesame oil
½ teaspoon onion powder
½ teaspoon garlic powder
Sea salt and cracked black pepper, to taste
½ teaspoon paprika

1. Start by preheating your Air Fryer to 400 degrees F/ 205 degrees C. 2. Toss the cauliflower with the remaining ingredients well until coat completely. 3. Arrange the coated cauliflower to the basket of the air fryer and cook for 12 minutes at 400 degrees F/ 205 degrees C, shaking the cooking basket halfway through the cooking time. 4. They will crisp up as they cool, Bon appétit!
Per serving: Calories: 66; Fat: 2.4g; Sodium: 46mg; Total Carbs: 9g; Net Carbs: 4.3g; Fiber: 4g; Sugars: 4.4g; Protein: 3.3g

Roasted Nut Mixture

Prep Time: 10 minutes | Cook time: 20 minutes| Serves: 6

½ cup walnuts
½ cup pecans
½ cup almonds
1 egg white
1 packet stevia
½-tablespoon ground cinnamon
A pinch of cayenne pepper

1. Mix up all of the ingredients in a bowl. 2. Arrange the nuts to the basket in the preheated air fryer (you can lay a piece of baking paper). 3. Cook the nuts for about 20 minutes at 320 degrees F/ 160 degrees C, stirring once halfway through. 4. Once done, transfer the hot nuts in a glass or steel bowl and serve.
Per serving: Calories: 121; Fat: 11g; Sodium: 3mg; Total Carbs: 3.4g; Net Carbs: 1g; Fiber: 2.1g; Sugars: 0.5g; Protein: 4.6g

Enticing Jalapeno Poppers

Prep Time: 15 minutes | Cook time: 13 minutes | Serves: 5

5 jalapeno peppers, slice in ½ and deseeded
2 tablespoons salsa
4 ounces goat cheese, crumbled
¼ teaspoon chili powder
½ teaspoon garlic, minced
Black pepper
Salt

1. In a suitable bowl, mix together cheese, salsa, chili powder, garlic, black pepper, and salt. 2. Spoon cheese mixture into each jalapeno halves and place in air fryer basket. 3. Cook jalapeno poppers at 350 degrees F/ 175 degrees C for 13 minutes. 4. Serve and enjoy.
Per serving: Calories: 111; Fat: 8.3g; Sodium: 486mg; Total Carbs: 2.1g; Net Carbs: 0g; Fiber: 0.7g; Sugars: 1.2g; Protein: 7.3g

Air-fried Sweet Potato Bites

Prep Time: 8 minutes | Cook time: 15 Minutes | Serves: 2

2 sweet potatoes, diced into 1-inch cubes
½ teaspoon red chili flakes
1½ teaspoon cinnamon
1 tablespoon olive oil
1½ tablespoon honey
½ cup fresh parsley, chopped

1. Heat your Air Fryer at 350 degrees F/ 175 degrees C ahead of time. 2. In a bowl, stir all of the ingredients well and then coat the sweet potato cubes entirely. 3. Put the sweet potato mixture into the basket. 4. Cook for 15 minutes at 350 degrees F/ 175 degrees C. 5. Serve and enjoy.
Per serving: Calories: 277; Fat: 7.4g; Sodium: 22mg; Total Carbs: 52.4g; Net Carbs: 13g; Fiber: 7.3g; Sugars: 9.5g; Protein: 2.8g

Cinnamon Almonds

Prep Time: 5 minutes | Cook time: 10 minutes | Serves: 4

½ tsp ground cinnamon
½ tsp smoked paprika
1 cup almonds
1 egg white
Sea salt to taste

1. In a bowl, beat the egg white and stir with the cinnamon, paprika and almonds well. 2. Spread the almonds on the oiled cooking basket. 3. Cook at 310 degrees F/ 95 degrees C for 12 minutes, flipping once or twice. 4. When cooked, sprinkle with sea salt and serve.
Per serving: Calories: 143; Fat: 11.9g; Sodium: 9mg; Total Carbs: 5.5g; Net Carbs: 1g; Fiber: 3.2g; Sugars: 1.1g; Protein: 6g

Cauliflower Bites

Prep Time: 5 minutes | Cook time: 15 minutes | Serves: 4

1 tbsp. Italian seasoning
1 cup flour
1 cup milk
1 egg, beaten
1 head cauliflower, cut into florets

1. After mixing the flour, milk, egg, and Italian seasoning well, coat the cauliflower with the mixture and drain the excess liquid. 2. Spray the florets with cooking spray and cook them in your air fryer at 390 degrees F/ 200 degrees C for 7 minutes. 3. After that, shake and cook for 5 minutes more. 4. Cool down before serving.
Per serving: Calories: 187; Fat: 3.8g; Sodium: 66mg; Total Carbs: 30.8g; Net Carbs: 5g; Fiber: 2.5g; Sugars: 4.8g; Protein: 7.9g

Caraway Bread

Prep Time: 15 minutes | Cook Time: 30 minutes | Servings: 10

3 cups whole-wheat flour
1 tbsp. sugar
2 tsps. caraway seeds
1 tsp. baking soda
1 tsp. sea salt
¼ cup chilled butter, cubed into small pieces
1 large egg, beaten
1½ cups buttermilk

1. In a suitable bowl, mix the flour, sugar, caraway seeds, baking soda and salt and mix well. 2. With a pastry cutter, add in the butter flour until coarse crumbs like mixture is formed. 3. Make a small-well in the center of the dry flour mixture. 4. In the well, add the egg, followed by the buttermilk and with a spatula, mix well. 5. With floured hand, shape the dough into a ball. 6. Then lightly knead the prepared dough on a floured surface. 7. Shape the dough into a 6-inch ball. 8. With a serrated knife, score an X on the top of the dough. 9. Arrange the dough in lightly greased the "Air Fryer Basket" and insert in the air fryer. 10. Cook the food at 350 degrees F/ 175 degrees C for 30 minutes on Air Crisp mode. 11. Carefully, invert the bread onto wire rack to cool completely before slicing. 12. Cut the bread into desired-sized slices and serve.
Per serving: Calories 205; Total Carbs 31.8 g; Net Carbs 6g; Protein 5.9 g; Fat 5 g; Sugar 1.2 g; Fiber 4 g

Cabbage Crackers

Prep Time: 10 minutes | Cook Time: 30 minutes | Servings: 6

1 large cabbage head, tear cabbage leaves into pieces
2 tbsps. olive oil
¼ cup parmesan cheese, grated
Pepper
Salt

1. Add all the recipe ingredients into the large mixing bowl and toss well. 2. Spray "Air Fryer Basket" with some cooking spray. 3. Divide cabbage in batches. 4. Add one cabbage batch in "Air Fryer Basket" and Air Fry for 25-30 minutes at 250 degrees F/ 120 degrees C. 5. Cook another batch with the same steps. 6. Serve and enjoy.
Per serving: Calories 96; Fat 5.1 g; Total Carbs 12.1 g; Net Carbs 3g; Sugar 6.7 g; Protein 3 g; Fiber 1 g

Broccoli Tots

Prep Time: 10 minutes | Cook Time: 15 minutes | Servings: 4

1 lb. broccoli, chopped
½ cup almond flour
¼ cup ground flaxseed
½ tsp. garlic powder
1 tsp. salt

1. Add broccoli into the microwave-safe bowl and microwave for 3 minutes. 2. Transfer steamed broccoli into the food processor and process until it looks like rice. 3. Transfer broccoli to a large mixing bowl. 4. Add the remaining ingredients into the bowl and mix well. 5. Spray the "Air Fryer Basket" with some cooking spray. 6. Make small tots from broccoli mixture and place into the Air Fryer Basket. 7. Cook broccoli tots for 12 minutes at 375 degrees F/ 190 degrees C. 8. Serve and enjoy.
Per serving: Calories 161; Fat 9.2 g; Total Carbs 12.8 g; Net Carbs 3g; Sugar 2.1 g; Protein 7.5 g; Fiber 0 g

Juicy Beef Meatballs

Prep Time: 10 minutes | Cook Time: 14 minutes | Servings: 5

1 lb. ground beef
1 tsp. garlic powder
1 egg, lightly beaten
½ onion, diced
¼ tsp. pepper
1 tsp. salt

1. Spray "Air Fryer Basket" with some cooking spray. 2. Add all the recipe ingredients into the bowl and mix well. 3. Make small balls from meat mixture and place into the Air Fryer Basket. 4. Cook meatballs for 14 minutes at 390 degrees F/ 200 degrees C on Air Fry mode. Shake the basket 3-4 times while cooking. 5. Serve and enjoy.
Per serving: Calories 259; Fat 18 g; Total Carbs 3 g; Sugar 0.5 g; Net Carbs 8g; Protein 17 g; Fiber 95 g

Bacon Poppers

Prep Time: 10 minutes | Cook Time: 8 minutes | Servings: 10

10 jalapeno peppers, cut in half and remove seeds
⅓ cup cream cheese, softened
5 bacon strips, cut in half

1. Stuff cream cheese into each jalapeno half. 2. Wrap each jalapeno half with half bacon strip and place in the Air Fryer Basket. 3. Air Fry the food at 370 degrees F/ 185 degrees C for 6-8 minutes. 4. Serve and enjoy.
Per serving: Calories 83; Fat 7.4 g; Total Carbs 1.3 g; Sugar 0.5 g; Net Carbs 2g; Protein 2.8 g; Fiber 9 g

Lemon Tofu

Prep Time: 10 minutes | Cook Time: 15 minutes | Servings: 4

1 lb. tofu, drained and pressed
1 tbsp. arrowroot powder
1 tbsp. tamari
For sauce:
2 tsps. arrowroot powder
2 tbsps. erythritol
½ cup water
⅓ cup lemon juice
1 tsp. lemon zest

1. Cut the tofu into cubes. Add tofu and tamari into the zip-lock bag and shake well. 2. Add 1 tablespoon of arrowroot into the bag and shake well to coat the tofu. Set aside for 15 minutes. 3. While marinating, in a suitable bowl, mix all sauce ingredients and then set aside for later use. 4. Spray "Air Fryer Basket" with some cooking spray. 5. Add tofu cubes into the "Air Fryer Basket" and Air Fry them at 390 degrees F/ 200 degrees C for 10 minutes. 6. Shake the basket halfway through for evenly cooking. 7. Add cooked tofu and sauce mixture into the skillet and cook over medium-high heat for 3-5 minutes. 8. Serve and enjoy.
Per serving: Calories 112; Fat 3 g; Total Carbs 13 g; Sugar 8 g; Net Carbs 8g; Protein 8 g; Fiber 0 g

BBQ Chicken Wings

Prep Time: 10 minutes | Cook Time: 15 minutes | Servings: 4

1 lb. chicken wings
½ cup BBQ sauce, sugar-free
¼ tsp. garlic powder
Pepper

1. Season chicken wings with garlic powder and pepper and place into the Air Fryer Basket. 2. Cook chicken wings for 15 minutes at 400 degrees F/ 205 degrees C on Air Fry mode. Shake basket 3-4 times while cooking. 3. Transfer cooked chicken wings in a large mixing bowl. 4. Pour BBQ sauce over chicken wings and toss to coat. 5. Serve and enjoy.
Per serving: Calories 263; Fat 8.5 g; Total Carbs 11.5 g; Sugar 8 g; Net Carbs 6g; Protein 32 g; Fiber 100 g

Vegetable Kabobs

Prep Time: 10 minutes | Cook Time: 10 minutes | Servings: 4

½ onion
1 zucchini
1 eggplant
2 bell peppers
Black pepper, to taste
Salt, to taste

1. Cut all vegetables into 1-inch pieces. 2. Thread vegetables onto the soaked wooden skewers and season with pepper and salt. 3. Place the skewers into the "Air Fryer Basket" and Air Fry them for 10 minutes at 390 degrees F/ 200 degrees C. 4. Turn the skewers halfway through cooking. 5. Serve and enjoy.
Per serving: Calories 61; Fat 0.5 g; Total Carbs 14 g; Sugar 8 g; Net Carbs 5g; Protein 2 g; Fiber 0 g

Shrimp Kabobs

Prep Time: 10 minutes | Cook Time: 8 minutes | Servings: 2

1 cup shrimp
1 lime juice
1 garlic clove, minced
¼ tsp. pepper
⅛ tsp. salt

1. At 350 degrees F/ 175 degrees C, preheat your Air Fryer. 2. Add shrimp, lime juice, garlic, pepper, and salt into the bowl and toss well. 3. Thread shrimp onto the soaked wooden skewers and place into the Air Fryer Basket. 4. Air Fry the food at 350 degrees F/ 175 degrees C for 8 minutes, flipping halfway through. 5. Serve and enjoy.
Per serving: Calories 75; Fat 1 g; Total Carbs 4 g; Sugar 0.5 g; Net Carbs 4g; Protein 13 g; Fiber 1 g

Mild Shishito Peppers

Prep Time: 5 minutes | Cook Time: 5 minutes | Servings: 2

20 shishito Peppers
1 tbsp. olive oil
Salt

1. Add shishito peppers into the bowl and toss with olive oil. 2. Add shishito peppers into the "Air Fryer Basket" and Air Fry them at 390 degrees F/ 200 degrees C for 5 minutes. 3. Shake the basket halfway through. 4. Season shishito peppers with salt. 5. Serve and enjoy.
Per serving: Calories 20; Fat 1 g; Total Carbs 5 g; Sugar 2 g; Net Carbs 6g; Protein 1 g; Fiber 0 g

Thai Chicken Wings

Prep Time: 10 minutes | Cook Time: 16 minutes | Servings: 6

½ lb. chicken wings
1 tsp. paprika
⅓ cup Thai chili sauce
2 tsps. garlic powder
2 tsps. ginger powder
2 ½ tbsp. dry sherry
Black pepper, to taste
Salt, to taste

1. Toss chicken wings with dry sherry, paprika, garlic powder, ginger, powder, pepper, and salt. 2. Add chicken wings into the "Air Fryer Basket" and Air Fry them at 365 degrees F/ 185 degrees C for 16 minutes. 3. Serve the chicken wings with Thai chili sauce and enjoy.
Per serving: Calories 120; Fat 2.9 g; Total Carbs 6 g; Sugar 3.9 g; Net Carbs 6g; Protein 11.2 g; Fiber 4 g

Tofu Steaks

Prep Time: 10 minutes | **Cook Time:** 35 minutes | **Servings:** 4

1 package tofu, press and remove excess liquid
¼ tsp. dried thyme
¼ cup lemon juice
2 tbsp. lemon zest
3 garlic cloves, minced
¼ cup olive oil
Black pepper, to taste
Salt, to taste

1. Cut the tofu into 8 pieces. 2. In a suitable bowl, mix olive oil, thyme, lemon juice, lemon zest, garlic, pepper, and salt. 3. Add tofu into the bowl and coat well and place in the refrigerator for overnight. 4. Spray "Air Fryer Basket" with some cooking spray. 5. Place marinated tofu into the "Air Fryer Basket" and Air Fry at 350 degrees F/ 175 degrees C for 30-35 minutes. Turn the tofu halfway through cooking. 6. Serve and enjoy.
Per serving: Calories 195; Fat 16 g; Total Carbs 5 g; Sugar 1 g; Net Carbs 2g; Protein 7 g; Fiber 0 g

Air Fried Cheese Sticks

Prep Time: 10 minutes | **Cook Time:** 8 minutes | **Servings:** 4 minutes

6 mozzarella cheese sticks
¼ tsp. garlic powder
1 tsp. Italian seasoning
⅓ cup almond flour
½ cup parmesan cheese, grated
1 large egg, lightly beaten
¼ tsp. sea salt

1. In a suitable bowl, whisk the egg. 2. In a shallow bowl, mix almond flour, parmesan cheese, Italian seasoning, garlic powder, and salt. 3. Dip the mozzarella cheese stick in egg then coat with almond flour mixture and place on a plate. 4. Refrigerate the coated sticks for 1 hour. 5. Spray "Air Fryer Basket" with some cooking spray. 6. Place prepared mozzarella cheese sticks into the "Air Fryer Basket" and Air Fry at 375 degrees F/ 190 degrees C for 8 minutes. 7. Serve and enjoy.
Per serving: Calories 245; Fat 18 g; Total Carbs 3 g; Sugar 2 g; Net Carbs 6g; Protein 19 g; Fiber 0 g

Broccoli Nuggets

Prep Time: 10 minutes | **Cook Time:** 15 minutes | **Servings:** 4

¼ cup almond flour
2 cups broccoli florets, cooked until soft
1 cup cheddar cheese, shredded
2 egg whites
⅛ tsp. salt

1. Spray "Air Fryer Basket" with some cooking spray. 2. Add cooked broccoli into the bowl and using masher mash broccoli into the small pieces. 3. Add the almond flour, cheddar cheese, egg whites, and salt together to the bowl and mix well to combine. 4. Make small nuggets from broccoli mixture and place into the air fryer basket. 5. Cook broccoli nuggets at 325 degrees F/ 160 degrees C for 15 minutes on Air Fry mode. 6. Turn the broccoli nuggets halfway through cooking. 7. Serve and enjoy.
Per serving: Calories 175; Fat 13 g; Total Carbs 5 g; Sugar 1 g; Net Carbs 6g; Protein 12 g; Fiber 3 g

Chicken Jalapeno Poppers

Prep Time: 10 minutes | **Cook Time:** 20 minutes | **Servings:** 12

½ cup chicken, cooked and shredded
6 jalapenos, halved and seed removed
¼ cup green onion, sliced
¼ cup Monterey jack cheese,
shredded
¼ tsp. garlic powder
4 oz. cream cheese
¼ tsp. dried oregano
¼ tsp. dried basil
¼ tsp. salt

1. Spray "Air Fryer Basket" with some cooking spray. 2. Mix all the recipe ingredients in a suitable bowl except jalapenos. 3. Spoon 1 tablespoon of mixture into each jalapeno halved and place into the Air Fryer Basket. 4. Air Fry the jalapeno for 20 minutes at 370 degrees F/ 185 degrees C. 5. Serve and enjoy.
Per serving: Calories 105; Fat 8.5 g; Total Carbs 1.5 g; Sugar 0.7 g; Net Carbs 6g; Protein 6.3 g; Fiber 5 g

Artichoke Dip

Prep Time: 10 minutes | **Cook Time:** 24 minutes | **Servings:** 6

15 oz. artichoke hearts, drained
1 tsp. Worcestershire sauce

3 cups arugula, chopped
1 cup cheddar cheese, shredded
1 tbsp. onion, minced
½ cup mayonnaise

1. At 325 degrees F/ 160 degrees C, preheat your Air Fryer. 2. Add all the recipe ingredients into the blender and blend until smooth. 3. Pour artichoke mixture into a suitable baking dish and then place the dish into the Air Fryer Basket. 4. Air Fry dip at 325 degrees F/ 160 degrees C for 24 minutes. 5. Serve with vegetables and enjoy.
Per serving: Calories 190; Fat 13 g; Total Carbs 13 g; Sugar 2.5 g; Net Carbs 5g; Protein 7.5 g; Fiber 5 g

Crab Mushrooms

Prep Time: 10 minutes | **Cook Time:** 8 minutes | **Servings:** 16

16 mushrooms, clean and chop stems
¼ tsp. chili powder
¼ tsp. onion powder
¼ cup mozzarella cheese, shredded
2 oz. crab meat, chopped
8 oz. cream cheese, softened
2 tsps. garlic, minced
¼ tsp. pepper

1. In a suitable mixing bowl, add the stems, chili powder, onion powder, pepper, cheese, crabmeat, cream cheese, and garlic, mix them well. 2. Stuff mushrooms with bowl mixture and then place them into the Air Fryer Basket. 3. Air Fry the stuffed mushrooms at 370 degrees F/ 185 degrees C for 8 minutes. 4. Serve and enjoy.
Per serving: Calories 59; Fat 5.1 g; Total Carbs 1.2 g; Sugar 0.4 g; Net Carbs 6g; Protein 2.2 g; Fiber 8 g

Chicken Dip

Prep Time: 10 minutes | **Cook Time:** 20 minutes | **Servings:** 6

2 cups chicken, cooked and shredded
¾ cup sour cream
¼ tsp. onion powder
8 oz. cream cheese, softened
3 tbsp. hot sauce
¼ tsp. garlic powder

1. At 325 degrees F/ 160 degrees C, preheat your Air Fryer. 2. Add all the recipe ingredients in a suitable bowl and mix well. 3. Transfer mixture in a suitable baking dish and then place the dish in the Air Fryer Basket. 4. Cook chicken dip at 325 degrees F/ 160 degrees C for 20 minutes. 5. Serve and enjoy.
Per serving: Calories 245; Fat 17 g; Total Carbs 1.5 g; Sugar 0.2 g; Net Carbs 2g; Protein 16 g; Fiber 5 g

Smoked Almonds

Prep Time: 5 minutes | **Cook Time:** 6 minutes | **Servings:** 6

1 cup almonds
¼ tsp. cumin
1 tsp. chili powder
¼ tsp. smoked paprika
2 tsp. olive oil

1. Add almonds into the bowl; add the remaining ingredients and toss to coat the almonds well. 2. Transfer the almonds into the "Air Fryer Basket" and Air Fry them at 320 degrees F/ 160 degrees C for 6 minutes. 3. Shake the basket halfway through for evenly cooking. 4. Serve and enjoy.
Per serving: Calories 107; Fat 9.6 g; Total Carbs 3.7 g; Sugar 0.7 g; Net Carbs 5g; Protein 3.4 g; Fiber 0 g

Parmesan Zucchini Bites

Prep Time: 10 minutes | **Cook Time:** 10 minutes | **Servings:** 6

4 zucchinis, grated and squeeze out all liquid
1 egg, lightly beaten
1 tsp. Italian seasoning
½ cup parmesan cheese, grated
1 cup shredded coconut

1. Grate all the zucchinis and then squeeze out all the liquid. Add all the recipe ingredients into the bowl and mix well. 2. Spray "Air Fryer Basket" with some cooking spray. 3. Make small balls from zucchini mixture and place into the "Air Fryer Basket" and Air Fry the balls at 400 degrees F/ 205 degrees C for 10 minutes. 4. Serve and enjoy.
Per serving: Calories 88; Fat 6.2 g; Total Carbs 6.6 g; Sugar 3.2 g; Net Carbs 4g; Protein 3.7 g; Fiber 2g

Broccoli Pop-corn

Prep Time: 10 minutes | Cook Time: 6 minutes | Servings: 4

2 cups broccoli florets
2 cups coconut flour
¼ cup butter, melted
4 eggs yolks
Pepper
Salt

1. In a suitable bowl, whisk egg yolk with melted butter, pepper, and salt. 2. Add coconut flour and stir to combine. 3. Spray "Air Fryer Basket" with some cooking spray. 4. Coat each broccoli floret with egg mixture. Place them into the "Air Fryer Basket" and then air-fry them at 400 degrees F/ 205 degrees C for 6 minutes. 5. Serve and enjoy.
Per serving: Calories 147; Fat 12 g; Total Carbs 7 g; Sugar 2 g; Net Carbs 6g; Protein 2 g; Fiber 3g

Rosemary Beans

Prep Time: 10 minutes | Cook Time: 5 minutes | Servings: 2

1 cup green beans, chopped
2 garlic cloves, minced
2 tbsps. rosemary, chopped
1 tbsp. butter, melted
½ tsp. salt

1. Add all the recipe ingredients into the bowl and toss well. 2. Transfer green beans into the "Air Fryer Basket" and Air Fry them at 390 degrees F/ 200 degrees C for 5 minutes. 3. Serve and enjoy.
Per serving: Calories 83; Fat 6.4 g; Total Carbs 7 g; Sugar 0.8 g; Net Carbs 6g; Protein 1.4 g; Fiber 1g

Cheesy Brussels sprouts

Prep Time: 10 minutes | Cook Time: 5 minutes | Servings: 2

1 cup Brussels sprouts, halved
¼ cup mozzarella cheese, shredded
1 tbsp. olive oil
¼ tsp. salt

1. Toss the halved Brussels sprouts with oil and season with salt. 2. Transfer Brussels sprouts into the "Air Fryer Basket" and top them with shredded cheese. 3. Air Fry the food at 375 degrees F/ 190 degrees C for 5 minutes. 4. When done, serve and enjoy.
Per serving: Calories 89; Fat 7.8 g; Total Carbs 4.1 g; Sugar 1 g; Net Carbs 8g; Protein 2.5 g; Fiber 2g

Mushrooms with Sauce

Prep Time: 10 minutes | Cook Time: 20 minutes | Servings: 5

1 ½ lbs. mushrooms
1 ½ tbsp. olive oil
1 ½ tbsp. vermouth
2 tbsps. fresh lemon juice
¼ tsp. cayenne pepper
½ tsp. turmeric
½ tbsp. Tahini
¼ tsp. pepper
1 tsp. kosher salt

1. In a suitable bowl, toss mushrooms with oil, turmeric, cayenne pepper, pepper, and salt. 2. Transfer mushrooms into the "Air Fryer Basket" and Air Fry the mushrooms at 350 degrees F/ 175 degrees C for 20 minutes. 3. Shake the basket halfway through cooking. 4. Meanwhile, in a suitable bowl, mix tahini, lemon juice, and vermouth. 5. Serve cooked mushrooms with tahini sauce.
Per serving: Calories 80; Fat 5.5 g; Total Carbs 5.2 g; Sugar 2.5 g; Net Carbs 2g; Protein 4.6 g; Fiber 0g

Baguette Bread

Prep Time: 15 minutes | Cook Time: 20 minutes | Servings: 8

¾ cup warm water
¾ tsp. quick yeast
½ tsp. demerara sugar
1 cup bread flour
½ cup whole-wheat flour
½ cup oat flour
1¼ tsp. salt

1. In a suitable bowl, add the warm water, yeast and sugar. 2. Add the bread flour and salt and mix until a stiff dough form. 3. Knead the dough onto a floured surface with your hands until smooth and elastic. 4. Now, shape the dough into a ball. 5. Place the dough into a slightly oiled bowl and turn to coat well. 6. With a plastic wrap, cover the bowl and place in a warm place for 1 hour or until doubled in size. 7. With your hands, punch down the dough and form into a long slender loaf. 8. Place the loaf onto a lightly greased baking pan and set aside in warm place, uncovered, for 30 minutes 9. Cook the loaf at 450 de-grees F/ 230 degrees C for 20 minutes on Bake mode. 10. Carefully, invert the bread onto wire rack to cool completely before slicing. 11. Cut the bread into desired-sized slices and serve.
Per serving: Calories 114; Total Carbs 22.8 g; Net Carbs 6g; Protein 3.8 g; Fat 5 g; Sugar 1.2 g; Fiber 4 g

Cheese Artichoke Dip

Prep Time: 10 minutes | Cook Time: 17 minutes | Servings: 10

½ cup mozzarella cheese, shredded
3 cups arugula leaves, chopped
½ cup mayonnaise
7 oz. brie cheese
⅓ tsp. dried basil
2 garlic cloves, minced
⅓ cup sour cream
⅓ can artichoke hearts, drained and chopped
⅓ tsp. pepper
1 tsp. sea salt

1. Add all the recipe ingredients except mozzarella cheese into the suitable baking dish and mix well. 2. Spread the mozzarella cheese on top and then place the dish in the Air Fryer Basket. 3. Air Fry the food at 325 degrees F/ 160 degrees C for 17 minutes. 4. Serve and enjoy.
Per serving: Calories 66; Fat 4 g; Total Carbs 6.6 g; Sugar 2.8 g; Net Carbs 5g; Protein 2.7 g; Fiber 1g

Crusted Onion Rings

Prep Time: 10 minutes | Cook Time: 10 minutes | Servings: 3

1 egg, lightly beaten
1 onion, cut into slices
¾ cup pork rind, crushed
1 cup coconut milk
1 tbsp. baking powder
1 ½ cups almond flour
Pepper
Salt

1. In a suitable bowl, mix almond flour, baking powder, salt and pepper. 2. In another suitable bowl, whisk the egg with milk. 3. Pour egg mixture into the almond flour mixture and stir to combine. 4. Add the crushed pork rinds in a shallow dish. 5. Spray "Air Fryer Basket" with some cooking spray. 6. Dip the onion rings into the almond flour batter and then coat them with pork rind and place into the Air Fryer Basket. 7. Cook onion rings for 10 minutes at 360 degrees F/ 180 degrees C on Air Fry mode. 8. Serve and enjoy.
Per serving: Calories 350; Fat 31 g; Total Carbs 13 g; Sugar 4 g; Net Carbs 6g; Protein 10 g; Fiber 6 g

Asparagus Pork Fries

Prep Time: 10 minutes | Cook Time: 10 minutes | Servings: 5

1 lb. asparagus spears
1 cup pork rinds, crushed
¼ cup almond flour
2 eggs, lightly beaten
½ cup parmesan cheese, grated
Black pepper, to taste
Salt, to taste

1. In a suitable bowl, mix up the parmesan cheese, almond flour, pepper, and salt. 2. In a shallow bowl, whisk eggs. 3. Add crushed pork rind into the shallow dish. 4. Spray "Air Fryer Basket" with some cooking spray. 5. First coat asparagus with parmesan mixture then into the eggs and finally coat with crushed pork rind. 6. Place coated asparagus into the "Air Fryer Basket" and Air Fry the food at 380 degrees F/ 195 degrees C for 10 minutes. 7. Serve and enjoy.
Per serving: Calories 102; Fat 6.1 g; Total Carbs 5 g; Sugar 1.9 g; Net Carbs 2g; Protein 8.1 g; Fiber 71 g

Pork Meatballs

Prep Time: 10 minutes | Cook Time: 10 minutes | Servings: 4

2 eggs, lightly beaten
2 tbsps. capers
½ lb. ground pork
3 garlic cloves, minced
2 tbsps. fresh mint, chopped
½ tbsp. cilantro, chopped
2 tsps. red pepper flakes, crushed
1 ½ tbsps. butter, melted
1 tsp. kosher salt

1. Add all the recipe ingredients into the mixing bowl and mix well. 2. Spray "Air Fryer Basket" with some cooking spray. 3. Make small balls from meat mixture and then place into the Air Fryer Basket. 4. Cook the meatballs at 395 degrees F/ 200 degrees C for 10 minutes. 5. Shake the basket halfway through cooking. 6. Serve and enjoy.
Per serving: Calories 159; Fat 8.7 g; Total Carbs 1.9 g; Sugar 0.3 g; Net Carbs 6g; Protein 18.1 g; Fiber 1 g

Chapter 3 Vegetables and Sides Recipes

Enticing Cauliflower Tots 29
Tasty Sweet Potato Wedges 29
Roasted Bell Peppers 29
Fava Beans and Bacon Medley 29
Cheese Cauliflower Tots 29
Balsamic Brussels Sprouts 29
Balsamic Sautéed Greens 29
Garlicky Mushrooms with Parsley 29
Buffalo Crusted Cauliflower 29
Mushroom Risotto Croquettes 30
Chinese Cabbage with Bacon 30
Apple Brussel Sprout Salad 30
Zucchini Tots with Mozzarella 30
Beans and Sweet Potato Boats 30
Awesome Mushroom Tots 30
Crispy Tofu with Soy Sauce 30
Pungent Mushroom Pizza 30
Herbed Potatoes Medley 31
Balsamic Tomatoes with Garlic 31
Zucchini and Potato Polenta 31
Mushroom Mozzarella Risotto 31
Roasted Pepper Salad with Pine Nuts 31
Cheddar Tomatillos with Lettuce 31
Cauliflower Bake with Basil Pesto 31
Turmeric Tofu Cubes 31
Sweet and Spicy Tofu 32
Coconut Brussels Sprouts 32
Parsley Cabbage 32
Cheese Broccoli with Basil 32
Turmeric Cauliflower Patties 32
Brussels Sprouts and Mushrooms 32
Turmeric Cauliflower with Cilantro 32
Creamy Garlic Bread 32
Lemon Fennel with Sunflower Seeds 33
Flavorful Radish Salad 33
Green Beans with Parsley 33
Garlic Brussel Sprouts with Celery 33
Lemony Cabbage Slaw 33
Creamy Cilantro Peppers Mix 33
Garlic Provolone Asparagus 33
Herbed Mushroom Pilau 33
Buffalo Cauliflower Bites 33
Tasty Spiced Tofu 34
Tomato Rolls 34
Provolone Zucchini Balls 34
Creamy Cauliflower Puree 34
Open-faced Sandwich 34
Mozzarella Broccoli and Cauliflower 34
Creamy Cauliflower Mash 34
Cheesy Zucchini Tots 34
Spiced Cauliflower Medley 34
Crispy Spiced Asparagus 35
Mozzarella Eggplant Gratin 35
Zucchinis and Arugula Salad 35

Mozzarella Spinach Mash 35
Lemon Cabbage with Cilantro 35
Rutabaga Fries 35
Stuffed Peppers 35
Creamy Spinach with Nutmeg 35
Parmesan Zucchini Gratin 35
Crispy Pickles with Parmesan 36
Maple Glazed Parsnips 36
Lemon Broccoli 36
Fried Brussel Sprouts 36
Carrots with Honey Glaze 36
Air-Fried Eggplant 36
Cauliflower Hash 36
Asparagus with Almonds 36
Roasted Garlic Head 36
Zucchini Cubes 37
Sweet Potato Onion Mix 37
Spicy Eggplant 37
Wrapped Asparagus 37
Baked Yams 37
Honey Onions 37
Roasted Garlic Slices 37
Air Fried Artichokes 37
Roasted Mushrooms 37
Shredded Cabbage 38
Fried Leeks 38
Brussels Sprouts Tomatoes Mix 38
Radish Hash 38
Broccoli Salad 38
Chili Broccoli 38
Broccoli and Asparagus 38
Broccoli Mix 38
Balsamic Kale 38
Kale Olives Salad 38
Kale Mushrooms Mix 38
Mashed Yams 39
Oregano Kale 39
Olives Avocado Mix 39
Olives, Green beans and Bacon 39
Parmesan Brussel Sprouts 39
Cajun Peppers 39
Crisp Kale 39
Basil Potatoes 39
Sweet Potato Fries 39
Green Bean Casserole 39

Enticing Cauliflower Tots

Prep Time: 15 minutes | Cook time: 8 minutes | Serves: 4

1 teaspoon cream cheese	1 cup cauliflower, chopped, boiled
5 ounces Monterey Jack cheese, shredded	¼ teaspoon garlic powder
	1 teaspoon sunflower oil

1. In a blender, add the boiled cauliflower, garlic powder, shredded Monterey Jack cheese, and cream cheese and mix until smooth. 2. Then make the cauliflower tots and cool them in the refrigerator for 10 minutes. 3. Before cooking, heat your air fryer to 365 degrees F/ 185 degrees C. 4. Transfer the broccoli tots inside the air fryer basket. 5. Sprinkle sunflower oil on the top and cook in your air fryer for 8 minutes. Flip to the other side halfway through cooking.
Per serving: Calories: 152; Fat: 12.2g; Sodium: 200mg; Total Carbs: 1g; Net Carbs: 0g; Fiber: 0.7g; Sugars: 0.8g; Protein: 9.3g

Tasty Sweet Potato Wedges

Prep Time: 15 minutes | Cook time: 25 minutes | Serves: 2

1 tablespoon olive oil	½ teaspoon smoked paprika
¼ teaspoon salt	½ teaspoon dried thyme
½ teaspoon chili powder	A pinch cayenne pepper
½ teaspoon garlic powder	

1. In a suitable bowl, mix olive oil, salt, chili and garlic powder, smoked paprika, thyme, and cayenne. 2. Toss in the potato wedges. Arrange the wedges on the air fryer, and cook for 25 minutes at 380 degrees F/ 195 degrees C, flipping once.
Per serving: Calories: 67; Fat: 7.2g; Sodium: 298mg; Total Carbs: 1g; Net Carbs: 0g; Fiber: 0.6g; Sugars: 0.3g; Protein: 0.3g

Roasted Bell Peppers

Prep Time: 15 minutes | Cook time: 8 minutes | Serves: 3

3 ½ cups bell peppers, cut into chunks	Black pepper
	Salt

1. Grease its air fryer basket with cooking spray. 2. Add bell peppers into the air fryer basket and cook at almost 360 degrees F/ 180 degrees C for 8 minutes. 3. Season bell peppers with black pepper and salt. 4. Serve and enjoy.
Per serving: Calories: 44; Fat: 0.4g; Sodium: 4mg; Total Carbs: 10.5g; Net Carbs: 0g; Fiber: 1.9g; Sugars: 7g; Protein: 1.4g

Fava Beans and Bacon Medley

Prep Time: 15 minutes | Cook time: 15 minutes | Serves: 4

3 pounds fava beans, shelled	crumbled
1 teaspoon olive oil	½ cup white wine
Black pepper and salt to taste	1 tablespoon parsley, chopped
4 ounces bacon, cooked and	

1. Place all of the recipe ingredients into a pan that fits your air fryer and mix well. 2. Put the pan in the preheated air fryer and cook at almost 380 degrees F/ 195 degrees C for almost 15 minutes. 3. Serve.
Per serving: Calories: 32; Fat: 13.5g; Sodium: 659mg; Total Carbs: 25g; Net Carbs: 16g; Fiber: 7.9g; Sugars: 0.2g; Protein: 19.9g

Cheese Cauliflower Tots

Prep Time: 15 minutes | Cook time: 12 minutes | Serves: 8

1 large head cauliflower	1 teaspoon seasoned salt
½ cup parmesan cheese, grated	1 egg
1 cup mozzarella cheese, shredded	

1. Set a suitable steamer basket over a pot of boiling water, ensuring the water is not high enough to enter the basket. 2. Cut the cauliflower into florets and transfer to the steamer basket. Cover the pot with a lid and leave to steam for seven minutes, making sure the cauliflower softens. 3. Place the florets on a cheesecloth and leave to cool. Remove as much moisture as possible. This is crucial as it ensures the cauliflower will harden. 4. In a suitable bowl, break up the cauliflower with a fork. 5. Add the parmesan, mozzarella, seasoned salt, and egg, incorporating the cauliflower well with all of the other ingredients. 6. Using your hand, mold about 2 tablespoons of the mixture into tots and repeat until you have used up all of the mixture. Put each tot into

your air fryer basket. They may need to be cooked in multiple batches. 7. Cook at almost 320 degrees F/ 160 degrees C for twelve minutes, turning them halfway through. Ensure they are brown in color before serving.
Per serving: Calories: 133; Fat: 5.6g; Sodium: 631mg; Total Carbs: 12g; Net Carbs: 7g; Fiber: 5.3g; Sugars: 5.1g; Protein: 12g

Balsamic Brussels Sprouts

Prep Time: 15 minutes | Cook time: 10 minutes | Serves: 6

2 cups Brussels sprouts, sliced	1 tablespoon olive oil
1 tablespoon balsamic vinegar	¼ teaspoon salt

1. Add all the recipe ingredients into the suitable bowl and toss well. 2. Grease its air fryer basket with cooking spray. 3. Transfer Brussels sprouts mixture into the air fryer basket. 4. Cook Brussels sprouts at 400 degrees F/ 205 degrees C for almost 10 minutes. Shake basket halfway through. 5. Serve and enjoy.
Per serving: Calories: 33; Fat: 2.4g; Sodium: 104mg; Total Carbs: 2g; Net Carbs: 0.5g; Fiber: 1.1g; Sugars: 0.6g; Protein: 1g

Balsamic Sautéed Greens

Prep Time: 15 minutes | Cook time: 15 minutes | Serves: 4

1 pound collard greens	A pinch of black pepper and salt
¼ cup cherry tomatoes, halved	2 tablespoons chicken stock
1 tablespoon balsamic vinegar	

1. In a suitable pan that fits your air fryer, mix the collard greens with the other ingredients, toss gently, introduce in the preheated air fryer, and cook at almost 360 degrees F/ 180 degrees C for almost 15 minutes. 2. Serve.
Per serving: Calories: 34; Fat: 0.8g; Sodium: 43mg; Total Carbs: 6g; Net Carbs: 2.5g; Fiber: 3.9g; Sugars: 0.3g; Protein 2.6g

Garlicky Mushrooms with Parsley

Prep Time: 15 minutes | Cook time: 12 minutes | Serves: 2

8 ounces mushrooms, sliced	1 tablespoon olive oil
1 tablespoon parsley, chopped	Black pepper
1 teaspoon soy sauce	Salt
½ teaspoon garlic powder	

1. Add all the recipe ingredients into the mixing bowl and toss well. 2. Transfer mushrooms in air fryer basket and cook at almost 380 degrees F/ 195 degrees C for almost 10-12 minutes. Shake basket halfway through. 3. Serve and enjoy.
Per serving: Calories: 89; Fat: 7.4g; Sodium: 157mg; Total Carbs: 4g; Net Carbs: 2g; Fiber: 1.3g; Sugars: 2.2g; Protein: 3.9g

Buffalo Crusted Cauliflower

Prep Time: 15 minutes | Cook time: 18 minutes | Serves: 4

3 tablespoons buffalo hot sauce	¼ teaspoon freshly black pepper
1 egg white	½ head of cauliflower, cut into
1 cup panko breadcrumbs	florets
½ teaspoon salt	Cooking spray

1. In a suitable bowl, add butter, hot sauce, and egg white. 2. Mix breadcrumbs with black pepper and salt, in a separate bowl. 3. Toss the florets in the hot sauce mixture until well-coated. 4. Toss the coated cauliflower in crumbs until coated, then transfer the coated florets to the air fryer. Spray with cooking spray. 5. Cook for 18 minutes at 340 degrees F/ 170 degrees C. Cook in batches if needed. 6. Serve.
Per serving: Calories: 94; Fat: 0.5g; Sodium: 592mg; Total Carbs: 19g; Net Carbs: 6.7g; Fiber: 2.9g; Sugars: 3.2g; Protein: 3.6g

Mushroom Risotto Croquettes

Prep Time: 10-15 minutes | Cook time: 15 minutes | Serves: 4

2 garlic cloves, peeled and minced	¼ teaspoon ground black pepper
½ cup mushrooms, chopped	1 tablespoon Colby cheese, grated
6 ounces cooked rice	1 egg, beaten
1 tablespoon rice bran oil	1 cup breadcrumbs
1 onion, chopped	½ teaspoon dried dill weed
Sea salt as needed	1 teaspoon paprika

1. Add oil, onion, and garlic in a medium sized saucepan. Heat the pan over medium heat for a few minutes until turn soft. 2. Then add the mushrooms in the pan. Cook until the liquid thickens. Cool down the mixture. 3. Add and combine salt, black pepper, dill, paprika, and the cooked rice together. 4. Then mix with cheese. Divide the mixture into risotto balls. 5. Dip in the beaten eggs and coat the balls with breadcrumbs. 6. On a flat kitchen surface, plug your air fryer and turn it on. 7. At 390 degrees F/ 200 degrees C, heat your air fryer for 4 to 5 minutes in advance. Gently grease your air fryer basket with cooking oil or spray. 8. Arrange the balls evenly on the basket. Then cook in your air fryer for 7 minutes. 9. If needed, cook 2 more minutes. 10. When cooked, remove from the air fryer and serve warm with marinara sauce.
Per serving: Calories: 332; Fat: 6.9g; Sodium: 228mg; Total Carbs: 57g; Net Carbs: 3g; Fiber: 2.7g; Sugars: 3.2g; Protein: 9.2g

Chinese Cabbage with Bacon

Prep Time: 5 minutes | Cook time: 12 minutes | Serves: 2

8 ounces Chinese cabbage, roughly chopped	2 ounces bacon, chopped
½ teaspoon onion powder	1 tablespoon sunflower oil
½ teaspoon salt	

1. In your air fryer, add the chopped bacon and cook at 400 degrees F/ 205 degrees C for 10 minutes. During cooking, stir from time to time. 2. Sprinkle the cooked bacon with salt and onion powder. 3. Then add Chinese cabbage and shake to mix well. 4. Cook for 2 minutes. 5. Before serving, add sunflower oil and stir. 6. Serve on plates.
Per serving: Calories: 232; Fat: 19.1g; Sodium: 1310mg; Total Carbs: 3g; Net Carbs: 1g; Fiber: 1.2g; Sugars: 1.6g; Protein: 12.3g

Apple Brussel Sprout Salad

Prep Time: 15 minutes | Cook time: 15 minutes | Serves: 4

1 pound Brussels sprouts	Dressing:
1 apple, cored and diced	¼ cup olive oil
½ cup mozzarella cheese, crumbled	2 tablespoons champagne vinegar
½ cup pomegranate seeds	1 teaspoon Dijon mustard
1 small-sized red onion, chopped	1 teaspoon honey
4 eggs, hardboiled and sliced	Salt and black pepper, to taste

1. At 380 degrees F/ 195 degrees C, preheat your air fryer. 2. Add the Brussels sprouts to the cooking basket. 3. Spritz with cooking spray and cook for almost 15 minutes. 4. Toss the Brussels sprouts with the apple, cheese, pomegranate seeds, and red onion. 5. Mix all the recipe ingredients for the dressing and toss to combine well. 6. Serve topped with the hard-boiled eggs. Serve
Per serving: Calories: 279; Fat: 18.1g; Sodium: 126mg; Total Carbs: 23g; Net Carbs: 11g; Fiber: 5.8g; Sugars: 11.6g; Protein: 10.7g

Zucchini Tots with Mozzarella

Prep Time: 15 minutes | Cook time: 6 minutes | Serves: 4

1 zucchini, grated	2 tablespoons. almond flour
½ cup Mozzarella, shredded	½ teaspoon black pepper
1 egg, beaten	1 teaspoon coconut oil, melted

1. Mix up grated zucchini, shredded Mozzarella, egg, almond flour, and black pepper. 2. Then make the small zucchini tots with the help of the fingertips. 3. At 385 degrees F/ 195 degrees C, preheat your air fryer. 4. Place the zucchini tots in the air fryer basket and cook for 3 minutes from each side or until the zucchini tots are golden brown. 5. Serve.
Per serving: Calories: 128; Fat: 9.6g; Sodium: 47mg; Total Carbs: 5g; Net Carbs: 2g; Fiber: 2.1g; Sugars: 0.9g; Protein: 6g

Beans and Sweet Potato Boats

Prep Time: 15 minutes | Cook time: 20 minutes | Serves: 4

2 tablespoons olive oil	¼ cup mozzarella cheese, grated
1 shallot, chopped	Black pepper and salt to taste
1 cup canned mixed beans	

1. At 400 degrees F/ 205 degrees C, preheat your air fryer. 2. Grease a suitable baking dish with the olive oil. Set aside. 3. Scoop out the flesh from potatoes, so shells are formed. 4. Chop the potato flesh and put it in a suitable bowl. 5. Add in shallot, mixed beans, salt, and black pepper and mix to combine. 6. Fill the hollow potato shells with the mixture and top with the cheese. Arrange on the baking dish. 7. Place this baking dish the preheated air fryer and cook for 20 minutes. 8. Serve.
Per serving: Calories: 142; Fat: 8.1g; Sodium: 11mg; Total Carbs: 11g; Net Carbs: 6.7g; Fiber: 3g; Sugars: 0g; Protein: 5.1g

Awesome Mushroom Tots

Prep Time: 15 minutes | Cook time: 6 minutes | Serves: 2

1 cup white mushrooms, grinded	½ teaspoon ground black pepper
1 teaspoon onion powder	1 teaspoon avocado oil
1 egg yolk	1 tablespoon coconut flour
3 teaspoons flax meal	

1. Add the onion powder, flax meal, ground black pepper, coconut flour, and grinded white mushrooms in a mixing bowl. Mix until smooth and homogenous. 2. Then make the mushroom tots from the mixture. 3. Before cooking, heat your air fryer to 400 degrees F/ 205 degrees C. 4. Brush the coconut oil over the inside of the air fryer basket. 5. Arrange evenly the mushroom tots on the air fryer basket. 6. Cook in your air fryer for 3 minutes. 7. Then flip the tots to the other side and continue cooking for 2to 3 minutes or until they are lightly brown.
Per serving: Calories: 88; Fat: 4.7g; Sodium: 7mg; Total Carbs: 8g; Net Carbs: 3.5g; Fiber: 4.7g; Sugars: 1.1g; Protein: 4.4g

Crispy Tofu with Soy Sauce

Prep Time: 15 minutes | Cook time: 35 minutes | Serves: 4

1 block firm tofu, pressed and diced	2 teaspoon sesame oil
1 tablespoon arrowroot flour	1 teaspoon vinegar
	2 tablespoon soy sauce

1. In a suitable bowl, toss tofu with oil, vinegar, and soy sauce and let sit for almost 15 minutes. 2. Toss marinated tofu with arrowroot flour. 3. Grease its air fryer basket with cooking spray. 4. Add tofu in air fryer basket and cook for 20 minutes at 370 degrees F/ 185 degrees C. Shake basket halfway through. 5. Serve and enjoy.
Per serving: Calories: 42; Fat: 3.2g; Sodium: 454mg; Total Carbs: 1g; Net Carbs: 0g; Fiber: 0.3g; Sugars: 0.3g; Protein: 2.4g

Pungent Mushroom Pizza

Prep Time: 8-10 minutes | Cook time: 8 minutes | Serves: 3-4

3 tablespoons olive oil	3 tablespoons mozzarella, shredded
3 cleaned portabella mushroom caps, scooped	1 pinch salt
3 tablespoons tomato sauce	1 pinch dried Italian seasonings
12 slices pepperoni	

1. On a flat kitchen surface, plug your air fryer and turn it on. 2. At 330 degrees F/ 165 degrees C, heat your air fryer for 4 to 5 minutes in advance. 3. Gently coat your air fryer basket with cooking oil or spray. 4. Toss the mushrooms with olive oil. 5. Season the inner side with Italian seasoning and salt. 6. Sprinkle the top with tomato sauce and cheese. 7. Arrange evenly the mushrooms onto the grease air fryer basket. 8. Cook in your air fryer at 330 degrees F/ 165 degrees C for 2 minutes. 9. When the cooking time is up, add the pepperoni slices and continue cooking for 4 to 5 minutes. 10. To serve, sprinkle the top with red pepper flakes and more cheese as you like.
Per serving: Calories: 242; Fat: 21.6g; Sodium: 499mg; Total Carbs: 2g; Net Carbs: 0.5g; Fiber: 0.2g; Sugars: 0.5g; Protein: 10.6g

Herbed Potatoes Medley

Prep Time: 15 minutes | Cook time: 30 minutes | Serves: 4

3 large potatoes, peeled and diced
1 teaspoon parsley, chopped
1 teaspoon chives, chopped
1 teaspoon oregano, chopped
1 tablespoon garlic, minced
Black pepper and salt to taste
2 tablespoons olive oil

1. Mix all of the recipe ingredients in your air fryer, and stir well. 2. Cook at almost 370 degrees F/ 185 degrees C for 30 minutes. Serve.
Per serving: Calories: 255; Fat: 7.3g; Sodium: 17mg; Total Carbs: 44g; Net Carbs: 21g; Fiber: 6.9g; Sugars: 3.2g; Protein: 4.8g

Balsamic Tomatoes with Garlic

Prep Time: 15 minutes | Cook time: 15 minutes | Serves: 4

1 tablespoon olive oil
1 pound cherry tomatoes, halved
1 tablespoon dill, chopped
6 garlic cloves, minced
1 tablespoon balsamic vinegar
Black pepper and salt to the taste

1. In a pan that fits the air fryer, combine all the recipe ingredients, toss gently. 2. Put the pan in your preheated air fryer and air fryer at almost 380 degrees F/ 195 degrees C for almost 15 minutes. 3. Divide between plates and serve.
Per serving: Calories: 60; Fat: 3.8g; Sodium: 8mg; Total Carbs: 6g; Net Carbs: 2.5g; Fiber: 1.6g; Sugars: 3.1g; Protein: 1.5g

Zucchini and Potato Polenta

Prep Time: 10-15 minutes | Cook time: 40 minutes | Serves: 5-6

½ pound zucchini, cut into bite-sized chunks
½ pound potatoes, make bite-sized chunks
½ teaspoon ground black pepper
½ teaspoon dried dill weed
1 tablespoon olive oil
1 cup onions, chopped
2 cloves garlic, finely minced
1 teaspoon paprika
½ teaspoon salt
14 ounces pre-cooked polenta tube, make slices
¼ cup cheddar cheese, shaved

1. On a flat kitchen surface, plug your air fryer and turn it on. 2. At 400 degrees F/ 205 degrees C, heat your air fryer for 4 to 5 minutes in advance. 3. Mix together the veggies, paprika, salt, olive oil, dill, and pepper in the air fryer basket until well-combined. 4. Cook in your air fryer for 6 minutes. 5. Shake for a while and continue cooking for 6 minutes or more. 6. Then add polenta and some cooking oil. Cook for 20 to 25 minutes. 7. Flip the polenta and continue cooking for 10 more minutes. 8. Cut the polenta into slices and top with the roasted vegetables and cheese. Serve and enjoy!
Per serving: Calories: 123; Fat: 6.1g; Sodium: 346mg; Total Carbs: 14g; Net Carbs: 9.5g; Fiber: 2.9g; Sugars: 3g; Protein: 4g

Mushroom Mozzarella Risotto

Prep Time: 5 minutes | Cook time: 20 minutes | Serves: 4

1-pound white mushrooms, sliced
¼ cup mozzarella, shredded
1 cauliflower head, florets separated and riced
1 cup chicken stock
1 tablespoon thyme, chopped
1 teaspoon Italian seasoning
A pinch of salt and black pepper
2 tablespoons olive oil

1. Grease a suitable baking pan with oil and then heat to medium heat. 2. Add the cauliflower rice and mushrooms. Toss and cook for a few minutes. 3. Add the shredded mozzarella, chicken stock, Italian seasoning, salt, and black pepper in the pan. 4. Cook in your air fryer at 360 degrees F/ 180 degrees C for 20 minutes. 5. To serve, sprinkle the chopped thyme on the top.
Per serving: Calories: 114; Fat: 8.2g; Sodium: 229mg; Total Carbs: 8g; Net Carbs: 3.5g; Fiber: 3.1g; Sugars: 3.8g; Protein: 5.6g

Roasted Pepper Salad with Pine Nuts

Prep Time: 10 minutes | Cook time: 25 Minutes | Serves: 4

2 yellow bell peppers
2 red bell peppers
2 green bell peppers
1 Serrano pepper
4 tbsps. olive oil
2 tbsps. cider vinegar
2 garlic cloves, peeled and pressed
1 tsp. cayenne pepper
Sea salt, to taste
½ tsp. mixed peppercorns, freshly crushed
½ cup pine nuts
¼ cup loosely packed fresh Italian parsley leaves, roughly chopped

1. Before cooking, heat your air fryer to 400 degrees F/ 205 degrees C. 2. Using cooking oil, lightly brush the air fryer basket. 3. Then transfer the peppers in the air fryer basket and roast in your air fryer for 5 minutes. 4. Turn the peppers and roast the other side for another 5 minutes. 5. Flip again and roast until it is soft and charred on the surface. 6. Peel the peppers and cool them to room temperature. 7. Whisk vinegar, olive oil, garlic, salt, crushed peppercorns, and cayenne pepper together. Then dress the salad and set it aside. 8. Then add the pine nuts inside the air fryer basket. Roast them in your air fryer at 360 degrees F/ 180 degrees C for 4 minutes. Toss the nuts well. 9. Roast again in the air fryer for 3 to 4 minutes. 10. Sprinkle the toasted nuts over the peppers. 11. Garnish with parsley. 12. Enjoy your meal.
Per serving: Calories: 270; Fat: 25.9g; Sodium: 72mg; Total Carbs: 10.5g; Net Carbs: 0g; Fiber: 2.6g; Sugars: 5.4g; Protein: 3.6g

Cheddar Tomatillos with Lettuce

Prep Time: 10 minutes | Cook time: 4 minutes | Serves: 4

2 tomatillos
¼ cup coconut flour
2 eggs, beaten
¼ teaspoon ground nutmeg
¼ teaspoon chili flakes
1 ounce Cheddar cheese, shredded
4 lettuce leaves

1. Cut the tomatillos into slices. 2. Mix ground nutmeg, chili flakes, and beaten eggs in a bowl. 3. Brush the tomatillo slices with the egg mixture. Then coat with coconut flour. 4. Repeat above steps with the rest slices. 5. Before cooking, heat your air fryer to 400 degrees F/ 205 degrees C. 6. Place the coated tomatillo slices in the air fryer basket in a single layer. 7. Cook in your air fryer for 2 minutes from each side. 8. When cooked, add the lettuce leaves on the top of the tomatillos. 9. To serve, sprinkle with shredded cheese.
Per serving: Calories: 127; Fat: 6.3g; Sodium: 75mg; Total Carbs: 11.5g; Net Carbs: 5g; Fiber: 6.4g; Sugars: 0.3g; Protein: 6.7g

Cauliflower Bake with Basil Pesto

Prep Time: 5 minutes | Cook time: 20 minutes | Serves: 6

1 cup heavy whipping cream
2 tablespoons basil pesto
Salt and black pepper to the taste
Juice of ½ lemon
1 pound cauliflower, florets
separated
4 ounces cherry tomatoes, halved
3 tablespoons ghee, melted
7 ounces cheddar cheese, grated

1. Drizzle a suitable baking pan with ghee. 2. Gently toss together the lemon juice, pesto, cream, and the cauliflower in the pan. 3. Add the tomatoes and cover the top with cheese. 4. Cook in your air fryer at 380 degrees F/ 195 degrees C for 20 minutes. 5. Serve on plates as a side dish.
Per serving: Calories: 281; Fat: 24.9g; Sodium: 237mg; Total Carbs: 5g; Net Carbs: 2g; Fiber: 2.1g; Sugars: 2.5g; Protein: 10.4g

Turmeric Tofu Cubes

Prep Time: 10 minutes | Cook time: 9 minutes | Serves: 2

6 ounces tofu, cubed
1 teaspoon avocado oil
1 teaspoon apple cider vinegar
1 garlic clove, diced
¼ teaspoon ground turmeric
¼ teaspoon ground paprika
½ teaspoon dried cilantro
¼ teaspoon lemon zest, grated

1. Before cooking, firstly heat your air fryer to 400 degrees F/ 205 degrees C. 2. Mix together apple cider vinegar, ground turmeric, diced garlic, paprika, avocado oil, lime zest, and cilantro in a bowl. 3. Coat the tofu cubes with the oil mixture. 4. Transfer the tofu cubes in the air fryer basket and cook in your air fryer for 9 minutes. 5. During cooking shake the basket from time to time.
Per serving: Calories: 67; Fat: 3.9g; Sodium: 11mg; Total Carbs: 2g; Net Carbs: 0.5g; Fiber: 1.1g; Sugars: 0.6g; Protein: 7.2g

Sweet and Spicy Tofu

Prep Time: 15 minutes | Cook time: 23 minutes | Serves: 3

For Tofu:
1 (14-ounce) block firm tofu, pressed and cubed
½ cup arrowroot flour
½ teaspoon sesame oil

For Sauce:
4 tablespoons low-sodium soy sauce
1½ tablespoons rice vinegar
1½ tablespoons chili sauce
1 tablespoon agave nectar
2 large garlic cloves, minced
1 teaspoon fresh ginger, peeled and grated
2 scallions (green part), chopped

1. Mix arrowroot flour, sesame oil, and tofu together in a bowl. 2. Before cooking, heat your air fryer to 360 degrees F/ 180 degrees C. 3. Gently grease an air fryer basket. 4. Place the tofu evenly on the air fryer basket in a layer. 5. Cook in your air fryer for 20 minutes. Halfway through cooking, shake the air fryer basket once. 6. To make the sauce, add soy sauce, rice vinegar, chili sauce, agave nectar, garlic, and ginger in a bowl. Beat the mixture to combine well. 7. When the tofu has cooked, remove from the air fryer and transfer to a skillet. 8. Add the sauce and heat the skillet over medium heat. Cook for about 3 minutes. Stir the meal from time to time. 9. Add the scallions to garnish and serve hot.
Per serving: Calories: 146; Fat: 6.5g; Sodium: 1894mg; Total Carbs: 7g; Net Carbs: 3g; Fiber: 1.9g; Sugars: 2.7g; Protein: 13.4g

Coconut Brussels Sprouts

Prep Time: 10 minutes | Cook time: 15 minutes | Serves: 4

8 ounces Brussels sprouts
2 tablespoons almonds, grinded
1 teaspoon coconut flakes
2 egg whites
½ teaspoon salt
½ teaspoon white pepper
Cooking spray

1. Whisk the egg whites together in a bowl. Season with white pepper and salt. 2. Cut the Brussels sprouts into halves and place in the halves the egg white mixture. 3. Shake the vegetables and coat the vegetables with coconut flakes and grinded almonds. 4. Before cooking, heat your air fryer to 380 degrees F/ 195 degrees C. 5. Transfer the Brussels sprouts in the air fryer basket. 6. Cook the prepared Brussels sprouts in your air fryer at 380 degrees F/ 195 degrees C for 15 minutes. 7. After cooking for 8 minutes, shake the basket.
Per serving: Calories: 52; Fat: 1.9g; Sodium: 322mg; Total Carbs: 6g; Net Carbs: 2.5g; Fiber: 2.6g; Sugars: 1.5g; Protein: 4.4g

Parsley Cabbage

Prep Time: 5 minutes | Cook time: 20 minutes | Serves: 4

2 ounces butter, melted
1 green cabbage head, shredded 1 and ½ cups heavy cream
¼ cup parsley, chopped
1 tablespoon sweet paprika
1 teaspoon lemon zest, grated

1. Heat butter on a suitable cooking pan. 2. Then add cabbage and cook for 5 minutes. 3. Place the remaining ingredients in the pan. Toss well and transfer the pan into your air fryer. 4. Cook in your air fryer at 380 degrees F/ 195 degrees C for 5 minutes. 5. Serve on plates as a side dish.
Per serving: Calories: 153; Fat: 11.9g; Sodium: 116mg; Total Carbs: 11g; Net Carbs: 6.7g; Fiber: 5.3g; Sugars: 6g; Protein: 2.8g

Cheese Broccoli with Basil

Prep Time: 10 minutes | Cook time: 7 minutes | Serves: 4

1 cup broccoli, chopped, boiled
1 teaspoon nut oil
1 teaspoon salt
1 teaspoon dried basil
½ cup Cheddar cheese, shredded
½ cup of coconut milk
½ teaspoon butter, softened

1. In the air fryer basket, place the broccoli, nut oil, dried dill, and salt. 2. Stir together the mixture and then pour in the coconut milk. 3. Drizzle butter and Cheddar cheese on the top of the meal. 4. Before cooking, heat your air fryer to 400 degrees F/ 205 degrees C. 5. Cook the mixture inside the preheated air fryer for 7 minutes.
Per serving: Calories: 148; Fat: 13.5g; Sodium: 685mg; Total Carbs: 3g; Net Carbs: 1g; Fiber: 1.3g; Sugars: 1.5g; Protein: 4.9g

Turmeric Cauliflower Patties

Prep Time: 15 minutes | Cook time: 10 minutes | Serves: 2

¼ cup cauliflower, shredded
1 egg yolk
½ teaspoon ground turmeric
¼ teaspoon onion powder
¼ teaspoon salt
2 ounces Cheddar cheese, shredded
¼ teaspoon baking powder
1 teaspoon heavy cream
1 tablespoon coconut flakes
Cooking spray

1. Squeeze the shredded cauliflower and put it in the bowl. 2. Add egg yolk, ground turmeric, baking powder, onion powder, heavy cream, salt, and coconut flakes. 3. Then melt Cheddar cheese and add it in the cauliflower mixture. 4. Stir the ingredients until you get the smooth mass. 5. After this, make the medium size cauliflower patties. 6. At 365 degrees F/ 185 degrees C, preheat your air fryer. 7. Grease its air fryer basket with cooking spray and put the patties inside. 8. Cook them for almost 5 minutes from each side. 9. Serve warm.
Per serving: Calories: 165; Fat: 13.5g; Sodium: 477mg; Total Carbs: 2g; Net Carbs: 0.5g; Fiber: 0.7g; Sugars: 0.8g; Protein: 8.9g

Brussels Sprouts and Mushrooms

Prep Time: 5 minutes | Cook time: 20 minutes | Serves: 4

1 pound Brussels sprouts, halved
1 tablespoon olive oil
8 ounces brown mushrooms, halved
8 ounces cherry tomatoes, halved
½ teaspoon rosemary, dried
A pinch of salt and black pepper
Juice of 1 lime

1. Mix Brussels sprouts, olive oil, mushrooms, cherry tomatoes, rosemary, salt, and pepper in the air fryer basket. 2. Cook the veggies in your air fryer at 380 degrees F/ 195 degrees C for 20 minutes. 3. Serve on plates as a side dish.
Per serving: Calories: 105; Fat: 4.1g; Sodium: 35mg; Total Carbs: 15g; Net Carbs: 5.6g; Fiber: 5.3g; Sugars: 4.9g; Protein: 5.8g

Turmeric Cauliflower with Cilantro

Prep Time: 10 minutes | Cook time: 8 minutes | Serves: 4

1 pound cauliflower head
1 tablespoon ground turmeric
1 tablespoon coconut oil
½ teaspoon dried cilantro
¼ teaspoon salt

1. Before cooking, heat your air fryer to 400 degrees F/ 205 degrees C. 2. Cut the cauliflower into 4 steaks. Rub together with salt, dried cilantro, ground turmeric, and the cauliflower steak. 3. Sprinkle the mixture with coconut oil. 4. Transfer the mixture inside the air fryer basket and cook in your air fryer for 4 minutes from each side.
Per serving: Calories: 105; Fat: 4.1g; Sodium: 35mg; Total Carbs: 15g; Net Carbs: 5.6g; Fiber: 5.3g; Sugars: 4.9g; Protein: 5.8g

Creamy Garlic Bread

Prep Time: 10 minutes | Cook time: 8 minutes | Serves: 4

1 ounce Mozzarella, shredded
2 tablespoons almond flour
1 teaspoon cream cheese
¼ teaspoon garlic powder
¼ teaspoon baking powder
1 egg, beaten
1 teaspoon coconut oil, melted
¼ teaspoon minced garlic
1 teaspoon dried dill
1 ounce Provolone cheese, grated

1. Mix almond flour, cream cheese, Mozzarella, baking powder, egg, dried dill, Provolone cheese, and garlic powder together in a mixing bowl until homogenous. 2. Line the baking paper over the air fryer basket. 3. Transfer the mixture onto the air fryer basket. 4. Shape the mixture into bread. 5. Then drizzle the garlic bread with coconut oil. 6. At 400 degrees F/ 205 degrees C, heat your air fryer in advance. 7. Cook the bread in the preheated air fryer for 8 minutes or until light brown. 8. When cooked, cut the bread into 4 servings. 9. Serve on plates.
Per serving: Calories: 159; Fat: 12.3g; Sodium: 128mg; Total Carbs: 4g; Net Carbs: 2g; Fiber: 1.6g; Sugars: 0.2g; Protein: 8.3g

Lemon Fennel with Sunflower Seeds

Prep Time: 5 minutes | Cook time: 15 minutes | Serves: 4

1 pound fennel, cut into small wedges	Salt and black pepper to the taste
A pinch of salt and black pepper	Juice of ½ lemon
3 tablespoons olive oil	2 tablespoons sunflower seeds

1. Mix fennel wedges, salt, black pepper, olive oil, and lemon in a suitable baking pan. 2. Cook the mixture in your air fryer at 400 degrees F/ 205 degrees C for 15 minutes. 3. When cooked, sprinkle on top with the sunflower seeds. 4. Serve on plates as a side dish.
Per serving: Calories: 134; Fat: 11.5g; Sodium: 59mg; Total Carbs: 8g; Net Carbs: 3.5g; Fiber: 3.7g; Sugars: 0g; Protein: 1.7g

Flavorful Radish Salad

Prep Time: 8-10 minutes | Cook time: 30 minutes | Serves: 4

1 ½ pounds radishes, trimmed and halved	1 teaspoon olive oil
2 tablespoons olive oil	1 tablespoon balsamic vinegar
Pepper and salt, as needed	½ pound mozzarella, sliced
For the Salad:	1 teaspoon honey
	Pepper and salt, as needed

1. Mix thoroughly the salt, black pepper, oil, and the radishes in medium sized bowl. 2. On a flat kitchen surface, plug your air fryer and turn it on. 3. Before cooking, heat your air fryer to 350 degrees F/ 175 degrees C for 4 to 5 minutes. 4. Place the mixture onto the air fryer basket. 5. Cook in your air fryer for 3 minutes. 6. In another medium sized bowl, mix thoroughly the cheese and fried radish. 7. Mix the remaining ingredients in a small bowl. Drizzle over the salad to serve.
Per serving: Calories: 103; Fat: 7.8g; Sodium: 88mg; Total Carbs: 7g; Net Carbs: 3g; Fiber: 2.7g; Sugars: 4.6g; Protein: 2.2g

Green Beans with Parsley

Prep Time: 5 minutes | Cook time: 20 minutes | Serves: 4

10 ounces green beans, trimmed	Zest of ½ lemon, grated
A pinch of salt and black pepper	¼ cup parsley, chopped
3 ounces butter, melted	2 garlic cloves, minced
1 cup coconut cream	

1. Add salt, black pepper, butter, coconut cream, lemon zest, parsley, and garlic cloves in a bowl. 2. Whisk them together. 3. Place the green beans in a suitable pan. Then add the butter mixture over the green beans. 4. Cook in your air fryer at 370 degrees F/ 185 degrees C for 20 minutes. 5. Serve on plates as a side dish.
Per serving: Calories: 316; Fat: 31.7g; Sodium: 138mg; Total Carbs: 9g; Net Carbs: 4.3g; Fiber: 3.9g; Sugars: 3.1g; Protein: 3.1g

Garlic Brussel Sprouts with Celery

Prep Time: 15 minutes | Cook time: 13 minutes | Serves: 6

1 pound Brussels sprouts	1 tablespoon butter, melted
1 teaspoon minced garlic	1 teaspoon cayenne pepper
2 ounces celery stalks, minced	¼ teaspoon salt

1. Roughly chop the Brussels sprouts with celery, cayenne pepper, butter, salt, and minced garlic. 2. Shake the mixture and marinate for 10 minutes. 3. Before cooking, heat the air fryer to 385 degrees F/ 195 degrees C. 4. Cook the marinated Brussels sprouts in your air fryer for 13 minutes. 5. During cooking, shake the basket from time to time.
Per serving: Calories: 53; Fat: 2.3g; Sodium: 137mg; Total Carbs: 7.5g; Net Carbs: 2.5g; Fiber: 3.1g; Sugars: 1.8g; Protein: 2.7g

Lemony Cabbage Slaw

Prep Time: 5 minutes | Cook time: 20 minutes | Serves: 4

1 green cabbage head, shredded	½ cup coconut cream
Juice of ½ lemon	½ teaspoon fennel seeds
A pinch of salt and black pepper	1 tablespoon mustard

1. Combine all the ingredients in a suitable baking pan. 2. Cook in your air fryer at 350 degrees F/ 175 degrees C for 20 minutes. 3. Serve on plates as a side dish.
Per serving: Calories: 128; Fat: 8.2g; Sodium: 37mg; Total Carbs: 13g; Net Carbs: 7g; Fiber: 5.6g; Sugars: 6.9g; Protein: 3.7g

Creamy Cilantro Peppers Mix

Prep Time: 5 minutes | Cook time: 20 minutes | Serves: 4

8 ounces mini bell peppers, halved	8 ounces cream cheese, soft
1 tablespoon olive oil	1 cup cheddar cheese, shredded
1 tablespoon cilantro, chopped	Salt and black pepper to the taste

1. Brush the olive oil gently over a suitable baking dish. 2. Arrange the bell pepper evenly inside the air fryer basket. 3. Mix the mini bell peppers, olive oil, cilantro, cream cheese, cheddar cheese, salt, and black pepper in a mixing bowl. 4. Then spread the mixture over the bell pepper. 5. Cook in your air fryer at 370 degrees F/ 185 degrees C for 20 minutes. 6. Serve on plate as a side dish.
Per serving: Calories: 358; Fat: 32.6g; Sodium: 343mg; Total Carbs: 5g; Net Carbs: 2g; Fiber: 0.7g; Sugars: 2.3g; Protein: 12g

Garlic Provolone Asparagus

Prep Time: 10 minutes | Cook time: 5 minutes | Serves: 3

9 ounces Asparagus	1 teaspoon olive oil
¼ teaspoon chili powder	4 Provolone cheese slices
¼ teaspoon garlic powder	

1. Sprinkle the trimmed asparagus with garlic powder and chili powder. 2. Before cooking, heat your air fryer to 400 degrees F/ 205 degrees C. 3. Transfer the asparagus in the air fryer basket. 4. Sprinkle with olive oil. 5. Cook the asparagus in your air fryer for 3 minutes. 6. Sprinkle the Provolone cheese on the top and continue cooking for 3 or more minutes.
Per serving: Calories: 163; Fat: 11.6g; Sodium: 331mg; Total Carbs: 4g; Net Carbs: 2g; Fiber: 1.9g; Sugars: 1.9g; Protein: 11.5g

Herbed Mushroom Pilau

Prep Time: 8 minutes | Cook time: 25 Minutes | Serves: 4

1 ½ cups cauliflower rice	2 garlic cloves
3 cups vegetable broth	1 onion, chopped
2 tbsps. olive oil	¼ cup dry vermouth
1 lb. fresh porcini mushrooms, sliced	1 tsp. dried thyme
	½ tsp. dried tarragon
2 tablespoons. olive oil	1 tsp. sweet Hungarian paprika

1. Lightly grease a suitable baking dish. 2. Mix all the ingredients in the dish until well combined. 3. Before cooking, heat your air fryer to 370 degrees F/ 185 degrees C. 4. Place the baking dish in your air fryer. Cook for 20 minutes. 5. Check periodically to make sure it is evenly cooked. 6. Serve your meal in bowls. Enjoy!
Per serving: Calories: 73; Fat: 1.9g; Sodium: 620mg; Total Carbs: 7g; Net Carbs: 3g; Fiber: 1.1g; Sugars: 3.6g; Protein: 6.2g

Buffalo Cauliflower Bites

Prep Time: 5 minutes | Cook Time: 20 minutes | Servings: 4

1 large chopped into florets cauliflower head	⅔ cup of cornstarch
3 beaten eggs	2 tbsp. of melted butter
	¼ cup of hot sauce

1. Preheat your air fryer to 360 degrees F/ 180 degrees C. 2. In a large mixing bowl, add and mix the eggs and the cornstarch a properly. 3. Add the cauliflower, gently toss it until it is properly covered with the batter, shake it off in case of any excess batter and set it aside. 4. Grease your "Air Fryer Basket" with a nonstick cooking spray and add the cauliflower bites which will require you to work in batches. 5. Cook the cauliflower bites at 360 degrees F/ 180 degrees C on Air Fry mode for 15 to 20 minutes or until it has a golden-brown color and a crispy texture, while still shaking occasionally. 6. Then, using a small mixing bowl, add and mix the melted butter and hot sauce properly. 7. Once the cauliflower bites are done, remove it from your air fryer and place it into a large bowl. 8. Drizzle the buffalo sauce over the cauliflower bites and toss it until it is properly covered. 9. Serve and enjoy!
Per serving: Calories 240, Fat 5.5g, Fiber: 6.3g,; Protein 8.8g; Total Carbs 37g; Sugar 1.2 g; Fiber 1g

Tasty Spiced Tofu

Prep Time: 15 minutes | Cook time: 13 Minutes | Serves: 3

1 (14-ounce) block extra-firm tofu, pressed and cut into ¾-inch cubes
3 teaspoons. cornstarch
1½ tablespoons avocado oil

1½ teaspoons paprika
1 teaspoon onion powder
1 teaspoon garlic powder
Salt and black pepper, to taste

1. Before cooking, heat your air fryer to 390 degrees F/ 200 degrees C. 2. Using cooking spray or the avocado oil, grease the air fryer basket. 3. In a bowl, add cornstarch, spices, and tofu and mix together. Toss to coat the tofu well. 4. Then evenly arrange the coated tofu inside the greased basket. 5. Cook in your air fryer for 13 minutes, tossing the tofu twice in between. 6. When cooked, dish out the meal and serve hot on plates.
Per serving: Calories: 273; Fat: 7.3g; Sodium: 17mg; Total Carbs: 45g; Net Carbs: 24g; Fiber: 3.8g; Sugars: 1.5g; Protein: 8.1g

Tomato Rolls

Prep Time: 5 minutes | Cook time: 15 minutes| Serves: 5

10 egg roll wrappers
1 tomato, diced

¼ tsp pepper
½ tsp salt

1. Add the diced tomato, salt, and pepper in a medium bowl. Use a fork to mash until smooth. It is also fine to leave chunks for the filling. 2. Then divide them onto the egg wrappers. 3. With your wet finger, brush along the edges to seal the rolls well. 4. Line a suitable baking sheet with baking paper. 5. Arrange the rolls evenly on the baking sheet. 6. Cook the rolls in your air fryer at 350 degrees F/ 175 degrees C for 5 minutes. 7. Serve the rolls with sweet chili dipping. Enjoy!
Per serving: Calories: 189; Fat: 0.2g Sodium: 599mg; Total Carbs: 37.6g; Net Carbs: 4.2 g Fiber1.3g; Sugars: 0.3g; Protein 6.4g

Provolone Zucchini Balls

Prep Time: 10 minutes | Cook time: 12 minutes | Serves: 4

¼ teaspoon salt
¼ teaspoon ground cumin
1 zucchini, grated
2 ounces Provolone cheese, grated

¼ teaspoon chili flakes
1 egg, beaten
¼ cup coconut flour
1 teaspoon sunflower oil

1. Mix ground cumin, zucchini, Provolone cheese, egg, chili flakes, and salt together. 2. Make them into small balls with a spoon. 3. Line baking paper over the air fryer basket. Brush the bottom of the baking paper with sunflower oil. 4. Cook in your air fryer at 375 degrees F/ 190 degrees C for 12 minutes. 5. To avoid burning, shake the balls every 2 minutes.
Per serving: Calories: 114; Fat: 6.9g; Sodium: 292mg; Total Carbs: 7g; Net Carbs: 3g; Fiber: 3.6g; Sugars: 1g; Protein: 6.6g

Creamy Cauliflower Puree

Prep Time: 10 minutes | Cook time: 8 minutes | Serves: 2

1 ½ cup cauliflower, chopped
1 tablespoon butter, melted
½ teaspoon salt
1 tablespoon fresh parsley,

chopped
¼ cup heavy cream
Cooking spray

1. Spritz the cooking spray over the inside of the air fryer basket. 2. Place the chopped cauliflower in the air fryer basket. 3. Cook in your air fryer at 400 degrees F/ 205 degrees C for 8 minutes. Stir the cauliflower every 4 minutes. 4. Heat the heavy cream until it is hot. Then pour in a blender, add parsley, butter, salt, and cauliflower. 5. Blend until it is smooth.
Per serving: Calories: 122; Fat: 11.4g; Sodium: 652mg; Total Carbs: 4.5g; Net Carbs: 0.5g; Fiber: 1.9g; Sugars: 1.8g; Protein: 1.9g

Open-faced Sandwich

Prep Time: 10 minutes | Cook time: 25 minutes | Serves: 4

1 can chickpeas, drained and rinsed
1 medium-sized head of cauliflower
1 tbsp. extra-virgin olive oil

2 ripe avocados, mashed
2 tbsps. lemon juice
4 flatbreads, toasted
salt and pepper to taste

1. Before cooking, heat your air fryer to 425 degrees F/ 220 degrees C. 2. Cut the cauliflower head into florets. Combine chickpea, olive oil, lemon juice, and the cauliflower together in a mixing bowl. 3. Transfer the mixture inside the air fryer basket. 4. Cook in your air fryer for 25 minutes. 5. When cooked, spread the mixture on half of the flatbread and then add avocado mash. 6. To season, add more salt and pepper as you like. 7. Serve the meal with hot sauce.
Per serving: Calories: 470; Fat: 26.3g; Sodium: 81mg; Total Carbs: 50.1g; Net Carbs: 0g; Fiber: 20.7g; Sugars: 10.9g; Protein: 15.7g

Mozzarella Broccoli and Cauliflower

Prep Time: 5 minutes | Cook time: 20 minutes | Serves: 4

15 ounces broccoli florets
10 ounces cauliflower florets
1 leek, chopped
2 spring onions, chopped
Salt and black pepper to the taste

2 ounces butter, melted
2 tablespoons mustard
1 cup sour cream
5 ounces mozzarella cheese, shredded

1. Spread butter on a suitable baking pan that fits in your air fryer. 2. Add cauliflower, broccoli florets, chopped leek, chopped spring onions, salt, black pepper, mustard, and sour cream in the baking pan. Toss together. 3. Then drizzle the mozzarella on the top. 4. Cook in your air fryer at 380 degrees F/ 195 degrees C for 20 minutes. 5. Serve on plates as a side dish.
Per serving: Calories: 421; Fat: 31.9g; Sodium: 387mg; Total Carbs: 20.2g; Net Carbs: 0g; Fiber: 6g; Sugars: 5g; Protein: 18.2g

Creamy Cauliflower Mash

Prep Time: 5 minutes | Cook time: 20 minutes | Serves: 4

2 pounds cauliflower florets
1 teaspoon olive oil
2 ounces parmesan, grated
4 ounces butter, soft

Juice of ½ lemon
Zest of ½ lemon, grated
Salt and black pepper to the taste

1. Before cooking, heat your air fryer with the air fryer basket to 380 degrees F/ 195 degrees C. 2. Add the cauliflower in the preheated air fryer basket and add oil to rub well. 3. Cook in your air fryer for 20 minutes. 4. When cooked, remove the cauliflower to a bowl. Mash well and place the remaining ingredients in the bowl. Stir well. 5. Serve on plates as a side dish.
Per serving: Calories: 316; Fat: 27.4g; Sodium: 363mg; Total Carbs: 12g; Net Carbs: 7g; Fiber: 5.7g; Sugars: 5.5g; Protein: 9.3g

Cheesy Zucchini Tots

Prep Time: 15 minutes | Cook time: 6 minutes | Serves: 4

1 zucchini, grated
½ cup Mozzarella, shredded
1 egg, beaten

2 tablespoons almond flour
½ teaspoon ground black pepper
1 teaspoon coconut oil, melted

1. Before cooking, heat your air fryer to 385 degrees F/ 195 degrees C. 2. Brush the coconut oil over the inside of the air fryer basket. 3. Mix the shredded Mozzarella, almond flour, egg, ground black pepper, and grated zucchini in a mixing bowl. Make small zucchini tots. Arrange evenly the zucchini tots on the air fryer basket. 4. Cook in your air fryer at 385 degrees F/ 195 degrees C for 3 minutes from each side or until golden brown.
Per serving: Calories: 128; Fat: 9.6g; Sodium: 47mg; Total Carbs: 5g; Net Carbs: 2g; Fiber: 2.1g; Sugars: 0.9g; Protein: 6g

Spiced Cauliflower Medley

Prep Time: 5 minutes | Cook time: 15 minutes | Serves: 4

1 pound cauliflower florets, roughly grated
3 eggs, whisked

3 tablespoons butter, melted
Salt and black pepper to the taste
1 tablespoon sweet paprika

1. Set heat to high and then melt the butter in a pan. 2. Then add the cauliflower in the pan and cook until brown for 5 minutes. 3. Add salt, the whisked eggs, paprika, and pepper. Toss well. 4. Cook in your air fryer at 400 degrees F/ 205 degrees C for 10 minutes. 5. Serve on plates.
Per serving: Calories: 157; Fat: 12.3g; Sodium: 142mg; Total Carbs: 7g; Net Carbs: 3g; Fiber: 3.5g; Sugars: 3.2g; Protein: 6.8g

Crispy Spiced Asparagus

Prep Time: 15 minutes | Cook time: 15 Minutes | Serves: 5

¼ cup almond flour
½ teaspoon garlic powder
½ teaspoon smoked paprika
10 medium asparagus, trimmed

2 large eggs, beaten
2 tablespoons parsley, chopped
Salt and pepper to taste

1. Before cooking, heat your air fryer to 350 degrees F/ 175 degrees C for about 5 minutes. 2. Combine garlic powder, smoked paprika, almond flour, and parsley in a mixing bowl. 3. To season, add salt and pepper. 4. Dredge the asparagus in the beaten eggs and then coat the asparagus with almond flour mixture. 5. Cook in your air fryer at 350 degrees F/ 175 degrees C for 15 minutes.
Per serving: Calories: 118; Fat: 5g; Sodium: 36mg; Total Carbs: 12g; Net Carbs: 7g; Fiber: 6.4g; Sugars: 5.3g; Protein: 9.8g

Mozzarella Eggplant Gratin

Prep Time: 10 minutes | Cook time: 30 minutes | Serves: 2

¼ cup chopped red pepper
¼ cup chopped green pepper
¼ cup chopped onion
⅓ cup chopped tomatoes
1 clove garlic, minced
1 tablespoon sliced pimiento-stuffed olives

1 teaspoon capers
¼ teaspoon dried basil
¼ teaspoon dried marjoram
Salt and pepper to taste
Cooking spray
¼ cup grated mozzarella cheese
1 tablespoon breadcrumbs

1. Before cooking, heat your air fryer to 300 degrees F/ 150 degrees C. 2. Add the green pepper, red pepper, eggplant, onion, olives, garlic, capers, basil marjoram, salt, tomatoes, and pepper in a large bowl. 3. Using olive oil cooking spray, lightly grease a suitable baking dish. 4. Evenly line the eggplant mixture into the baking dish. 5. Then flatten the mixture. 6. Add the mozzarella cheese on the top and spread over with breadcrumbs. 7. Cook in your air fryer for 20 minutes.
Per serving: Calories: 47; Fat: 1.3g; Sodium: 92mg; Total Carbs: 7g; Net Carbs: 3g; Fiber: 1.3g; Sugars: 2.7g; Protein: 2.3g

Zucchinis and Arugula Salad

Prep Time: 5 minutes | Cook time: 20 minutes | Serves: 4

1-pound zucchinis, sliced
1 tablespoon olive oil
Salt and white pepper to the taste

4 ounces arugula leaves
¼ cup chives, chopped
1 cup walnuts, chopped

1. Combine the chopped chives, zucchini, olive oil, salt, and white pepper in the air fryer basket. Toss well. 2. Cook in your air fryer at 360 degrees F/ 180 degrees C for 20 minutes. 3. Place the cooked veggies in a salad bowl and toss with the walnuts and arugula. 4. Serve as a side salad.
Per serving: Calories: 249; Fat: 22.4g; Sodium: 20mg; Total Carbs: 8g; Net Carbs: 3.5g; Fiber: 3.9g; Sugars: 2.9g; Protein: 9.7g

Mozzarella Spinach Mash

Prep Time: 10 minutes | Cook time: 13 minutes | Serves: 4

3 cups spinach, chopped
½ cup Mozzarella, shredded
4 bacon slices, chopped
1 teaspoon butter

1 cup heavy cream
½ teaspoon salt
½ jalapeno pepper, chopped

1. In the air fryer basket, place the chopped bacon slices. 2. Cook in your air fryer at 400 degrees F/ 205 degrees C for 8 minutes. 3. During cooking, stir the bacon with a spatula from time to time. 4. In the air fryer casserole mold, add the cooked bacon. 5. Add spinach, heavy cream, salt, and jalapeno pepper, Mozzarella, and butter. Gently stir the mixture. 6. Cook the mash at 400 degrees F/ 205 degrees C for 5 minutes. 7. Using a spoon, carefully stir the spinach mash.
Per serving: Calories: 230; Fat: 20.7g; Sodium: 787mg; Total Carbs: 2g; Net Carbs: 0.5g; Fiber: 0.6g; Sugars: 0.2g; Protein: 9.3g

Lemon Cabbage with Cilantro

Prep Time: 4 minutes | Cook time: 25 minutes | Serves: 4

1 green cabbage head, shredded and cut into large wedges
2 tablespoons olive oil

1 tablespoon cilantro, chopped
1 tablespoon lemon juice
A pinch of salt and black pepper

1. Before cooking, heat your air fryer to 370 degrees F/ 185 degrees C. 2. In the air fryer basket, mix all the ingredients. 3. Cook in your air fryer for 25 minutes. 4. Serve on plates as a side dish.
Per serving: Calories: 106; Fat: 7.2g; Sodium: 33mg; Total Carbs: 10.5g; Net Carbs: 0g; Fiber: 4.5g; Sugars: 5.8g; Protein: 2.3g

Rutabaga Fries

Prep Time: 5 minutes | Cook time: 20 minutes | Serves: 4

15 ounces rutabaga, cut into fries
4 tablespoons olive oil

½ teaspoon chili powder
A pinch of salt and black pepper

1. Mix the rutabaga, olive oil, chili powder, salt, and black pepper in a bowl. 2. Transfer into your air fryer basket. 3. Cook the seasoned rutabaga in your air fryer at 400 degrees F/ 205 degrees C for 20 minutes. 4. Serve on plates as a side dish.
Per serving: Calories: 159; Fat: 14.3g; Sodium: 25mg; Total Carbs: 8g; Net Carbs: 3.5g; Fiber: 2.8g; Sugars: 6g; Protein: 1.3g

Stuffed Peppers

Prep Time: 5 minutes | Cook time: 16 Minutes | Serves: 1

1 bell pepper
½ tablespoon diced onion
½ diced tomato, plus one tomato slice

¼ teaspoon smoked paprika
Salt and pepper, to taste
1 teaspoon olive oil
¼ teaspoon dried basil

1. Before cooking, heat your air fryer to 350 degrees F/ 175 degrees C. 2. The bell pepper should be cored and cleaned for stuffing. 3. Using half of the olive oil to brush the pepper on the outside. 4. Combine together the diced onion, the diced tomato, smoked paprika, salt, and pepper in a small bowl. 5. Then stuff the cored pepper with the mixture and add the tomato slice on the top. 6. Using the remaining olive oil, brush the tomato slice. 7. Sprinkle the stuffed pepper with basil. 8. Cook the stuffed peppers in your air fryer for 10 minutes or until thoroughly cooked.
Per serving: Calories: 87; Fat: 5.1g; Sodium: 5mg; Total Carbs: 11g; Net Carbs: 6.7g; Fiber: 2.3g; Sugars: 7.1g; Protein: 1.6g

Creamy Spinach with Nutmeg

Prep Time: 15 minutes | Cook time: 15 minutes| Serves: 2

10 ounces frozen spinach, thawed
¼ cup parmesan cheese, shredded
½ teaspoon ground nutmeg
1 teaspoon black pepper

4 ounces cream cheese, diced
2 teaspoons garlic, minced
1 small onion, chopped
1 teaspoon salt

1. Spray 6-inch pan with cooking spray and set aside. 2. In a suitable bowl, mix together spinach, cream cheese, garlic, onion, nutmeg, black pepper, and salt. 3. Pour spinach mixture into the prepared pan. 4. Place dish in air fryer basket and air fry the mixture at 350 degrees F/ 175 degrees C for almost 10 minutes. 5. Open air fryer basket and sprinkle parmesan cheese on top of spinach mixture and air fry them at 400 degrees F/ 205 degrees C for 5 minutes more. 6. Serve and enjoy.
Per serving: Calories: 217; Fat: 16.3g; Sodium: 401mg; Total Carbs: 6g; Net Carbs: 2.5g; Fiber: 2.2g; Sugars: 1.2g; Protein: 13.5g

Parmesan Zucchini Gratin

Prep Time: 10 minutes | Cook time: 15 Minutes | Serves: 2

5 ounces parmesan cheese, shredded
1 tablespoon coconut flour

1 tablespoon dried parsley
2 zucchinis
1 teaspoon butter, melted

1. In a bowl, add the coconut flour and parmesan cheese together. 2. To season, add parsley. 3. Cut the zucchini lengthwise in half and slice the halves into four slices. 4. Before cooking, heat your air fryer to 400 degrees F/ 205 degrees C. 5. Then coat the zucchinis with the melted butter and dip in the parmesan-flour mixture to thoroughly coat the zucchini slices. 6. Cook in your air fryer for 13 minutes.
Per serving: Calories: 292; Fat: 17.8g; Sodium: 692mg; Total Carbs: 11g; Net Carbs: 6.7g; Fiber: 3.7g; Sugars: 3.4g; Protein: 25.7g

Crispy Pickles with Parmesan

Prep Time: 15 minutes | Cook time: 6 minutes | Serves: 4

16 dill pickles, sliced
1 egg, lightly beaten
½ cup almond flour
3 tablespoon parmesan cheese, grated
½ cup pork rind, crushed

1. Take 3 bowls. Mix together pork rinds and cheese in the first bowl. 2. In a second bowl, add the egg. 3. In the third bowl, spread the almond flour for coating. 4. Coat each pickle slice with almond flour then dip in egg and finally coat with pork and cheese mixture. 5. Grease its air fryer basket with cooking spray. 6. Place coated pickles in the air fryer basket. 7. Cook pickles for 6 minutes at 370 degrees F/ 185 degrees C. 8. Serve and enjoy.
Per serving: Calories: 206; Fat: 13.4g; Sodium: 3390mg; Total Carbs: 9g; Net Carbs: 4.3g; Fiber: 4.6g; Sugars: 2.8g; Protein: 13.1g

Maple Glazed Parsnips

Prep Time: 10 minutes | Cook time: 44 Minutes | Serves: 6

2 pounds parsnips, peeled
1 tablespoon butter, melted
2 tablespoons maple syrup
1 tablespoon dried parsley flakes, crushed
¼ teaspoon red pepper flakes, crushed

1. Before cooking, heat your air fryer to 355 degrees F/ 180 degrees C. 2. Using cooking spray, spray the air fryer basket. Cut the peeled parsnips into 1-inch chunks. 3. In a bowl, add butter and parsnips and toss well to coat. 4. Then evenly arrange the parsnips on the air fryer basket. 5. Cook in your air fryer for about 40 minutes. 6. Then mix the remaining ingredients in a large bowl. 7. Transfer the mixture inside the air fryer basket. 8. Cook for about 4 minutes or more. 9. When cooked, remove from the air fryer and serve warm.
Per serving: Calories: 148; Fat: 2.4g; Sodium: 30mg; Total Carbs: 31g; Net Carbs: 15g; Fiber: 7.5g; Sugars: 11.3g; Protein: 1.9g

Lemon Broccoli

Prep Time: 10 minutes | Cook time: 20 Minutes | Serves: 3

1 tablespoon butter
2 teaspoons vegetable bouillon granules
1 large head broccoli
1 tablespoon fresh lemon juice
3 garlic cloves, sliced
½ teaspoon fresh lemon zest, finely grated
½ teaspoon red pepper flakes, crushed

1. Before cooking, heat your air fryer to 355 degrees F/ 180 degrees C. 2. Using cooking spray, lightly grease a suitable baking pan. Cut the broccoli into bite-sized pieces. 3. In the baking pan, add bouillon granules, lemon juice, and butter. 4. Cook in your air fryer for 1½ minutes. Then add garlic and stir. 5. Cook for about 30 seconds and add lemon zest, red pepper flakes, and broccoli. 6. Cook for about 18 minutes. 7. When cooked, remove from the air fryer and serve hot in a bowl.
Per serving: Calories: 51; Fat: 4.1g; Sodium: 58mg; Total Carbs: 3g; Net Carbs: 1g; Fiber: 1g; Sugars: 0.7g; Protein: 1.2g

Fried Brussel Sprouts

Prep Time: 5 minutes | Cook time: 20 minutes | Serves: 4

1 pound Brussels sprouts, trimmed and halved
Salt and black pepper to the taste
2 tablespoons ghee, melted
½ cup coconut cream
2 tablespoons garlic, minced
1 tablespoon chives, chopped

1. Grease the air fryer basket with the melted ghee. 2. Mix the Brussels sprouts with the remaining ingredients in the air fryer basket. 3. Cook in your air fryer at 370 degrees F/ 185 degrees C for 20 minutes. 4. Serve on plates as a side dish.
Per serving: Calories: 181; Fat: 13.9g; Sodium: 34mg; Total Carbs: 13g; Net Carbs: 7g; Fiber: 5g; Sugars: 3.5g; Protein: 4.9g

Carrots with Honey Glaze

Prep Time: 5 minutes | Cook Time: 10 minutes | Servings: 1

1 tbsp. of olive oil
3 cups of chopped into ½-inch pieces' carrots
salt and black pepper, to taste
2 tbsps. of honey
1 tbsp. of brown sugar

1. At 390 degrees F/ 200 degrees C, preheat your air fryer. 2. Using a bowl, add and toss the carrot pieces, olive oil, honey, brown sugar, salt, and the black pepper until it is properly covered. 3. Place it inside your air fryer and add the seasoned glazed carrots. 4. Cook it for 12 minutes at 390 degrees F/ 200 degrees C, shaking the basket halfway through. 5. Serve and enjoy!
Per serving: Calories 90, Fat 3.5g, Fiber: 2g; Total Carbs 13g; Protein 1g; Sugar 1.2 g; Fiber 1g

Air-Fried Eggplant

Prep Time: 5 minutes | Cook Time: 20 minutes | Servings: 4

2 thinly sliced or chopped into chunks eggplants
1 tsp. of salt
1 tsp. of black pepper
1 cup of rice flour
1 cup of white wine

1. In a bowl, add the rice flour, white wine and mix properly until it gets smooth. 2. Add the salt, black pepper and stir again. 3. Dredge the eggplant slices or chunks into the batter and remove any excess batter. 4. At 390 degrees F/ 200 degrees C, preheat your Air Fryer. 5. Grease your "Air Fryer Basket" with a nonstick cooking spray. 6. Add the eggplant slices or chunks into your air fryer and cook them at 390 degrees F/ 200 degrees C on Air Fry mode for 15 to 20 minutes or until it has a golden brown and crispy texture, while still shaking it occasionally. 7. Carefully remove it from your air fryer and allow it to cool off. 8. Serve and enjoy!
Per serving: Calories 380; Total Carbs 51g, Net Carb 2g; Fat 15g; Protein 13g; Sugar 1g; Fiber: 6.1g

Cauliflower Hash

Prep Time: 10 minutes | Cook Time: 15 minutes | Servings: 6

1-lb. cauliflower
2 eggs
1 tsp. salt
½ tsp. ground paprika
4-oz. turkey fillet, chopped

1. Wash the cauliflower, chop, and set aside. 2. Whisk together the 2 eggs in a bowl and mix well; add the salt and ground paprika and stir well. 3. Place the chopped turkey in the "Air Fryer Basket" and cook them for 4 minutes at 365 degrees F/ 185 degrees C on Air Fry mode, stirring halfway through. 4. After this, add the chopped cauliflower and stir the prepared mixture. 5. Air Fry the turkey/cauliflower mixture for 6 minutes more at 370 degrees F/ 185 degrees C, stirring it halfway through. 6. Then pour in the whisked egg mixture and stir it carefully. 7. Air Fry the cauliflower hash for 5 minutes more at 365 degrees F/ 185 degrees C. 8. When the cauliflower hash is done, let it cool and transfer to serving bowls. 9. Serve and enjoy.
Per serving: Calories 143; Total Carbs 4.5g; Net Carbs 2g; Protein 10.4; Fat 9.5g; Sugar 2g; Fiber 2

Asparagus with Almonds

Prep Time: 10 minutes | Cook Time: 5 minutes | Servings: 2

9 oz. asparagus
1 tsp. almond flour
1 tbsp. almond flakes
¼ tsp. salt
1 tsp. olive oil

1. Combine the almond flour and almond flakes; stir the prepared mixture well. 2. Sprinkle the asparagus with the olive oil and salt. 3. Shake it gently and coat in the almond flour mixture. 4. Place the asparagus in the "Air Fryer Basket" and Air Fry them at 400 degrees F/ 205 degrees C for 5 minutes, stirring halfway through. 5. Then cool a little and serve.
Per serving: Calories 143; Total Carbs 8.6g; Net Carbs 2g; Protein 6.4; Fat 11g; Sugar 2g; Fiber 4.6

Roasted Garlic Head

Prep Time: 5 minutes | Cook Time: 10 minutes | Servings: 4

1-lb. garlic head
1 tbsp. olive oil
1 tsp. thyme

1. Cut the ends of the garlic head and place it in the Air Fryer Basket. 2. Then sprinkle the garlic head with the olive oil and thyme. 3. Air Fry the garlic head for 10 minutes at 400 degrees F/ 205 degrees C. 4. When the garlic head is cooked, it should be soft and aromatic. 5. Serve immediately.
Per serving: Calories 200; Total Carbs 37.7g; Net Carbs 2g; Protein 7.2g; Fat 4.1g; Sugar 2g; Fiber 2.5g

Zucchini Cubes

Prep Time: 7 minutes | Cook Time: 8 minutes | Servings: 2

1 zucchini	2 tbsp. chicken stock
½ tsp. ground black pepper	½ tsp. coconut oil
1 tsp. oregano	

1. Chop the zucchini into cubes. 2. Combine the ground black pepper, and oregano; stir the prepared mixture. 3. Sprinkle the zucchini cubes with the spice mixture and stir well. 4. After this, sprinkle the vegetables with the chicken stock. 5. Place the coconut oil in the "Air Fryer Basket" and heat it to 360 degrees F/ 180 degrees C for 20 seconds. 6. Then add the zucchini cubes and Air Fry the vegetables for 8 minutes at 390 degrees F/ 200 degrees C, stirring halfway through. 7. Transfer to serving plates and enjoy!
Per serving: Calories 30; Total Carbs 4.3g; Net Carbs 2g; Protein 1.4; Fat 1.5g; Sugar 2g; Fiber 1.6g

Sweet Potato Onion Mix

Prep Time: 10 minutes | Cook Time: 15 minutes | Servings: 4

2 sweet potatoes, peeled	1 tsp. olive oil
1 red onion, peeled	¼ cup almond milk
1 white onion, peeled	

1. Chop the sweet potatoes and the onions into cubes. 2. Sprinkle the sweet potatoes with olive oil. 3. Place the peeled and diced sweet potatoes in the "Air Fryer Basket" and Air Fry them for 5 minutes at 400 degrees F/ 205 degrees C. 4. When the time is up, stir the sweet potatoes and add the chopped onions; pour in the almond milk and stir gently. 5. Air Fry the mix for 10 minutes more at 400 degrees F/ 205 degrees C. 6. When the mix is cooked, let it cool a little and serve.
Per serving: Calories 56; Total Carbs 3.5g; Net Carbs 2g; Protein 0.6; Fat 4.8g; Sugar 2g; Fiber 0.9g

Spicy Eggplant

Prep Time: 10 minutes | Cook Time: 20 minutes | Servings: 2

12 oz. eggplants	½ tsp. cilantro
½ tsp. cayenne pepper	½ tsp. ground paprika
½ tsp. ground black pepper	

1. Rinse the eggplants and slice them into cubes. 2. Sprinkle the eggplant cubes with the cayenne pepper and ground black pepper. 3. Add the cilantro and ground paprika. 4. Stir the prepared mixture well and let it rest for 10 minutes. 5. After this, sprinkle the eggplants with olive oil and place in the air fryer basket. 6. Cook the eggplants for 20 minutes at 380 degrees F/ 195 degrees C on Air Fry mode, stirring halfway through. 7. When the eggplant cubes are done, serve them right away!
Per serving: Calories 67; Total Carbs 10.9g; Net Carbs 2g; Protein 1.9; Fat 2.8g; Sugar 2g; Fiber 6.5g

Wrapped Asparagus

Prep Time: 10 minutes | Cook Time: 5 minutes | Servings: 4

12 oz. asparagus	3-oz. turkey fillet, sliced
½ tsp. ground black pepper	¼ tsp. chili flakes

1. Sprinkle the asparagus with the ground black pepper and chili flakes. 2. Stir carefully. 3. Wrap the asparagus in the sliced turkey fillet and place in the Air Fryer Basket. 4. Cook the asparagus at 400 degrees F/ 205 degrees C for 5 minutes, turning halfway through cooking. 5. Let the wrapped asparagus cool for 2 minutes before serving.
Per serving: Calories 133; Total Carbs 3.8g; Net Carbs 2g; Protein 9.8; Fat 9g; Sugar 2g; Fiber 1.9g

Baked Yams

Prep Time: 10 minutes | Cook Time: 8 minutes | Servings: 2

2 yams	1 tsp. coconut oil
1 tbsp. fresh dill	½ tsp. minced garlic

1. Wash the yams carefully and cut them into halves. 2. Sprinkle the yam halves with the coconut oil and then rub with the minced garlic. 3. Place the yams in the "Air Fryer Basket" and Air Fry for 8 minutes at 400 degrees F/ 205 degrees C. 4. After this, mash the yams gently with a fork and then sprinkle with the fresh dill. 5. Serve the yams immediately.
Per serving: Calories 25; Total Carbs 1.2g; Net Carbs 2g; Protein 0.4; Fat 2.3g; Sugar 2g; Fiber 0.2g

Honey Onions

Prep Time: 10 minutes | Cook Time: 20 minutes | Servings: 2

2 large white onions	1 tsp. water
1 tbsp. raw honey	1 tbsp. paprika

1. Peel the onions and using a knife, make cuts in the shape of a cross. 2. Then combine the raw honey and water; stir. 3. Add the paprika and stir the prepared mixture until smooth. 4. Place the onions in the "Air Fryer Basket" and sprinkle them with the honey mixture. 5. Cook the onions for 16 minutes at 380 degrees F/ 195 degrees C on Air Fry mode. 6. When the onions are cooked, they should be soft. 7. Transfer the cooked onions to serving plates and serve.
Per serving: Calories 102; Total Carbs 24.6g; Net Carbs 2g; Protein 2.2g; Fat 0.6g; Sugar 2g; Fiber 4.5g

Roasted Garlic Slices

Prep Time: 10 minutes | Cook Time: 8 minutes | Servings: 4

1 tsp. coconut oil	¼ tsp. cayenne pepper
½ tsp. dried cilantro	12 oz. garlic cloves, peeled

1. Sprinkle the garlic cloves with the cayenne pepper and dried cilantro. 2. Mix up the garlic and the spices, and then transfer to the Air Fryer Basket. 3. Add the coconut oil and Air Fry the garlic mixture for 8 minutes at 400 degrees F/ 205 degrees C, stirring halfway through. 4. When the garlic cloves are done, transfer them to serving plates and serve.
Per serving: Calories 137; Total Carbs 28.2g; Net Carbs 2g; Protein 5.4; Fat 1.6g; Sugar 2g; Fiber 1.8g

Air Fried Artichokes

Prep Time: 10 minutes | Cook Time: 13 minutes | Servings: 4

1-lb. artichokes	½ tsp. minced garlic
1 tbsp. coconut oil	¼ tsp. cayenne pepper
1 tbsp. water	

1. Trim the ends of the artichokes, sprinkle them with the water, and rub them with the minced garlic. 2. Sprinkle with the cayenne pepper and the coconut oil. 3. After this, wrap the artichokes in foil and place in the Air Fryer Basket. 4. Air Fry the artichokes for 10 minutes at 370 degrees F/ 185 degrees C. 5. When the time is up, remove the artichokes from the foil and Air Fry them for 3 minutes more at 400 degrees F/ 205 degrees C. 6. Transfer the cooked artichokes to serving plates and allow to cool a little. 7. Serve!
Per serving: Calories 83; Total Carbs 12.1g; Net Carbs 2g; Protein 3.7; Fat 3.6g; Sugar 2g; Fiber 6.2g

Roasted Mushrooms

Prep Time: 10 minutes | Cook Time: 5 minutes | Servings: 2

12 oz. mushroom hats	1 tsp. olive oil
¼ cup fresh dill, chopped	¼ tsp. turmeric
¼ tsp. onion, chopped	

1. Combine the chopped dill and onion in a suitable bowl. 2. Add the turmeric and stir the prepared mixture. 3. After this, add the olive oil and mix until homogenous. 4. Then fill the mushroom hats with the dill mixture and place them in the Air Fryer Basket. 5. Cook the mushrooms for 5 minutes at 400 degrees F/ 205 degrees C on Air Fry mode. 6. When the vegetables are cooked, let them cool to room temperature before serving.
Per serving: Calories 73; Total Carbs 9.2g; Net Carbs 2g; Protein 6.6; Fat 3.1g; Sugar 2g; Fiber 2.6g

Shredded Cabbage

Prep Time: 15 minutes | Cook Time: 15 minutes | Servings: 4

15 oz. cabbage	¼ cup chicken stock
¼ tsp. salt	½ tsp. paprika

1. Shred the cabbage and sprinkle it with the salt and paprika. 2. Stir the cabbage and let it sit for 10 minutes. 3. Then transfer the cabbage to the "Air Fryer Basket" and add the chicken stock. 4. Air Fry the food for 15 minutes at 250 degrees F/ 120 degrees C, stirring halfway through. 5. When the cabbage is soft, it is done. 6. Serve immediately.
Per serving: Calories 132; Fat 2.1g; Total Carbs 32.1 g; Net Carbs 2g; Protein 1.78g; Sugar 2g; Fiber 2.5g

Fried Leeks

Prep Time: 5 minutes | Cook Time: 10 minutes | Servings: 4

4 leeks; ends cut off and halved	1 tbsp. lemon juice
1 tbsp. butter; melted	Salt and black pepper to the taste

1. Coat the leeks with melted butter, flavor with black pepper and salt, put in your air fryer and Air Fry at 350 degrees F/ 175 degrees C for 7 minutes. 2. When cooked, arrange on a platter, drizzle lemon juice all over and serve.
Per serving: Calories 100; Fat 4; Fiber: 2g; Total Carbs 6g; Net Carbs 2g; Protein 2 g; Sugar 2g; Fiber 2.5g

Brussels Sprouts Tomatoes Mix

Prep Time: 5 minutes | Cook Time: 10 minutes | Servings: 4

1 lb. Brussels sprouts; trimmed	1 tbsp. olive oil
6 cherry tomatoes; halved	Salt and black pepper to the taste
¼ cup green onions; chopped.	

1. Season Brussels sprouts with black pepper and salt, put them in your air fryer and Air Fry them at 350 degrees F/ 175 degrees C for 10 minutes 2. Transfer them to a bowl, add salt, pepper, cherry tomatoes, green onions and olive oil, toss well and serve.
Per serving: Calories 121; Fat 4; Fiber: 4g; Total Carbs 11g; Net Carbs 2g; Protein 4 g; Sugar 2g; Fiber 2.5g

Radish Hash

Prep Time: 5 minutes | Cook Time: 7 minutes | Servings: 4

½ tsp. onion powder	4 eggs
⅓ cup parmesan; grated	1 lb. radishes; sliced
Salt and black pepper to the taste	

1. In a bowl, mix the radishes with salt, pepper, onion, eggs and parmesan. 2. Transfer radishes to a suitable pan and Air Fry them at 350 degrees F/ 175 degrees C for 7 minutes 3. Divide hash on plates and serve.
Per serving: Calories 80; Fat 5; Fiber: 2g; Total Carbs 5g; Net Carbs 2g; Protein 7 g; Sugar 2g; Fiber 2.5g

Broccoli Salad

Prep Time: 5 minutes | Cook Time: 10 minutes | Servings: 4

1 broccoli head; florets separated	6 garlic cloves; minced
1 tbsp. Chinese rice wine vinegar	Salt and black pepper to the taste
1 tbsp. peanut oil	

1. In a bowl; mix broccoli with salt, pepper and half of the oil, toss. 2. Transfer the food to your air fryer and Air Fry them at 350 degrees F/ 175 degrees C for 8 minutes, shaking the fryer halfway 3. When cooked, transfer broccoli to a salad bowl, add the rest of the peanut oil, garlic and rice vinegar, toss really well and serve.
Per serving: Calories 121; Fat 3; Fiber: 4g; Total Carbs 4g; Net Carbs 2g; Protein 4 g; Sugar 2g; Fiber 2.5g

Chili Broccoli

Prep Time: 5 minutes | Cook Time: 15 minutes | Servings: 4

1-lb. broccoli florets	Juice of 1 lime
2 tbsps. olive oil	A pinch of salt and black pepper
2 tbsps. chili sauce	

1. Mix all of the recipe ingredients in a suitable bowl, and toss well. 2. Put the broccoli florets in your "Air Fryer Basket" and Air Fry them at 400 degrees F/ 205 degrees C for 15 minutes. 3. Divide between plates and serve.
Per serving: Calories 173g; Total Carbs 6g; Net Carbs 2g; Protein 8 Fat 6g; Sugar 2g; Fiber 2g

Broccoli and Asparagus

Prep Time: 5 minutes | Cook Time: 15 minutes | Servings: 4

1 broccoli head, florets separated	Salt and black pepper to the taste
½ lb. asparagus, trimmed	2 tbsps. olive oil
Juice of 1 lime	3 tbsps. parmesan, grated

1. In a suitable bowl, combine the asparagus with the broccoli and all the other ingredients except the parmesan, toss well. 2. Transfer the food to your "Air Fryer Basket" and Air Fry them at 400 degrees F/ 205 degrees C for 15 minutes. 3. Divide between plates, sprinkle the parmesan on top and serve.
Per serving: Calories 172g; Total Carbs 4g; Net Carbs 2g; Protein 9 Fat 5g; Sugar 2g; Fiber 2g

Broccoli Mix

Prep Time: 5 minutes | Cook Time: 15 minutes | Servings: 4

1-lb. broccoli florets	1 tsp. sweet paprika
A pinch of salt and black pepper	½ tbsp. butter, melted

1. In a suitable bowl, combine the broccoli with the rest of the ingredients, and toss well. 2. Put the broccoli in your "Air Fryer Basket", Air Fry the food at 350 degrees F/ 175 degrees C for 15 minutes, 3. When cooked, divide between plates and serve.
Per serving: Calories 130g; Total Carbs 4g; Net Carbs 2g; Protein 8 ; Fat 3g; Sugar 2g; Fiber 3g

Balsamic Kale

Prep Time: 2 minutes | Cook Time: 12 minutes | Servings: 6

2 tbsps. olive oil	Salt and black pepper to the taste
3 garlic cloves, minced	2 tbsps. balsamic vinegar
2 and ½ lbs. kale leaves	

1. In a pan that fits the air fryer, combine all the recipe ingredients and toss. 2. Put this pan in your air fryer and Air Fry the food at 300 degrees F/ 150 degrees C for 12 minutes. 3. Divide between plates and serve.
Per serving: Calories 122g; Total Carbs 4g; Net Carbs 2g; Protein 5; Fat 4g; Sugar 2g; Fiber 3g

Kale Olives Salad

Prep Time: 5 minutes | Cook Time: 15 minutes | Servings: 4

1 an ½ lbs. kale, torn	1 tbsp. hot paprika
2 tbsp. olive oil	2 tbsp. black olives, pitted and
Salt and black pepper to the taste	sliced

1. In a pan that fits the air fryer, combine all the recipe ingredients and toss well. 2. Put this pan in your air fryer, Air Fry the food at 370 degrees F/ 185 degrees C for 15 minutes. 3. When cooked, divide between plates and serve.
Per serving: Calories 154g; Total Carbs 4g; Net Carbs 2g; Protein 6; Fat 3g; Sugar 2g; Fiber 2 g

Kale Mushrooms Mix

Prep Time: 5 minutes | Cook Time: 15 minutes | Servings: 4

1 lb. brown mushrooms, sliced	2 tbsps. olive oil
1-lb. kale, torn	14 oz. coconut milk
Salt and black pepper to the taste	

1. In a pot that fits your air fryer, mix the kale with the rest of the ingredients and toss. 2. Put this pan in the fryer, Air Fry the food at 380 degrees F/ 195 degrees C for 15 minutes. 3. When cooked, divide between plates and serve.
Per serving: Calories 162g; Total Carbs 3g; Net Carbs 2g; Protein 5; Fat 4g; Sugar 2g; Fiber 1g

Mashed Yams

Prep Time: 10 minutes | Cook Time: 10 minutes | Servings: 5

1 lb. yams	¾ tsp. salt
1 tsp. olive oil	1 tsp. dried parsley
1 tbsp. almond milk	

1. Peel the yams and chop. 2. Place the chopped yams in the "Air Fryer Basket" and sprinkle with the salt and dried parsley. 3. Add the olive oil and stir the prepared mixture. 4. Cook the yams at 400 degrees F/ 205 degrees C for 10 minutes on Air Fry mode, stirring twice during cooking. 5. When the yams are done, blend them well with a hand blender until smooth. 6. Add the almond milk and stir carefully. 7. Serve, and enjoy!
Per serving: Calories 120; Total Carbs 25.1g; Net Carbs 2g; Protein 1.4; Fat 1.8g; Sugar 2g; Fiber 3.6g

Oregano Kale

Prep Time: 5 minutes | Cook Time: 10 minutes | Servings: 4

1-lb. kale, torn	A pinch of salt and black pepper
1 tbsp. olive oil	2 tbsps. oregano, chopped

1. In a pan that fits the air fryer, combine all the recipe ingredients and toss well. 2. Put this pan in the air fryer and Air Fry the food at 380 degrees F/ 195 degrees C for 10 minutes. 3. Divide between plates and serve.
Per serving: Calories 140g; Total Carbs 3g; Net Carbs 2g; Protein 5; Fat 3; Fiber 2 g; Sugar 2g; Fiber 2.5g

Olives Avocado Mix

Prep Time: 5 minutes | Cook Time: 15 minutes | Servings: 4

2 cups kalamata olives, pitted	¼ cup cherry tomatoes, halved
2 small avocados, pitted, peeled and sliced	Juice of 1 lime
	1 tbsp. coconut oil, melted

1. In a pan that fits the air fryer, combine the olives with the other ingredients and toss well. 2. Put this pan in your air fryer and Air Fry the food at 370 degrees F/ 185 degrees C for 15 minutes. 3. Divide the mix between plates and serve.
Per serving: Calories 153g; Total Carbs 4g; Net Carbs 2g; Protein 6; Fat 3g; Sugar 2g; Fiber 3g

Olives, Green beans and Bacon

Prep Time: 5 minutes | Cook Time: 15 minutes | Servings: 4

½ lb. green beans, trimmed and halved	¼ cup bacon, cooked and crumbled
1 cup black olives, pitted and halved	1 tbsp. olive oil
	¼ cup tomato sauce

1. In a pan that fits the air fryer, combine all the recipe ingredients and toss well. 2. Put this pan in the air fryer and Air Fry the food at 380 degrees F/ 195 degrees C for 15 minutes. 3. Divide between plates and serve.
Per serving: Calories 160g; Total Carbs 5g; Net Carbs 2g; Protein 4; Fat 4g; Sugar 2g; Fiber 3g

Parmesan Brussel Sprouts

Prep Time: 10minutes | Cook Time: 20 minutes | Servings: 4

10 Brussel sprouts halved	3 cloves garlic, minced
3 tbsps. olive oil, divided	½ tbsp. Parmesan cheese, grated
¼ tsp. kosher salt	3 cups of water

1. Add 2 tablespoons of olive oil, salt, garlic, and Parmesan in a suitable bowl and mix well. 2. Boil Brussel sprouts in 3 cups of water for 5 minutes, then set aside. 3. At 400 degrees F/ 205 degrees C, preheat your Air Fryer. 4. Place Brussel sprouts into the Air Fryer Basket and brush with the remaining olive oil. 5. Cook the Brussel sprouts for 15 minutes at 400 degrees F/ 205 degrees C on Air Fry mode. 6. Brush Parmesan mixture on each Brussel sprout half when there are 7 minutes of cook time left. 7. Remove when done and serve immediately.
Per serving: Calories 127; Total Carbs 5g; Net Carbs 2g; Protein 2; Fat 3g; Sugar 2g; Fiber 2g

Cajun Peppers

Prep Time: 4 minutes | Cook Time: 12 minutes | Servings: 4

1 tbsp. olive oil	halved
½ lb. mixed bell peppers, sliced	½ tbsp. Cajun seasoning
1 cup black olives, pitted and	

1. In a pan that fits the air fryer, combine all the recipe ingredients. 2. Put this pan it in your air fryer and Air Fry the food at 390 degrees F/ 200 degrees C for 12 minutes. 3. Divide the mix between plates and serve.
Per serving: Calories 151g; Total Carbs 4g; Net Carbs 2g; Protein 5; Fat 3g; Sugar 2g; Fiber 2g

Crisp Kale

Prep Time: 5 minutes | Cook Time: 8 minutes | Servings: 4-5

4 handfuls kale, washed & stemless	1 tbsp. olive oil
	Pinch Sea Salt

1. Combine your ingredients together making sure your kale is coated evenly. 2. Place the kale in your air fryer and Air Fry them at 360 degrees F/ 180 degrees C for 8 minutes.
Per serving: Calories 121 Fat 4g; Total Carbs 5; Net Carb 2g; Protein 8; Fat 3g; Sugar 2g; Fiber 2g

Basil Potatoes

Prep Time: 15 minutes | Cook Time: 40 minutes | Servings: 5

8 medium potatoes	1-½ tsp. garlic powder
5 tbsp. olive oil	salt & pepper to taste
4 tsp. basil, dried	butter

1. Cut your potatoes lengthwise, and make sure to cut them thin. 2. Lightly coat your potatoes with both your butter and oil. 3. Add in black pepper and salt, and then Air Fry them at 390 degrees F/ 200 degrees C for 40 minutes. 4. When done, serve and enjoy.
Per serving: Calories 140 Fat 5g; Total Carbs 8; Net Carb 2g; Protein 9; Fat 3g; Sugar 2g; Fiber 2g

Sweet Potato Fries

Prep Time: 10 minutes | Cook Time: 12-15 minutes | Servings: 4

3 large sweet potatoes, peeled	A pinch tsp. sea salt
1 tbsp. olive oil	

1. Cut the sweet potatoes in quarters, cutting them lengthwise to make fries. 2. Combine the uncooked fries with a tbsp. of sea salt and olive oil. Make sure all of your fries are coated well. 3. Place your sweet potato pieces in the Air Fryer Basket, cook them at 390 degrees F/ 200 degrees C on Air Fry mode for 12 minutes. 4. Air Fry the food for 2 to 3 minutes more if you want it to be crispier. 5. Add more salt to taste, and serve when cooled.
Per serving: Calories 150; Fat 6g; Total Carbs 8; Net Carb 2g; Protein 9; Fat 3g; Sugar 2g; Fiber 2g

Green Bean Casserole

Prep Time: 5minutes | Cook Time: 34 minutes | Servings: 4

1 lb. green beans, diced	1½ cups crispy fried onions
1 can (10.5-oz.) cream of mushroom soup	¼ tsp. black pepper
¾ cup milk	⅛ tsp. kosher salt

1. Add the green beans to the preheated air fryer and Air Fry them at 400 degrees F/ 205 degrees C for 14 minutes. 2. Mix cream of mushroom soup, half of the crispy fried onions, green beans, milk, black pepper, and salt until fully incorporated, then place in the casserole dish. 3. Place casserole dish in your preheated air fryer and cook the food at 400 degrees F/ 205 degrees C for 20 minutes on Bake mode. 4. Place the remaining crispy fried onions on top of the casserole after 14 minutes of cooking time. 5. Serve immediately.
Per serving: Calories 926; Total Carbs 70.3g; Net Carbs 2g; Protein 13; Fat 3g; Sugar 2g; Fiber 2

Chapter 4 Fish and Seafood Recipes

Halibut Soy Treat with Rice 41

Tilapia Fillets with Mayonnaise 41

Tuna Steak with Niçoise Salad 41

Tasty Coconut Prawns 41

Glazed Fillets 41

Flounder Fillets with Coconut Aminos 41

Salmon with Sweet Potato 41

Pollock Fillets with Rosemary & Oregano 42

Beer Squid 42

Crusty Catfish with Parmesan Cheese 42

Fish Mania with Mustard 42

Salmon Bowl with Lime Drizzle 42

Delicious Fillets with Avocado Sauce 42

Chip-crusted Tilapia with Parmesan Cheese 42

Typical Cod Nuggets 43

Pasta Shrimp 43

Sea Bream Fillet with Tomato Sauce 43

Crumbed Fish Fillets with Parmesan Cheese 43

Bean Burritos with Cheddar Cheese 43

Thai Coconut Fish 43

Catfish Fillets with Tortilla Chips 43

Spicy Salmon and Fennel Salad 43

Lemon Salmon Fillet 44

Spicy Jumbo Shrimps 44

Salmon Burgers 44

Chunky Fish with Mustard 44

Homemade Lobster Tails Ever 44

Shrimp with Parsley 44

Trimmed Mackerel with Spring Onions 44

Rosemary Salmon 44

Tasty Juicy Salmon 44

Cajun Lemon Branzino 45

Simple Fish Sticks 45

Flavored Salmon Grill with Oregano & Cumin 45

Red Snapper with Hot Chili Paste 45

Buttered Shrimp Fry 45

Clams with Spring Onions 45

Ginger-garlic Swordfish 45

Herbed and Garlic Salmon Fillets 45

Baked Sardines 45

Garlic Scallops with Parsley 46

Cajun Fish Cakes 46

Old Bay Cod Fish Fillets 46

Greek Sardines with Sauce 46

Garlic Tilapia Fillets 46

Tasty Anchovies and Cheese Wontons 46

Healthy Hot Salmon 46

Grouper with Miso-Honey Sauce 46

Lemon Jumbo Scallops 47

Typical Crab Cakes with Lemon Wedges 47

Garlic Butter Scallops with Lemon Zest 47

Cajun Shrimp with Veggie 47

Flavor Moroccan Harissa Shrimp 47

Pancetta-Wrapped Scallops with Pancetta Slices 47

Flavor Calamari with Mediterranean Sauce 47

Salmon Fillets 47

Southwestern Prawns with Asparagus 48

Haddock Cakes 48

Flounder Filets with Parmesan Cheese 48

Delicious Grouper Filets 48

Mayo Shrimp 48

Hot Sauce Crab Dip 48

Fish Packets 48

Air Fried Scallops 48

Spicy Prawns 49

Air Fried Prawns 49

Spicy Shrimp 49

Cheese Salmon 49

Crab Patties 49

Air Fried Catfish 49

Bacon Shrimp 49

Basil Parmesan Shrimp 49

Cajun Cheese Shrimp 49

Creamy Shrimp 49

Lemon Butter Salmon 50

Cheesy Dip 50

Almond Shrimp 50

Chili Shrimp 50

Thai Shrimp 50

Lemon Cajun Cod 50

Savory Breaded Shrimp 50

Steamed Salmon with Sauce 50

Breaded Salmon Patties 51

Indian Fish Fingers 51

Fish with Chips 51

Spicy Shrimp Kebab 51

Fish Fillets with Tarragon 51

Smoked White Fish 51

Paprika Baked Tilapia 51

Tangy Cod Fillets 51

Halibut Soy Treat with Rice

Prep Time: 15-20 minutes | Cook time: 12 minutes | Serves: 4

16-ounce Halibut steak
To make the marinade:
⅔ cup soy sauce
½ cup cooking vine
¼ cup sugar
2 tablespoon lime juice

¼ cup orange juice
¼ teaspoon red pepper flakes, crushed
¼ teaspoon ginger ground
1 clove garlic (smashed)

1. Add the marinade ingredients in a medium-size saucepan. 2. Heat the pan over medium heat for a few minutes. Cool down completely. 3. To marinate, in a zip-lock bag, combine the steak and marinade. Seal and refrigerate for 30-40 minutes. 4. Coat the air-frying basket gently with cooking oil or spray. 5. Place the steak in the basket of your air fryer and cook for 12 minutes at 355 degrees F/ 180 degrees C. 6. When done, serve warm with cooked rice!
Per serving: Calories: 396; Fat: 6.8g; Sodium: 2552mg; Total Carbs: 17g; Net Carbs: 8g; Fiber: 0.4g; Sugars: 14.5g; Protein: 63.3g

Tilapia Fillets with Mayonnaise

Prep Time: 5 minutes | Cook time: 12 minutes | Serves: 4

1 tablespoon olive oil, extra-virgin
4 tilapia fillets
Celery salt, as needed
Freshly cracked pink peppercorns, as needed
For the Sauce:

½ cup crème fraiche
¼ cup Cottage cheese
2 tablespoons mayonnaise
1 tablespoon capers, finely chopped

1. Thoroughly mix up the olive oil, celery salt, and cracked peppercorns in a medium-sized bowl, then let the fillets be coated with the mixture. 2. Coat the air-frying basket with the cooking oil and spray. 3. Arrange the fillets to the basket and cook for 12 minutes at 360 degrees F/ 180 degrees C. 4. To make a sauce, in a bowl of medium size, thoroughly mix the remaining ingredients to make a sauce. 5. When the time is up, serve warm with the sauce!
Per serving: Calories: 194; Fat: 8.5g; Sodium: 241mg; Total Carbs: 2g; Net Carbs: 0.5g; Fiber: 0.1g; Sugars: 0.5g; Protein: 29.2g

Tuna Steak with Niçoise Salad

Prep Time: 10 minutes | Cook time: 15 minutes | Serves 4

1 pound tuna steak
Sea salt, to taste
Ground black pepper, to taste
½ teaspoon red pepper flakes, crushed
¼ teaspoon dried dill weed
½ teaspoon garlic paste
1-pound green beans, trimmed
2 handfuls baby spinach
2 handfuls iceberg lettuce, torn into pieces

½ red onion, sliced
1 cucumber, sliced
2 tablespoons lemon juice
1 tablespoon olive oil
1 teaspoon Dijon mustard
1 tablespoon balsamic vinegar
1 tablespoon roasted almonds, coarsely chopped
1 tablespoon fresh parsley, coarsely chopped

1. Pat the tuna steak dry. 2. Combine the salt, black pepper, red pepper, dill, garlic paste and toss with the tuna steak well. 3. Spritz the coated tuna steak with a nonstick cooking spray. 4. Cook the tuna steak at 400 degrees F/ 205 degrees C for 10 minutes, flipping halfway through. 5. When the time is up, remove the tuna steak and add the green beans. 6. Spritz green beans with a nonstick cooking spray. 7. Cook at 400 degrees F/ 205 degrees C for 5 minutes, shaking once or twice for evenly cooking. 8. Cut your tuna into thin strips and transfer to a salad bowl; add in the green beans. 9. Add in the onion, cucumber, baby spinach and iceberg lettuce. 10. Whisk the lemon juice, olive oil, mustard and vinegar. 11. Dress the salad and garnish with roasted almonds and fresh parsley. Bon appétit!
Per serving: Calories: 307; Fat: 11.8g; Sodium: 94mg; Total Carbs: 13g; Net Carbs: 7g; Fiber: 5.2g; Sugars: 3.8g; Protein: 37.5g

Tasty Coconut Prawns

Prep Time: 8-10 minutes | Cook time: 10 minutes | Serves: 4-5

1 medium-sized egg, whisked
⅓ cup beer
½ cup all-purpose flour
12 prawns, cleaned and deveined

Salt and ground black pepper as needed
½ teaspoon cumin powder
1 teaspoon lemon juice

1 teaspoon baking powder
1 tablespoon curry powder

½ teaspoon fresh ginger, grated
1 cup flaked coconut

1. Thoroughly mix the prawns with salt, pepper, cumin powder, and lemon juice in a medium-size bowl. 2. Prepare another medium-size bowl, thoroughly whisk the egg. Mix the beer, ¼ cup of flour, baking powder, curry, and the ginger well. 3. In another mixing bowl, place the remaining flour. Add the coconut into a third bowl. 4. Dip the prawns in the flour, then dip them in the beer mix. Lastly, roll them over flaked coconut. 5. Arrange them to the basket which has been coated with cooking oil or spray of your air fryer. 6. Cook them for 5 minutes at 360 degrees F/ 180 degrees C. 7. When the time is up, turn and continue cooking for 4 minutes. 8. Serve warm!
Per serving: Calories: 239; Fat: 9.4g; Sodium: 184mg; Total Carbs: 18g; Net Carbs: 9.5g; Fiber: 2.8g; Sugars: 1.5g; Protein: 19.1g

Glazed Fillets

Prep Time: 8-10 minutes | Cook time: 15 minutes | Serves: 4

4 flounder fillets
1 ½ tablespoons dark sesame oil
2 tablespoons sake
Sea salt and cracked mixed peppercorns, as needed

¼ cup soy sauce
1 teaspoon brown sugar
1 tablespoon grated lemon rind
2 garlic cloves, minced
Fresh chopped chives, to serve

1. To marinate, prepare a large deep dish, add the ingredients except for chives and stir a little. Cover and refrigerate for 2-3 hours. 2. Add the fish to the basket that has been coated with the cooking oil or spray. 3. Arrange it to the air fryer and cook at 360 degrees F/ 180 degrees C for 12 minutes, flipping halfway through. 4. Pour the remaining marinade into a saucepan; simmer over medium-low heat until it has thickened. 5. Serve the fish with the marinade and chives on top!
Per serving: Calories: 208; Fat: 7.1g; Sodium: 1032mg; Total Carbs: 2g; Net Carbs: 0.5g; Fiber: 0.3g; Sugars: 1.1g; Protein 31.8g

Flounder Fillets with Coconut Aminos

Prep Time: 15 minutes | Cook time: 12 Minutes | Serves: 2

2 flounder fillets, boneless
2 garlic cloves, minced
2 teaspoons coconut aminos
2 tablespoons lemon juice

A pinch of salt and black pepper
½-teaspoon stevia
1 tablespoon olive oil

1. Mix up the flounder fillets, garlic cloves, coconut aminos, lemon juice, salt, black pepper, stevia, and olive oil in the cooking pan of your air fryer. 2. Arrange the pan to the air fryer and cook for 12 minutes at 390 degrees F/ 200 degrees C. 3. Divide into bowls and serve.
Per serving: Calories: 155; Fat 2g; Sodium 135mg; Total Carbs 1.2g; Net Carbs: 0.8g; Fiber 0.1g; Sugars: 0.2g; Protein: 30.9g

Salmon with Sweet Potato

Prep Time: 10 minutes | Cook time: 40 minutes | Serves: 4

For the Fillets:
2 tablespoons capers
1 teaspoon celery salt
4 (6 ounces) skin-on salmon fillets
1 tablespoon extra-virgin olive oil
1 teaspoon smoked cayenne pepper
¼ teaspoon black pepper

A pinch of dry mustard
A pinch of ground mace
For the Potatoes:
4 sweet potatoes, peeled and make wedges
1 tablespoon sesame oil
Kosher salt and pepper, as needed

1. Oil the salmon on all sides, season as needed. 2. Place the salmon in the basket that has been coated with cooking oil or spray. 3. Arrange the basket to the air fryer and cook at 360 degrees F/ 180 degrees C for 5 minutes. 4. When the time is up, set aside and clean the basket. 5. In the basket, add the sweet potatoes, oil, salt and pepper. 6. Toss and cook for 30 minutes at 380 degrees F/ 195 degrees C, flipping halfway through. 7. Serve warm with salmon fillets!
Per serving: Calories: 600; Fat: 12.8g; Sodium: 776mg; Total Carbs: 28g; Net Carbs: 11.5g; Fiber: 4.2g; Sugars: 0.5g; Protein: 93.6g

Pollock Fillets with Rosemary & Oregano

Prep Time: 18 minutes | Cook time: 15 Minutes | Serves: 3

1 tablespoon olive oil
1 red onion, sliced
2 cloves garlic, chopped
1 Florina pepper, deveined and minced
3 pollock fillets, skinless
2 ripe tomatoes, diced
12 Kalamata olives, pitted and chopped
1 tablespoon capers
1 teaspoon oregano
1 teaspoon rosemary
Sea salt, to taste
½ cup white wine

1. Start by preheating your Air Fryer to 360 degrees F/ 180 degrees C. 2. Heat the oil in a baking pan. Once hot, sauté the onion, garlic, and pepper for 2 to 3 minutes or until fragrant. 3. Add the fish fillets to the baking pan, then top with the tomatoes, olives, and capers. 4. After sprinkling with the oregano, rosemary and salt, pour in white wine and transfer to the pan. 5. Cook for 10 minutes at 395 degrees F/ 200 degrees C. 6. Taste for seasoning and serve on individual plates, garnished with some extra Mediterranean herbs if desired. 7. Enjoy!
Per serving: Calories: 229; Fat: 7.9g; Sodium: 390mg; Total Carbs: 10.2g; Net Carbs: 0g; Fiber: 2.8g; Sugars: 4.1g; Protein: 23.6g

Beer Squid

Prep Time: 10 minutes | Cook time: 20 Minutes | Serves: 3

1 cup beer
1 lb. squid
1 cup all-purpose flour
2 eggs
½ cup cornstarch
Sea salt, to taste
½-teaspoon ground black pepper
1 tablespoon Old Bay seasoning

1. At 390 degrees F/ 200 degrees C, heat your air fryer in advance. 2. Clean the squid and then cut them into rings. Add the beer and squid in a glass bowl, cover and let it sit in your refrigerator for 1 hour. 3. Rinse the squid before patting it dry. 4. Add the flour in a shallow bowl; in another bowl, whisk the eggs. Lastly, in a third shallow bowl, add the cornstarch and seasonings. 5. Dredge the calamari in the flour. 6. Then dip the rings into the egg mixture and coat them with the cornstarch on all sided. 7. Arrange them in the cooking basket. Spritz with cooking oil and cook for 9 to 12 minutes, depending on the desired level of doneness. Work in batches. 8. Serve warm with your favorite dipping sauce. Enjoy!
Per serving: Calories: 449; Fat: 5.4g; Sodium: 832mg; Total Carbs: 59g; Net Carbs: 26g; Fiber: 1.4g; Sugars: 0.3g; Protein 32g

Crusty Catfish with Parmesan Cheese

Prep Time: 15 minutes | Cook time: 50 Minutes | Serves: 2

½ lb. catfish
½ cup bran cereal
¼ cup Parmesan cheese, grated
Sea salt, to taste
Ground black pepper, to taste
1 teaspoon smoked paprika
½ teaspoon garlic powder
¼-teaspoon ground bay leaf
1 egg
½ tablespoon butter, melted
4 sweet potatoes, cut French fries

1. Use the kitchen towel to pat the catfish dry. 2. In a shallow bowl, combine the bran cereal with the Parmesan cheese and all spices in a shallow bowl. 3. In another shallow bowl, whisk the egg. 4. Coat the fish evenly and completely with the egg mixture, then dredge in the bran cereal mixture, turning a couple of times to coat evenly. 5. Arrange the catfish to the basket that has been sprayed and cook at 390 degrees F/ 200 degrees C for 10 minutes; flip them and cook for 4 minutes more. 6. After that, drizzle the melted butter all over the sweet potatoes; cook them at 380 degrees F/ 195 degrees C for 30 minutes, shaking occasionally. 7. Serve over the warm fish fillets. Bon appétit!
Per serving: Calories: 755; Fat: 25g; Sodium: 489mg; Total Carbs: 106g; Net Carbs: 43g; Fiber: 18.6g; Sugars: 5.1g; Protein: 31.4g

Fish Mania with Mustard

Prep Time: 10-15 minutes | Cook time: 10 minutes | Serves: 4-5

1 cup soft bread crumbs
1 teaspoon whole-grain mustard
2 cans canned fish
2 celery stalks, chopped
1 egg, whisked
½ teaspoon sea salt
¼ teaspoon black peppercorns, cracked
1 teaspoon paprika

1. Thoroughly mix the fish, breadcrumbs, celery and other ingredients in a large bowl. 2. Make four cakes shapes from the mixture and

refrigerate for 45-50 minutes. 3. Place the cakes in the basket that has been coated with cooking oil or spray. 4. Arrange it to air fryer and cook for 5 minutes at 360 degrees F/ 180 degrees C. 5. After 5 minutes, flip the cakes gently and cook for another 4 minutes 6. Serve over mashed potatoes.
Per serving: Calories: 152; Fat: 4g; Sodium: 640mg; Total Carbs: 5g; Net Carbs: 2g; Fiber: 0.6g; Sugars: 0.6g; Protein: 22.5g

Salmon Bowl with Lime Drizzle

Prep Time: 10 minutes | Cook time: 10 minutes | Serves 3

1 pound salmon steak
2 teaspoons sesame oil
Sea salt and Sichuan pepper, to taste
½ teaspoon coriander seeds
1 lime, juiced
2 tablespoons reduced-sodium soy sauce
1 teaspoon honey

1. Drizzle the salmon which has been patted dry in advance with 1 teaspoon of sesame oil. 2. After seasoning the salmon with coriander seeds, salt and pepper, transfer the salmon to the basket of your air fryer. 3. Cook the salmon at 400 degrees F/ 205 degrees C for 10 minutes, flipping halfway through. 4. In a small saucepan, warm the remaining ingredients to make the lime drizzle. 5. Cut the fish into bite-sized strips, drizzle with the sauce. 6. Serve and enjoy!
Per serving: Calories: 240; Fat: 12.4g; Sodium: 467mg; Total Carbs: 2g; Net Carbs: 0.5g; Fiber: 0.1g; Sugars: 2.1g; Protein 30g

Delicious Fillets with Avocado Sauce

Prep Time: 25 minutes | Cook time: 20 Minutes | Serves: 2

2 cod fish fillets
1 egg
Sea salt, to taste
1 teaspoon olive oil
½ avocado, peeled, pitted, and mashed
½ tablespoon mayonnaise
1 tablespoon sour cream
½-teaspoon yellow mustard
½ teaspoon lemon juice
1 garlic clove, minced
¼-teaspoon black pepper
¼-teaspoon salt
¼-teaspoon hot pepper sauce

1. Coat the basket of your air fryer with cooking oil. 2. Use a kitchen towel to pat dry the fish fillets. 3. In a shallow bowl, beat the egg, add in the salt and olive oil. 4. Coat the fillets with the egg mixture thoroughly. 5. Place the fillets in the basket and then arrange it to the air fryer. 6. Cook the fillets at 360 degrees F/ 180 degrees C for 12 minutes or until turn pink. 7. Meanwhile, in another clean bowl, make the avocado sauce by mixing the remaining ingredients in a bowl. Place the bowl in your refrigerator until ready to serve. 8. Serve the fish fillets with chilled avocado sauce on the side. Bon appétit!
Per serving: Calories: 389; Fat: 19.7g; Sodium: 652mg; Total Carbs: 7g; Net Carbs: 3g; Fiber: 3.5g; Sugars: 1g; Protein: 45.3g

Chip-crusted Tilapia with Parmesan Cheese

Prep Time: 10 minutes | Cook time: 10 minutes | Serves 3

1 ½ pounds tilapia, slice into 4 portions
Sea salt, to taste
Ground black pepper, to taste
½ teaspoon cayenne pepper
1 teaspoon granulated garlic
¼ cup almond flour
¼ cup parmesan cheese, preferably freshly grated
1 egg, beaten
2 tablespoons buttermilk
1 cup tortilla chips, crushed

1. Season the tilapia with cayenne pepper, salt and black pepper generously and orderly. 2. On a bread station, add the granulated garlic, almond flour and parmesan cheese to a rimmed plate. 3. Add the egg and buttermilk in another bowl and mix well. 4. In the third bowl, place the crushed tortilla chips. 5. Coat the tilapia pieces with the flour mixture and egg mixture in order and then roll them in the crushed chips, press to adhere well. 6. Cook the tilapia pieces in your air fryer at 400 degrees F/ 205 degrees C for 10 minutes, flipping halfway through. 7. Serve with chips if desired. Bon appétit!
Per serving: Calories: 217; Fat: 4g; Sodium: 112mg; Total Carbs: 0.9g; Net Carbs: 0g; Fiber: 0.2g; Sugars: 0.6g; Protein: 44.6g

Typical Cod Nuggets

Prep Time: 10-15 minutes | Cook time: 10 minutes | Serves: 4

16-ounce cod
To make the breading:
1 cup all-purpose flour
2 tablespoons olive oil

2 eggs, beaten
1 pinch salt
¾ cup panko breadcrumbs, finely processed

1. Thoroughly mix the oil, salt and crumbs in a medium-size bowl. 2. Take the cod, make pieces from it of about 2.5 inches by 1 inch. 3. In a bowl of medium size, thoroughly mix the salt, oil and crumbs. 4. Side by side place three bowls; add the flour in the first bowl, crumb mixture in the second and eggs in the third. Dip the fish in the flour, one by one, and then mix in the egg mix. 5. Lastly coat with the crumb mixture completely. 6. Place the fish pieces in the basket that has been coated with cooking oil or spray. 7. Arrange the basket to the air fryer and cook at 390 degrees F/ 200 degrees C for 10 minutes or until turn pink. 8. Serve the crispy fish!
Per serving: Calories: 377; Fat: 10.9g; Sodium: 261mg; Total Carbs: 35g; Net Carbs: 20g; Fiber: 2.3g; Sugars: 0.6g; Protein: 33.4g

Pasta Shrimp

Prep Time: 10 minutes | Cook time: 5 minutes | Serves: 4

½ teaspoon hot paprika
2 garlic cloves, peeled and minced
1 teaspoon onion powder
½ teaspoon salt
1 teaspoon lemon-pepper seasoning
18 shrimps, shelled and deveined

2 tablespoons extra-virgin olive oil
¼ teaspoon cumin powder
2 tablespoons squeezed lemon juice
½ cup parsley, coarsely chopped

1. Thoroughly mix the ingredients in a medium-size bowl, then cover it with a foil and refrigerate for 30-45 minutes. 2. Place the shrimps in the basket that has been coated with cooking oil or spray. 3. Arrange the basket to the air fryer and cook at 400 degrees F/ 205 degrees C for 5 minutes or until turn pink. 4. Serve warm with cooked pasta or just shrimps!
Per serving: Calories: 187; Fat: 8.8g; Sodium: 537mg; Total Carbs: 3g; Net Carbs: 1g; Fiber: 0.5g; Sugars: 0.3g; Protein: 23g

Sea Bream Fillet with Tomato Sauce

Prep Time: 10 minutes | Cook time: 8 Minutes | Serves: 4

1 tablespoon keto tomato sauce
1 tablespoon avocado oil
1 teaspoon ground black pepper

½-teaspoon salt
12 oz. sea bream fillet

1. Cut the sea bream fillet on 4 servings. 2. After that, mix up tomato sauce, avocado oil, salt, and ground black pepper in a mixing bowl. 3. Rub the fish fillets with tomato mixture on both sides. 4. Line the air fryer basket with foil. 5. Put the sea bream fillets on the foil and cook them for 8 minutes at 390 degrees F/ 200 degrees C.
Per serving: Calories: 499; Fat: 23.3g; Sodium: 212mg; Total Carbs: 47g; Net Carbs: 22g; Fiber: 3g; Sugars: 3.9g; Protein: 23.9g

Crumbed Fish Fillets with Parmesan Cheese

Prep Time: 10 minutes | Cook time: 25 Minutes | Serves: 4

2 eggs, beaten
½-teaspoon tarragon
4 fish fillets, halved
½ tablespoon dry white wine

⅓ cup Parmesan cheese, grated
1 teaspoon seasoned salt
⅓-teaspoon mixed peppercorns
½-teaspoon fennel seed

1. Add the Parmesan cheese, salt, peppercorns, fennel seeds, and tarragon to your food processor; blitz for about 20 seconds. 2. Drizzle dry white wine on the top of these fish fillets. 3. In a shallow dish, dump the egg. 4. Now, coat the fish fillets with the beaten egg on all sides, then coat them with the seasoned cracker mix. 5. Air-fry at 345 degrees F/ 175 degrees C for about 17 minutes. Bon appétit!
Per serving: Calories: 254; Fat: 13.9g; Sodium: 917mg; Total Carbs: 16g; Net Carbs: 7g; Fiber: 0.6g; Sugars: 0.2g; Protein: 16.9g

Bean Burritos with Cheddar Cheese

Prep Time: 5 minutes | Cook time: 15 Minutes | Serves: 4

4 tortillas
1 can beans

1 cup cheddar cheese, grated
¼-teaspoon paprika

¼-teaspoon chili powder
¼-teaspoon garlic powder

Salt and pepper to taste

1. Heat the Air Fryer to 350 degrees F/ 175 degrees C ahead of time. 2. Mix up the paprika, chili powder, garlic powder, salt and pepper in a suitable bowl. 3. Before adding the spice mixture and cheddar cheese, fill each tortilla with an equal portion of beans. 4. Roll the tortilla wraps into burritos. 5. Use the parchment paper to cover the base of a baking dish. 6. Arrange the burritos to the baking dish and place the dish in the air fryer. 7. Cook the burritos for about 5 minutes at 350 degrees F/ 175 degrees C. 8. When cooked, serve hot.
Per serving: Calories: 168; Fat: 10.1g; Sodium: 188mg; Total Carbs: 11.5g; Net Carbs: 5g; Fiber: 1.7g; Sugars: 0.4g; Protein: 8.5g

Thai Coconut Fish

Prep Time: 10 minutes | Cook time: 20 Minutes | Serves: 2

1 cup coconut milk
1 tablespoon lime juice
1 tablespoon Shoyu sauce
Salt and white pepper, to taste
1 teaspoon turmeric powder

½-teaspoon ginger powder
½ Thai Bird's Eye chili
1 lb. tilapia
1 tablespoon olive oil

1. Remove the seeds from the chili and finely chop them. Prepare a mixing bowl, thoroughly combine the coconut milk with the lime juice, Shoyu sauce, salt, pepper, turmeric, ginger, and chili pepper. 2. Coat the tilapia with the mixture and let it marinate for 1 hour. 3. Brush the basket of your air fryer with olive oil. 4. Take the tilapia fillets out of the marinade and place them in the basket. 5. Cook the tilapia fillets in the preheated Air Fryer at 400 degrees F/ 205 degrees C for 12 minutes, flipping halfway through. 6. Working in batches is suggested. 7. Serve with some extra lime wedges if desired. Enjoy!
Per serving: Calories: 474; Fat: 30.8g; Sodium: 99mg; Total Carbs: 9.5g; Net Carbs: 5g; Fiber: 3g; Sugars: 4.4g; Protein: 45.2g

Catfish Fillets with Tortilla Chips

Prep Time: 20 minutes | Cook time: 30 Minutes | Serves: 4

2 catfish fillets [catfish]
1 medium egg, beaten
1 cup bread crumbs
1 cup tortilla chips

1 lemon, juiced and peeled
1 teaspoon parsley
Salt and pepper to taste

1. Slice the catfish fillets neatly and then drizzle lightly with the lemon juice. 2. Mix up the bread crumbs with the lemon rind, parsley, tortillas, salt and pepper in a bowl, then pour into your food processor and pulse. 3. Distributes the fillets evenly on the base of the cooking tray. 4. Cover the fish fillets well with the prepared mixture. 5. Arrange the tray to your air fryer and cook the fillets at 350 degrees F/ 175 degrees C for 15 minutes. 6. When done, serve with chips and a refreshing drink.
Per serving: Calories: 160; Fat: 7.6g; Sodium: 120mg; Total Carbs: 7g; Net Carbs: 3g; Fiber: 0.6g; Sugars: 0.5g; Protein: 14.8g

Spicy Salmon and Fennel Salad

Prep Time: 10 minutes | Cook time: 20 minutes | Serves 3

1 pound salmon
1 fennel, quartered
1 teaspoon olive oil
Sea salt, to taste
Ground black pepper, to taste
½ teaspoon paprika
1 tablespoon balsamic vinegar

1 tablespoon lime juice
1 tablespoon extra-virgin olive oil
1 tomato, sliced
1 cucumber, sliced
1 tablespoon sesame seeds, lightly toasted

1. Combine the olive oil, salt, black pepper and paprika well, then stir the salmon and fennel with the spice mixture. 2. Cook the salmon at 380 degrees F/ 195 degrees C for 12 minutes, shaking the basket once or twice for even cooking. 3. After cutting the salmon into bite-sized strips, transfer them to a nice salad bowl. 4. In the same bowl, add in the fennel, balsamic vinegar, lime juice, 1 tablespoon of extra-virgin olive oil, tomato and cucumber, then combine well. 5. Serve garnished with lightly toasted sesame seeds. Enjoy!
Per serving: Calories: 260; Fat: 12.6g; Total Carbs: 7.5g; Net Carbs: 2.5g; Fiber: 2.1g; Sugars: 2.3g; Protein: 31.1g

Lemon Salmon Fillet

Prep Time: 10 minutes | Cook time: 15 Minutes | Serves: 1

1 salmon fillet
½ teaspoon Cajun seasoning
½ lemon, juiced
¼-teaspoon sugar
2 lemon wedges, for serving

1. Heat the Air Fryer to 350 degrees F/ 175 degrees C ahead of time. 2. Combine the lemon juice and sugar, then coat the salmon with the sugar mixture. 3. Coat the salmon with the Cajun seasoning. 4. Place a sheet of parchment paper on the base of your air fryer. 5. Arrange the salmon to the air fryer and cook for 7 minutes.
Per serving: Calories: 239; Fat: 11g; Sodium: 129mg; Total Carbs: 1g; Net Carbs: 0g; Fiber: 0g; Sugars: 1g; Protein: 34.6g

Spicy Jumbo Shrimps

Prep Time: 15 minutes | Cook time: 6 Minutes | Serves: 4

¼-teaspoon cayenne pepper
¼-teaspoon red chili flakes
1 teaspoon cumin
1 teaspoon oregano
1 teaspoon salt
1 teaspoon thyme
1 tablespoon coconut oil
1 teaspoon cilantro
1 teaspoon onion powder
1 teaspoon smoked paprika
20 jumbo shrimps, peeled and deveined

1. In addition to the shrimps, combine the other ingredients well and then coat the shrimps. 2. Place the shrimps on the cooking pan and arrange the pan to your air fryer. 3. Cook for 6 minutes at 390 degrees F/ 200 degrees C. 4. When done, serve and enjoy.
Per serving: Calories: 237; Fat: 3.7g; Sodium: 234mg; Total Carbs: 1.5g; Net Carbs: 0g; Fiber: 0.6g; Sugars: 5.3g; Protein: 50.3g

Salmon Burgers

Prep Time: 15 minutes | Cook time: 15 Minutes | Serves: 4

1 lb. salmon
1 egg
1 garlic clove, minced
2 green onions, minced
1 cup parmesan cheese
Sauce:
1 teaspoon rice wine
1 ½-tablespoon soy sauce
A pinch of salt
1 teaspoon gochutgaru (Korean red chili pepper flakes)

1. Start by preheating your Air Fryer to 380 degrees F/ 195 degrees C. Spritz the Air Fryer basket with cooking oil. 2. Oil the basket of your air fryer. 3. Mix up the salmon with egg, garlic, green onions, and Parmesan cheese in a bowl. 4. Knead it with your hands until everything comes together nicely. 5. Shape the mixture into equally sized patties. 6. Transfer your patties to the basket and arrange the basket to the air fryer. 7. Cook the fish patties for 10 minutes, flipping halfway through. 8. Make the sauce by whisking all ingredients. 9. With the sauce on the side, serve and enjoy the warm fish patties.
Per serving: Calories: 197; Fat: 9.6g; Sodium: 520mg; Total Carbs: 2g; Net Carbs: 0.5g; Fiber: 0.3g; Sugars: 0.7g; Protein: 26.2g

Chunky Fish with Mustard

Prep Time: 15 minutes | Cook time: 10 Minutes | Serves: 4

2 cans canned fish
2 celery stalks, trimmed and finely chopped
1 egg, whisked
1 cup bread crumbs
1 teaspoon whole-grain mustard
½-teaspoon sea salt
¼-teaspoon freshly cracked black peppercorns
½ teaspoon paprika

1. Add all of the ingredients one by one and combine well. 2. Form four equal-sized cakes from the mixture, then leave to chill in the refrigerator for 50 minutes. 3. Spray all sides of each cake after putting them on the cooking pan of your air fryer. 4. Arrange the pan to the air fryer and grill at 360 degrees F/ 180 degrees C for 5 minutes. 5. After 5 minutes, turn the cakes over and resume cooking for an additional 3 minutes. 6. Serve with mashed potatoes if desired.
Per serving: Calories: 150; Fat: 3.9g; Sodium: 640mg; Total Carbs: 4g; Net Carbs: 2g; Fiber: 0.4g; Sugars: 0.6g; Protein: 22.4g

Homemade Lobster Tails Ever

Prep Time: 10 minutes | Cook time: 7 minutes | Serves 2

2 (6-ounce) lobster tails
1 teaspoon fresh cilantro, minced

½ teaspoon dried rosemary
½ teaspoon garlic, pressed
1 teaspoon deli mustard
Sea salt, to taste
Ground black pepper, to taste
1 teaspoon olive oil

1. In addition to the lobster tails, combine the remaining ingredients well and coat the lobster tails well on all sides. 2. Cook the lobster tails at 370 degrees F/ 185 degrees C for 7 minutes, flipping halfway through. 3. Serve warm and enjoy!
Per serving: Calories: 174; Fat: 3.8g; Sodium: 827mg; Total Carbs: 0.4g; Net Carbs: 0g; Fiber: 0.1g; Sugars: 0g; Protein: 32.4g

Shrimp with Parsley

Prep Time: 15 minutes | Cook time: 12 Minutes | Serves: 4

1 lb. shrimp, peeled and deveined
1 teaspoon cumin, ground
1 tablespoon parsley, chopped
1 tablespoon olive oil
A pinch of salt and black pepper
4 garlic cloves, minced
1 tablespoon lime juice

1. Mix the shrimp, ground cumin, chopped parsley, olive oil, salt, black pepper, minced garlic, and lemon juice in a pan that fits your air fryer, toss well. 2. Arrange the pan to the air fryer and cook at 370 degrees F/ 185 degrees C for 12 minutes, flipping halfway through. 3. Divide into bowls and serve.
Per serving: Calories: 172; Fat: 5.6g; Sodium: 279mg; Total Carbs: 3g; Net Carbs: 1g; Fiber: 0.2g; Sugars: 0.1g; Protein: 26.1g

Trimmed Mackerel with Spring Onions

Prep Time: 10 minutes | Cook time: 20 Minutes | Serves: 5

1 pound mackerel, trimmed
1 tablespoon ground paprika
1 green bell pepper
½ cup spring onions, chopped
1 tablespoon avocado oil
1 teaspoon apple cider vinegar
½-teaspoon salt

1. Sprinkle the clean mackerel with ground paprika. 2. Chop the green bell pepper. 3. Fill the mackerel with bell pepper and spring onion. 4. After this, sprinkle the fish with avocado oil, salt and apple cider vinegar. 5. At 375 degrees F/ 190 degrees C, heat your air fryer in advance. 6. Place the mackerel in the basket and arrange the basket to the air fryer. 7. Cook the mackerel for 20 minutes at 375 degrees F/ 190 degrees C. 8. When cooked, serve and enjoy.
Per serving: Calories: 256; Fat: 16.8g; Sodium: 311mg; Total Carbs: 3.5g; Net Carbs: 0.5g; Fiber: 1.2g; Sugars: 1.6g; Protein: 22.3g

Rosemary Salmon

Prep Time: 10 minutes | Cook time: 15 Minutes | Serves: 4

½-teaspoon dried rosemary
½-teaspoon dried thyme
½-teaspoon dried basil
½-teaspoon ground coriander
½-teaspoon ground cumin
½-teaspoon ground paprika
½-teaspoon salt
1 pound salmon
1 tablespoon olive oil

1. Mixed up the dried rosemary, thyme, basil, coriander, cumin, paprika, and salt in a suitable bowl. 2. Rub the salmon with the spice mixture gently and sprinkle it with the olive oil. 3. At 375 degrees F/ 190 degrees C, heat your air fryer in advance. 4. Put the prepared salmon on the cooking pan with the baking paper under it. 5. Cook the fish at 375 degrees F/ 190 degrees C for 15 minutes, or until you get the light crunchy crust. 6. Once done, serve and enjoy.
Per serving: Calories: 153; Fat: 7.1g; Sodium: 341mg; Total Carbs: 0.4g; Net Carbs: 0g; Fiber: 0.2g; Sugars: 0g; Protein: 22.1g

Tasty Juicy Salmon

Prep Time: 15 minutes | Cook time: 13 Minutes | Serves: 2

2 salmon fillets
4 asparagus stalks
¼ cup champagne
Salt and black pepper, to taste
¼ cup white sauce
1½ teaspoon olive oil

1. Heat the air fryer ahead of time. 2. In a bowl, mix the salmon fillets, asparagus, champagne, salt, black pepper, white sauce, and olive oil together and divide this mixture evenly over 2 foil papers. 3. Arrange the foil papers in the basket of your air fryer and cook for about 13 minutes at 355 degrees F/ 180 degrees C. 4. Dish out in a platter and serve hot.
Per serving: Calories: 319; Fat: 16.7g; Sodium: 190mg; Total Carbs: 4g; Net Carbs: 2g; Fiber: 0.7g; Sugars: 2g; Protein: 36.4g

Cajun Lemon Branzino

Prep Time: 10 minutes | Cook time: 8 Minutes | Serves: 4

1-pound branzino, trimmed, washed	1 tablespoon sesame oil
1 teaspoon Cajun seasoning	1 tablespoon lemon juice
	1 teaspoon salt

1. Carefully coat the branzino with salt and Cajun seasoning. 2. Drizzle the lemon juice and sesame oil over the branzino. 3. At 380 degrees F/ 195 degrees C, heat your air fryer in advance. 4. Place the branzino in the air fryer and cook it for 8 minutes at 380 degrees F/ 195 degrees C. 5. When done, serve and enjoy.
Per serving: Calories: 196; Fat: 7.2g; Sodium: 707mg; Total Carbs: 0.1g; Net Carbs: 0g; Fiber: 0g; Sugars: 0.1g; Protein: 31.5g

Simple Fish Sticks

Prep Time: 10 minutes | Cook time: 10 minutes | Serves 2

½ pound fish sticks, frozen	4 tablespoons mayonnaise
½ pound Vidalia onions, halved	4 tablespoons Greek-style yogurt
1 teaspoon sesame oil	¼ teaspoon mustard seeds
Sea salt, to taste	1 teaspoon chipotle chili in adobo, minced
Ground black pepper, to taste	
½ teaspoon red pepper flakes	

1. Drizzle the fish sticks and Vidalia onions with sesame oil. 2. Toss the fish sticks with red pepper flakes, salt and black pepper. 3. Transfer the fish sticks to the cooking basket and arrange the basket to the air fryer. 4. Cook the fish sticks and onions at 400 degrees F/ 205 degrees C for 10 minutes, shaking the basket halfway through. 5. Mix up the mayonnaise, Greek-style yogurt, mustard seeds and chipotle chili at the same time. 6. Garnish the warm sticks with Vidalia onions and the sauce on the side. 7. Bon appétit!
Per serving: Calories: 402; Fat: 28g; Sodium: 242mg; Total Carbs: 22g; Net Carbs: 10g; Fiber: 1.6g; Sugars: 14.4g; Protein: 13.2g

Flavored Salmon Grill with Oregano & Cumin

Prep Time: 15 minutes | Cook time: 15 Minutes | Serves: 4

1 ½ lbs. skinless salmon fillet (preferably wild), cut into 1" pieces	2 lemons, very thinly sliced into rounds
1 teaspoon ground cumin	1 tablespoon chopped fresh oregano
1 teaspoon kosher salt	1 tablespoon olive oil
¼-teaspoon crushed red pepper flakes	1 teaspoon sesame seeds

1. Prepare a small bowl, mix well oregano, sesame seeds, cumin, salt, and pepper flakes. 2. Thread salmon and folded lemon slices in a skewer. 3. Brush the salmon with oil and sprinkle with spice. 4. Arrange the skewers to the air fryer and cook for 5 minutes at 360 degrees F/ 180 degrees C. 5. Serve and enjoy.
Per serving: Calories: 240; Fat: 16.1g; Sodium: 648mg; Total Carbs: 1g; Net Carbs: 0g; Fiber: 0.7g; Sugars: 0.1g; Protein: 22.4g

Red Snapper with Hot Chili Paste

Prep Time: 15 minutes | Cook time: 15 Minutes | Serves: 4

4 red snapper fillets, boneless	1 tablespoon lime juice
A pinch of salt and black pepper	1 tablespoon hot chili paste
2 garlic cloves, minced	1 tablespoon olive oil
1 tablespoon coconut aminos	

1. In addition to the fish, mix up the other ingredients in a bowl and stir well. 2. Use the mixture to rub the fish, then place the fish in the basket of your air fryer. 3. Cook for 15 minutes at 380 degrees F/ 195 degrees C. 4. Serve with a side salad.
Per serving: Calories: 262; Fat: 7.1g; Sodium: 142mg; Total Carbs: 2g; Net Carbs: 0.5g; Fiber: 0g; Sugars: 1g; Protein: 45.1g

Buttered Shrimp Fry

Prep Time: 15 minutes | Cook time: 15 Minutes | Serves: 4

1 tablespoon chopped chives or 1-teaspoon dried chives	or 1 teaspoon dried basil, plus more for sprinkling
1 tablespoon lemon juice	1 tablespoon minced garlic
1 tablespoon basil leaves, minced,	21-25 count defrosted shrimp

1 tablespoon chicken stock (or white wine)	1 teaspoon red pepper flakes
	1 tablespoon butter

1. Lightly spray the baking pan of your air fryer. 2. Melt butter for 2 minutes at 330 degrees F/ 165 degrees C. 3. After stirring in red pepper flakes and garlic, cook for 3 minutes. 4. Add remaining ingredients in pan and toss well to coat. 5. Cook for 5 minutes at 330 degrees F/ 165 degrees C. 6. Stir and let it stand for another 5 minutes. 7. When done, serve and enjoy.
Per serving: Calories: 168; Fat: 5g; Sodium: 315mg; Total Carbs: 2g; Net Carbs: 0.5g; Fiber: 0.2g; Sugars: 0.2g; Protein: 26.6g

Clams with Spring Onions

Prep Time: 10 minutes | Cook time: 20 Minutes | Serves: 4

15 small clams	10 oz. coconut cream
1 tablespoon spring onions, chopped	1 tablespoon cilantro, chopped
Juice of 1 lime	1 teaspoon olive oil

Heat up a suitable pan that fits your air fryer with the oil over medium heat, add the spring onions and sauté for 2 minutes. Add lime juice, coconut cream and the cilantro, stir and cook for 2 minutes more. Add the clams, toss, introduce in the fryer and cook at 390 degrees F/ 200 degrees C for 15 minutes. Divide into bowls and serve hot.
Per serving: Calories: 193; Fat: 18.2g; Sodium: 161mg; Total Carbs: 8g; Net Carbs: 3.5g; Fiber: 1.8g; Sugars: 3.8g; Protein: 1.9g

Ginger-garlic Swordfish

Prep Time: 10 minutes | Cook time: 10 Minutes | Serves: 3

1 pound swordfish steak	¼ teaspoon cayenne pepper
1 teaspoon ginger-garlic paste	¼ teaspoon dried dill weed
Sea salt, to taste	½ pound mushrooms
Ground black pepper, to taste	

1. Mix up the ginger-garlic paste; season with salt, black pepper, cayenne pepper and dried dill, then rub the swordfish steak with the mixture. 2. Spritz the fish with a nonstick cooking spray and transfer to the Air Fryer cooking basket. Cook the swordfish at 400 degrees F/ 205 degrees C for 5 minutes. 3. Now, add the mushrooms to the cooking basket and continue to cook for 5 minutes longer until tender and fragrant. Eat warm.
Per serving: Calories: 262; Fat: 9g; Sodium: 178mg; Total Carbs: 3g; Net Carbs: 1g; Fiber: 0.8g; Sugars: 1.3g; Protein: 40.9g

Herbed and Garlic Salmon Fillets

Prep Time: 10 minutes | Cook time: 12 minutes | Serves: 3

1 pound salmon fillets	1 sprig thyme
Sea salt, to taste	2 sprigs rosemary
Ground black pepper, to taste	2 cloves garlic, minced
1 tablespoon olive oil	1 lemon, sliced

1. Season the salmon fillets that have been patted dry with salt and pepper. 2. Drizzle the salmon fillets with olive oil and place them in the cooking basket of your air fryer. 3. Cook the salmon fillets at 380 degrees F/ 195 degrees C for 12 minutes. 4. After 7 minutes of cooking time, turn them over, top with thyme, rosemary and garlic and continue to cook them for 5 minutes more. 5. Serve topped with lemon slices and enjoy!
Per serving: Calories: 243; Fat: 14g; Sodium: 67mg; Total Carbs: 0.7g; Net Carbs: 0g; Fiber: 0g; Sugars: 0g; Protein: 29.5g

Baked Sardines

Prep Time: 10 minutes | Cook time: 40 minutes | Serves: 3

1-pound fresh sardines	2 cloves garlic, minced
Sea salt, to taste	3 tablespoons olive oil
Ground black pepper, to taste	½ lemon, freshly squeezed
1 teaspoon Italian seasoning mix	

1. Toss salt, black pepper, Italian seasoning mix and the sardines well. 2. Cook the sardines in your air fryer at 325 degrees F/ 160 degrees C for 35 to 40 minutes or until skin is crispy. 3. To make the sauce, whisk the remaining ingredients. 4. Serve warm sardines with the sauce on the side. Bon appétit!
Per serving: Calories: 437; Fat: 31.3g; Sodium: 764mg; Total Carbs: 0.7g; Net Carbs: 0g; Fiber: 0g; Sugars: 0g; Protein: 37.4g

Garlic Scallops with Parsley

Prep Time: 20 minutes | Cook time: 10 Minutes | Serves: 4

1 cup bread crumbs
¼ cup chopped parsley
16 sea scallops, rinsed and drained
2 shallots, chopped
3 pinches ground nutmeg

1½ tablespoons olive oil
5 cloves garlic, minced
2 tablespoons butter, melted
salt and pepper to taste

1. Coat the baking pan that fits your air fryer with cooking spray lightly. 2. Mix in melted butter, shallots, garlic and scallops, then season with nutmeg, salt and pepper. 3. Whisk the olive oil and bread crumbs well in a small bowl, then sprinkle over the processed scallops. 4. Cook the scallops at 390 degrees F/ 200 degrees C for 10 minutes or until the tops are lightly browned. 5. Sprinkle the parsley, serve and enjoy.
Per serving: Calories: 276; Fat: 8.9g; Sodium: 414mg; Total Carbs: 23g; Net Carbs: 11g; Fiber: 1.5g; Sugars: 1.8g; Protein: 24.1g

Cajun Fish Cakes

Prep Time: 10 minutes | Cook time: 30 Minutes | Serves: 4

2 catfish fillets
1 cup all-purpose flour
1 ounce butter
1 teaspoon baking powder

1 teaspoon baking soda
½ cup buttermilk
1 teaspoon Cajun seasoning
1 cup Swiss cheese, shredded

1. Boil a pot of water, the put in the fish fillets and boil for 5 minutes or until it is opaque. 2. When done, flake the fish into small pieces. 3. In a bowl, mix up the other ingredients, then add the fish and mix them well. 4. Form 12 fish patties from the mixture. 5. Place the patties to the cooking pan and arrange the pan to your air fryer. 6. Cook at 380 degrees F/ 195 degrees C for 15 minutes. 7. Working in batches is suggested. 8. Enjoy!
Per serving: Calories: 389; Fat: 19.9g; Sodium: 496mg; Total Carbs: 27g; Net Carbs: 19g; Fiber: 0.9g; Sugars: 1.9g; Protein: 24g

Old Bay Cod Fish Fillets

Prep Time: 10 minutes | Cook time: 12 minutes | Serves 2

2 cod fish fillets
1 teaspoon butter, melted
1 teaspoon Old Bay seasoning
1 egg, beaten

2 tablespoons coconut milk, unsweetened
⅓ cup coconut flour, unsweetened

1. Prepare a Ziploc bag, add the cod fish fillets, butter and Old Bay seasoning, shake to coat the fillets well on all sides. 2. Whisk the egg and coconut milk until frothy in a shallow bowl. 3. In another bowl, place the coconut flour. 4. Coat the fish fillets with the egg mixture and coconut flour in order, pressing to adhere. 5. Cook the fish fillets at 390 degrees F/ 200 degrees C until the fish fillets flake easily when poking it with a fork, for 12 minutes. 6. Flip halfway through. 7. Bon appétit!
Per serving: Calories: 352; Fat: 11.2g; Sodium: 507mg; Total Carbs: 14g; Net Carbs: 9.5g; Fiber: 8.3g; Sugars: 0.7g; Protein: 46.9g

Greek Sardines with Sauce

Prep Time: 10 minutes | Cook time: 55 minutes | Serves 2

4 sardines, cleaned
¼ cup all-purpose flour
Sea salt, to taste
Ground black pepper, to taste
4 tablespoons extra-virgin olive oil
½ red onion, chopped
½ teaspoon fresh garlic, minced

¼ cup sweet white wine
1 tablespoon fresh coriander, minced
¼ cup baby capers, drained
1 tomato, crushed
¼ teaspoon chili pepper flakes

1. Coat your sardines with all-purpose flour on all sides. 2. Drizzle salt and black pepper on the sardines and then transfer them to the cooking basket. 3. Arrange the basket to the air fryer and cook the sardines at 325 degrees F/ 160 degrees C for 35 to 40 minutes or until the skin is crispy. 4. While cooking the sardines, heat the olive oil in a frying pan over a moderate flame, then sauté the onion and garlic together for 4 to 5 minutes or until tender and aromatic. 5. Add the white wine, fresh coriander, baby capers, the crushed tomato, and chili pepper flakes and stir well, cover and let the mixture simmer for about 15 minutes or until thickened and reduced. 6. When simmered, spoon the sauce over the warm sardines. 7. Serve warm and enjoy!
Per serving: Calories: 496; Fat: 13.2g; Sodium: 468mg; Total Carbs: 61g; Net Carbs: 25g; Fiber: 10.4g; Sugars: 10.8g; Protein: 25.6g

Garlic Tilapia Fillets

Prep Time: 10 minutes | Cook time: 10 Minutes | Serves: 5

1 tablespoon all-purpose flour
Sea salt and white pepper, to taste
1 teaspoon garlic paste

1 tablespoon extra-virgin olive oil
½ cup cornmeal
5 tilapia fillets, slice into halves

1. Prepare a Ziploc bag and mix up the flour, salt, white pepper, garlic paste, olive oil, and cornmeal. 2. Add the fish fillets to the Ziploc bag and coat them well with the spice mixture. 3. Oil the basket of your air fryer with cooking spray and then put the coated fillets in it. 4. Arrange the basket to the air fryer and cook at 400 degrees F/ 205 degrees C for 10 minutes. 5. After 10 minutes, flip the fillets and cook for more 6 minutes. 6. Working in batches is suggested. 7. When done, serve with lemon wedges if desired. 8. Enjoy!
Per serving: Calories: 197; Fat: 5.5g; Sodium: 72mg; Total Carbs: 10.8g; Net Carbs: 0g; Fiber: 0.9g; Sugars: 0.1g; Protein: 28.3g

Tasty Anchovies and Cheese Wontons

Prep Time: 10 minutes | Cook time: 10 Minutes | Serves 4

½ pound anchovies
½ cup cheddar cheese, grated
1 cup fresh spinach
2 tablespoons scallions, minced
1 teaspoon garlic, minced

1 tablespoon Shoyu sauce
Himalayan salt, to taste
Ground black pepper, to taste
½ pound wonton wrappers
1 teaspoon sesame oil

1. Mix the mashed anchovies with the cheese, spinach, scallions, garlic and Shoyu sauce, then season with salt and black pepper. 2. Fill the wontons with 1 tablespoon of the filling mixture and fold into triangle shape, then brush the side with a bit of oil and water to seal the edges. 3. Cook the wontons at 390 degrees F/ 200 degrees C for 10 minutes, flipping halfway through for even cooking. 4. When done, serve with the seasoned anchovies and enjoy!
Per serving: Calories: 355; Fat: 12.2g; Sodium: 2498mg; Total Carbs: 33g; Net Carbs: 12g; Fiber: 1.3g; Sugars: 0.2g; Protein: 25.8g

Healthy Hot Salmon

Prep Time: 10 minutes | Cook time: 25 Minutes | Serves: 2

1 teaspoon olive oil
Juice of 1 lime
1 teaspoon chili flakes
Salt and black pepper

1 lb. salmon fillets
1 teaspoon olive oil
1 tablespoon soy sauce

1. Mix up the oil, lime juice, flakes, salt and black pepper in a bowl, then rub the fillets with the mixture. 2. Lay the florets into your air fryer and drizzle with oil. 3. Arrange the fillets around or on top and cook at 340 degrees F/ 170 degrees C for 10 minutes. Drizzle the florets with soy sauce to serve!
Per serving: Calories: 325; Fat: 16.3g; Sodium: 551mg; Total Carbs: 0.7g; Net Carbs: 0g; Fiber: 0.1g; Sugars: 0.2g; Protein: 44.5g

Grouper with Miso-Honey Sauce

Prep Time: 10 minutes | Cook time: 10 minutes | Serves 2

¾ pound grouper fillets
Salt and white pepper, to taste
1 tablespoon sesame oil
1 teaspoon water
1 teaspoon deli mustard or Dijon

mustard
¼ cup white miso
1 tablespoon mirin
1 tablespoon honey
1 tablespoon Shoyu sauce

1. Sprinkle salt and white pepper on the grouper fillets, then drizzle them with a nonstick cooking oil. 2. Arrange the fillets to the air fryer and cook them at 400 degrees F/ 205 degrees C for 10 minutes, flipping halfway through. 3. Meanwhile, whisk the other ingredients to make the sauce. 4. Serve the warm fish with the miso-honey sauce on the side. Bon appétit!
Per serving: Calories: 375; Fat: 11.2g; Sodium: 1466mg; Total Carbs: 21g; Net Carbs: 9g; Fiber: 2g; Sugars: 12.8g; Protein: 46.4g

Lemon Jumbo Scallops

Prep Time: 10 minutes | Cook time: 11 minutes | Serves 4

8 jumbo scallops	1 teaspoon garlic, minced
1 teaspoon sesame oil	1 tablespoon oyster sauce
Sea salt and red pepper flakes, to season	1 tablespoon soy sauce
1 tablespoon coconut oil	¼ cup coconut milk
1 Thai chili, deveined and minced	2 tablespoons fresh lime juice

1. Mix up the 1 teaspoon of sesame oil, salt, red pepper and the jumbo scallops that have been patted dry in advance. 2. Cook the jumbo scallops in your Air Fryer at 400 degrees F/ 205 degrees C for 4 minutes. 3. After that, turn them over and cook an additional 3 minutes. 4. While cooking the scallops, in a frying pan, heat the coconut oil over medium-high heat. 5. Once hot, add the Thai chili, garlic and cook for 1 minute or so until just tender and fragrant. 6. Add in the soy sauce, coconut milk, and oyster sauce and continue to simmer, partially covered, for 5 minutes longer. 7. Lastly, add fresh lime juice and stir to combine well. 8. Add the warm scallops to the sauce and serve immediately.
Per serving: Calories: 337; Fat: 18.1g; Sodium: 795mg; Total Carbs: 11.5g; Net Carbs: 5g; Fiber: 0.4g; Sugars: 6.6g; Protein: 20.6g

Typical Crab Cakes with Lemon Wedges

Prep Time: 10 minutes | Cook time: 10 minutes | Serves 3

1 egg, beaten	1 teaspoon deli mustard
2 tablespoons milk	1 teaspoon Sriracha sauce
2 crustless bread slices	Sea salt, to taste
1 pound lump crabmeat	Ground black pepper, to taste
2 tablespoons scallions, chopped	4 lemon wedges, for serving
1 garlic clove, minced	

1. Beat the egg and milk until white and frothy, then add the bread in and let it soak for a few minutes. 2. In addition to the lemon wedges, stir in the remaining ingredients. 3. Form 4 equal-size patties, place the patties in the cooking basket of your air fryer and then spray them with a non-stick cooking spray. 4. Arrange the basket to the air fryer and cook the patties at 400 degrees F/ 205 degrees C for 10 minutes, flipping halfway through. 5. Serve warm, garnished with lemon wedges. Bon appétit!
Per serving: Calories: 239; Fat: 5.1g; Sodium: 582mg; Total Carbs: 12g; Net Carbs: 7g; Fiber: 1.1g; Sugars: 1.6g; Protein: 35g

Garlic Butter Scallops with Lemon Zest

Prep Time: 10 minutes | Cook time: 8 minutes | Serves 2

½ pound scallops	¼ teaspoon dried basil
Coarse sea salt, to taste	2 tablespoons butter pieces, cold
Ground black pepper, to taste	1 teaspoon garlic, minced
¼ teaspoon cayenne pepper	1 teaspoon lemon zest
¼ teaspoon dried oregano	

1. Sprinkle the salt, black pepper, cayenne pepper, oregano and basil on the scallops. 2. Spray the scallops with a nonstick cooking oil and transfer them to the cooking basket of your air fryer. 3. Cook the scallops at 400 degrees F/ 205 degrees C for 6 to 7 minutes, shaking the air fryer basket halfway through the cooking time. 4. At the same time, in a small saucepan, melt the butter over medium-high heat. 5. Once hot, add in the garlic and continue to sauté for about 1 minute, until fragrant. 6. Add in lemon zest, taste and adjust the seasonings. 7. Spoon the garlic butter over the warm scallops and serve.
Per serving: Calories: 104; Fat: 0.9g; Sodium: 183mg; Total Carbs: 3g; Net Carbs: 1g; Fiber: 0.2g; Sugars: 0.1g; Protein: 19.2g

Cajun Shrimp with Veggie

Prep Time: 15 minutes | Cook time: 20 minutes | Serves: 4

50 small shrimp	1 bag of frozen mix vegetables
1 tablespoon Cajun seasoning	1 tablespoon olive oil

1. Line air fryer basket with aluminum foil. 2. Add all the recipe ingredients into the suitable mixing bowl and toss well. 3. Transfer shrimp and vegetable mixture into the air fryer basket and cook at almost 350 degrees F/ 175 degrees C for almost 10 minutes. 4. Toss well and cook for almost 10 minutes more. 5. Serve and enjoy.
Per serving: Calories: 357; Fat: 8.2g; Sodium: 709mg; Total Carbs: 4g; Net Carbs: 2g; Fiber: 0g; Sugars: 0g; Protein: 62.7g

Flavor Moroccan Harissa Shrimp

Prep Time: 10 minutes | Cook time: 10 minutes | Serves 3

1-pound breaded shrimp, frozen	1 teaspoon coriander seeds
1 teaspoon extra-virgin olive oil	1 teaspoon caraway seeds
Sea salt, to taste	1 teaspoon crushed red pepper
Ground black pepper, to taste	1 teaspoon fresh garlic, minced

1. Arrange the breaded shrimp tossed with olive oil to the cooking basket and then arrange the basket to the air fryer. 2. Cook the shrimp at 400 degrees F/ 205 degrees C for 5 minutes. 3. After 5 minutes, shake the basket and cook an additional 4 minutes. 4. During cooking, mix the remaining ingredients until well combined. 5. Taste and adjust seasonings. 6. Toss the warm shrimp with the harissa sauce and serve immediately. Enjoy!
Per serving: Calories: 438; Fat: 24.7g; Sodium: 1334mg; Total Carbs: 37g; Net Carbs: 19g; Fiber: 0.5g; Sugars: 0.1g; Protein: 17.7g

Pancetta-Wrapped Scallops with Pancetta Slices

Prep Time: 10 minutes | Cook time: 10 minutes | Serves 3

1 pound sea scallops	½ teaspoon dried dill
1 tablespoon deli mustard	Sea salt, to taste
2 tablespoons soy sauce	Ground black pepper, to taste
¼ teaspoon shallot powder	4 ounces' pancetta slices
¼ teaspoon garlic powder	

1. Transfer the sea scallops that have patted dry in advance to a mixing bowl, the add the deli mustard, soy sauce, shallot powder, garlic powder, dill, salt, black pepper and toss well. 2. Use a bacon slice to wrap one scallop, when finished, transfer the scallop wraps to the cooking basket. 3. Cook the scallop wraps in your Air Fryer at 400 degrees F/ 205 degrees C for 7 minutes. 4. After 4 minutes of cooking time, turn them over and cook an additional 3 minutes. 5. Serve with hot sauce for dipping if desired. Bon appétit!
Per serving: Calories: 145; Fat: 1.2g; Sodium: 895mg; Total Carbs: 4g; Net Carbs: 2g; Fiber: 0.1g; Sugars: 0.2g; Protein: 26.1g

Flavor Calamari with Mediterranean Sauce

Prep Time: 10 minutes | Cook time: 4 minutes | Serves 4

½ pound calamari tubes cut into rings, cleaned	¼ teaspoon cayenne pepper
Sea salt, to taste	½ cup breadcrumbs
Ground black pepper, to season	¼ cup mayonnaise
½ cup almond flour	¼ cup Greek-style yogurt
½ cup all-purpose flour	1 clove garlic, minced
4 tablespoons parmesan cheese, grated	1 tablespoon fresh lemon juice
½ cup ale beer	1 teaspoon fresh parsley, chopped
	1 teaspoon fresh dill, chopped

1. Sprinkle salt and black pepper on the calamari. 2. In a bowl, mix the flour, cheese and beer until well combined. 3. In another bowl, mix cayenne pepper and breadcrumbs. 4. Coat the calamari pieces with the flour mixture and then roll them onto the breadcrumb mixture, pressing to coat on all sides. 5. Lightly oil the cooking basket and transfer the calamari pieces in it. 6. Cook the calamari pieces at 400 degrees F/ 205 degrees C for 4 minutes, shaking the basket halfway through. 7. Meanwhile, thoroughly mix the remaining ingredients well. 8. Serve warm calamari with the sauce for dipping. 9. Enjoy!
Per serving: Calories: 446; Fat: 21g; Sodium: 504mg; Total Carbs: 34g; Net Carbs: 18g; Fiber: 2.6g; Sugars: 2.6g; Protein: 24.9g

Salmon Fillets

Prep Time: 10 minutes | Cook Time: 7 minutes | Serving: 2

2 salmon fillets	Pepper
2 tsps. olive oil	Salt
2 tsps. paprika	

1. Rub salmon fillet with oil, paprika, pepper, and salt. 2. Place prepared salmon fillets in the "Air Fryer Basket" and Air Fry them at 390 degrees F/ 200 degrees C for 7 minutes. 3. Serve and enjoy.
Per serving: Calories 280; Fat 15 g; Total Carbs 1.2 g; Net Carbs 2g; Sugar 0.2 g; Protein 35 g; Fiber 75 g

Southwestern Prawns with Asparagus

Prep Time: 10 minutes | Cook time: 5 minutes | Serves 3

1-pound prawns, deveined
½ pound asparagus spears, cut
into 1-inch chinks
1 teaspoon butter, melted
¼ teaspoon oregano
½ teaspoon mixed peppercorns,

crushed
Salt, to taste
1 ripe avocado
1 lemon, sliced
½ cup chunky-style salsa

1. Toss your prawns and asparagus with melted butter, oregano, salt and mixed peppercorns. 2. Cook the prawns and asparagus at 400 degrees F/ 205 degrees C for 5 minutes, shaking the air fryer basket halfway through the cooking time. 3. Divide the prawns and asparagus between serving plates and garnish with avocado and lemon slices. Serve with the salsa on the side. Bon appétit!
Per serving: Calories: 343; Fat: 17g; Sodium: 434mg; Total Carbs: 11g; Net Carbs: 6.7g; Fiber: 6.1g; Sugars: 1.8g; Protein: 37.4g

Haddock Cakes

Prep Time: 10 minutes | Cook time: 10 minutes | Serves 3

1 pound haddock
1 egg
2 tablespoons milk
1 bell pepper, deveined and finely
chopped
2 stalks fresh scallions, minced
½ teaspoon fresh garlic, minced

Sea salt, to taste
Ground black pepper, to taste
½ teaspoon cumin seeds
¼ teaspoon celery seeds
½ cup breadcrumbs
1 teaspoon olive oil

1. In addition to the breadcrumbs and olive oil, thoroughly combine the other ingredients. 2. Form 3 patties from the mixture and coat them with breadcrumbs, pressing to adhere. 3. Place the patties on the cooking basket and then drizzle the olive oil on them. 4. Arrange the basket to the air fryer and cook at 400 degrees F/ 205 degrees C for 10 minutes, flipping halfway through. 5. Bon appétit!
Per serving: Calories: 241; Fat: 5.4g; Sodium: 248mg; Total Carbs: 17g; Net Carbs: 8g; Fiber: 1.7g; Sugars: 3.9g; Protein: 29.5g

Flounder Filets with Parmesan Cheese

Prep Time: 10 minutes | Cook time: 10 minutes | Serves 3

1 pound flounder filets
1 teaspoon garlic, minced
2 tablespoons soy sauce
1 teaspoon Dijon mustard
¼ cup malt vinegar
1 teaspoon granulated sugar

Salt and black pepper, to taste
½ cup plain flour
1 egg
2 tablespoons milk
½ cup parmesan cheese, grated

1. In a suitable bowl, combine the flounder filets with garlic, soy sauce, mustard, vinegar and sugar. 2. Marinate the flounder filets by refrigerating it for at least 1 hour. 3. When marinated, take the flounder filets out of the marinade and season with salt and pepper. 4. Place the plain flour in a suitable shallow bowl. 5. In another bowl, beat the egg and add milk until pale and well combined, then in the third bowl, place the Parmesan cheese. 6. Coat the flounder filet with the flour, egg mixture and Parmesan in order, pressing to adhere. 7. Coat the remaining flounder filets with the same steps. 8. Cook the flounder filets in the preheated Air Fryer at 400 degrees F/ 205 degrees C for 10 minutes, flipping halfway through. 9. When done, serve and enjoy.
Per serving: Calories: 374; Fat: 6.9g; Sodium: 957mg; Total Carbs: 19g; Net Carbs: 6.7g; Fiber: 0.7g; Sugars: 2.2g; Protein: 57.3g

Delicious Grouper Filets

Prep Time: 10 minutes | Cook time: 10 minutes | Serves 3

1 pound grouper filets
¼ teaspoon shallot powder
¼ teaspoon porcini powder
1 teaspoon fresh garlic, minced
½ teaspoon cayenne pepper
½ teaspoon hot paprika

¼ teaspoon oregano
½ teaspoon marjoram
½ teaspoon sage
1 tablespoon butter, melted
Sea salt and black pepper, to taste

1. Use the kitchen towels to pat dry the grouper filets. 2. Mix up the remaining ingredients until well incorporated, then rub the grouper filets on all sides with the mixture. 3. Cook the grouper filets in the preheated Air Fryer at 400 degrees F/ 205 degrees C for 10 minutes,

flipping halfway through. 4. Serve over hot rice if desired. Bon appétit!
Per serving: Calories: 355; Fat: 7.4g; Sodium: 170mg; Total Carbs: 0.7g; Net Carbs: 0g; Fiber: 0.2g; Sugars: 0.1g; Protein: 67.1g

Mayo Shrimp

Prep Time: 10 minutes | Cook Time: 8 minutes | Serving: 2

½ lb. shrimp, peeled
½ tbsp. ketchup
1 ½ tbsps. mayonnaise
¼ tsp. paprika

½ tsp. sriracha
½ tbsp. garlic, minced
¼ tsp. salt

1. In a suitable bowl, mix mayonnaise, paprika, sriracha, garlic, ketchup, and salt. 2. Add shrimp into the bowl and coat well. 3. Spray "Air Fryer Basket" with some cooking spray. 4. Transfer shrimps into the "Air Fryer Basket" and Air Fry them at 325 degrees F/ 160 degrees C for 8 minutes. 5. Shake the basket halfway through cooking. 6. Serve and enjoy.
Per serving: Calories 185; Total Carbs 6 g; Net Carbs 2g; Protein 25 g; Fat 5.7g; Sugar 1.6 g; Fiber 2g

Hot Sauce Crab Dip

Prep Time: 10 minutes | Cook Time: 7 minutes | Serving: 2

½ cup crabmeat, cooked
½ tsp. pepper
1 tbsp. hot sauce
¼ cup scallions
1 cup cheese, grated

1 tbsp. mayonnaise
1 tbsp. parsley, chopped
1 tbsp. lemon juice
¼ tsp. salt

1. In an air fryer baking dish, mix crabmeat, hot sauce, scallions, cheese, mayonnaise, pepper, and salt. 2. Place dish into the "Air Fryer Basket" and Air Fry the food at 400 degrees F/ 205 degrees C for 7 minutes. 3. Add parsley and lemon juice. Stir well. 4. Serve and enjoy.
Per serving: Calories 295; Fat 21 g; Total Carbs 4 g; Net Carbs 2g; Sugar 1.3 g; Protein 20 g; Fiber 9 g

Fish Packets

Prep Time: 10 minutes | Cook Time: 15 minutes | Serving: 2

2 cod fish fillets
½ tsp. dried tarragon
½ cup bell peppers, sliced
¼ cup celery, cut into julienne
½ cup carrots, cut into julienne

1 tbsp. olive oil
1 tbsp. lemon juice
2 pats butter, melted
Pepper
Salt

1. In a suitable bowl, mix the butter, lemon juice, tarragon, and salt. Add vegetables and toss well. Set aside. 2. Take 2 parchments paper pieces to fold vegetables and fish. 3. Spray fish with some cooking spray and season with pepper and salt. 4. Place a fish fillet on each baking paper piece and top with vegetables. 5. Fold baking paper around the fish and vegetables. 6. Place vegie fish packets into the "Air Fryer Basket" and Air Fry them at 350 degrees F/ 175 degrees C for 15 minutes. 7. Serve and enjoy.
Per serving: Calories 281; Fat 8 g; Total Carbs 6 g; Net Carbs 2g; Sugar 3 g; Protein 41 g; Fiber 1g

Air Fried Scallops

Prep Time: 10 minutes | Cook Time: 10 minutes | Serving: 2

8 sea scallops
1 tbsp. tomato paste
¾ cup heavy whipping cream
12 oz. frozen spinach, thawed and drained

1 tsp. garlic, minced
1 tbsp. fresh basil, chopped
½ tsp. pepper
½ tsp. salt

1. Spray "Air Fryer Basket" with some cooking spray. 2. Add spinach in the pan. Spray scallops with some cooking spray and season with pepper and salt. 3. Place scallops on top of spinach. 4. In a suitable bowl, mix garlic, basil, tomato paste, whipping cream, pepper, and salt and pour over scallops and spinach. 5. Place pan into the air fryer and Air Fry the food at 350 degrees F/ 175 degrees C for 10 minutes. 6. Serve and enjoy.
Per serving: Calories 311; Fat 18.3 g; Total Carbs 12 g; Net Carbs 2g; Sugar 1 g; Protein 26 g; Fiber 1 g

Spicy Prawns

Prep Time: 10 minutes | Cook Time: 8 minutes | Serving: 2

6 prawns
¼ tsp. pepper
½ tsp. chili powder

1 tsp. chili flakes
¼ tsp. salt

1. At 350 degrees F/ 175 degrees C, preheat your Air Fryer. 2. In a suitable bowl, mix spices add prawns. 3. Spray "Air Fryer Basket" with some cooking spray. 4. Transfer prawns into the "Air Fryer Basket" and Air Fry them for 8 minutes. 5. Serve and enjoy.
Per serving: Calories 80; Fat 1.2 g; Total Carbs 1 g; Net Carbs 2g; Sugar 0.1 g; Protein 15.2 g; Fiber 1 g

Air Fried Prawns

Prep Time: 10 minutes | Cook Time: 6 minutes | Serving: 4

12 king prawns
1 tbsp. vinegar
1 tbsp. ketchup
3 tbsps. mayonnaise

½ tsp. pepper
1 tsp. chili powder
1 tsp. red chili flakes
½ tsp. sea salt

1. At 350 degrees F/ 175 degrees C, preheat your Air Fryer. 2. Spray "Air Fryer Basket" with some cooking spray. 3. Add prawns, chili flakes, chili powder, pepper, and salt to the bowl and toss well. 4. Transfer the prawns to the "Air Fryer Basket" and Air Fry them for 6 minutes. 5. In a suitable bowl, mix mayonnaise, ketchup, and vinegar. 6. Serve with mayo mixture and enjoy.
Per serving: Calories 130; Fat 5 g; Total Carbs 5 g; Net Carbs 2g; Sugar 1 g; Protein 15 g; Fiber 0 g

Spicy Shrimp

Prep Time: 10 minutes | Cook Time: 6 minutes | Serving: 2

½ lb. shrimp, peeled and deveined
½ tsp. old bay seasoning
1 tsp. cayenne pepper

1 tbsp. olive oil
¼ tsp. paprika
⅛ tsp. salt

1. At 390 degrees F/ 200 degrees C, preheat your Air Fryer. 2. Add all the recipe ingredients into the bowl and toss well. 3. Transfer shrimps into the "Air Fryer Basket" and Air Fry them for 6 minutes. 4. Serve and enjoy.
Per serving: Calories 195; Fat 9 g; Total Carbs 2 g; Net Carbs 2g; Sugar 0.1 g; Protein 26 g; Fiber 0 g

Cheese Salmon

Prep Time: 10 minutes | Cook Time: 10 minutes | Serving: 5

5 salmon fillets
1 tsp. Italian seasoning
2 garlic cloves, minced
1 cup parmesan cheese, shredded
1 tsp. paprika

1 tbsp. olive oil
¼ cup fresh parsley, chopped
Pepper
Salt

1. At 425 degrees F/ 220 degrees C, preheat your Air Fryer. 2. Add salmon, seasoning, and olive oil to the bowl and mix well. 3. Place salmon fillet into the Air Fryer Basket. 4. In another bowl, mix cheese, garlic, and parsley. 5. Sprinkle cheese mixture on top of salmon and Air Fry for 10 minutes. 6. Serve and enjoy.
Per serving: Calories 333; Fat 18 g; Total Carbs 2 g; Net Carbs 2g; Sugar 0.4 g; Protein 40 g; Fiber 0 g

Crab Patties

Prep Time: 10 minutes | Cook Time: 10 minutes | Serving: 4

1 egg
12 oz. crabmeat
2 green onions, chopped
¼ cup mayonnaise

1 cup almond flour
1 tsp. old bay seasoning
1 tsp. red pepper flakes
1 tbsp. fresh lemon juice

1. At 400 degrees F/ 205 degrees C, preheat your Air Fryer. 2. Spray the "Air Fryer Basket" with some cooking spray. 3. Add ½ cup of almond flour into the mixing bowl. 4. Add the remaining ingredients and mix well. 5. Make patties from mixture and coat with remaining almond flour and place into the Air Fryer Basket. 6. Cook the crab patties for 10 minutes, flipping them halfway through. 7. Serve and enjoy.

Per serving: Calories 184 Fat 11 g; Total Carbs 5 g; Net Carbs 2g; Sugar 1 g; Protein 12 g; Fiber 0 g

Air Fried Catfish

Prep Time: 10 minutes | Cook Time: 20 minutes | Serving: 4

4 catfish fillets
1 tbsp. olive oil

¼ cup fish seasoning
1 tbsp. fresh parsley, chopped

1. At 400 degrees F/ 205 degrees C, preheat your Air Fryer. 2. Spray "Air Fryer Basket" with some cooking spray. 3. Seasoned fish with seasoning and place into the Air Fryer Basket. 4. Drizzle fish fillets with oil and Air Fry them for 20 minutes, turning the fillets halfway through. 5. Garnish with parsley and serve.
Per serving: Calories 245 Fat 15 g; Total Carbs 0.1 g; Net Carbs 2g; Sugar 0 g; Protein 24 g; Fiber 0 g

Bacon Shrimp

Prep Time: 10 minutes | Cook Time: 7 minutes | Serving: 4

16 shrimp, deveined
¼ tsp. pepper

16 bacon slices

1. At 390 degrees F/ 200 degrees C, preheat your Air Fryer. 2. Spray "Air Fryer Basket" with some cooking spray. 3. Wrap each shrimp with one bacon slice and then place them into the "Air Fryer Basket". 4. Air Fry for 5 minutes. 5. Turn shrimp to another side and Air Fry for 2 minutes more. Season shrimp with pepper. 6. Serve and enjoy.
Per serving: Calories 515 Fat 33 g; Total Carbs 2 g; Net Carbs 2g; Sugar 0 g; Protein 45 g; Fiber 0 g

Basil Parmesan Shrimp

Prep Time: 10 minutes | Cook Time: 10 minutes | Serving: 6

2 lbs. shrimp, peeled and deveined
1 tsp. basil
½ tsp. oregano
1 tsp. pepper

⅔ cup parmesan cheese, grated
2 garlic cloves, minced
2 tbsps. olive oil
1 tsp. onion powder

1. Add all the recipe ingredients into the bowl and toss well. 2. Spray "Air Fryer Basket" with some cooking spray. 3. Transfer the shrimps into the "Air Fryer Basket" and Air Fry them at 350 degrees F/ 175 degrees C for 10 minutes. 4. Serve and enjoy.
Per serving: Calories 290 Fat 10 g; Total Carbs 3 g; Net Carbs 2g; Sugar 0.3 g; Protein 40 g; Fiber 0 g

Cajun Cheese Shrimp

Prep Time: 10 minutes | Cook Time: 5 minutes | Serving: 4

1 lb. shrimp
½ cup almond flour
1 tsp. olive oil

1 tbsp. Cajun seasoning
2 tbsps. parmesan cheese
2 garlic cloves, minced

1. Add all the recipe ingredients into the bowl and toss well. 2. Spray "Air Fryer Basket" with some cooking spray. 3. Transfer shrimp mixture into the "Air Fryer Basket" and Air Fry the food at 390 degrees F/ 200 degrees C for 5 minutes. 4. Shake the basket halfway through. 5. Serve and enjoy.
Per serving: Calories 175 Fat 5 g; Total Carbs 3 g; Net Carbs 2g; Sugar 0.2 g; Protein 27 g; Fiber 0 g

Creamy Shrimp

Prep Time: 10 minutes | Cook Time: 8 minutes | Serving: 4

1 lb. shrimp, peeled
1 tbsp. garlic, minced
1 tbsp. tomato ketchup
3 tbsp. mayonnaise

½ tsp. paprika
1 tsp. sriracha
½ tsp. salt

1. In a suitable bowl, mix mayonnaise, paprika, sriracha, garlic, ketchup, and salt. Add shrimp and stir well. 2. Add shrimp mixture into the air fryer baking dish and place in the air fryer. 3. Air Fry the food at 325 degrees F/ 160 degrees C for 8 minutes, stirring halfway through cooking. 4. Serve and enjoy.
Per serving: Calories 185 Fat 5 g; Total Carbs 6 g; Net Carbs 2g; Sugar 1 g; Protein 25 g; Fiber 0 g

Lemon Butter Salmon

Prep Time: 10 minutes | Cook Time: 11 minutes | Serving: 2

2 salmon fillets	2 tbsps. fresh lemon juice
½ tsp. olive oil	¼ cup white wine
2 tsps. garlic, minced	Pepper
2 tbsps. butter	Salt

1. At 350 degrees F/ 175 degrees C, preheat your Air Fryer. 2. Spray the "Air Fryer Basket" with some cooking spray. 3. Season salmon with pepper and salt and place into the "Air Fryer Basket" and Air Fry for 6 minutes. 4. Meanwhile, in a saucepan, add the remaining ingredients and heat over low heat for 4-5 minutes. 5. Place cooked salmon on serving dish then pour prepared sauce over salmon. 6. Serve and enjoy.
Per serving: Calories 379; Fat 23 g; Total Carbs 2 g; Net Carbs 2g; Sugar 0.5 g; Protein 35 g; Fiber 0 g

Cheesy Dip

Prep Time: 10 minutes | Cook Time: 7 minutes | Serving: 4

1 cup crabmeat, cooked	2 tbsps. hot sauce
2 tbsps. fresh parsley, chopped	½ cup green onions, sliced
2 tbsps. fresh lemon juice	¼ cup mayonnaise
2 cups Jalapeno jack cheese, grated	1 tsp. pepper
	½ tsp. salt

1. Add all the recipe ingredients except parsley and lemon juice in air fryer baking dish and stir well. 2. Place prepared dish in the "Air Fryer Basket" and Air Fry the food at 400 degrees F/ 205 degrees C for 7 minutes. 3. Add parsley and lemon juice. Mix well. 4. Serve and enjoy.
Per serving: Calories 305 Fat 22 g; Total Carbs 5 g; Net Carbs 2g; Sugar 1 g; Protein 20 g; Fiber 0 g

Almond Shrimp

Prep Time: 10 minutes | Cook Time: 5 minutes | Serving: 4

16 oz. shrimp, peeled	½ cup unsweetened shredded
½ cup almond flour	coconut
2 egg whites	½ tsp. salt
¼ tsp. cayenne pepper	

1. At 400 degrees F/ 205 degrees C, preheat your Air Fryer. 2. Spray "Air Fryer Basket" with some cooking spray. 3. Whisk egg whites in a shallow dish. 4. In a suitable bowl, mix the shredded coconut, almond flour, and cayenne pepper. 5. Dip shrimps into the prepared egg mixture and then coat them with coconut mixture. 6. Place coated shrimp into the "Air Fryer Basket" and Air Fry for 5 minutes. 7. Serve and enjoy.
Per serving: Calories 200 Fat 7 g; Total Carbs 4 g; Net Carbs 2g; Sugar 1 g; Protein 28 g; Fiber 0 g

Chili Shrimp

Prep Time: 10 minutes | Cook Time: 5 minutes | Serving: 4

1 lb. shrimp, peeled and deveined	½ tsp. garlic powder
1 tbsp. olive oil	Pepper
1 lemon, sliced	Salt
1 red chili pepper, sliced	

1. At 400 degrees F/ 205 degrees C, preheat your Air Fryer. 2. Spray "Air Fryer Basket" with some cooking spray. 3. Add all the recipe ingredients into the bowl and toss well. 4. Add the coated shrimps into the "Air Fryer Basket" and Air Fry them for 5 minutes. 5. Shake the basket twice during cooking. 6. Serve and enjoy.
Per serving: Calories 170 Fat 5 g; Total Carbs 3 g; Net Carbs 2g; Sugar 0.5 g; Protein 25 g; Fiber 0 g

Thai Shrimp

Prep Time: 10 minutes | Cook Time: 10 minutes | Serving: 4

1 lb. shrimp, peeled and deveined	2 tbsps. Thai chili sauce
1 tsp. sesame seeds, toasted	1 tbsp. arrowroot powder
2 garlic cloves, minced	1 tbsp. green onion, sliced
2 tbsps. soy sauce	⅛ tsp. ginger, minced

1. Spray "Air Fryer Basket" with some cooking spray. 2. Toss shrimp with arrowroot powder and place into the Air Fryer Basket. 3. Cook shrimp at 350 degrees F/ 175 degrees C for 10 minutes, shaking the basket halfway through. 4. Meanwhile, in a suitable bowl, mix soy sauce, ginger, garlic, and chili sauce. 5. Add shrimp to the bowl and toss well. 6. Garnish with green onions and sesame seeds. 7. Serve and enjoy.
Per serving: Calories 155 Fat 2 g; Total Carbs 6 g; Net Carbs 2g; Sugar 2 g; Protein 25 g; Fiber 0 g

Lemon Cajun Cod

Prep Time: 5 minutes | Cook Time: 12 minutes | Servings: 2

2 (8-oz.) cod fillets, cut to fit into the "Air Fryer Basket"	1 tsp. salt
1 tbsp. Cajun seasoning	½ tsp. freshly ground black pepper
½ tsp. lemon pepper	2 tbsps. unsalted butter, melted
	1 lemon, cut into 4 wedges

1. Combine the Cajun seasoning, lemon pepper, salt, and pepper in a small mixing bowl. 2. Rub the seasoning mix onto the fish. 3. Place the cod into the greased Air Fryer Basket. 4. Brush the top of each fillet with melted butter. 5. Set the cooking temperature of your air fryer to 360 degrees F/ 180 degrees C. 6. Set the timer and Air Fry for 6 minutes. 7. After 6 minutes, open up your air fryer drawer and flip the fish. 8. Brush the top of each fillet with more melted butter. 9. Reset the timer and Air Fry the fillets for 6 minutes more. 10. Squeeze fresh lemon juice over the fillets.
Per serving: Calories 283; Fat 14g; Total Carbs 0g; Net Carb: 0g; Sugar 0g; Protein 40g; Fiber 6g

Savory Breaded Shrimp

Prep Time: 5 minutes | Cook Time: 20 minutes | Servings: 2

½ lb. of fresh shrimp, peeled from their shells and rinsed	½ tsp. of turmeric powder
2 raw eggs	½ tsp. of red chili powder
½ cup of breadcrumbs	½ tsp. of cumin powder
½ white onion, peeled and rinsed and chopped	½ tsp. of black pepper powder
1 tsp. of ginger-garlic paste	½ tsp. of dry mango powder
	Pinch of salt

1. Cover the Air Fryer Basket with a lining of tin foil, leaving the edges uncovered to allow air to circulate through the basket. 2. At 350 degrees F/ 175 degrees C, preheat your Air Fryer. 3. In a large mixing bowl, beat the eggs until fluffy and until the yolks and whites are fully combined. 4. Dunk all the shrimp in the prepared egg mixture, fully submerging. 5. In a separate mixing bowl, combine the bread crumbs with all the dry ingredients until evenly blended. 6. One by one, coat the egg-covered shrimp in the mixed dry ingredients so that fully covered, and place on the foil-lined air-fryer basket. 7. Set the air-fryer timer to 20 minutes. 8. Halfway through the Cook Time, shake the handle of the air-fryer so that the breaded shrimp jostles inside and fry-coverage is even. 9. After 20 minutes, when the fryer shuts off, the shrimp will be perfectly cooked and their breaded crust golden-brown and delicious! 10. Using tongs, remove from the air fryer and set on a serving dish to cool.
Per serving: Calories: 190; Fat: 9.5g; Total Carbs 0.6g; Net Carbs 2g; Protein: 24g; Fiber: 0.3g; Sugar: 0.2g

Steamed Salmon with Sauce

Prep Time: 5 minutes | Cook Time: 10 minutes | Servings: 2

1 cup water	½ cup plain Greek yogurt
2 (6 oz.) fresh salmon	½ cup sour cream
2 tsps. vegetable oil	2 tbsps. chopped dill
A pinch of salt for each fish	Salt to taste

1. Pour the water into the bottom of the air fryer and start heating to 285 degrees F/ 140 degrees C. 2. Drizzle oil over the salmons and spread it. Salt the fish to taste. 3. Now pop them into the fryer and Air Fry them at 285 degrees F/ 140 degrees C for 10 minutes. 4. In the meantime, mix the yogurt, cream, dill and a bit of salt to make the sauce. 5. When done, serve the salmons with the sauce and garnish with sprigs of dill.
Per serving: Calories 322; Fat 22 g; Total Carbs 5 g; Net Carbs 2g; Sugar 1 g; Protein 20 g; Fiber 0 g

Breaded Salmon Patties

Prep Time: 5 minutes | Cook Time: 10 minutes | Servings: 4

1 (14.75-oz.) can wild salmon, drained
1 large egg
¼ cup diced onion
½ cup bread crumbs
1 tsp. dried dill
½ tsp. freshly ground black pepper
1 tsp. salt
1 tsp. Old Bay seasoning

1. Put the salmon in a suitable bowl and remove any bones or skin. 2. Add the egg, onion, bread crumbs, dill, pepper, salt, and Old Bay seasoning and mix well. 3. Form the salmon mixture into 4 equal patties. 4. Place the patties in the greased Air Fryer Basket. 5. Set the cooking temperature to 370 degrees F/ 185 degrees C. 6. Set the timer and cook for 10 minutes, flipping the patties halfway through. 7. When cooked, serve and enjoy.
Per serving: Calories 239; Total Carbs 11g; Fat 9g; Net Carbs 2g;; Protein 27g; Fiber: 1g; Sugar 1g

Indian Fish Fingers

Prep Time: 35 minutes | Cook Time: 15 minutes | Servings: 4

½lb. fish fillet
1 tbsp. chopped fresh mint
⅓ cup bread crumbs
1 tsp. ginger garlic paste
1 hot green chili chopped
½ tsp. paprika
Generous pinch of black pepper
Salt to taste
¾ tbsp. lemon juice
¾ tsp. garam masala powder
⅓ tsp. rosemary
1 egg

1. Remove any skin on the fish, wash and then pat the fish fillet dry. 2. Cut the fish fillet into fingers. 3. In a suitable bowl, mix all the recipe ingredients except for fish, mint, and bread crumbs. 4. Bury the fingers in the prepared mixture and refrigerate for 30 minutes. 5. Remove from the bowl from the fridge and mix in mint leaves. 6. In a separate bowl beat the egg, pour bread crumbs into a third bowl. 7. Dip the fingers in the egg bowl then toss them in the bread crumbs bowl. 8. Air Fry the food at 360 degrees F/ 180 degrees C for 15 minutes, tossing the fingers halfway through. 9. When done, serve and enjoy.
Per serving: Calories: 246; Fat: 8.5g; Total Carbs 3.7g; Net Carbs 2g; Protein: 36.6g; Fiber: 1g; Sugar: 1.9g

Fish with Chips

Prep Time: 5 minutes | Cook Time: 15 minutes | Servings: 3

Old Bay seasoning
½ cup panko breadcrumbs
1 egg
2 tbsps. almond flour
4-6-oz. tilapia fillets
Frozen crinkle cut fries

1. Add almond flour to one bowl, beat egg in another bowl 2. Add panko breadcrumbs to the third bowl, mixed with Old Bay seasoning. 3. Dredge tilapia in flour, then egg, and then breadcrumbs. 4. Place coated fish in Air Fryer Basket along with fries. 5. Set temperature to 390 degrees F/ 200 degrees C and set time to 15 minutes. 6. When cooked, serve and enjoy.
Per serving: Calories: 267; Fat: 12.5g; Total Carbs 5.1g; Net Carbs 3g; Protein: 30.8g ; Fiber: 2g; Sugar: 1.7g

Spicy Shrimp Kebab

Prep Time: 25 minutes | Cook Time: 20 minutes | Servings: 4

½ lbs. jumbo shrimp, cleaned, shelled and deveined
1-lb. cherry tomatoes
1 tbsp. butter, melted
1 tbsp. sriracha sauce
Salt and black pepper, to taste
½ tsp. dried oregano
½ tsp. dried basil
1 tsp. dried parsley flakes
½ tsp. marjoram
½ tsp. mustard seeds

1. Toss all the recipe ingredients in a suitable mixing bowl until the shrimp and tomatoes are covered on all sides. 2. Soak the wooden skewers in water for 15 minutes. 3. Thread the jumbo shrimp and cherry tomatoes onto skewers. 4. Air Fry the skewers at 400 degrees F/ 205 degrees C for 5 minutes, working with batches. 5. When cooked, serve and enjoy.
Per serving: Calories 247 Fat 8.4g; Total Carbs 6g; Net Carbs 2g; Protein 36.4 Sugars: 3.5g; Fiber: 1.8 g

Fish Fillets with Tarragon

Prep Time: 25 minutes | Cook Time: 20 minutes | Servings: 4

2 eggs, beaten
½ tsp. tarragon
4 fish fillets, halved
2 tbsps. dry white wine
⅓ cup parmesan cheese, grated
1 tsp. seasoned salt
⅓ tsp. mixed peppercorns
½ tsp. fennel seed

1. Add the parmesan cheese, salt, peppercorns, fennel seeds, and tarragon to your food processor; blitz for 20 seconds. 2. Drizzle fish fillets with dry white wine. 3. Dump the egg into a shallow dish. 4. Now, coat the fish fillets with the beaten egg on all sides. 5. Then, coat them with the seasoned cracker mix. 6. Air Fry the coated fillets at 345 degrees F/ 175 degrees C for 17 minutes. 7. When done, serve and enjoy.
Per serving: Calories: 209; Fat: 5g; Total Carbs 0g; Net Carbs 1.2g; Protein: 39.8g; Fiber: 0g; Sugar: 0g

Smoked White Fish

Prep Time: 20 minutes | Cook Time: 15 minutes | Servings: 4

½ tbsp. yogurt
⅓ cup spring garlic, chopped
Fresh chopped chives, for garnish
3 eggs, beaten
½ tsp. dried dill weed
1 tsp. dried rosemary
⅓ cup scallions, chopped
⅓ cup smoked whitefish, chopped
1 ½ tbsps. crème fraiche
1 tsp. kosher salt
1 tsp. dried marjoram
⅓ tsp. ground black pepper, or more to taste
Cooking spray

1. Firstly, spritz 4 oven-safe ramekins with some cooking spray. 2. Then, divide smoked whitefish, spring garlic, and scallions among greased ramekins. 3. Crack one egg into each ramekin; add the crème, yogurt, and all seasonings. 4. Air Fry the food for about 13 minutes at 355 degrees F/ 180 degrees C. 5. Taste for doneness and eat warm garnished with fresh chives.
Per serving: Calories: 215; Fat: 5.1g; Total Carbs 1g; Net Carbs 2g; Protein: 40g; Fiber: 0.3g; Sugar: 0.2g

Paprika Baked Tilapia

Prep Time: 20 minutes | Cook Time: 15 minutes | Servings: 6

1 cup parmesan cheese, grated
1 tsp. paprika
1 tsp. dried dill weed
2 lbs. tilapia fillets
⅓ cup mayonnaise
½ tbsp. lime juice
Salt and ground black pepper, to taste

1. Mix the mayonnaise, parmesan, paprika, salt, black pepper, and dill weed until everything is combined. 2. Then, drizzle tilapia fillets with the lime juice. 3. Cover each fish fillet with parmesan/mayo mixture; roll them in parmesan/paprika mixture. 4. Cook the food at 335 degrees F/ 170 degrees C for 10 minutes on Bake mode. 5. Serve and eat warm.
Per serving: Calories: 242; Fat: 8.5g; Total Carbs 0.4g; Net Carbs 2g; Protein: 39.9g; Fiber: 0.1g; Sugar: 0.2g

Tangy Cod Fillets

Prep Time: 20 minutes | Cook Time: 10 minutes | Servings: 2

½ tbsp. sesame oil
½ heaping tsp. dried parsley flakes
⅓ tsp. fresh lemon zest, grated
2 medium-sized cod fillets
1 tsp. sea salt flakes
A pinch of black pepper and salt
⅓ tsp. ground black pepper, or more to savor
½ tbsp. fresh lemon juice

1. At 375 degrees F/ 190 degrees C, preheat your Air Fryer. 2. Season each cod fillet with sea salt flakes, black pepper, and dried parsley flakes. 3. Now, drizzle them with sesame oil. 4. Place the seasoned cod fillets in a single layer at the bottom of the Air Fryer Basket. 5. Air Fry the cod fillets for approximately 10 minutes. 6. While the fillets are cooking, prepare the sauce by mixing the other ingredients. 7. Serve cod fillets on 4 individual plates garnished with the creamy citrus sauce.
Per serving: Calories: 212; Fat: 8.1g; Total Carbs 0.5g; Net Carbs 2g; Protein: 33.3g; Fiber: 0.3g; Sugar: 0.1g

Chapter 5 Poultry Mains Recipes

Flavorful Chicken with Bacon 53
Tasty Pasta Chicken 53
Honey-Mustard Duck Breasts 53
Sweet Marinated Chicken Wings 53
Peanut Butter Turkey Wings................................ 53
Turmeric Chicken Sticks 53
Roasted Turkey Thighs and Cauliflower 53
Simple Chicken Burgers 54
Basic BBQ Chicken.. 54
Chicken and Carrot 54
Basil Turkey with Chili Mayo 54
Marinated Chicken with Peppercorns 54
Awesome Duck with Potato Rösti 54
Crusted Chicken Tenders 54
Classical Buffalo Wings 55
Grilled Chicken Legs with Coconut Cream 55
Garlic-Basil Turkey Breast 55
Creamy Turkey Sausage Cups 55
Mayonnaise Taco Chicken 55
Spicy and Crispy Duck...................................... 55
Herbs Chicken Drumsticks with Tamari Sauce.............. 55
Chicken and Veggies Salad 55
Turkey Sausage Casserole 56
Cojita Chicken Taquitos 56
Chicken in Soy Sauce 56
Balsamic Turkey in Hoisin Sauce........................... 56
Grilled Curried Chicken Wings 56
Air-fried Whole Chicken 56
Marjoram Chicken Drumsticks 56
Chicken Wings with Garlic Butter Sauce 56
Tasty Chicken Fajitas 57
Chicken Quesadillas with Ricotta Cheese.................. 57
Grilled Cajun Chicken 57
Crunchy Chicken Bites 57
Crispy Chicken Nuggets 57
Rosemary Chicken with Sweet Potatoes 57
Awesome Chicken with Mustard Rosemary Sauce 57
Alfredo Chicken with Mushrooms 58
Barbecued Chicken Skewers 58
Balsamic Chicken Drumsticks 58
Garlic Chicken with Bacon 58
Marjoram Butter Chicken.................................... 58
Spiced Duck Legs 58
Parmesan Turkey Meatballs 58
Mayonnaise Chicken Drumettes with Peppers 58
Crispy Chicken Nuggets with Turnip 59
Simple Meatballs 59
Tender Chicken with Parmesan Cheese 59
Flavorful Cornstarch Chicken 59
Honey Turkey Tenderloin.................................... 59
Dijon Turkey with Gravy 59
Simple Grilled Chicken 59
Simple & Delicious Chicken Wings 59
Mediterranean Fried Chicken 60
Classical Greek Keftedes 60
Baked Chicken with Parmesan Cheese....................... 60

Chicken and Onion Sausages 60
Herbed Chicken and Broccoli 60
Roasted Turkey with Veggies 60
Spiced Chicken with Pork Rind 60
Sriracha Chicken Thighs 61
Za'atar Chives Chicken with Lemon Zest 61
Herbed Cornish Game Hens.................................. 61
Turkey Breast with Fresh Herbs 61
Turkey Breasts 61
Southern Fried Chicken 61
BBQ Chicken Breasts 61
Honey-Mustard Chicken Breasts 61
Chicken Parmesan Wings..................................... 61
Air Fryer Chicken Wings 62
Whole Chicken 62
Light and Airy Breaded Chicken Breasts 62
Honey Duck Breasts 62
Creamy Coconut Chicken 62
Buffalo Chicken Tenders 62
Teriyaki Wings 62
Lemon Chicken Drumsticks................................... 62
Parmesan Chicken Tenders 62
Simple Lemon Chicken Thighs 63
Air Fryer Chicken Breasts 63
Crispy Air Fryer Butter Chicken 63
Cheesy Chicken Tenders 63
Bacon Lovers' Stuffed Chicken 63
Chicken Fillets, Brie & Ham 63
Air Fryer Cornish Hen 63
Air Fried Turkey Wings 63
Air Fryer Turkey Breast 64
Mustard Chicken Tenders.................................... 64
Homemade Breaded Nugget in Doritos 64
Chicken Breast... 64
Breaded Chicken without Flour 64
Roasted Chicken Thighs 64
Coxinha Fit 64
Herb Air Fried Chicken Thighs 64
Chicken in Beer 64
Chicken Fillet 65
Rolled Turkey Breast 65
Chicken with Lemon and Bahian Seasoning 65
Chicken Meatballs 65
Pretzel Crusted Chicken with Spicy Mustard Sauce 65
Simple Marinated Chicken Wings 65
Western Chicken Wings 65
Perfect Chicken Thighs 65
Perfectly Spiced Chicken Tenders 65
Chinese-Style Sticky Turkey Thighs........................ 66
Classic No Frills Turkey Breast 66
Easy Hot Chicken Drumsticks 66
Crunchy Chicken Tenders with Peanuts 66
Tarragon Turkey Tenderloins with Baby Potatoes........... 66
Mediterranean Chicken Breasts with Roasted Tomatoes ... 66
Asian Chicken Filets with Cheese 66

Flavorful Chicken with Bacon

Prep Time: 8-10 minutes | Cook time: 25 minutes | Serves: 4

4 medium-sized skin-on chicken drumsticks	Salt and pepper as needed
1 ½ teaspoons herbs de Provence	2 garlic cloves, crushed
1 tablespoon rice vinegar	12 ounces crushed canned tomatoes
2 tablespoons olive oil	1 leek, thinly sliced
	2 slices smoked bacon, chopped

1. Mix thoroughly the herbs de Provence, salt, chicken, and pepper in a medium sized bowl. 2. Then add rice vinegar and olive oil inside and mix to toss well. 3. On a flat kitchen surface, plug your air fryer and turn it on. 4. Before cooking, heat your air fryer to 360 degrees F/ 180 degrees C for about 4 to 5 minutes. 5. Gently coat an air fryer basket with cooking oil or spray. 6. Then add the chicken mixture inside. 7. Insert the basket inside your air fryer and cook for 10 minutes. 8. When cooked, remove the basket from the air fryer and then add the remaining ingredients inside. Stir well. 9. Cook in the air fryer for 15 more minutes. 10. Serve the chicken warm with lemon wedges or steamed rice.
Per serving: Calories: 303; Fat: 19.2g; Sodium: 208mg; Total Carbs: 6g; Net Carbs: 2.5g; Fiber: 1.4g; Sugars: 0.9g; Protein: 24.2g

Tasty Pasta Chicken

Prep Time: 8-10 minutes | Cook time: 15 minutes | Serves: 4

¼ cup green onions, chopped	¼ teaspoon mixed peppercorns, ground
1 green garlic, minced	1 package penne pasta, cooked
4 tablespoons seasoned breadcrumbs	1 tablespoon coriander, minced
½ teaspoon cumin powder	½ teaspoon sea salt
1 cup chicken meat, ground	
1 sweet red pepper, minced	

1. Mix thoroughly red pepper, garlic, green onions, and the chicken in a medium sized bowl. 2. Mix in seasonings and the breadcrumbs until well combined. 3. Make small balls out from the mixture. 4. On a flat kitchen surface, plug your air fryer and turn it on. 5. Before cooking, heat your air fryer to 350 degrees F/ 175 degrees C for about 4 to 5 minutes. 6. Gently coat an air fryer basket with cooking oil or spray. 7. Arrange the balls to the greased basket. 8. When cooked, remove the balls from the air fryer and serve warm with cooked pasta as you like.
Per serving: Calories: 457; Fat: 6g; Sodium: 331mg; Total Carbs: 74g; Net Carbs: 41g; Fiber: 0.7g; Sugars: 1.7g; Protein: 25.4g

Honey-Mustard Duck Breasts

Prep Time: 15 minutes | Cook time: 21 minutes | Serves: 2

1 smoked duck breast, halved	1 tablespoon mustard
1 teaspoon honey	½ teaspoon apple vinegar
1 teaspoon tomato paste	

1. Mix tomato paste, honey, mustard, and vinegar in a suitable bowl. 2. Whisk well. Add duck breast pieces and coat well. 3. Cook in the preheated Air Fryer at about 370 degrees F/ 185 degrees C for almost 15 minutes. 4. Remove the duck breast from the air fryer and add to the honey mixture. 5. Coat again. Cook again at 370 degrees F/ 185 degrees C for 6 minutes. 6. Serve.
Per serving: Calories: 642; Fat: 34.3 g; Sodium: 551 mg; Total Carbs: 12.9g; Net Carbs: 3g; Fiber: 2.9g; Sugar: 9.1g; Protein: 70.8g

Sweet Marinated Chicken Wings

Prep Time: 8-10 minutes | Cook time: 12 minutes | Serves: 6-8

16 chicken wings	½ teaspoon sea salt
To make the marinade:	¼ teaspoon black pepper
2 tablespoons honey	¼ teaspoon white pepper, ground
2 tablespoons light soya sauce	2 tablespoons lemon juice

1. To marinate, combine the marinade ingredients with the chicken wings in the zip-log bag. Then seal and refrigerate for 4 to 6 minutes. 2. On a flat kitchen surface, plug your air fryer and turn it on. 3. Before cooking, heat the air fryer to 355 degrees F/ 180 degrees C for 4 to 5 minutes. 4. Gently coat the air fryer basket with cooking oil or spray. 5. Place the chicken wings inside the air fryer basket. Cook in your air fryer for 5 to 6 minutes. 6. When cooked, remove the air fryer basket from the air fryer and serve warm with lemon wedges as you like.
Per serving: Calories: 152; Fat: 5.2g; Sodium: 105mg; Total Carbs: 4g; Net Carbs: 2g; Fiber: 0.1g; Sugars: 4.5g; Protein: 20.5g

Peanut Butter Turkey Wings

Prep Time: 10-15 minutes | Cook time: 40 minutes | Serves: 4

1 teaspoon garlic powder	Sea salt flakes, to season
¾ teaspoon paprika	Ground black pepper, to savor
2 tablespoons soy sauce	1 tablespoon sesame oil
¾ pound turkey wings, make pieces	½ cup sweet chili sauce
1 teaspoon ginger powder	2 tablespoons rice wine vinegar
1 handful lemongrass, minced	¼ cup peanut butter

1. Pour enough water in a saucepan and bring together to a boil. Add the turkey wings and cook for 18 to 20 minutes. 2. In a large mixing dish, place the turkey wings and toss them with garlic powder, paprika, soy sauce, ginger powder, lemongrass, sea salt flakes, ground black pepper, sesame oil, rice wine vinegar, and peanut butter. 3. On a flat kitchen surface, plug your air fryer and turn it on. 4. Before cooking, heat your air fryer to 350 degrees F/ 175 degrees C for 4 to 5 minutes. 5. Place the turkey mixture inside the air fryer basket. 6. Cook in your air fryer for 20 minutes. 7. When cooked, remove from the air fryer and serve warm with lemon wedges and chili sauce.
Per serving: Calories: 233; Fat: 13.5g; Sodium: 766mg; Total Carbs: 16g; Net Carbs: 7g; Fiber: 1.3g; Sugars: 13.9g; Protein: 9.1g

Turmeric Chicken Sticks

Prep Time: 20-30 minutes | Cook time: 20 minutes | Serves: 4-5

¼ teaspoon turmeric powder	2 tablespoons vinegar
1 lemon juice	1 teaspoon each chili powder
2 eggs	1 teaspoon corn flour
1 tablespoon ginger paste	Breadcrumbs as required
8 medium pieces (make horizontal slits) chicken drumsticks	Salt as required
1 tablespoon garlic paste	Oil as required to brush

1. Mix thoroughly the vinegar, chili powder, lemon juice, garlic, drumsticks, ginger paste, salt, and turmeric powder in a medium sized bowl. 2. To marinate, add the bowl mixture in a zip-lock bag. Seal it and refrigerate for 4 to 6 hours. 3. On a flat kitchen surface, plug your air fryer and turn it on. 4. Gently coat the air fryer basket with cooking oil or spray. 5. Before cooking, heat your air fryer to 355 degrees F/ 180 degrees C for 4 to 5 minutes. 6. Mix thoroughly a dash of chili powder, eggs, and salt in a medium sized bowl. In a separate bowl, place the breadcrumbs. 7. Dip the chicken sticks in the egg mixture and dredge in the crumb mixture until coat well. 8. Arrange the drumsticks inside the air fryer basket. 9. Cook in your air fryer for 10 to 15 minutes. 10. When cooked, remove from the air fryer and serve warm.
Per serving: Calories: 466; Fat: 26.3g; Sodium: 308mg; Total Carbs: 2g; Net Carbs: 0.5g; Fiber: 0.3g; Sugars: 0.3g; Protein: 49.1g

Roasted Turkey Thighs and Cauliflower

Prep Time: 10 minutes | Cook time: 53 minutes | Serves 4

1 tablespoon butter, room temperature	Ground black pepper, to taste
2 pounds turkey thighs	1 pound cauliflower, broken into small florets
½ teaspoon smoked paprika	⅓ cup Pecorino Romano cheese, freshly grated
½ teaspoon dried marjoram	1 teaspoon garlic, minced
¼ teaspoon dried dill	
Sea salt, to taste	

1. Before cooking, heat your air fryer to 360 degrees F/ 180 degrees C. Toss the turkey thighs with butter. To season, rub the turkey thighs with marjoram, smoked paprika, salt, black pepper, and dill. 2. Roast the turkey thighs at 360 degrees F/ 180 degrees C for about 20 minutes. 3. Then flip to cook the other side for 20 minutes. 4. Mix the cauliflower, garlic, and Pecorino Romano, and salt together. Toss well. 5. Cook in your air fryer at 400 degrees F/ 205 degrees C for 12 to 13 minutes. 6. When cooked, serve the turkey with the cauliflower. Enjoy!
Per serving: Calories: 192; Fat: 12.2g; Sodium: 197mg; Total Carbs: 6g; Net Carbs: 2.5g; Fiber: 3g; Sugars: 2.9g; Protein: 15.1g

Simple Chicken Burgers

Prep Time: 10 minutes | Cook time: 11 minutes | Serves 4

1 ¼ pounds chicken white meat, ground
½ white onion, finely chopped
1 teaspoon fresh garlic, finely chopped
Sea salt, to taste
Ground black pepper, to taste
1 teaspoon paprika
½ cup cornmeal
1 ½ cups breadcrumbs
4 burger buns
4 lettuce leaves
2 small pickles, sliced
2 tablespoons ketchup
1 teaspoon yellow mustard

1. In a mixing dish, combine thoroughly the onion, salt, black pepper, garlic, and chicken. Then make 4 equal patties from the mixture. 2. Mix cornmeal, breadcrumbs, and paprika in a shallow bowl. 3. Dredge the patties in the breadcrumb mixture. Press the patties to coat the both sides. 4. Using a non-stick cooking spray, spritz an air fryer basket. 5. Place the coated patties inside the air fryer basket. 6. Cook the patties in your air fryer at 370 degrees F/ 185 degrees C for 11 minutes or until it reaches the doneness as you desired. 7. When cooked, remove from the air fryer and place on burger buns. Serve with toppings. Enjoy! 8. Place your burgers on burger buns and serve with toppings. Bon appétit!
Per serving: Calories: 424; Fat: 17.8g; Sodium: 1098mg; Total Carbs: 16g; Net Carbs: 7g; Fiber: 1.9g; Sugars: 2.7g; Protein: 48.8g

Basic BBQ Chicken

Prep Time: 5 minutes | Cook Time: 20 minutes | Servings: 4

2 tbsps. Worcestershire Sauce
1 tbsp. honey
¾ cup ketchup
2 tsps. chipotle chili powder
6 chicken drumsticks

1. At 370 degrees F/ 185 degrees C, preheat your Air Fryer. 2. In a big bowl, mix up the Worcestershire sauce, honey, ketchup and chili powder. 3. Drop in the drumsticks and turn them so they are all coated with the prepared mixture. 4. Grease the Air Fryer Basket with nonstick spray and then place 3 chicken drumsticks in. 5. Air Fry the chicken drumsticks at 370 degrees F/ 185 degrees C for 17 minutes for large drumsticks or 15 minutes for smaller ones, flipping when it reaches half the time. 6. Repeat with the other 3 drumsticks. 7. When done, serve and enjoy.
Per serving: Calories 145; Total Carbs 4.5g; Fat 2.6g; Net Carbs 5g; Protein 13g; fibers: 3g; Sugars: 6g

Chicken and Carrot

Prep Time: 10-15 minutes | Cook time: 30-35 minutes | Serves: 4

2 chicken breasts, make bite-sized chunks
1 cup scallions, chopped
1 parsnip, chopped
⅓ cup cornstarch
⅓ cup flour
1 carrot, thinly sliced
For the Sauce:
¼ cup dry white wine
¼ cup soy sauce
¼ cup honey
⅓ cup chicken broth

1. On a flat kitchen surface, plug your air fryer and turn it on. 2. Before cooking, heat your air fryer to 365 degrees F/ 185 degrees C for about 4 to 5 minutes. Gently coat the air fryer basket with cooking oil or spray. 3. Mix thoroughly the cornstarch, flour, and chicken chunks. 4. Place the chicken to the air fryer basket. 5. Cook in your air fryer for 20 minutes. 6. When cooked, remove from the air fryer and add the veggies. 7. Cook for 7 minutes. 8. To make the sauce, whisk the sauce ingredients in a saucepan over moderate heat. 9. Serve the chicken with the sauce.
Per serving: Calories: 339; Fat: 5.6g; Sodium: 1043mg; Total Carbs: 46g; Net Carbs: 23g; Fiber: 3.2g; Sugars: 20.8g; Protein: 23.8g

Basil Turkey with Chili Mayo

Prep Time: 10 minutes | Cook time: 40 minutes | Serves 4

3 teaspoons olive oil
½ teaspoon marjoram
1 teaspoon basil
½ teaspoon garlic powder
1 teaspoon shallot powder
Coarse salt, to taste
Ground black pepper, to taste
2 pounds turkey breast, boneless
Chili mayo:
¼ cup mayonnaise
¼ cup sour cream
1 tablespoon chili sauce
½ teaspoon stone-ground mustard

1. Before cooking, heat your air fryer to 360 degrees F/ 180 degrees

C. 2. Combine thoroughly the spices with olive oil in a mixing bowl. 3. Using the spice mixture, rub the turkey to coat the turkey on all sides. 4. Cook in your air fryer for 40 minutes. Flip the turkey halfway through cooking. When cooked, the internal temperature should be 165 degrees F/ 75 degrees C. 5. To make the chili mayo, mix all the ingredients. Cool the sauce in the refrigerator until ready to serve. 6. Slice the turkey breast against the grain skin-side up. 7. Serve the meal with chili mayo. Enjoy your meal.
Per serving: Calories: 356; Fat: 15.2g; Sodium: 2509mg; Total Carbs: 14g; Net Carbs: 9.5g; Fiber: 1.2g; Sugars: 9.1g; Protein: 39.4g

Marinated Chicken with Peppercorns

Prep Time: 10-15 minutes | Cook time: 15 minutes | Serves: 4

1 ½ cups all-purpose flour
Salt, as needed
½ teaspoon peppercorns, cracked
1 teaspoon shallot powder
¾ cup of buttermilk
1 pound chicken tenders
½ teaspoon cumin powder
1 tablespoon sesame oil
1 ½ teaspoon smoked cayenne pepper

1. In a deep marinade dish, add chicken and the buttermilk and stir gently to coat well. Marinate the chicken for 1 hour. 2. Mix thoroughly all seasonings with the flour in a medium sized bowl. 3. Dredge the chicken in the seasoning-flour mixture and coat well. 4. Then add in the buttermilk and put in the flour mixture to coat. 5. Using sesame oil, grease the chicken. 6. On a flat kitchen surface, plug your air fryer and turn it on. 7. Before cooking, heat your air fryer to 365 degrees F/ 185 degrees C for about 4 to 5 minutes. 8. Spread the chicken tenders in the air fryer basket and insert the basket inside your air fryer. 9. Cook for 15 minutes. 10. During cooking, shake the basket every 5 minutes. 11. When cooked, remove from the air fryer and serve warm.
Per serving: Calories: 436; Fat: 12.7g; Sodium: 186mg; Total Carbs: 38g; Net Carbs: 23.5g; Fiber: 1.4g; Sugars: 2.3g; Protein: 39.3g

Awesome Duck with Potato Rösti

Prep Time: 10 minutes | Cook time: 15 minutes | Serves 2

½ pound duck breast, skin-on, boneless
1 clove garlic, halved
Coarse sea salt, to taste
Ground black pepper, to taste
½ teaspoon marjoram
¼ teaspoon mustard seeds
¼ teaspoon fennel seeds
Potato Rösti:
½ pound potatoes, grated
2 tablespoons butter, melted
1 teaspoon fresh rosemary, chopped
Coarse sea salt, to taste
Ground black pepper, to taste

1. Butterfly the duck breast to render the fat: and season with fresh garlic on all sides. 2. To season, add salt, marjoram, mustard seeds, fennel seeds, and pepper. 3. Transfer the duck breast onto the air fryer basket skin-side up. Cook the duck breast in your air fryer at 400 degrees F/ 205 degrees C for 10 minutes. Flip the duck breast halfway through cooking. 4. When cooked, rest for 5 to 8 minutes before serving. 5. To make the potato rösti, mix all the ingredients in a bowl until well combined. Then make 2 equal patties from the mixture. 6. Cook the potato rösti at 400 degrees F/ 205 degrees C for 15 minutes. 7. When cooked, remove from the air fryer and serve the warm duck breast with potato rösti.
Per serving: Calories: 334; Fat: 16.4g; Sodium: 90mg; Total Carbs: 19g; Net Carbs: 6.7g; Fiber: 3.2g; Sugars: 1.4g; Protein: 27.3g

Crusted Chicken Tenders

Prep Time: 10 minutes | Cook time: 10 minutes | Serves 3

1 pound chicken tenders
Sea salt and black pepper, to taste
½ teaspoon shallot powder
½ teaspoon porcini powder
½ teaspoon dried rosemary
⅓ cup tortilla chips, crushed

1. Before cooking, heat your air fryer to 360 degrees F/ 180 degrees C. 2. Rub salt, shallot powder, dried rosemary, pepper, tortilla chips, and porcini powder over the chicken tenders. 3. Using a nonstick cooking spray, spritz the air fryer basket. 4. Transfer the chicken tenders inside the air fryer basket. 5. Cook the coated chicken in your air fryer for 10 minutes. Flip halfway through cooking. 6. Serve warm with your favorite dipping sauce.
Per serving: Calories: 293; Fat: 11.3g; Sodium: 131mg; Total Carbs: 1g; Net Carbs: 0g; Fiber: 0.2g; Sugars: 0g; Protein: 43.9g

Classical Buffalo Wings

Prep Time: 10 minutes | Cook time: 22 minutes | Serves 4

1 ½ pounds chicken wings
Coarse salt and ground black pepper, to season
½ teaspoon onion powder
½ teaspoon cayenne pepper
1 teaspoon granulated garlic
4 tablespoons butter, at room temperature
2 tablespoons hot pepper sauce
1 (1-inch) piece ginger, peeled and grated
2 tablespoons soy sauce
2 tablespoons molasses

1. Using kitchen towels, dry the chicken wings and then set aside. 2. To season, add pepper, salt, cayenne pepper, granule garlic, and onion powder to toss the chicken wings. 3. Place the seasoned chicken wings evenly in the air fryer basket. 4. Cook in your air fryer at 380 degrees F/ 195 degrees C for 22 minutes until both sides are golden brown. 5. Meanwhile, mix together hot pepper sauce, soy sauce, molasses, butter, and ginger. 6. Drizzle the sauce mixture over the chicken wings. 7. Serve hot. Enjoy!
Per serving: Calories: 464; Fat: 24.2g; Sodium: 683mg; Total Carbs: 9g; Net Carbs: 4.3g; Fiber: 0.3g; Sugars: 6g; Protein: 50.1g

Grilled Chicken Legs with Coconut Cream

Prep Time: 15 minutes | Cook time: 25 minutes | Serves: 4

4 big chicken legs
5 teaspoons turmeric powder
2 tablespoons ginger grated
Black pepper and salt to taste
4 tablespoons coconut cream

1. In a suitable bowl, mix salt, black pepper, ginger, turmeric, and cream, whisk well. 2. Add chicken pieces, coat and marinate for 2 hours. 3. Transfer chicken to the preheated air fryer and cook at almost 370 degrees F/ 185 degrees C for 25 minutes. 4. Serve.
Per serving: Calories: 301; Fat: 11.2g; Sodium: 413 mg; Total Carbs: 4.7g; Net Carbs: 3g; Fiber: 0.3g; Sugar: 3.5g; Protein: 42.9g

Garlic-Basil Turkey Breast

Prep Time: 10 minutes | Cook time: 42 minutes | Serves 4

1 ½ pounds turkey breast
2 tablespoons olive oil
2 cloves garlic, minced
Sea salt, to taste
Ground black pepper, to taste
1 teaspoon basil
2 tablespoons lemon zest, grated

1. Using paper towels pat dry the turkey breast. 2. Toss the turkey breast with salt, pepper, lemon zest, basil, garlic, and olive oil. 3. Before cooking, heat your air fryer to 380 degrees F/ 195 degrees C. 4. Arrange the chicken breast inside the air fryer basket. 5. Cook in your air fryer for 20 minutes. 6. Then flip the turkey breast and cook for 20 to 22 minutes. 7. Enjoy!
Per serving: Calories: 241; Fat: 9.9g; Sodium: 1727mg; Total Carbs: 8g; Net Carbs: 3.5g; Fiber: 1.1g; Sugars: 6.2g; Protein: 29.2g

Creamy Turkey Sausage Cups

Prep Time: 10 minutes | Cook time: 11 minutes | Serves 2

1 smoked turkey sausage, chopped
4 eggs
4 tablespoons cream cheese
4 tablespoons cheddar cheese, shredded
4 tablespoons fresh scallions, chopped
½ teaspoon garlic, minced
¼ teaspoon mustard seeds
¼ teaspoon chili powder
Salt and red pepper, to taste

1. In the 4 silicone baking cups, add the chopped sausage. 2. Beat the eggs in a suitable mixing bowl until frothy. 3. Then mix together with the rest of the ingredients until well combined. 4. Then divide the egg mixture into the four cups. 5. Cook in your air fryer at 330 degrees F/ 165 degrees C for 10 to 11 minutes. 6. When cooked, remove the cups to a wire rack and cool slightly before unmolding.
Per serving: Calories: 441; Fat: 31.7g; Sodium: 1335mg; Total Carbs: 6g; Net Carbs: 2.5g; Fiber: 0.5g; Sugars: 4.3g; Protein: 33.1g

Mayonnaise Taco Chicken

Prep Time: 10 minutes | Cook time: 20 minutes | Serves 3

1 pound chicken legs, skinless, boneless
½ cup mayonnaise
½ cup milk
⅓ cup all-purpose flour
Sea salt, to season
Ground black pepper, to season
½ teaspoon cayenne pepper
⅓ cup tortilla chips, crushed
1 teaspoon Taco seasoning blend
½ teaspoon dried Mexican oregano

1. Before cooking, heat your air fryer to 385 degrees F/ 195 degrees C. 2. Pat the chicken legs dry and set aside. 3. Combine milk, flour, black pepper, cayenne pepper, salt, and mayonnaise together in a mixing bowl. 4. Mix taco seasoning blend, Mexican oregano, and the crushed tortilla chip in another shallow bowl. 5. Dredge the chicken legs with the mayonnaise mixture. Coat the tortilla chip mixture over the chicken legs. Shake off any excess crumbs. 6. Cook for 20 minutes. Flip halfway through cooking. 7. Serve and enjoy!
Per serving: Calories: 530; Fat: 25.6g; Sodium: 432mg; Total Carbs: 25g; Net Carbs: 16g; Fiber: 1.1g; Sugars: 4.5g; Protein: 47.4g

Spicy and Crispy Duck

Prep Time: 10 minutes | Cook time: 20 minutes | Serves 3

2 tablespoons peanuts, chopped
1 tablespoon honey
1 tablespoon olive oil
1 tablespoon hoisin sauce
1 pound duck breast
1 small-sized white onion, sliced
1 teaspoon garlic, chopped
1 celery stick, diced
1 thumb ginger, sliced
4 baby potatoes, diced

1. Using cooking oil, lightly grease the air fryer basket. 2. In a mixing bowl, combine honey, hoisin sauce, peanuts, and olive oil. 3. Rub the duck breast with mixture and transfer to the air fryer basket. 4. Spread garlic, celery, potatoes, ginger and onion over the duck breast. 5. Cook at 400 degrees F/ 205 degrees C for 20 minutes. 6. Serve the duck breast with Mandarin pancakes.
Per serving: Calories: 333; Fat: 13.9g; Sodium: 93mg; Total Carbs: 15g; Net Carbs: 5.6g; Fiber: 2g; Sugars: 7.5g; Protein: 36.4g

Herbs Chicken Drumsticks with Tamari Sauce

Prep Time: 15 minutes | Cook time: 35 minutes | Serves: 6

6 chicken drumsticks
Sauce:
6 oz. hot sauce
3 tablespoons olive oil
3 tablespoons tamari sauce
1 teaspoon dried thyme
½ teaspoon dried oregano

1. Spritz a nonstick cooking spray over the sides and bottom of the cooking basket. 2. Cook the chicken drumsticks at 380 degrees F/ 195 degrees C for 35 minutes, flipping them over halfway through. 3. Meanwhile, heat the hot sauce, olive oil, tamari sauce, thyme, and oregano in a pan over medium-low heat; reserve. 4. Drizzle the sauce over the prepared chicken drumsticks; toss to coat well and serve.
Per serving: Calories: 297; Fat: 18.4 g; Sodium: 1151 mg; Total Carbs: 11.6g; Net Carbs: 3g; Fiber: 0.6g; Sugar: 10.9g; Protein: 20.5g

Chicken and Veggies Salad

Prep Time: 10 minutes | Cook time: 12 minutes | Serves 2

½ pound chicken breasts, boneless and skinless
1 cup grape tomatoes, halved
1 Serrano pepper, deveined and chopped
2 bell peppers, deveined and chopped
2 tablespoons olives, pitted and sliced
1 cucumber, sliced
1 red onion, sliced
1 cup arugula
1 cup baby spinach
¼ cup mayonnaise
2 tablespoons Greek-style yogurt
1 teaspoon lime juice
¼ teaspoon oregano
¼ teaspoon basil
¼ teaspoon red pepper flakes, crushed
Sea salt, to taste
Ground black pepper, to taste

1. Before cooking, heat your air fryer to 380 degrees F/ 195 degrees C. 2. Using a nonstick cooking oil, spray the chicken breasts. 3. Transfer the chicken breasts inside the air fryer basket. 4. Cook in your air fryer for 12 minutes. 5. When the cooking time is up, cool for a while and cut into strips. 6. In a salad bowl, add the chicken strips and the remaining ingredients. Then place in your refrigerator. 7. When ready, serve and enjoy!
Per serving: Calories: 447; Fat: 20g; Sodium: 407mg; Total Carbs: 32g; Net Carbs: 12g; Fiber: 5.6g; Sugars: 15.5g; Protein: 37.5g

Turkey Sausage Casserole

Prep Time: 10 minutes | Cook time: 12 minutes | Serves 5

4 tablespoons bacon bits	½ teaspoon smoked paprika
1 pound turkey sausage, chopped	Sea salt, to taste
½ cup sour cream	Ground black pepper, to your
1 cup milk	liking
5 eggs	1 cup Colby cheese, shredded

1. Lightly grease a suitable baking dish. 2. Add the bacon bites and chopped sausage in the dish. 3. Combine thoroughly milk, eggs, salt, black pepper, and paprika in a mixing dish. 4. Add the mixture inside the baking dish. 5. Cook in your air fryer at 310 degrees F/ 95 degrees C for about 10 minutes. 6. Sprinkle Colby cheese on the top and continue cooking for 2 minutes or until the cheese is bubbly. 7. Enjoy!
Per serving: Calories: 513; Fat: 41.3g; Sodium: 1053mg; Total Carbs: 3g; Net Carbs: 1g; Fiber: 0.1g; Sugars: 2.3g; Protein: 30.4g

Cojita Chicken Taquitos

Prep Time: 10 minutes | Cook time: 18 minutes | Serves 3

1 pound chicken breast, boneless	½ teaspoon garlic powder
Sea salt, to taste	½ teaspoon mustard powder
Ground black pepper, to taste	1 cup Cotija cheese, shredded
½ teaspoon cayenne pepper	6 corn tortillas
½ teaspoon onion powder	

1. Before cooking, heat your air fryer to 380 degrees F/ 195 degrees C. 2. To season, rub the chicken with black pepper, onion powder, mustard power, garlic powder, cayenne paper, and salt. 3. Cook the seasoned chicken in the preheated air fryer for 12 minutes. Halfway through cooking, flip the chicken to evenly cook the meal. 4. Then remove the chicken from the air fryer and cool. On a cutting board, shred the chicken with two forks. 5. Place the chicken and Cojita cheese on the taquitos. Then roll them up. 6. Bake in your air fryer at 390 degrees F/ 200 degrees C for 5 to 6 minutes. 7. When cooked, remove from your air fryer and serve immediately.
Per serving: Calories: 216; Fat: 4.3g; Sodium: 95mg; Total Carbs: 16g; Net Carbs: 7g; Fiber: 2.4g; Sugars: 0.5g; Protein: 26.5g

Chicken in Soy Sauce

Prep Time: 10 minutes | Cook time: 50 minutes | Serves 3

1 pound chicken cutlets	1 teaspoon ginger, peeled and
1 teaspoon sesame oil	grated
1 tablespoon lemon juice	2 garlic cloves, minced
1 tablespoon Mirin	1 teaspoon cornstarch
1 tablespoon soy sauce	

1. Before cooking, heat your air fryer to 360 degrees F/ 180 degrees C. 2. Pat the chicken cutlets dry and set aside. 3. Combine sesame oil, lemon juice, mirin, soy sauce, ginger, garlic cloves, and cornstarch in a mixing bowl until well incorporated. 4. Brush the chicken cutlets with the oil mixture. Transfer to the refrigerator for 30 to 40 minutes. 5. Cook the chicken cutlets in your air fryer for 10 minutes. Flip halfway through cooking. 6. Serve the chicken cutlets with shirataki noodles.
Per serving: Calories: 321; Fat: 12.8g; Sodium: 475mg; Total Carbs: 4g; Net Carbs: 2g; Fiber: 0.2g; Sugars: 1.6g; Protein: 44.3g

Balsamic Turkey in Hoisin Sauce

Prep Time: 20 minutes | Cook time: 50 Minutes | Serves: 4

2 pounds turkey drumsticks	Ground black pepper, to your
2 tablespoons balsamic vinegar	liking
2 tablespoons dry white wine	2 ½ tablespoons butter, melted
1 tablespoon sesame oil	For the Hoisin Sauce:
1 sprig rosemary, chopped	2 tablespoons hoisin sauce
Salt, to taste	1 tablespoon mustard

1. Before cooking, heat your air fryer to 350 degrees F/ 175 degrees C. 2. In a mixing dish, add the turkey drumsticks, vigar, sesame oil, rosemary, and wine. Marinate the mixture for 3 hours. 3. To season, add salt and pepper in the marinate. 4. Drizzle over with the melted butter. 5. Transfer the turkey drumsticks inside an air fryer basket. 6. Cook in the preheated air fryer at 350 degrees F/ 175 degrees C for 30 to 35 minutes, in batches if possible. 7. During cooking, flip the drumsticks from to time to ensure even cook. 8. To make the hoisin sauce, mix all the sauce ingredients. 9. When the cooking time is up, drizzle the sauce over the turkey and cook again for 5 minutes. 10. When cooked, let it rest for about 10 minutes. 11. Carve the turkey into your desired size and serve. Enjoy! 12. While the turkey drumsticks are roasting, prepare the Hoisin sauce by mixing the ingredients. After that, drizzle the turkey with the sauce mixture; roast for a further 5 minutes. 13. Then allow the turkey to rest for about 10 minutes before carving and serving. Bon appétit!
Per serving: Calories: 376; Fat: 27.4g; Sodium: 362mg; Total Carbs: 9g; Net Carbs: 4.3g; Fiber: 1.3g; Sugars: 4.9g; Protein: 21.1g

Grilled Curried Chicken Wings

Prep Time: 5 minutes | Cook time: 35 minutes | Serves: 4

½ cup plain yogurt	2 pounds chicken wings
1 tablespoon curry powder	Salt and pepper to taste

1. To season, rub curry powder, salt, yogurt, and pepper over the chicken wings. Toss well to season. 2. Refrigerate the seasoned chicken wings for at least 2 hours. 3. Before cooking, hear your air fryer to 390 degrees F/ 200 degrees C. 4. When ready, transfer the marinated chicken wings onto a grill pan that fits your air fryer. 5. Grill in the preheated air fryer for 35 minutes and flip halfway through cooking to cook evenly. 6. Serve and enjoy!
Per serving: Calories: 458; Fat: 17.4g; Sodium: 217mg; Total Carbs: 3g; Net Carbs: 1g; Fiber: 0.5g; Sugars: 2.2g; Protein: 67.6g

Air-fried Whole Chicken

Prep Time: 15 minutes | Cook time: 45 minutes | Serves: 8

1-2 ½ pounds Whole chicken,	1 teaspoon Salt
washed and pat dried	Cooking spray
2 tablespoons Dry rub	

1. At 350 degrees F/ 175 degrees C, preheat your Air Fryer. 2. Rub the dry rub on the chicken, then rub with salt. 3. Cook it at 350 degrees F/ 175 degrees C for 45 minutes. 4. After 30 minutes, flip the chicken and resume cooking. 5. Serve.
Per serving: Calories: 457; Fat: 28.8 g; Sodium: 712 mg; Total Carbs: 7.8g; Net Carbs: 3g; Fiber: 2.9g; Sugar: 3.9g; Protein: 42g

Marjoram Chicken Drumsticks

Prep Time: 10 minutes | Cook time: 30 minutes | Serves 3

3 chicken drumsticks	½ teaspoon onion powder
Sea salt, to taste	½ teaspoon garlic powder
Ground black pepper, to season	1 teaspoon dried marjoram
½ teaspoon red pepper flakes,	¼ cup cornstarch
crushed	2 tablespoons balsamic vinegar
½ teaspoon shallot powder	2 tablespoons milk

1. Before cooking, heat your air fryer to 380 degrees F/ 195 degrees C. 2. Using the paper towels, pat the chicken dry. To season, rub the chicken drumsticks with all seasonings. 3. Mix balsamic vinegar, milk, and cornstarch together in a shallow bowl. 4. Dredge the chicken drumsticks in the cornstarch mixture and press the drumsticks to coat thoroughly. Then shake off any excess mixture. 5. Set the temperature to 380 degrees F/ 195 degrees C and timer for 30 minutes. 6. Halfway through cooking, flip the chicken. 7. Serve and enjoy!
Per serving: Calories: 130; Fat: 2.9g; Sodium: 44mg; Total Carbs: 11g; Net Carbs: 6.7g; Fiber: 0.3g; Sugars: 0.8g; Protein: 13.2g

Chicken Wings with Garlic Butter Sauce

Prep Time: 10 minutes | Cook time: 18 minutes | Serves 3

1 pound chicken wings	1 teaspoon garlic paste
Salt and black pepper, to taste	1 lemon, cut into slices
2 tablespoons butter	

1. Before cooking, heat your air fryer to 380 degrees F/ 195 degrees C. 2. Using a kitchen towel, pat the chicken wings dry and add black pepper and salt to taste. 3. Mix the garlic paste and butter together in a bowl. Dredge the wings thoroughly in the mixture to toss well. 4. Set the cooking temperature to 380 degrees F/ 195 degrees C and timer for 18 minutes. Then cook. 5. Garnish the chicken wings with lemon slices and serve.
Per serving: Calories: 357; Fat: 18.9g; Sodium: 185mg; Total Carbs: 0.3g; Net Carbs: 0g; Fiber: 0g; Sugars: 0g; Protein: 43.9g

Tasty Chicken Fajitas

Prep Time: 10 minutes | Cook time: 22 minutes | Serves 3

1 pound chicken breast, skinless and boneless	crushed
1 teaspoon butter, melted	½ teaspoon Mexican oregano
Sea salt, to taste	½ teaspoon garlic powder
Ground black pepper, to taste	3 bell peppers, thinly sliced
½ teaspoon red pepper flakes,	1 red onion, sliced

1. Before cooking, heat your air fryer to 380 degrees F/ 195 degrees C. 2. Using the melted butter, brush all sides of the chicken. 3. To season, rub black pepper, salt, oregano, garlic powder, and red pepper. 4. Set the cooking temperature to 380 degrees F/ 195 degrees C and timer for 12 minutes. Cook the seasoned chicken breast in your air fryer until golden brown. Flip halfway through cooking. 5. Set the chicken aside to cool for 10 minutes. Then slice into strips and reserve to keep it warm. 6. In the air fryer basket, add peppers and onions. Cook in your air fryer at 400 degrees F/ 205 degrees C for 10 minutes. Taste to adjust the seasonings and add some seasoning as you like. 7. When cooked, place the vegetables on a bowl. Stir to combine well and serve immediately!
Per serving: Calories: 240; Fat: 5.5g; Sodium: 91mg; Total Carbs: 13g; Net Carbs: 7g; Fiber: 2.6g; Sugars: 7.7g; Protein: 33.8g

Chicken Quesadillas with Ricotta Cheese

Prep Time: 10 minutes | Cook time: 10 minutes | Serves 2

½ pound chicken breasts, boneless and skinless	4 ounces Ricotta cheese
Salt to taste	2 tablespoons flaxseed meal
3 eggs	1 teaspoon psyllium husk powder
	Black pepper, to taste

1. Before cooking, heat your air fryer to 380 degrees F/ 195 degrees C. 2. Transfer the chicken inside an air fryer basket. Then cook it in the preheated air fryer at 380 degrees F/ 195 degrees C. Flip the chicken halfway through cooking. 3. Add salt to season and cut the chicken into small strips. 4. Whisk the eggs, cheese, psyllium husk powder, black pepper, and flaxseed meal in a mixing bowl. 5. Gently grease a baking pan that fits in your air fryer. 6. Transfer the mixture inside the baking pan. 7. Bake in your air fryer at 380 degrees F/ 195 degrees C for 9 to 10 minutes. 8. Spread the chicken pieces onto the quesadilla. Then pour the cheese mixture on the top and fold the quesadilla in half. 9. Cut into two pieces and serve.
Per serving: Calories: 425; Fat: 21.6g; Sodium: 340mg; Total Carbs: 5.5g; Net Carbs: 1g; Fiber: 1.9g; Sugars: 0.8g; Protein 48.9g

Grilled Cajun Chicken

Prep Time: 5 minutes | Cook time: 20 Minutes | Serves: 2

2 medium skinless, boneless chicken breasts	3 tablespoons Cajun spice
½ teaspoon salt	1 tablespoon olive oil

1. Before cooking, heat your air fryer to 370 degrees F/ 185 degrees C. 2. Rub the chicken breasts with Cajun sauce and salt. Drizzle olive oil over the chicken breast. 3. Transfer the chicken breasts in an air fryer basket. 4. Cook in the preheated air fryer for 7 minutes. 5. When the cooking time is over, flip the both chicken breasts to the other side and cook again for 3 to 4 minutes. 6. When cooked, remove onto a cutting board and slice into your desired size. 7. Serve and enjoy!
Per serving: Calories: 200; Fat: 11g; Sodium: 846mg; Total Carbs: 0g; Net Carbs: 0g; Fiber: 0g; Sugars: 0g; Protein: 25.2g

Crunchy Chicken Bites

Prep Time: 10 minutes | Cook time: 10 minutes | Serves 3

1 pound chicken tenders	Sea salt, to taste
¼ cup all-purpose flour	Ground black pepper, to taste
½ teaspoon onion powder	½ cup breadcrumbs
½ teaspoon garlic powder	1 egg
½ teaspoon cayenne pepper	1 tablespoon olive oil

1. Using kitchen towels, pat the chicken dry and cut the chicken into bites. 2. Mix the onion powder, cayenne pepper, garlic powder, black pepper, and salt in a shallow bowl. 3. Dip the chicken bites in the mixture and rub to coat the bites well. 4. Add the breadcrumbs into a separate bowl. 5. Then beat the egg in a third bowl. 6. Dip the chicken firstly in the whisked egg, and then dredge in the breadcrumbs pressing to coat well. 7. Brush olive oil over the chicken fingers. 8. Cook the chicken bites in the air fryer at 360 degrees F/ 180 degrees C for 8 to 10 minutes. Halfway through cooking, turn the chicken fingers over to cook evenly. 9. As you desired, serve the chicken fingers with your favorite dipping sauce.
Per serving: Calories: 461; Fat: 18.4g; Sodium: 283mg; Total Carbs: 21g; Net Carbs: 9g; Fiber: 1.2g; Sugars: 1.5g; Protein: 49.2g

Crispy Chicken Nuggets

Prep Time: 10 minutes | Cook time: 40 Minutes | Serves: 4

2 slices bread crumbs	1 tablespoon olive oil
9 ounces chicken breast, chopped	1 teaspoon. paprika
1 teaspoon garlic, minced	1 teaspoon parsley
1 teaspoon tomato ketchup	Salt and pepper to taste
2 medium egg	

1. To make the batter, combine together the paprika, pepper, salt, oil, and breadcrumbs. 2. Whisk one egg in a separate bowl. 3. Whisk the egg, with ketchup and parsley over the chopped chicken and press to coat well. 4. Make several nuggets from the chicken mixture and dip each in the egg. 5. Then coat the chicken with breadcrumbs. 6. Cook the breaded chicken in your air fryer at 390 degrees F/ 200 degrees C for 10 minutes. 7. If desired, serve the chicken nuggets with your favorite sauce.
Per serving: Calories: 273; Fat: 14.6g; Sodium: 155mg; Total Carbs: 1.5g; Net Carbs: 0g; Fiber: 0.1g; Sugars: 0.9g; Protein: 32.7g

Rosemary Chicken with Sweet Potatoes

Prep Time: 10 minutes | Cook time: 35 minutes | Serves 2

2 chicken legs, bone-in	Ground black pepper, to taste
2 garlic cloves, minced	2 sprigs rosemary, leaves picked and crushed
1 teaspoon sesame oil	½ pound sweet potatoes
Sea salt, to taste	

1. Before cooking, heat your air fryer to 380 degrees F/ 195 degrees C. 2. Rub the chicken legs with the garlic cloves. 3. Drizzle the sesame oil over the chicken legs and sweet potatoes. Then sprinkle rosemary and salt over them. Transfer the sweet potatoes and chicken legs inside the air fryer basket. 4. Then set the cooking temperature to 380 degrees F/ 195 degrees C and the timer for 30 minutes. Cook in your air fryer until the sweet potatoes are completely cooked and the internal temperature of the chicken legs is 165 degrees F/ 75 degrees C. 5. When cooked, remove from the air fryer and serve. Enjoy!
Per serving: Calories: 424; Fat: 12.9g; Sodium: 131mg; Total Carbs: 32g; Net Carbs: 12g; Fiber: 4.7g; Sugars: 0.6g; Protein: 42.4g

Awesome Chicken with Mustard Rosemary Sauce

Prep Time: 15 minutes | Cook time: 20 Minutes | Serves: 4

½ cup full-fat sour cream	rosemary, minced
1 teaspoon ground cinnamon	½ cup white wine
½ teaspoon whole grain mustard	3 cloves garlic, minced
1 ½ tablespoons mayonnaise	½ teaspoon smoked paprika
1 pound chicken thighs, boneless, skinless, and cut into pieces	Salt, to taste
1 ½ tablespoons olive oil	Freshly cracked black pepper, to taste
2 heaping tablespoons fresh	

1. Toss the chicken thighs with white wine and olive oil in a mixing dish and stir well to coat. 2. Then add the smoked paprika, salt, ground cinnamon, black pepper, and garlic in a bowl. Put the bowl in your refrigerator to let the chicken thigh marinate for 1 to 3 hours. 3. Roast the chicken thighs in your air fryer at 375 degrees F/ 190 degrees C for 18 minutes. Flip the chicken wings halfway through cooking. Cook in batches if possible. 4. For the sauce, mix together the whole grain, mayonnaise, mustard, rosemary, and sour cream. 5. Sprinkle the sauce on the top to serve. Enjoy!
Per serving: Calories: 348; Fat: 15.8g; Sodium: 167mg; Total Carbs: 9g; Net Carbs: 4.3g; Fiber: 1.2g; Sugars: 2.7g; Protein: 34.2g

Alfredo Chicken with Mushrooms

Prep Time: 10 minutes | Cook time: 15 minutes | Serves 3

1 pound chicken breasts, boneless	½ pound mushrooms, cleaned
1 medium onion, quartered	12 ounces Alfredo sauce
1 teaspoon butter, melted	Salt and black pepper, to taste

1. Before cooking, heat your air fryer to 380 degrees F/ 195 degrees C. 2. In the air fryer basket, add the onion and chicken and drizzle over with melted butter. 3. Cook for 6 minutes. When the cooking time is up, add mushrooms in the air fryer basket and cook again for 5 to 6 minutes or more. 4. Cut the chicken into strips. Add the chopped mushrooms and onions and stir in the Alfredo sauce. Add pepper and salt as you desired to taste. 5. Serve the chicken with the hot cooked fettuccine. Enjoy!
Per serving: Calories: 478; Fat: 20g; Sodium: 3399mg; Total Carbs: 35g; Net Carbs: 20g; Fiber: 0.9g; Sugars: 1.7g; Protein: 38g

Barbecued Chicken Skewers

Prep Time: 15 minutes | Cook time: 15 Minutes | Serves: 4

4 cloves garlic, chopped	½ cup pineapple juice
4 scallions, chopped	½ cup soy sauce
2 tablespoons sesame seeds, toasted	⅓ cup sesame oil
1 tablespoon fresh ginger, grated	A pinch of black pepper

1. Skew the tenders with any excess fat: trimmed. 2. In a bowl, mix the chopped garlic, scallions, sesame seeds, fresh ginger, the pineapple juice, soy sauce, sesame oil, and black pepper. Add the chicken skewers together with the mixture in the bowl and refrigerate for about 4 hours. 3. Before cooking, heat your air fryer to 375 degrees F/ 190 degrees C. 4. Cook the chicken skewers in the preheated air fryer for 12 minutes.
Per serving: Calories: 234; Fat: 20.6g; Sodium: 1802mg; Total Carbs: 10.6g; Net Carbs: 0g; Fiber: 1.5g; Sugars: 4.1g; Protein: 3.5g

Balsamic Chicken Drumsticks

Prep Time: 10 minutes | Cook time: 40 Minutes | Serves: 2

½ cup balsamic vinegar	2 green onions, sliced thinly
½ cup soy sauce	2 tbsps. sesame seeds
2½ pounds chicken drumsticks	3 tbsps. honey
2 cloves of garlic, minced	

1. To marinate, combine the balsamic vinegar, garlic, honey, and chicken in a zip-lock bag and refrigerate for at least 30 minutes. 2. Before cooking, heat your air fryer to 330 degrees F/ 165 degrees C. 3. Transfer the marinated chicken onto a grill grate that fits in your air fryer. 4. Cook in the preheated air fryer for 30 to 40 minutes. Flip the chicken every 10 minutes to ensure even cook. 5. While cooking, transfer the remaining marinate sauce in a sauce pan and simmer to thicken. 6. When the cooking time is over, serve the chicken with the sauce. Sprinkle green onions and sesame seeds over the meal to garnish. 7. Enjoy!
Per serving: Calories: 439; Fat: 13g; Sodium: 3781mg; Total Carbs: 7.5g; Net Carbs: 2.5g; Fiber: 1g; Sugars: 1.7g; Protein: 66.8g

Garlic Chicken with Bacon

Prep Time: 30 minutes | Cook time: 15 minutes | Serves: 2

4 rashers smoked bacon	1 (2-inch) piece ginger, peeled and minced
2 chicken filets	
½ teaspoon coarse sea salt	1 teaspoon. black mustard seeds
¼ teaspoon black pepper, preferably freshly ground	1 teaspoon mild curry powder
	½ cup coconut milk
1 teaspoon garlic, minced	½ cup parmesan cheese, grated

1. Before cooking, heat your air fryer to 400 degrees F/ 205 degrees C. 2. In the air fryer basket, place the smoked bacon. 3. Cook in your air fryer for 5 to 7 minutes. Set aside for later use. 4. Add the salt, chicken fillets, garlic, mustard seed, milk, curry powder, black pepper, and ginger in a mixing dish. 5. Refrigerate for about 30 minutes to make the marinate. 6. Add the grated parmesan cheese in a second separate bowl. 7. Then dip the parmesan bowl and coat well. Place in the air fryer basket. Decrease the air fryer to 380 degrees F/ 195 degrees C and set the timer for 6 minutes. Start to cook. 8. When the cooking time is up, flip and cook again for 6 minutes. 9. Repeat the prepare cooking steps for the remaining ingredients. 10. Serve with the cooked bacon.

Per serving: Calories: 543; Fat: 37.7g; Sodium: 936mg; Total Carbs: 19g; Net Carbs: 6.7g; Fiber: 3g; Sugars: 2.1g; Protein: 32.6g

Marjoram Butter Chicken

Prep Time: 30 to 60 minutes | Cook time: 30 minutes | Serves: 2

2 skinless, boneless small chicken breasts	½ teaspoon red pepper flakes, crushed
2 tablespoons butter	2 teaspoon marjoram
1 teaspoon sea salt	¼ teaspoon lemon pepper

1. Before cooking, heat your air fryer to 390 degrees F/ 200 degrees C. 2. Combine chicken breasts, butter, sea salt, red pepper flakes, marjoram, and lemon pepper together in a bowl and toss together to coat well. 3. Let it marinate for 30 to 60 minutes. 4. Cook in your air fryer for 20 minutes, and flip the chicken halfway through cooking. Check the doneness with an instant-read thermometer. 5. When cooked, serve with jasmine rice.
Per serving: Calories: 38; Fat: 19.7g; Sodium: 1099mg; Total Carbs: 0.8g; Net Carbs: 0g; Fiber: 0.4g; Sugars: 0.1g; Protein: 50.3g

Spiced Duck Legs

Prep Time: 10 minutes | Cook time: 30 minutes | Serves: 2

½ tbsp. fresh thyme, chopped	1 garlic clove, minced
½ tbsp. fresh parsley, chopped	1 tsp. five spice powder
2 duck legs	Salt and black pepper, as required

1. Gently grease an air fryer basket. 2. Before cooking, heat your air fryer to 340 degrees F/ 170 degrees C. 3. In a bowl, combine together herbs, salt, black pepper, garlic, and five spice powder. 4. Rub the garlic mixture over the duck legs. Then transfer to the air fryer basket. 5. Cook in the preheated air fryer at 390 degrees F/ 200 degrees C for 25 minutes. 6. When the cooking time is up, cook for 5 more minutes if needed. 7. Remove from the air fryer and serve hot. Enjoy !
Per serving: Calories: 138; Fat: 4.5g; Sodium: 82mg; Total Carbs: 1g; Net Carbs: 0g; Fiber: 0.3g; Sugars: 0g; Protein: 22g

Parmesan Turkey Meatballs

Prep Time: 10 minutes | Cook time: 10 minutes | Serves 5

1 ½ pounds ground turkey	1 egg, beaten
½ cup parmesan cheese, grated	2 cloves garlic, minced
½ cup tortilla chips, crumbled	1 tablespoon soy sauce
1 yellow onion, finely chopped	1 teaspoon Italian seasoning mix
2 tablespoons Italian parsley, finely chopped	1 teaspoon olive oil

1. Combine all the ingredients thoroughly. 2. Form 10 equal meatballs from the mixture. 3. Using a non-stick cooking spray, spritz an air fryer basket. 4. Place the meatballs inside the air fryer basket. 5. Cook in your air fryer at 360 degrees F/ 180 degrees C for about 10 minutes or as your desired. 6. Enjoy!
Per serving: Calories: 356; Fat: 19.5g; Sodium: 449mg; Total Carbs: 7g; Net Carbs: 3g; Fiber: 1.2g; Sugars: 1.2g; Protein: 43.1g

Mayonnaise Chicken Drumettes with Peppers

Prep Time: 10 minutes | Cook time: 45 minutes | Serves 3

½ cup all-purpose four	1 tablespoon hot sauce
1 teaspoon kosher salt	¼ cup mayonnaise
1 teaspoon shallot powder	¼ cup milk
½ teaspoon dried basil	1 pound chicken drumettes
½ teaspoon dried oregano	2 bell peppers, sliced
½ teaspoon smoked paprika	

1. Before cooking, heat your air fryer to 380 degrees F/ 195 degrees C. 2. Mix salt, shallot powder, oregano, smoked paprika, basil, and flour in a shallow bowl. 3. Mix mayonnaise, milk, and hot sauce in another bowl. 4. Coat the chicken drumettes with the flour mixture, then dip in the milk mixture thoroughly. 5. Cook the chicken drumettes in the preheated air fryer for 28 to 30 minutes. Flip to the other side halfway through cooking. 6. Keep warm and reserve the chicken drumettes. 7. Cook the pepper slices at 400 degrees F/ 205 degrees C for 13 to 15 minutes. Flip once and shake the peppers halfway cooking.
Per serving: Calories: 489; Fat: 30.8g; Sodium: 1555mg; Total Carbs: 15g; Net Carbs: 5.6g; Fiber: 1.5g; Sugars: 5.5g; Protein: 34.9g

Crispy Chicken Nuggets with Turnip

Prep Time: 10 minutes | Cook time: 32 minutes | Serves 3

1 egg
½ teaspoon cayenne pepper
⅓ cup panko crumbs
¼ teaspoon Romano cheese, grated
2 teaspoons canola oil
1 pound chicken breast, cut into

slices
1 medium-sized turnip, trimmed and sliced
½ teaspoon garlic powder
Sea salt, to taste
Ground black pepper, to taste

1. Whisk the egg together with the cayenne pepper until frothy in a bowl. 2. Mix the cheese together with the panko crumbs in another shallow until well combined. 3. Dredge the chicken slices firstly in the egg mixture, then in the panko mixture until coat well. 4. Then using 1 teaspoon of canola oil brush the slices. 5. To season, add salt and pepper. 6. Before cooking, heat your air fryer to 380 degrees F/ 195 degrees C. 7. Cook the chicken slices in the air fryer for 12 minutes. Shake the basket halfway through cooking. 8. When done, the internal temperature of their thickest part should read 165 degrees F/ 75 degrees C. 9. Remove from the air fryer and reserve. Keep warm. 10. With the remaining canola oil, drizzle over the turnip slices. 11. To season, add salt, pepper, and garlic powder. 12. Cook the slices in your air fryer at 370 degrees F/ 185 degrees C for about 20 minutes. 13. Serve the parsnip slices with chicken nuggets. Enjoy!
Per serving: Calories: 229; Fat: 8.9g; Sodium: 208mg; Total Carbs: 6g; Net Carbs: 2.5g; Fiber: 0.8g; Sugars: 1.6g; Protein: 29.1g

Simple Meatballs

Prep Time: 15 minutes | Cook time: 10 minutes | Serves: 4

1-pound ground chicken
1 egg, lightly beaten
½ cup mozzarella cheese, shredded
1 ½ tablespoon taco seasoning
3 garlic cloves, minced

3 tablespoons fresh parsley, chopped
1 small onion, minced
Black pepper
Salt

1. Add all the recipe ingredients into the suitable mixing bowl and mix until well combined. 2. Make small balls from mixture and place in the air fryer basket. 3. Cook meatballs for almost 10 minutes at 400 degrees F/ 205 degrees C. 4. Serve and enjoy.
Per serving: Calories: 253; Fat: 12.2g; Sodium: 587mg; Total Carbs: 12.2g; Net Carbs: 3g; Fiber: 1g; Sugar: 0.9g; Protein: 25.8g

Tender Chicken with Parmesan Cheese

Prep Time: 15 minutes | Cook time: 20 minutes | Serves: 2

1 tablespoon butter, melted
2 chicken breasts

2 tablespoons parmesan cheese
6 tablespoons almond flour

1. At 350 degrees F/ 175 degrees C, preheat your Air Fryer. 2. Combine the 6 tablespoons of almond flour and parmesan cheese in a plate. 3. Drizzle the chicken breasts with butter. 4. Dredge in the almond flour mixture. 5. Place in the air fryer basket. 6. Cook for 20 minutes at 350 degrees F/ 175 degrees C. 7. When cooked, serve and enjoy.
Per serving: Calories: 546; Fat: 40 g; Sodium: 231 mg; Total Carbs: 3.1g; Net Carbs: 3g; Fiber: 0.2g; Sugar: 0.9g; Protein: 40.4g

Flavorful Cornstarch Chicken

Prep Time: 10 minutes | Cook time: 40-45 minutes | Serves: 3-4

¼ cup soy sauce
¼ cup honey
¼ cup tomato puree
1 tablespoon water
1 tablespoon cornstarch
1 teaspoon garlic paste
½ teaspoon ginger, grated

1 teaspoon lemon juice
1 teaspoon garam masala
3 chicken legs
1 tablespoon peanut oil
Sea salt, to taste
Ground black pepper as needed

1. Add soy sauce, water, honey, ginger, cornstarch, garlic, and tomato puree in a medium sized saucepan. Cook to thicken until it reduces to half. Then completely cool down the sauce. 2. To marinate, combine the pan mixture, chicken, and other ingredients. Then seal the bag and set aside at room temperature for 30 minutes. 3. On a flat kitchen surface, plug your air fryer and turn it on. 4. Gently coat an air fryer basket with cooking oil or spray. 5. Before cooking, heat your air fryer

to 390 degrees F/ 200 degrees C for 4 to 5 minutes. 6. When cooked, remove from the air fryer and Place the chicken marinate inside the air fryer basket. Cook in your air fryer for 20 minutes. 7. When cooked, remove from the air fryer and serve warm with naan (Indian-style bread) or other bread as your like.
Per serving: Calories: 318; Fat: 11.2g; Sodium: 996mg; Total Carbs: 22g; Net Carbs: 10g; Fiber: 0.5g; Sugars: 18.5g; Protein: 31.8g

Honey Turkey Tenderloin

Prep Time: 10-15 minutes | Cook time: 55 minutes | Serves: 4

1 tablespoon honey
¼ cup vermouth
2 tablespoons lemon juice
1 teaspoon marjoram
1 teaspoon oregano, dried
1 turkey tenderloin, quartered

1 tablespoon sesame oil
Sea salt flakes as needed
¾ teaspoon smoked paprika
1 teaspoon crushed sage leaves, dried
½ teaspoon ground pepper

1. To marinate, combine honey, vermouth, lemon juice, marjoram, and oregano together in a zip-lock bag. 2. Seal and marinate at room temperature for 3 hours. 3. On a flat kitchen surface, plug your air fryer and turn it on. 4. Before cooking, heat your air fryer to 355 degrees F/ 180 degrees C for 4 to 5 minutes. 5. Gently coat the air fryer basket with cooking oil or spray. 6. Place the turkey tenderloin inside the air fryer basket. 7. Cook in your air fryer for 50 to 55 minutes. 8. When cooked, remove from the air fryer and serve warm.
Per serving: Calories: 175; Fat: 5g; Sodium: 67mg; Total Carbs: 5g; Net Carbs: 2g; Fiber: 0.5g; Sugars: 4.5g; Protein: 28.3g

Dijon Turkey with Gravy

Prep Time: 10 minutes | Cook time: 50 minutes | Serves 4

1 ½ pounds turkey breast
1 tablespoon Dijon mustard
2 tablespoons butter, at room temperature
Sea salt, to taste
Ground black pepper, to taste
Freshly ground black pepper, to taste

1 teaspoon cayenne pepper
½ teaspoon garlic powder
Gravy:
2 cups vegetable broth
¼ cup all-purpose flour

1. Before cooking, heat your air fryer to 360 degrees F/ 180 degrees C. 2. Rub the turkey breast with butter and Dijon mustard. 3. To season, toss the turkey with black pepper, cayenne pepper, garlic powder, and salt. 4. Transfer the turkey breast inside the air fryer basket. Cook the turkey breast in your air fryer at 360 degrees F/ 180 degrees C for about 50 minutes. Flip halfway through cooking. 5. Transfer the fat drippings to a sauté pan. Add in 1 cup of broth and ⅛ cup of all-purpose flour. Cook and whisk continuously until smooth. 6. Add in the remaining ingredients and simmer to thicken the gravy to half.
Per serving: Calories: 281; Fat: 9.6g; Sodium: 2194mg; Total Carbs: 14g; Net Carbs: 9.5g; Fiber: 1.3g; Sugars: 6.5g; Protein: 32.6g

Simple Grilled Chicken

Prep Time: 15 minutes | Cook time: 35 minutes | Serves: 4

2 pounds' chicken wings
Black pepper and salt, to taste

Cooking spray

1. Flavor the chicken wings with black pepper and salt. 2. Grease its air fryer basket with cooking spray. 3. Add chicken wings and cook at 400 degrees F/ 205 degrees C for 35 minutes. 4. Flip 3 times during cooking for even cooking. 5. Serve.
Per serving: Calories: 499; Fat: 23.8 g; Sodium: 197 mg; Total Carbs: 0.9g; Net Carbs: 3g; Fiber: 0.3g; Sugar: 0.1g; Protein: 65.6g

Simple & Delicious Chicken Wings

Prep Time: 15 minutes | Cook time: 20 minutes | Serves: 8

1 ½ pounds chicken wings
2 tablespoons olive oil

Black pepper
Salt

1. Toss chicken wings with oil and place in the air fryer basket. 2. Cook chicken wings at 370 degrees F/ 185 degrees C for almost 15 minutes. 3. Shake basket and cook at 400 degrees F/ 205 degrees C for 5 minutes more. 4. Season cooked chicken wings with black pepper and salt. 5. Serve and enjoy.
Per serving: Calories: 192; Fat: 17.7g; Sodium: 1516mg; Total Carbs:

1.7g; Net Carbs: 3g; Fiber: 0.5g; Sugar: 0.4g; Protein: 24.6g

Mediterranean Fried Chicken

Prep Time: 15 minutes | Cook time: 21 Minutes | Serves: 2

2 (6-ounce) boneless skinless chicken breast halves	2 tablespoons. capers, drained
3 tablespoons olive oil	½-pint grape tomatoes
6 pitted Greek or ripe olives, sliced	¼ teaspoon salt
	¼ teaspoon. pepper

1. Before cooking, heat your air fryer to 390 degrees F/ 200 degrees C. 2. Using the cooking spray, gently grease a baking pan that fits in your air fryer. 3. To season, add salt and pepper, as well as the chicken inside the baking pan and toss well. 4. Brown in the preheated air fryer for 6 minutes, flipping to the other side halfway through cooking. 5. Add olives, oil, capers, and tomatoes in the baking pan and stir to combine. 6. Cook in your air fryer at 330 degrees F/ 165 degrees C for 15 minutes. 7. When cooked, remove from the air fryer and serve.
Per serving: Calories: 477; Fat: 33g; Sodium: 531mg; Total Carbs: 4g; Net Carbs: 2g; Fiber: 1.5g; Sugars: 2.4g; Protein: 41.4g

Classical Greek Keftedes

Prep Time: 10 minutes | Cook time: 10 minutes | Serves 2

½ pound ground chicken	chopped
1 egg	1 teaspoon olive oil
1 slice stale bread, cubed and soaked in milk	½ teaspoon dried oregano
1 teaspoon fresh garlic, pressed	½ teaspoon dried basil
2 tablespoons Romano cheese, grated	⅛ teaspoon grated nutmeg
	Sea salt, to taste
1 bell pepper, deveined and	Ground black pepper, to taste
	2 pita bread

1. Combine together the ground chicken, egg, stale bread slice, fresh garlic, Romano cheese, bell pepper, olive oil, oregano, basil, nutmeg, salt, and black pepper thoroughly in a mixing bowl. Stir well. 2. Lightly grease an air fryer basket. 3. Make 6 meatballs from the mixture and arrange the meatballs inside the air fryer basket. 4. Cook the meatballs in your air fryer at 390 degrees F/ 200 degrees C for 10 minutes. During cooking, shake the basket from time to time to cook evenly. 5. When cooked, add the keftedes inside the pita bread. 6. If desired, serve the meal with tomato and tzatziki sauce.
Per serving: Calories: 399; Fat: 14.7g; Sodium: 572mg; Total Carbs: 30.4g; Net Carbs: 0g; Fiber: 2.2g; Sugars: 3.3g; Protein: 35.1g

Baked Chicken with Parmesan Cheese

Prep Time: 10 minutes | Cook time: 12 minutes | Serves 2

2 chicken fillets	chopped
1 egg, beaten	½ cup seasoned breadcrumbs
2 tablespoons milk	4 tablespoons marinara sauce
1 teaspoon garlic paste	4 slices parmesan cheese
1 tablespoon fresh cilantro,	

1. Before cooking, heat your air fryer to 380 degrees F/ 195 degrees C. 2. Using a nonstick cooking oil, spritz the air fryer basket. 3. Beat the egg in a medium shallow bowl, and add milk, cilantro, and garlic paste. 4. Place the seasoned breadcrumbs in a separate bowl. 5. Dredge the chicken fillet in the egg mixture and then in the seasoned breadcrumbs to coat well the fillet. Press to ensure the fillet is well coated. 6. Set the temperature to 380 degrees F/ 195 degrees C and the timer to 6 minutes. Turn the chicken over halfway cooking. 7. Drizzle the marinara sauce and parmesan cheese over the chicken fillet and cook again in the air fryer for 6 minutes. 8. Serve immediately and enjoy!
Per serving: Calories: 312; Fat: 14.6g; Sodium: 579mg; Total Carbs: 12g; Net Carbs: 7g; Fiber: 0.9g; Sugars: 1.8g; Protein: 32.7g

Chicken and Onion Sausages

Prep Time: 10 minutes | Cook time: 10 Minutes | Serves: 4

1 garlic clove, diced	½ teaspoon ground black pepper
1 spring onion, chopped	4 sausage links
1 cup ground chicken	1 teaspoon olive oil
½ teaspoon salt	

1. Mix together the ground chicken, ground black pepper, onion, and the diced garlic clove in a mixing dish to make the filling. 2. Fill the sausage links with the chicken mixture. 3. Then cut the sausages into halves and make sure the endings of the sausage halves are secured. 4. Before cooking, heat your air fryer to 365 degrees F/ 185 degrees C. 5. Brush olive oil over the sausages. Arrange the chicken and onion sausage in the air fryer basket and cook in the preheated air fryer for 10 minutes. 6. Then flip the sausage to ensure even cook. Cook again for 5 minutes or more. Or increase the temperature to 390 degrees F/ 200 degrees C and cook for 8 minutes for a faster result.
Per serving: Calories: 130; Fat: 8.3g; Sodium: 454mg; Total Carbs: 1g; Net Carbs: 0g; Fiber: 0.2g; Sugars: 0.3g; Protein: 12.2g

Herbed Chicken and Broccoli

Cook time: 15 minutes | Serves: 6

3 tablespoons dried parsley, crushed	en breasts, sliced
1 tablespoon onion powder	3 cups instant white rice
1 tablespoon garlic powder	¾ cup cream soup
½ teaspoon red chili powder	3 cups small broccoli florets
½ teaspoon paprika	⅓ cup butter
2 pounds boneless, skinless chick-	3 cups water

1. In a large mixing dish, add spices and the parsley together. 2. Dredge the chicken slices in the spice mixture until coat well. 3. Line 6 large foil pieces on a flat table. 4. Arrange ½ cup of rice over each foil piece. Then add the, 2 tablespoons of cream soup, ½ cup of broccoli, ⅙ of chicken, ½ cup of water, and 1 tablespoon of butter. 5. Then fold tightly the foil to ensure the rice mixture is sealed. 6. Arrange onto the air fryer basket. 7. Air fry the foil packets in your air fryer at 390 degrees F/ 200 degrees C for about 15 minutes. 8. When the cooking time runs out, remove from the air fryer and serve hot on plates.
Per serving: Calories: 424; Fat: 22.7g; Sodium: 710mg; Total Carbs: 7g; Net Carbs: 3g; Fiber: 0.6g; Sugars: 0.8g; Protein: 45.2g

Roasted Turkey with Veggies

Prep Time: 15 minutes | Cook time: 1 hour 15 minutes | Serves: 4

1 red onion, cut into wedges	2 turkey thighs
1 carrot, trimmed and sliced	½ teaspoon. mixed peppercorns, freshly cracked
1 celery stalk, trimmed and sliced	1 teaspoon fine sea salt
1 cup Brussel sprouts, trimmed and halved	1 teaspoon cayenne pepper
1 cup roasted vegetable broth	1 teaspoon onion powder
1 tablespoon. apple cider vinegar	½ teaspoon garlic powder
1 teaspoon. maple syrup	⅓ teaspoon mustard seeds

1. Arrange the veggies on a baking dish that fits in your air fryer. 2. Pour roasted vegetable broth in the dish. 3. Place the remaining ingredients in a large-sized bowl. Then set it aside to marinate for about 30 minutes. 4. Then add over the veggies. 5. Roast in your air fryer at 330 degrees F/ 165 degrees C for 40 to 45 minutes. 6. Serve and enjoy!
Per serving: Calories: 167; Fat: 3.8g; Sodium: 1068mg; Total Carbs: 10.3g; Net Carbs: 0g; Fiber: 3.1g; Sugars: 3.8g; Protein: 22g

Spiced Chicken with Pork Rind

Prep Time: 15 minutes | Cook time: 12 minutes | Serves: 6

4 eggs	1 teaspoon onion powder
1 ½ pounds chicken breasts, diced into small chunks	2 ½ cups pork rind, crushed
1 teaspoon paprika	¼ cup coconut flour
½ teaspoon garlic powder	Black pepper
	Salt

1. In a suitable bowl, mix together coconut flour, black pepper, and salt. 2. In another bowl, whisk eggs until combined. 3. Take 1 more bowl and mix together pork panko, paprika, garlic powder, and onion powder. 4. Add chicken pieces in a suitable mixing bowl. Sprinkle coconut flour mixture over chicken and toss well. 5. Dip chicken pieces in the prepared egg mixture and coat with pork panko mixture and place on a plate. 6. Grease its air fryer basket with cooking spray. 7. At 400 degrees F/ 205 degrees C, preheat your Air fryer. 8. Add ½ prepared chicken in air fryer basket and cook for almost 10-12 minutes. Shake basket halfway through. 9. Cook remaining ½ using the same method. 10. Serve and enjoy.
Per serving: Calories: 314; Fat: 14g; Sodium: 251mg; Total Carbs: 4g; Net Carbs: 2g; Fiber: 2.2g; Sugars: 0.5g; Protein: 41.1g

Sriracha Chicken Thighs

Prep Time: 10 minutes | Cook time: 12 minutes | Serves 2

1 pound chicken thighs	Ground black pepper, to taste
1 cup buttermilk	1 teaspoon cayenne pepper
½ teaspoon garlic paste	¼ cup corn flour
¼ cup Sriracha sauce	¼ cup all-purpose flour
Sea salt, to taste	

1. Using kitchen towel, pat the chicken thighs dry. 2. Combine the garlic paste, Sriracha sauce, black pepper, cayenne pepper, and the buttermilk thoroughly. 3. Place the chicken into the mixture and dredge until it is well coated. Refrigerate for 2 hours. 4. Add the flour in a separate suitable shallow bowl and place the chicken thighs in to coat well. 5. Set your air fryer at 395 degrees F/ 200 degrees C and timer for 12 minutes. Cook. 6. Serve and enjoy!
Per serving: Calories: 594; Fat: 18.8g; Sodium: 325mg; Total Carbs: 29g; Net Carbs: 14.3g; Fiber: 1.7g; Sugars: 6.1g; Protein: 72.4g

Za'atar Chives Chicken with Lemon Zest

Prep Time: 15 minutes | Cook time: 18 minutes | Serves: 4

1-pound chicken drumsticks, bone-in	½ teaspoon lemon zest, grated
1 tablespoon za'atar	1 teaspoon chives, chopped
1 teaspoon garlic powder	1 tablespoon avocado oil

1. In the mixing bowl mix up za'atar, garlic powder, lemon zest, chives, and avocado oil. 2. Then rub the chicken drumsticks with the za'atar mixture. 3. At 375 degrees F/ 190 degrees C, heat your air fryer in advance. 4. Put the prepared chicken drumsticks in the air fryer basket and cook for 15 minutes. 5. Then flip the drumsticks on another side and cook them for 3 minutes more. 6. Serve.
Per serving: Calories: 319; Fat: 14.7 g; Sodium: 92 mg; Total Carbs: 30.3g; Net Carbs: 3g; Fiber: 4g; Sugar: 12.3g; Protein: 24g

Herbed Cornish Game Hens

Prep Time: 15 minutes | Cook time: 16 Minutes | Serves: 4

1 teaspoon fresh rosemary, chopped	¼ teaspoon sugar
1 teaspoon fresh thyme, chopped	¼ teaspoon red pepper flakes, crushed
2 pounds Cornish game hen, backbone removed and halved	Salt and black pepper, to taste
½ cup olive oil	1 teaspoon fresh lemon zest, finely grated

1. Lightly grease an air fryer basket with cooking spray or oil. 2. Before cooking, heat your air fryer to 390 degrees F/ 200 degrees C. 3. In a mixing dish, add the herbs, olive oil, sugar, spices, and lemon zest. 4. Dredge the Cornish game hen in and stir well. Then marinate in the fridge for about 24 hours. 5. Place the marinated Cornish game hen inside the air fryer basket. 6. Cook in your air fryer for about 16 minutes. 7. When cooked, remove from the air fryer and serve hot on plates. Enjoy!
Per serving: Calories: 440; Fat: 38.2g; Sodium: 94mg; Total Carbs: 0.5g; Net Carbs: 0g; Fiber: 0.2g; Sugars: 0.2g; Protein: 25.4g

Turkey Breast with Fresh Herbs

Prep Time: 15 minutes | Cook time: 35 minutes | Serves: 4

2 pounds' turkey breast	1 teaspoon fresh thyme, chopped
1 teaspoon fresh sage, chopped	Black pepper
1 teaspoon fresh rosemary, chopped	Salt

1. Grease its air fryer basket with cooking spray. 2. In a suitable bowl, mix together sage, rosemary, and thyme. 3. Season turkey breast with black pepper and salt and herb mixture. 4. Set the seasoned turkey breast in air fryer basket and cook at almost 390 degrees F/ 200 degrees C for 30-35 minutes. 5. Slice and serve.
Per serving: Calories: 264; Fat: 17g; Sodium: 129mg; Total Carbs: 0.9g; Net Carbs: 3g; Fiber: 0.3g; Sugar: 0g; Protein: 27g

Turkey Breasts

Prep Time: 5 minutes | Cook Time: 1 hour| Servings: 4

3 lbs. boneless turkey breast	black pepper and salt to taste
¼ cup mayonnaise	½ tsp. garlic powder
2 tsps. poultry seasoning	

1. At 360 degrees F/ 180 degrees C, preheat your Air Fryer. 2. Season the turkey with mayonnaise, seasoning, salt, garlic powder, and black pepper. 3. Cook the mayo turkey breasts in the air fryer for 1 hour at 360 degrees F/ 180 degrees C on Air Fry mode, turning the turkey breasts every 15 minutes. 4. The turkey breasts are done when they reach 165 degrees F/ 75 degrees C.
Per serving: Calories 558 g; Total Carbs 1g; Fat 18g; Protein 98g; Fat 22.4g; fibers: 3g; Sugars: 6g

Southern Fried Chicken

Cook time: 30 Minutes | Serves: 2

2 x 6-oz. boneless skinless chicken breasts	½ tsp. onion powder
2 tbsp. hot sauce	1 tbsp. chili powder
	2 oz. pork rinds, finely ground

1. Lengthwise cut the chicken breasts in half and rub in the hot sauce. Combine the onion powder with the chili powder, then rub into the chicken. Leave to marinate for at least a half hour. 2. Use the ground pork rinds to coat the chicken breasts in the ground pork rinds, covering them thoroughly. Place the chicken in your air fryer. 3. Set the fryer at 350 degrees F/ 175 degrees C and cook the chicken for 13 minutes. Flip the chicken and then cook the other side for another 13 minutes or until golden. 4. Test the chicken with a meat thermometer. When fully cooked, it should reach 165 degrees F/ 75 degrees C. Serve hot, with the sides of your choice.
Per serving: Calories: 327; Fat: 13.8g; Sodium: 2376mg; Total Carbs: 5g; Net Carbs: 2g; Fiber: 1.4g; Sugars: 0.7g; Protein: 45.8g

BBQ Chicken Breasts

Prep Time: 5 minutes | Cook Time: 15 minutes | Servings: 4

4 boneless (about 6 oz.) chicken breasts,	2 tbsps. BBQ seasoning
	Cooking spray

1. Rub the chicken breasts with BBQ seasoning and marinate them in the refrigerator for 45 minutes. 2. At 400 degrees F/ 205 degrees C, preheat your Air Fryer. 3. Grease the air fryer basket with oil and place in the chicken breasts. 4. Spray oil on top. 5. Air Fry the chicken breasts for 13 to 14 minutes, flipping halfway through cooking. 6. Serve.
Per serving: Calories 131 g; Total Carbs 2g; Fat 3g; Protein 24g; Fat 22.4g; fibers: 3g; Sugars: 6g

Honey-Mustard Chicken Breasts

Prep Time: 5 minutes | Cook Time: 25 minutes | Servings: 6

6 (6-oz., each) boneless, chicken breasts	3 tbsps. honey
	1 tbsp. Dijon mustard
2 tbsps. fresh rosemary minced	black pepper and salt to taste

1. Combine the mustard, honey, pepper, rosemary and salt in a suitable bowl. 2. Rub the chicken breasts with this mixture. 3. Grease the "Air Fryer Basket" with oil. 4. Air Fry the chicken breasts at 350 degrees F/ 175 degrees C for 20 to 24 minutes or until the chicken reaches 165 degrees F/ 75 degrees C. 5. Serve.
Per serving: Calories 236 g; Total Carbs 9.8g; Fat 5g; Protein 38g; Fat 22.4g; fibers: 3g; Sugars: 6g

Chicken Parmesan Wings

Prep Time: 5 minutes | Cook Time: 15 minutes | Servings: 4

2 lbs. chicken wings. cut into drumettes, pat dried	1 tsp. herbs de Provence
	1 tsp. paprika
½ cup parmesan, plus 6 tbsps. grated	Salt to taste

1. Combine the parmesan, herbs, paprika, and salt in a suitable bowl and rub the chicken with this mixture. 2. At 350 degrees F/ 175 degrees C, preheat your Air Fryer. 3. Grease the air fryer basket with some cooking spray. 4. Air Fry the coated chicken wings for 15 minutes, flipping halfway through. 5. Garnish with parmesan and serve.
Per serving: Calories 490 g; Total Carbs 1g; Fat 22g; Protein 72g; Fat 22.4g; fibers: 3g; Sugars: 6g

Air Fryer Chicken Wings

Prep Time: 5 minutes | Cook Time: 35 minutes | Servings: 4

2 lbs. chicken wings   Cooking spray
Black pepper and salt to taste

1. Flavor the chicken wings with black pepper and salt. 2. Add the seasoned chicken wings to your air fryer basket and Air Fry them at 400 degrees F/ 205 degrees C for 35 minutes. 3. Flip 3 times during cooking for even cooking. 4. Serve.
Per serving: Calories 277 g; Total Carbs 1g; Fat 8g; Protein 50g; Fat 22.4g; fibers: 3g; Sugars: 6g

Whole Chicken

Prep Time: 5 minutes | Cook Time: 45 minutes | Servings: 6

1 (2 ½ lbs.) whole chicken,   1 tsp. salt
washed and pat dried   Cooking spray
2 tbsps. dry rub

1. At 350 degrees F/ 175 degrees C, preheat your Air Fryer. 2. Rub the dry rub on the chicken. Then rub with salt. Cook it at 350 degrees F/ 175 degrees C for 45 minutes on Air Fry mode. 3. After 30 minutes of cooking time, flip the chicken and finish cooking. 4. Chicken is done when it reaches 165 degrees F/ 75 degrees C. 5. Serve and enjoy.
Per serving: Calories 412 g; Total Carbs 1g; Fat 28g; Protein 35g; Fat 22.4g; fibers: 3g; Sugars: 6g

Light and Airy Breaded Chicken Breasts

Prep Time: 5 minutes | Cook Time: 15 minutes | Servings: 2

2 large eggs   4 to 5 tbsp. vegetable oil
1cup bread crumbs or panko bread   2 boneless, skinless, chicken
crumbs   breasts
1 tsp. Italian seasoning

1. At 370 degrees F/ 185 degrees C, preheat your Air Fryer. 2. In a suitable bowl, whisk the eggs until frothy. 3. Mix the bread crumbs, Italian seasoning, and oil in a separate small mixing bowl. 4. Dip the chicken in the prepared egg mixture, then in the bread crumb mixture. 5. Place the chicken directly into the greased air fryer basket, or on the greased baking pan set into the basket. 6. Grease the chicken generously and with olive oil to avoid powdery, uncooked breading. 7. Air Fry the chicken breasts at 370 degrees F/ 185 degrees C for 14 minutes; after 7 minutes of cooking time, flip the chicken breasts and generously spray them with the olive oil. 8. When cooked, the chicken breasts should reach an internal temperature of 165 degrees F/ 75 degrees C. 9. Remove the chicken breasts from the air fryer with thongs and serve.
Per serving: Calories 833; Fat 46g; Total Carbs 40g; Protein 65g; Fat 22.4g; fibers: 3g; Sugars: 6g

Honey Duck Breasts

Prep Time: 5 minutes | Cook Time: 25 minutes | Servings: 2

1 smoked duck breast, halved   1 tbsp. mustard
1 tsp. honey   ½ tsp. apple vinegar
1 tsp. tomato paste

1. Mix tomato paste, honey, mustard, and vinegar in a suitable bowl. 2. Whisk well. Add duck breast pieces and coat well. 3. Cook in your air fryer at 370 degrees F/ 185 degrees C for 15 minutes on Air Fry mode. 4. Remove the duck breast from the air fryer and add to the honey mixture, coat well. 5. Cook again at 370 degrees F/ 185 degrees C for 6 minutes more. 6. Serve.
Per serving: Calories 274 g; Total Carbs 22g; Fat 11g; Protein 13g; Fat 22.4g; fibers: 3g; Sugars: 6g

Creamy Coconut Chicken

Prep Time: 5 minutes | Cook Time: 25 minutes | Servings: 4

4 big chicken legs   salt and black pepper to taste
5 tsps. turmeric powder   4 tbsps. coconut cream
2 tbsps. Ginger, smashed

1. In a suitable bowl, mix salt, pepper, ginger, turmeric and cream. 2. Add chicken pieces, coat and marinate them for 2 hours. 3. Transfer the chicken pieces to your preheated air fryer and Air Fry them at 370 degrees F/ 185 degrees C for 25 minutes. 4. Serve.
Per serving: Calories 300 g; Total Carbs 22g; Fat 4g; Protein 20g; Fat 22.4g; fibers: 3g; Sugars: 6g

Buffalo Chicken Tenders

Prep Time: 5 minutes | Cook Time: 20 minutes | Servings: 4

1 lb. boneless chicken tenders   1 ½ oz. pork rinds, ground
¼ cup hot sauce   1 tsp. chili powder
1 tsp. garlic powder

1. Put the chicken breasts in a suitable bowl and pour hot sauce over them. Toss to coat. 2. Mix ground pork rinds, chili powder and garlic powder in another bowl. 3. Place each tender in the ground pork rinds, and coat well. 4. With wet hands, press down the pork rinds into the chicken. 5. Place the tenders in a single layer into the air fryer basket. 6. Air Fry the chicken tenders at 375 degrees F/ 190 degrees C for 20 minutes, flipping halfway through. 7. Serve.
Per serving: Calories 160 g; Total Carbs 0.6g; Fat 4.4g; Protein 27.3g; Fat 22.4g; fibers: 3g; Sugars: 6g

Teriyaki Wings

Prep Time: 5 minutes | Cook Time: 25 minutes | Servings: 4

2 lbs. chicken wings   ¼ tsp. ground ginger
½ cup teriyaki sauce   2 tsps. baking powder
2 tsp. minced garlic

1. Except for the baking powder, place all the recipe ingredients in a suitable bowl and marinate for 1 hour in the refrigerator. 2. Place the seasoned wings into the "Air Fryer Basket" and sprinkle with baking powder. 3. Gently rub into wings. 4. Air Fry the chicken wings at 400 degrees F/ 205 degrees C for 25 minutes. 5. Shake the basket 2 or 3-times during cooking. 6. Serve.
Per serving: Calories 446 g; Total Carbs 3.1g; Fat 29.8g; Protein 41.8g; Fat 22.4g; fibers: 3g; Sugars: 6g

Lemon Chicken Drumsticks

Prep Time: 5 minutes | Cook Time: 25 minutes | Servings: 2

2 tsps. baking powder   4 tbsps. salted butter melted
½ tsp. garlic powder   1 tbsp. lemon pepper seasoning
8 chicken drumsticks

1. Sprinkle garlic powder and baking powder over drumsticks and rub into chicken skin. 2. Place drumsticks into the air fryer basket. 3. Air Fry the chicken drumsticks at 375 degrees F/ 190 degrees C for 25 minutes. 4. Flip the drumsticks once halfway through cooking. 5. Mix seasoning and butter in a suitable bowl. 6. When cooked, add drumsticks to the bowl and toss to coat. 7. Serve.
Per serving: Calories 532 g; Total Carbs 1.2g; Fat 32.3g; Protein 48.3g; Fat 22.4g; fibers: 3g; Sugars: 6g

Parmesan Chicken Tenders

Prep Time: 5 minutes | Cook Time: 10 minutes | Servings: 4

1 lb. chicken tenderloins   ½ cup Italian-style bread crumbs
3 large egg whites   ¼ cup grated Parmesan cheese

1. Trim off any white, fat from the chicken tenderloins. 2. In a suitable bowl, whisk the egg whites until frothy. 3. In a separate small mixing bowl, combine the bread crumbs and Parmesan cheese. Mix well. 4. Dip the chicken tenderloins into the prepared egg mixture, then into the Parmesan and bread crumbs. 5. Shake off any excess breading. 6. Place the chicken tenderloins in the greased "Air Fryer Basket" in a single layer. 7. Generously Grease the chicken with olive oil to avoid powdery, uncooked breading. 8. At 370 degrees F/ 185 degrees C, preheat your Air Fryer. 9. Air Fry the chicken tenderloins for 4 minutes. 10. Using tongs, flip the chicken tenders and Air Fry for 4 minutes more. 11. Test if the internal temperature of the thickest part reaches 165 degrees F/ 75 degrees C. 12. Add Cook Time if needed. 13. Once the chicken is fully cooked, plate, serve, and enjoy.
Per serving: Calories 210; Fat 4g; Net Carbs 1g; Total Carbs 10g; Protein 33g;; Fiber: 1g; Sugar 1g

Simple Lemon Chicken Thighs

Prep Time: 5 minutes | Cook Time: 25 minutes | Servings: 4

Salt and black pepper to taste
2 tbsps. olive oil
2 tbsps. Italian seasoning
2 tbsps. freshly squeezed lemon
juice
1 lb. chicken thighs
1 lemon, sliced

1. Set the chicken thighs in a medium mixing bowl and season them with the black pepper and salt. 2. Add the olive oil, Italian seasoning, and lemon juice and toss until the chicken thighs are coated with oil. 3. Add the sliced lemons. Add the chicken thighs into the "Air Fryer Basket" in a single layer. 4. At 350 degrees F/ 175 degrees C, preheat your Air Fryer. 5. Air Fry the food for 10 minutes. 6. Using tongs, flip the chicken. Air Fry for 10 minutes more. 7. Add Cook Time if needed. 8. Once the chicken is fully cooked, plate, serve, and enjoy.
Per serving: Calories 325g; Total Carbs 1g; Fat 26g; Protein 20g; Fat 22.4g; fibers: 3g; Sugars: 6g

Air Fryer Chicken Breasts

Prep Time: 5 minutes | Cook Time: 14 minutes | Servings: 4

salt and black pepper to taste
1 tsp. dried parsley
½ tsp. garlic powder
2 tbsps. olive oil, divided
3 boneless, chicken breasts

1. In a suitable bowl, combine together the garlic powder, salt, pepper, and parsley. 2. Rub each chicken breast with oil and seasonings. 3. Place the prepared chicken breasts in the air fryer basket. 4. At 370 degrees F/ 185 degrees C, preheat your Air Fryer. 5. Air Fry the chicken breasts for 14 minutes, flipping the chicken breasts halfway through and brushing the remaining olive oil and spices onto them. 6. When cooked, the chicken breasts should reach an internal temperature of 165 degrees F/ 75 degrees C. 7. Transfer it to a platter and serve.
Per serving: Calories 182g; Total Carbs 0g; Fat 9g; Protein 26g; Fat 22.4g; fibers: 3g; Sugars: 6g

Crispy Air Fryer Butter Chicken

Prep Time: 5 minutes | Cook Time: 15 minutes | Servings: 4

2 (8-oz.) boneless, chicken breasts
1 sleeve Ritz crackers
4 tbsps. (½ stick) cold unsalted
butter, cut into 1-tbsp. slices

1. Dip the chicken breasts in water. Put the crackers in a Ziploc bag. 2. Using a mallet or your hands, crush the crackers. 3. Place the chicken breasts inside the bag one at a time and coat them with the cracker crumbs. 4. Place the chicken in the greased air fryer basket, or on the greased baking pan set into the air fryer basket. 5. Put 1 to 2 tablespoons of butter onto each piece of chicken. 6. At 370 degrees F/ 185 degrees C, preheat your Air Fryer. Set the timer and Air Fry the chicken breasts for 14 minutes; after 7 minutes of cooking time, flip them and grease them generously with olive oil to avoid uncooked breading. 7. When cooked, the chicken breasts should reach an internal temperature of 165 degrees F/ 75 degrees C. 8. Serve.
Per serving: Calories 750; Fat 40g; Total Carbs 38g; Protein 57g;; Fat 22.4g; fibers: 3g; Sugars: 6g

Cheesy Chicken Tenders

Prep Time: 10 minutes | Cook Time: 30 minutes | Servings: 4

1 large white meat chicken breast
1 cup of breadcrumbs
2 medium-sized eggs
Pinch of black pepper and salt
1 tbsp. of grated or powdered
parmesan cheese

1. Cover the Air Fryer Basket with a layer of tin foil, leaving the edges open to allow air to flow through the basket. 2. At 350 degrees F/ 175 degrees C, preheat your Air Fryer. 3. In a suitable bowl, whisk the eggs until fluffy and until the yolks and whites are fully combined, and set aside. 4. In a separate bowl, mixt he breadcrumbs, parmesan, black pepper and salt. 5. Dip each piece chicken into the bowl with dry ingredients. 6. Then submerge into the bowl with wet ingredients, then dip again into the dry ingredients. 7. Put the coated chicken pieces on the foil covering the Air Fryer Basket, in a single flat layer. 8. Air Fry the chicken pieces at 350 degrees F/ 175 degrees C for 15 minutes. 9. Flip each piece of chicken over to ensure a full all over fry. 10. Reset the air fryer to 320 degrees F/ 160 degrees C and resume cooking on Air Fry mode for 15 minutes more. 11. Remove the fried chicken

strips using tongs and set on a serving plate. 12. Eat once cool enough to handle, and enjoy.
Per serving: Calories 278; Fat 15g; Protein 29g; Sugar 7g; Fat 22.4g; fibers: 3g; Sugars: 6g

Bacon Lovers' Stuffed Chicken

Prep Time: 10 minutes | Cook Time: 20 minutes | Servings: 4

4 (5-oz.) boneless, chicken breasts,
sliced into ¼ inch thick
2 packages Boursin cheese
8 slices thin-cut bacon or beef
bacon
Sprig of fresh cilantro, for garnish

1. Grease the "Air Fryer Basket" with avocado oil. 2. At 400 degrees F/ 205 degrees C, preheat your Air Fryer. 3. Put one of the chicken breasts on a cutting board. 4. Make a 1-inch-wide cut at the top of the breast. 5. Carefully cut into the breast to form a large pocket, leaving a ½-inch border along the sides and bottom. 6. Repeat with the other 3 chicken breasts. 7. Cut the corner of a large Ziploc bag to form a ¾-inch hole. 8. Add Boursin cheese in the bag and pipe the cheese into the pockets in the chicken breasts, dividing the cheese evenly among them. 9. Wrap 2 slices of bacon around each chicken breast and secure the ends with toothpicks. 10. Transfer the bacon-wrapped chicken to the "Air Fryer Basket" and cook for 18 to 20 minutes, flipping after 10 minutes of cooking time. 11. Garnish with a sprig of cilantro before serving, if desired.
Per serving: Calories 446; Total Carbs 13g; Net Carbs 6g; Protein 36g; Fat 22.4g; fibers: 3g; Sugars: 6g

Chicken Fillets, Brie & Ham

Prep Time: 5 minutes | Cook Time: 15 minutes | Servings: 4

2 large chicken fillets
freshly ground black pepper
4 slices cured ham
4 small slices of brie
1 tbsp. freshly chopped chives

1. Slice the fillets into 4 and make incisions as you would for a hamburger bun. 2. Leave a little "hinge" uncut at the back. 3. Season the inside and pop some brie and chives in there. 4. Close them, and wrap them each in a slice of ham. 5. Brush with oil and pop them into the air fryer basket. 6. At 350 degrees F/ 175 degrees C, preheat your Air Fryer. 7. Roast the food for 15 minutes until they look tasty. 8. Serve and enjoy.
Per serving: Calories 850g; Total Carbs 43 g; Net Carbs 5g; Protein 76 g; Fat 22.4g; fibers: 3g; Sugars: 6g

Air Fryer Cornish Hen

Prep Time: 5 minutes | Cook Time: 30 minutes | Servings: 2

2 tbsp. Montreal chicken seasoning
1 (1½ to 2-lb.) Cornish hen

1. At 390 degrees F/ 200 degrees C, preheat your Air Fryer. 2. Rub the prepared seasoning over the chicken, coating it thoroughly. 3. Put the chicken in the air fryer basket. 4. Air Fry the chicken at 390 degrees F/ 200 degrees C for 30 minutes, flipping halfway through. 5. Add Cook Time if needed. 6. When done, the chicken should reach an internal temperature of 165 degrees F/ 75 degrees C. 7. Serve and enjoy.
Per serving: Calories 520; Fat 36g; Total Carbs 0g; Protein 45g;; Fat 22.4g; fibers: 3g; Sugars: 6g

Air Fried Turkey Wings

Prep Time: 5 minutes | Cook Time: 26 minutes | Servings: 4

2 lbs. turkey wings
3 tbsps. olive oil or sesame oil
3 to 4 tbsps. chicken rub

1. Put the turkey wings in a large mixing bowl. 2. Pour the olive oil into the bowl and add the rub. 3. Using your hands, rub the oil mixture over the turkey wings. 4. Place the prepared turkey wings in the air fryer basket. 5. Air Fry the turkey wings at 380 degrees F/ 195 degrees C for 26 minutes, flipping the wings halfway through. 6. Serve and enjoy.
Per serving: Calories 521; Fat 34g; Total Carbs 4g; Protein 52g;; Fat 22.4g; fibers: 3g; Sugars: 6g

Air Fryer Turkey Breast

Prep Time: 5 minutes | Cook Time: 60 minutes | Servings: 6

Pepper and salt   Turkey seasonings of choice
1 oven-ready turkey breast

1. At 350 degrees F/ 175 degrees C, preheat your Air Fryer. 2. Season the turkey breast with pepper, salt, and other desired seasonings. 3. Place turkey in Air Fryer Basket. 4. Set the cooking temperature to 350 degrees F/ 175 degrees C, and set time to 60 minutes. 5. Cook the food for 60 minutes. 6. The meat shall be at 165 degrees F/ 75 degrees C when done. 7. Allow to rest 10-15 minutes before slicing. Enjoy.
Per serving: Calories 212; Total Carbs 13g; Net Carbs 6g; Protein24g; Sugar 0g; Fat 22.4g; fibers: 3g; Sugars: 6g

Mustard Chicken Tenders

Prep Time: 5 minutes | Cook Time: 20 minutes | Servings: 4

½ cup coconut flour   2 beaten eggs
1 tbsp. spicy brown mustard   1 lb. of chicken tenders

1. Season tenders with pepper and salt. 2. Place a thin layer of mustard onto tenders and then dredge in flour and dip in egg. 3. Arrange the food to the Air Fryer Basket in air fryer and cook them at 390 degrees F/ 200 degrees C for 20 minutes on Air Fry mode. 4. When cooked, serve and enjoy.
Per serving: Calories 346; Fat 10g; Total Carbs 12g; Net Carbs 4g; Protein 31g; Fat 22.4g; fibers: 3g; Sugars: 6g

Homemade Breaded Nugget in Doritos

Prep Time: 10 minutes | Cook Time: 15 minutes | Servings: 4

½ lb. boneless, chicken breast   1 egg
¼ lb. Doritos snack   Salt, garlic and black pepper to
1 cup of wheat flour   taste.

1. Cut the chicken breast in the width direction, 1 to 1.5 cm thick, so that it is already shaped like pips. 2. Season with salt, garlic, black pepper to taste and some other seasonings if desired. 3. You can also season with those seasonings or powdered onion soup. 4. Put the Doritos snack in a food processor or blender and beat until everything is crumbled, but don't beat too much, you don't want flour. 5. Now bread, passing the pieces of chicken breast first in the wheat flour, then in the beaten eggs and finally in the Doritos, without leaving the excess flour, eggs or Doritos. 6. Add the food in the "Air Fryer Basket" and Air Fry them for 15 minutes at 400 degrees F/ 205 degrees C, and half the time they brown evenly.
Per serving: Calories 42; Total Carbs 1.65g; Fat 1.44g; Net Carbs 2g; Protein 5.29g; Sugar 0.1g; Fiber: 2g

Chicken Breast

Prep Time: 30 minutes | Cook Time: 25 minutes | Servings: 6

1 lb. diced clean chicken breast   Black pepper or chili powder, to
½ lemon   taste
Smoked paprika to taste   Salt to taste

1. Flavor the chicken breasts with salt, paprika and pepper and marinate. 2. Transfer the marinated chicken breasts to the Air Fryer Basket in the air fryer and Air Fry them at 350 degrees F/ 175 degrees C for 15 minutes. 3. When the time is up, reset the cooking temperature to 200 degrees F F/ 95 degrees C, flip the food and Air Fry them for 5 minutes more or until golden. 4. Serve warm.
Per serving: Calories 124; Total Carbs 0g; Fat 1.4g; Net Carbs 4g; Protein 26.1g; Sugar 0g; Fiber: 6g

Breaded Chicken without Flour

Prep Time: 10 minutes | Cook Time: 30 minutes | Servings: 6

1 ¹⁄₆ oz. of grated parmesan cheese   1 lb. of chicken breast
1 unit of egg   Salt and black pepper to taste

1. Cut the chicken breast into 6 fillets and season with a little black pepper and salt. 2. Beat the egg in a suitable bowl. 3. Pass the chicken breast in the egg and then in the grated cheese, sprinkling the fillets. 4. Transfer the chicken breast slices to the Air Fryer Basket in air fryer and Air Fry them at 400 degrees F/ 205 degrees C for 30 minutes or

until golden brown, 5. When cooked, serve warm.
Per serving: Calories 114; Total Carbs 13g; Fat 5.9g; Net Carbs 6g; Protein 2.3g; Sugar 3.2g; Fiber: 1g

Roasted Chicken Thighs

Prep Time: 5 minutes | Cook Time: 20-30 minutes | Servings: 1

3 chicken thighs   ½ tsp. of salt
2 red seasonal bags   1 pinch of black pepper
1 clove garlic

1. Season chicken thighs with red season, minced garlic, salt, and pepper. 2. Marinated the thighs for 5-10 minutes. 3. Put the prepared chicken thighs in the Air Fryer Basket and Roast them at 390 degrees F/ 200 degrees C for 20 minutes. 4. After that time, remove the "Air Fryer Basket" and check the chicken spot. 5. If the thighs are still raw or not golden enough, turn them over and cook them for 10 minutes more at 350 degrees F/ 175 degrees C. 6. You can enjoy the cooked thighs with doré potatoes and leaf salad.
Per serving: Calories 278; Total Carbs 0.1g; Fat 18g; Net Carbs 6g; Protein 31g; Sugar 0g; Fiber: 6g

Coxinha Fit

Prep Time: 10 minutes | Cook Time: 10-15 minutes | Servings: 4

½ lb. seasoned and minced chick-   1 egg
en   Condiments to taste
1 cup light cottage cheese   Flaxseed or oatmeal

1. In a suitable bowl, mix all the ingredients together except flour. 2. Knead well with your hands and mold into coxinha format. 3. If you prefer you can fill it, add chicken or cheese. 4. Repeat the process until all the dough is gone. 5. Pass the drumsticks in the flour and then transfer them to the air fryer. 6. Air Fry them for 10 to 15 minutes at 390 degrees F/ 200 degrees C or until golden. 7. Serve and enjoy!
Per serving: Calories 220; Total Carbs 40g; Fat 18g; Net Carbs 6g; Protein 100g; Sugar 5g; Fiber:0g

Herb Air Fried Chicken Thighs

Prep Time: 30 minutes | Cook Time: 20 minutes | Servings: 4

2 lbs. deboned chicken thighs   1 tsp. garlic powder
1 tsp. rosemary   1 large lemon
1 tsp. thyme   black and salt

1. Trim fat from thighs; season with the black pepper and salt all sides. 2. In a suitable bowl, combine the rosemary, thyme, and garlic powder. 3. Sprinkle over the chicken thighs and press the prepared mixture in putting them on a baking pan. 4. Cut the lemon and squeeze the juice over all the chicken thighs. 5. Cover with plastic wrap and put in the refrigerator for 30 minutes. 6. At 360 degrees F/ 180 degrees C, preheat your Air Fryer. 7. Spray the Air Fryer Basket with butter flavored cooking spray. 8. Place the prepared thighs in the Air Fryer Basket, as many will fit in one layer. 9. Air Fry the food at 360 degrees F/ 180 degrees C for 15 minutes, turning after 7 minutes. 10. When cooked, serve and enjoy.
Per serving: Calories 534; Fat 27.8g; Total Carbs 2.5 g; Sugar 0.5 g; Net Carbs 6g; Protein 66.2 g; Fiber 2 g

Chicken in Beer

Prep Time: 5 minutes | Cook Time: 45 minutes | Servings: 4

2 ¼ lbs. chicken thighs   1 large onion
½ can of beer   Pepper and salt to taste
4 cloves of garlic

1. Wash the chicken thighs and, if desired, remove the skin to be healthier. 2. Place the clean chicken thighs on an ovenproof plate. 3. In the blender, add the beer, onion, garlic, and add black pepper and salt, mix all together. 4. Cover the chicken thighs with this mixture; it has to stay like swimming in the beer. 5. Cook the chicken thighs at 390 degrees F/ 200 degrees C for 45 minutes under Roast mode. 6. The thighs are done when they have a brown cone on top and the beer has dried a bit.
Per serving: Calories 674; Total Carbs 5.47g; Fat 41.94g; Net Carbs 4g; Protein 61.94g; Sugar 1.62g; Fiber: 20g

Chicken Fillet

Prep Time: 5 minutes | Cook Time: 20 minutes | Servings: 4

4 chicken fillets
salt to taste
1 garlic clove, crushed

thyme, to taste
black pepper, to taste

1. Add seasoning to fillets, wrapping well for flavor. 2. At 350 degrees F/ 175 degrees C, preheat your Air Fryer. 3. Place the chicken fillets in the air fryer basket and cook them for 20 minutes at 350 degrees F/ 175 degrees C on Air Fry mode. 4. After 15 minutes of cooking time, turn the fillets and raise the temperature to 390 degrees F/ 200 degrees C. 5. Serve!
Per serving: Calories 90; Total Carbs 1g; Fat 1g; Net Carbs 2g; Protein 17g; Sugar 0g; Fiber: 4g

Rolled Turkey Breast

Prep Time: 5 minutes | Cook Time: 10 minutes | Servings: 4

1 box of cherry tomatoes
¼ lb. turkey breast, sliced

1. Wrap the turkey in the tomatoes, close with the help of toothpicks. 2. Air Fry the food in the air fryer for 10 minutes at 390 degrees F/ 200 degrees C. 3. You can increase the filling with ricotta and other preferred light ingredients.
Per serving: Calories 172; Total Carbs 3g; Fat 2g; Net Carbs 6g; Protein 34g; Sugar 1g; Fiber: 30g

Chicken with Lemon and Bahian Seasoning

Prep Time: 2 hours Cook Time: 20 minutes | Servings: 4

5 pieces of chicken to bird;
2 garlic cloves, crushed;
4 tbsps. of lemon juice;

1 coffee spoon of Bahian spices;
salt and black pepper to taste.

1. Place the chicken pieces in a covered bowl and add the spices. 2. Add the lemon juice. Cover the container and let the chicken marinate for 2 hours. 3. Place each piece of chicken in the Air Fryer Basket, without overlapping the pieces. 4. Air Fry the chicken pieces at 390 degrees F/ 200 degrees C for 20 minutes, flipping halfway through cooking. 5. Serve!
Per serving: Calories 316.2; Total Carbs 4.9g; Fat 15.3g; Net Carbs 6g; Protein 32.8g; Sugar 0g; Fiber: 4g

Chicken Meatballs

Prep Time: 5 minutes | Cook Time: 15 minutes | Servings: 2

½ lb. chicken breast
1 tbsp. of garlic
1 tbsp. of onion
½ chicken broth

1 tbsp. of oatmeal, whole wheat flour or of your choice
1 pinch of paprika
Salt and black pepper

1. Place all of the recipe ingredients in a food processor and beat well until well mixed and ground. 2. Make balls from the mixture and place them in the Air Fryer Basket. 3. Cook the food for 15 minutes at 400 degrees F/ 205 degrees C on Air Fry mode. 4. Shake the basket halfway through cooking so that the meatballs loosen and fry evenly. 5. When done, serve and enjoy.
Per serving: Calories 45; Total Carbs 1.94g; Fat 1.57g; Net Carbs 6g; Protein 5.43g; Sugar 0.41g; Fiber: 23g

Pretzel Crusted Chicken with Spicy Mustard Sauce

Prep Time: 15 minutes | Cook Time: 20 minutes | Servings: 6

2 eggs
1 ½ lb. chicken breasts, boneless, diced
½ cup crushed pretzels
1 tsp. shallot powder
1 tsp. paprika
Salt and black pepper, to taste
½ cup vegetable broth

1 tbsp. cornstarch
3 tbsps. Worcestershire sauce
3 tbsps. tomato paste
1 tbsp. apple cider vinegar
2 tbsps. olive oil
2 garlic cloves, chopped
1 jalapeno pepper, minced
1 tsp. yellow mustard

1. At 390 degrees F/ 200 degrees C, preheat your Air Fryer. 2. In a mixing dish, whisk the eggs until frothy; toss the chicken chunks into the whisked eggs and coat well. 3. In another dish, combine the crushed pretzels with shallot powder, paprika, black pepper and salt. 4. Then, lay the chicken chunks in the pretzel mixture; turn it over until well coated. 5. Place the chicken pieces in the Air Fryer Basket. Air Fry the chicken pieces at 390 degrees F/ 200 degrees C for 12 minutes, shaking the basket halfway through. 6. Meanwhile, whisk the vegetable broth with cornstarch, Worcestershire sauce, tomato paste, and apple cider vinegar. 7. Preheat a cast-iron skillet over medium flame. 8. Add the olive oil to heat and sauté the garlic with jalapeno pepper for 30 to 40 seconds, stirring frequently. 9. Add the cornstarch mixture and let it simmer until the sauce has thickened a little. 10. Now, add the air-fried chicken and mustard; let it simmer for 2 minutes more or until heated through. 11. Serve immediately and enjoy!
Per serving: Calories 357; Fat 20.3g; Total Carbs 28.1g; Net Carbs 6g; Protein 2.8g; Sugars 1g; Fiber: 4g

Simple Marinated Chicken Wings

Prep Time: 5 minutes | Cook Time: 15 minutes | Servings: 4

2 tsps. salt
2 tsps. fresh ground pepper

2 lbs. chicken wings

1. In a suitable bowl, mix the wings with black pepper and salt. 2. Put half of the chicken wings in the "Air Fryer Basket" that has been sprayed with nonstick cooking spray. 3. Air Fry the chicken wings at 350 degrees F/ 175 degrees C for 15 minutes, flipping halfway through cooking, 4. Cook the left chicken wings with the same steps. 5. Serve hot.
Per serving: Calories 342; Fat 14.8g; Total Carbs 1 g; Sugar 0 g; Net Carbs 4g; Protein 49.2 g; Fiber 6 g

Western Chicken Wings

Prep Time: 10 minutes | Cook Time: 15 minutes Serve: 4

2 lbs. chicken wings
1 tsp. Herb de Provence
1 tsp. paprika

½ cup parmesan cheese, grated
Black pepper and salt

1. Add cheese, paprika, herb de Provence, pepper, and salt into the large mixing bowl. 2. Place the chicken wings into the bowl and toss well to coat. 3. At 350 degrees F/ 175 degrees C, preheat your Air Fryer. 4. Place the chicken wings into the air fryer basket. 5. Spray top of chicken wings with some cooking spray. 6. Air Fry the chicken wings at 350 degrees F/ 175 degrees C for 15 minutes. 7. Turn chicken wings halfway through cooking. 8. Serve and enjoy.
Per serving: Calories 473; Fat 19.6g; Total Carbs 0.8 g; Sugar 0.1 g; Net Carbs 6g; Protein 69.7 g; Fiber 1 g

Perfect Chicken Thighs

Prep Time: 10 minutes | Cook Time: 15 minutes | Serve: 4

4 chicken thighs, bone-in & skinless
¼ tsp. ground ginger

2 tsps. paprika
2 tsps. garlic powder
black pepper and salt

1. In a suitable bowl, mix ginger, paprika, garlic powder, pepper, and salt together and rub all over chicken thighs. 2. Spray chicken thighs with some cooking spray. 3. Place the prepared chicken thighs into the "Air Fryer Basket" and Air Fry them at 400 degrees F/ 205 degrees C for 10 minutes. 4. When the time is up, turn chicken thighs and Air Fry for 5 minutes more. 5. Serve and enjoy.
Per serving: Calories 286; Fat 11g; Total Carbs 1.8 g; Sugar 0.5 g; Net Carbs 2g; Protein 42.7 g; Fiber 1 g

Perfectly Spiced Chicken Tenders

Prep Time: 10 minutes | Cook Time: 13 minutes Serve: 4

6 chicken tenders
1 tsp. onion powder
1 tsp. garlic powder

1 tsp. paprika
1 tsp. kosher salt

1. At 380 degrees F/ 195 degrees C, preheat your Air Fryer. 2. In a suitable bowl, mix onion powder, garlic powder, paprika and salt together and rub all over chicken tenders. 3. Spray chicken tenders with some cooking spray. 4. Place the prepared chicken tenders into the "Air Fryer Basket" and Air Fry them at 380 degrees F/ 195 degrees C for 13 minutes. 5. Serve and enjoy.
Per serving: Calories 423; Fat 16.4g; Total Carbs 1.5 g; Sugar 0.5 g; Net Carbs 6g; Protein 63.7 g; Fiber 1 g

Chinese-Style Sticky Turkey Thighs

Prep Time: 20 minutes | Cook Time: 35 minutes | Servings: 6

1 tbsp. sesame oil	6 tbsps. honey
2 lbs. turkey thighs	1 tbsp. Chinese rice vinegar
1 tsp. Chinese Five-spice powder	2 tbsps. soy sauce
1 tsp. pink Himalayan salt	1 tbsp. sweet chili sauce
¼ tsp. Sichuan pepper	1 tbsp. mustard

1. Brush the turkey thighs with sesame oil. Season them with spices. 2. Air Fry the turkey thighs at 360 degrees F/ 180 degrees C for 23 minutes, turning over once or twice. Make sure to work in batches to ensure even cooking 3. In the meantime, combine the remaining ingredients in a wok (or similar type pan) that is preheated over medium-high heat. 4. Cook and stir until the sauce reduces by about a third. 5. Add the fried turkey thighs to the wok; gently stir to coat with the sauce. 6. Allow the turkey thighs to rest for 10 minutes before slicing and serving. Enjoy!
Per serving: Calories 279; Fat 19g; Total Carbs 27.7g; Net Carbs 6g; Protein 17.9g; Sugars 1g; Fiber: 4g

Classic No Frills Turkey Breast

Prep Time: 5 minutes | Cook Time: 50 minutes | Servings: 4

1 bone in turkey breast (about 8 lbs.)	2 tbsps. sea salt
2 tbsps. olive oil	1 tbsp. black pepper

1. At 360 degrees F/ 180 degrees C, preheat your Air Fryer . 2. Rub the washed turkey breast with the olive oil both on the skin and on the inside of the cavity. 3. Add sea salt and black pepper on top. 4. Spray the Air Fryer Basket with butter or olive oil flavored nonstick spray. 5. Put the turkey in with the breast side down. 6. Air Fry the turkey breast at 360 degrees F/ 180 degrees C for 40 minutes; after 20 minutes of cooking, turn the food over and spray with the oil. 7. When done, check with thermometer and it should read 165 degrees F/ 75 degrees C. If not, put it back in for a few minutes. 8. Let the breast rest at least 15 minutes before cutting and serving.
Per serving: Calories 375; Total Carbs 8.2g; Fat 6.8g; Net Carbs 5g; Protein 15g; fibers: 3g; Sugars: 6g

Easy Hot Chicken Drumsticks

Prep Time: 40 minutes | Cook Time: 40 minutes | Servings: 6

6 chicken drumsticks	3 tbsps. tamari sauce
Sauce:	1 tsp. dried thyme
6 oz. hot sauce	½ tsp. dried oregano
3 tbsps. olive oil	

1. Spray the Air Fryer Basket with the non-stick cooking spray and then arrange the chicken drumsticks to it. 2. Air Fry the chicken drumsticks at 380 degrees F/ 195 degrees C for 35 minutes, flipping them over halfway through. 3. Meanwhile, heat the hot sauce, olive oil, tamari sauce, thyme, and oregano in a pan over medium-low heat; reserve. 4. Drizzle the sauce over the prepared chicken drumsticks; toss to coat well and serve. 5. Bon appétit!
Per serving: Calories 280; Fat 2.6g; Total Carbs 24.1g; Net Carbs 6g; Protein 1.4g; Sugars 1g; Fiber: 4g

Crunchy Chicken Tenders with Peanuts

Prep Time: 25 minutes | Cook Time: 20 minutes | Servings: 4

1 ½ lbs. chicken tenderloins	½ tsp. garlic powder
2 tbsps. peanut oil	1 tsp. red pepper flakes
½ cup tortilla chips, crushed	2 tbsps. peanuts, roasted and
Salt and black pepper, to taste	roughly chopped

1. At 360 degrees F/ 180 degrees C, preheat your Air Fryer. 2. Brush the chicken tenderloins with peanut oil on all sides. 3. In a suitable mixing bowl, combine the crushed chips, salt, black pepper, garlic powder, and red pepper flakes. 4. Dredge the chicken tenderloin pieces in the breading, shaking off any residual coating. 5. Lay the chicken tenderloins into the Air Fryer Basket. 6. Air Fry the chicken tenderloins at 360 degrees F/ 180 degrees C for 12 to 13 minutes or until it is no longer pink in the center. 7. Work in batches; an instant-read thermometer should read at least 165 degrees F/ 75 degrees C. 8. Serve

garnished with roasted peanuts. Bon appétit!
Per serving: Calories 343; Fat 10.6g; Total Carbs 36.8g; Net Carbs 6g; Protein 1g; Sugar 2g; Fiber: 4g

Tarragon Turkey Tenderloins with Baby Potatoes

Prep Time: 50 minutes | Cook Time: 50 minutes | Servings: 6

2 lbs. turkey tenderloins	2 tbsps. dry white wine
2 tsps. olive oil	1 tbsp. fresh tarragon leaves,
Salt and ground black pepper, to taste	chopped
1 tsp. smoked paprika	1-lb. baby potatoes, rubbed

1. Place the turkey tenderloins in a suitable cooking pan. Brush the turkey tenderloins with 1 teaspoon of olive oil. Season the turkey tenderloins with salt, black pepper, and paprika. 2. Afterwards, add the white wine and tarragon leaves. 3. Air Fry the turkey tenderloins at 350 degrees F/ 175 degrees C for 30 minutes, flipping them over halfway through. 4. Let them rest for 5 to 9 minutes before slicing and serving. 5. After that, spritz the sides and bottom of the "Air Fryer Basket" with the remaining olive oil. Arrange the baby potatoes to the basket. 6. Air Fry the potatoes at 400 degrees F/ 205 degrees C for 15 minutes. 7. When cooked, serve with the turkey and enjoy!
Per serving: Calories 317; Fat 14.2g; Total Carbs 45.7g; Net Carbs 6g; Protein 1.1g; Sugars 1g; Fiber: 4g

Mediterranean Chicken Breasts with Roasted Tomatoes

Prep Time: 1 hour | Cook Time: 35 minutes | Servings: 8

2 tsps. olive oil, melted	2 tbsps. fresh parsley, minced
3 lbs. chicken breasts, bone-in	1 tsp. fresh basil, minced
½ tsp. black pepper, freshly ground	1 tsp. fresh rosemary, minced
½ tsp. salt	4 medium-sized Roma tomatoes, halved
1 tsp. cayenne pepper	

1. At 370 degrees F/ 185 degrees C, preheat your Air Fryer. 2. Brush the "Air Fryer Basket" with 1 teaspoon of olive oil and then arrange the chicken breasts to it. 3. Sprinkle the chicken breasts with all seasonings listed above. 4. Air Fry the chicken breasts at 370 degrees F/ 185 degrees C for 25 minutes or until chicken breasts are slightly browned. Work in batches. 5. Arrange the tomatoes in the "Air Fryer Basket" and brush them with the remaining olive oil. Season with sea salt. 6. Air Fry the tomatoes at 350 degrees F/ 175 degrees C for 10 minutes, shaking halfway through. 7. Serve with chicken breasts. Bon appétit!
Per serving: Calories 315; Fat 2.7g; Total Carbs 36g; Net Carbs 8g; Protein 1.7g; Sugars 1g; Fiber: 4g

Asian Chicken Filets with Cheese

Prep Time: 50 minutes | Cook Time: 20 minutes | Servings: 2

4 rashers smoked bacon	minced
2 chicken filets	1 tsp. black mustard seeds
½ tsp. coarse sea salt	1 tsp. mild curry powder
¼ tsp. black pepper, preferably freshly ground	½ cup coconut milk
1 tsp. garlic, minced	⅓ cup tortilla chips, crushed
1 (2-inch) piece ginger, peeled and	½ cup Pecorino Romano cheese, grated

1. At 400 degrees F/ 205 degrees C, preheat your Air Fryer. 2. Add the smoked bacon and cook in your preheated air fryer for 5 to 7 minutes on Air Fry mode. Reserve. 3. In a suitable mixing bowl, place the chicken fillets, salt, black pepper, garlic, ginger, mustard seeds, curry powder, and milk. Let the chicken fillets marinate in your refrigerator about 30 minutes. 4. In another bowl, mix the crushed chips and grated Pecorino Romano cheese. 5. Dredge the chicken fillets through the chips mixture and transfer them to the Air Fryer Basket. 6. Air Fry the chicken fillets at 380 degrees F/ 195 degrees C for 12 minutes, turning them over halfway through. 7. Repeat the same until you have run out of ingredients. 8. Serve with reserved bacon. Enjoy!
Per serving: Calories 376; Fat 12.1g; Total Carbs 36.2g; Net Carbs 4g; Protein 3.4g; Sugars 1g; fibers 1g

Chapter 6 Beef, Pork, and Lamb Recipes

Flavor Beef Ribs 68
BBQ Pork Chops with Vegetables 68
Meat Burger with Salad 68
Delectable Beef with Kale Pieces............................ 68
Pork Tenderloins with Soy Sauce 68
Beef Cubes with Vegetables 68
Cube Steak 68
Garlicky Rosemary Lamb Chops 68
Pork Cutlets 69
Air-fried Pork with Wine Sauce 69
Pork Tenderloin with Bell Pepper........................... 69
Beer Beef.................................... 69
Delicious Pork Shoulder with Molasses Sauce 69
Garlic Pork Roast.................................... 69
Beef Sausage with Tomato Puree 69
Liver Muffins 70
Pork Meatloaf with Onion 70
Creole Pork Chops 70
Garlic Beef Meatloaf 70
Spicy Pork Belly Pieces 70
Festive Pork Fillets 70
Country-style Pork Ribs 70
Filet Mignon with Peanut Sauce 70
Lamb Chops with Mustard Mixture 71
Spiced Rib Eye Steak 71
Steak with Onion and Bell Peppers 71
Marinated Beef and Vegetable Stir Fry...................... 71
Roasted Garlic Ribeye with Mayo 71
Cajun Spareribs with Coriander 71
Montreal Steak.................................... 71
Pork Chops with Soy Sauce 71
Porterhouse Steak with Mustard and Butter 71
Moroccan-style Steak with Salad 72
Italian-style Honey Pork 72
Beef Tenderloin Steaks with Marjoram 72
Garlic Lamb Rack 72
Delicious Baby Back Ribs 72
Tender Pork Ribs with BBQ Sauce 72
Glazed Meatloaf 72
Simple Pork Chops 73
Garlic Beef Cubes 73
Spiced Pork Chops 73
Unique Beef Cheeseburgers 73
Pork Sausages with Mustard Sauce 73
Tasty Spaghetti with Beef Meatballs 73
Delectable Pork Chops.................................... 73
Lemon Beef Schnitzel 73
Paprika Pork Chops 73
Spice Meatloaf.................................... 74
Flank Steak with Honey and Paprika 74

Spiced Lamb Kebabs 74
Flank Steak with Tamari Sauce 74
Simple and Tasty Hamburgers 74
Delicious Empanadas 74
Steak Kabobs with Vegetables 74
Cajun Pork 74
Simple Rib-Eye Steak 75
Flank Steaks with Capers 75
Homemade Steak.................................... 75
Marinated Beef with BBQ Sauce 75
Garlic Beef with Sauce.................................... 75
Broccoli Pork Chops 75
Spiced Beef Chuck Roast.................................... 75
Pork Tenderloins 75
Pork Curry 75
Teriyaki Pork 76
Garlic Beef with Egg and Bell Pepper 76
Asian Pork 76
Great Garlicky Pork Roast 76
Bratwurst with Vegetables 76
Air Fried Pork Strips 76
Spicy Steak 76
Greek Vegetable Mix 76
Keto Crispy Pork Chops 76
Beef Chops with Broccoli 77
Air Fried Pork Loin 77
Pork Chops with Seasoning marinade 77
Honey Mustard Meatballs 77
Adorable Air Fried Steak 77
Classic Burger 77
Teriyaki Steak 77
Tasty & Spicy Lamb 77
Gorgeous Lamb Meatballs 77
Nourishing Lamb with Potatoes 78
Roast Lamb with Rosemary.................................... 78
Steak Bites with Mushrooms 78
Beef with Creamed Mushroom Sauce 78
Simple Air Fryer Steak.................................... 78
Savoury Apple Pork Bites 78
Crisp Pork Chops.................................... 78
Easy Pork & Parmesan Meatballs 78
Classic Pork 78
Coconut Butter Pork Chops 79
Mushrooms Meatballs 79
Mustard Pork Tenderloin 79
Spanish-style Pork with Padrón Peppers 79
McCormick Pork Chops 79
Dreamy Beef Roast 79
St. Louis-style Pork Ribs with Roasted Peppers 79
Hawaiian Cheesy Meatball Sliders 79

Flavor Beef Ribs

Prep Time: 10-15 minutes | Cook time: 12 minutes | Serves: 4

1 cup coriander, finely chopped	1 teaspoon fennel seeds
1 tablespoon basil leaves, chopped	1 teaspoon hot paprika
2 garlic cloves, finely chopped	Kosher salt and black pepper, as
1-pound meaty beef ribs	needed
3 tablespoons apple cider vinegar	½ cup vegetable oil
1 chipotle powder	

1. Thoroughly mix the coriander, basil leaves, garlic cloves, meaty beef ribs, apple cider vinegar, chipotle powder, fennel seeds, hot paprika, salt, black pepper, and vegetable oil together in a medium-size bowl and then coat the ribs well. Cover and refrigerate for 3-4 hours. 2. Coat the cooking basket of your air fryer with cooking oil or spray. 3. Once marinated, take the ribs out of the marinade and place on the cooking basket. 4. Cook the ribs at 360 degrees F/ 180 degrees C for 8 minutes. 5. If the meat is not tender, then cook for 3-4 more minutes. 6. Top with the leftover marinade and serve warm!
Per serving: Calories: 404; Fat 32.9g; Sodium 49mg; Total Carbs 0.7g; Net Carbs: 0g; Fiber 0.2g; Sugars 0.1g; Protein 25g

BBQ Pork Chops with Vegetables

Prep Time: 10-15 minutes | Cook time: 20 minutes | Serves: 5-6

6 pork chops	needed
1 teaspoon onion powder	½ teaspoon cayenne pepper
½ teaspoon garlic powder	1 teaspoon brown sugar
Ground black pepper and salt as	⅓ cup all-purpose flour

1. To marinate, prepare a Ziploc bag, add the ingredients, seal and shake well. 2. Coat the cooking basket of your air fryer with cooking oil or spray. 3. Place the chops on the basket and then arrange the basket to the air fryer. 4. Cook the chops at 375 degrees F/ 190 degrees C for 20 minutes. 5. When done, serve warm with sautéed vegetables!
Per serving: Calories: 286; Fat 20g; Sodium 57mg; Total Carbs 6g; Net Carbs: 2.5g; Fiber 0.3g; Sugars 0.7g; Protein 18.8g

Meat Burger with Salad

Prep Time: 10-15 minutes | Cook time: 45 minutes | Serves: 4

1 teaspoon garlic puree	1 teaspoon tomato puree
4 bread buns	1 teaspoon mixed herbs
1 teaspoon mustard	4 ounces cheddar cheese
1 onion, diced	1 teaspoon basil
10-ounce mixed mince (beef and	Pepper and salt as required
pork)	Salad of your choice

1. Thoroughly mix up the seasoning ingredients and coat the meat well in a medium-size bowl. 2. Form the burger patties from the mixture and flatten them. 3. Coat the cooking basket of your air fryer with cooking oil or spray. 4. Place the patties on the basket and then arrange the basket to the air fryer. 5. Cook the patties at 390 degrees F/ 200 degrees C for 20-25 minutes. 6. When the time is up, turn the patties and cook for 20 more minutes. 7. Make burgers using buns, patties, cheese, and salads!
Per serving: Calories: 501; Fat 12.2g; Sodium 812mg; Total Carbs 80.2g; Net Carbs: 0g; Fiber 10.8g; Sugars 15.3g; Protein 24.6g

Delectable Beef with Kale Pieces

Prep Time: 5-8 minutes | Cook time: 15-20 minutes | Serves: 4

1 cup kale, make pieces and wilted	4 eggs, beaten
1 tomato, chopped	4 tablespoons heavy cream
¼ teaspoon brown sugar	½ teaspoon turmeric powder
½ pound leftover beef, coarsely	Salt and ground black pepper, as
chopped	needed
2 garlic cloves, pressed	⅛ teaspoon ground allspice

1. Make 4 ramekins and lightly oil them. 2. Divide the remaining ingredients among the ramekins. 3. Coat the cooking basket of your air fryer with cooking oil or spray. 4. Place the ramekins on the basket and then arrange the basket to the air fryer. 5. Cook the ramekins at 360 degrees F/ 180 degrees C for 15 minutes. 6. When done, serve warm!
Per serving: Calories: 209; Fat 12.6g; Sodium 104mg; Total Carbs 4g; Net Carbs: 2g; Fiber 0.5g; Sugars 1g; Protein 19.5g

Pork Tenderloins with Soy Sauce

Prep Time: 15 minutes. | Cook time: 60 Minutes | Serves: 4

1 apple, wedged	1 tablespoon soy sauce
1 cinnamon quill	Salt and black pepper
1 tablespoon olive oil	1 lb. pork tenderloin

1. Prepare a suitable bowl, mix up the apple, cinnamon, olive oil, soy sauce, salt, and black pepper, then add the pork and coat well. 2. Marinate the pork for 25-35 minutes at room temperature. 3. Place the pork, apples and add a little bit of marinade on the cooking basket. 4. Cook at 380 degrees F/ 195 degrees C for 14 minutes, flipping halfway through. 5. Serve hot!
Per serving: Calories: 223; Fat 7.6g; Sodium 291mg; Total Carbs 8g; Net Carbs: 3.5g; Fiber 1.4g; Sugars 5.9g; Protein 30.1g

Beef Cubes with Vegetables

Prep Time: 10-15 minutes | Cook time: 20 minutes | Serves: 4

1 tablespoon apple cider vinegar	smoked
1 teaspoon fine sea salt	¼ pound broccoli, make florets
1-pound top round steak, make	¼ pound mushrooms, sliced
cubes	1 teaspoon dried basil
2 tablespoons olive oil	½ teaspoon garlic powder
½ teaspoon black pepper, ground	¼ teaspoon ground cumin
1 teaspoon shallot powder	1 teaspoon celery seeds
¾ teaspoon cayenne pepper,	

1. To marinate, prepare a zip-lock bag, combine the beef with olive oil, vinegar, salt, black pepper, shallot powder, cayenne pepper, garlic powder and cumin. 2. Seal and marinate at room temperature for 3 hours. 3. Coat the cooking basket of your air fryer with cooking oil or spray. 4. Place the beef cubes on the basket and then arrange the basket to the air fryer. 5. Cook the beef cubes at 365 degrees F/ 185 degrees C for 12 minutes. 6. When cooked, transfer the cubes to a prepared bowl. 7. Clean the basket, arrange the vegetables in it and sprinkle basil and celery seeds on them. 8. Cook the vegetables at 400 degrees F/ 205 degrees C for 5 to 6 minutes. 9. When done, serve with the reserved meat cubes.
Per serving: Calories: 326; Fat 17.5g; Sodium 550mg; Total Carbs 3g; Net Carbs: 1g; Fiber 1.3g; Sugars 1.1g; Protein 37.9g

Cube Steak

Prep Time: 15 minutes. | Cook time: 20 Minutes | Serves: 4

1 ½ lbs. cube steak	2 scallions, finely chopped
Salt, to taste	2-tablespoon fresh parsley, finely
¼-teaspoon ground black pepper,	chopped
or more to taste	1 tablespoon fresh horseradish,
4 ounces' butter	grated
2 garlic cloves, finely chopped	1 teaspoon cayenne pepper

1. Use the kitchen to pat the cube steak dry, then season it with salt and black pepper. 2. Coat the cooking basket of your air fryer with cooking oil or spray. 3. Place the cube steak on the basket and arrange the basket to the air fryer. 4. Cook the cube steak at 400 degrees F/ 205 degrees C for 14 minutes. 5. While cooking the cube steak, melt the butter in a skillet over a moderate heat. 6. Add the remaining ingredients and simmer them, until the sauce has thickened and reduced slightly. 7. When done, serve the cube steak and drizzle the Cowboy sauce on the top. 8. Serve and enjoy.
Per serving: Calories: 447; Fat 20.1g; Sodium 211mg; Total Carbs 1g; Net Carbs: 0g; Fiber 0.4g; Sugars 0.5g; Protein 61.9g

Garlicky Rosemary Lamb Chops

Prep Time: 10 minutes | Cook Time: 12 minutes | Servings: 4

4 lamb chops	2 garlic cloves, minced
2 tsps. olive oil	2 tsps. garlic puree
1 tsp. fresh rosemary	Salt and black pepper

1. Rub them with olive oil, rosemary, garlic, garlic puree, salt, and black pepper 2. Place lamb chops in the Air Fryer Basket. 3. Air Fry the chops at 350 degrees F/ 175 degrees C for 12 minutes. 4. Flip the chops when cooked halfway through then resume cooking. 5. Serve warm.
Per serving: Calories 297; Fat 14 g; Total Carbs 8 g; Net Carbs 6g; Fiber 1 g; Sugar 3 g; Protein 32 g

Pork Cutlets

Prep Time: 15 minutes. | Cook time: 1 Hour 20 Minutes | Serves: 2

1 cup water
1 cup red wine
1 tablespoon sea salt
2 pork cutlets
½ cup all-purpose flour
½ teaspoon shallot powder
½-teaspoon porcini powder
Sea salt, to taste
Ground black pepper, to taste
1 egg
¼ cup yogurt
1 teaspoon brown mustard
1 cup tortilla chips, crushed

1. In a large ceramic dish, combine the water, wine and salt. After adding the pork cutlets, refrigerating the mixture for 1 hour. 2. In a shallow bowl, mix the flour, shallot powder, porcini powder, salt, and ground pepper. 3. In another bowl, whisk the eggs with yogurt and mustard. 4. In the third bowl, place the crushed tortilla chips. 5. Evenly coat the pork cutlets with the flour mixture and egg mixture in order, then, roll them over the crushed tortilla chips. 6. Lightly grease the bottom of the cooking basket with cooking oil. 7. Place the breaded pork cutlets on the basket and cook them at 395 degrees F/ 200 degrees C and for 10 minutes. 8. Flip and cook for 5 minutes more on the other side. 9. Serve warm.
Per serving: Calories: 331; Fat 12.1g; Sodium 1993mg; Total Carbs 32g; Net Carbs: 12g; Fiber 2.4g; Sugars 2.7g; Protein 10.8g

Air-fried Pork with Wine Sauce

Prep Time: 8-10 minutes | Cook time: 20 minutes | Serves: 4

For the Ribs:
½ teaspoon cracked black peppercorns
½ teaspoon Hickory-smoked salt
1 pound pork ribs
For the Sauce:
1 teaspoon brown sugar
1 teaspoon balsamic vinegar
1 ½ cups beef stock
2 tablespoons olive oil
1 tablespoon Dijon honey mustard
¼ cup soy sauce
1 clove garlic, minced

1 cup red wine
¼ teaspoon salt

1. To marinate, prepare a large dish, add the ingredients and seal and refrigerate for 3-4 hours or overnight. 2. Coat the cooking basket of your air fryer with cooking oil or spray. 3. Place the ribs on the basket and then arrange the basket to the air fryer. 4. Cook the ribs at 320 degrees F/ 160 degrees C for 10 minutes. 5. Add the stock in a deep saucepan and boil over medium flame until half reduces it. 6. Add the remaining sauce ingredients. Cook for 10 minutes over high heat or until the sauce is reduced by half. 7. Serve the air fried pork ribs with the wine sauce.
Per serving: Calories: 438; Fat 27.3g; Sodium 1408mg; Total Carbs 3g; Net Carbs: 1g; Fiber 0.2g; Sugars 1.5g; Protein 32.2g

Pork Tenderloin with Bell Pepper

Prep Time: 8-10 minutes | Cook time: 18 minutes | Serves: 2

1 red onion, make thin slices
1 yellow or red bell pepper, make thin strips
2 teaspoons herbs
1 tablespoon olive oil
½ tablespoon mustard
Black pepper, ground as required
11-ounce pork tenderloin

1. Make the tenderloin into four pieces, spread the oil, mustard and sprinkle some pepper and salt on them. 2. Thoroughly mix the herbs, pepper strips, oil, onion, salt and pepper in a medium-size bowl. 3. Coat the cooking basket of your air fryer with cooking oil or spray. 4. Add the mixture on the basket, put the tenderloin pieces on and then arrange the basket to the air fryer. 5. Cook the tenderloin pieces at 390 degrees F/ 200 degrees C for 16-18 minutes. 6. When done, serve warm!
Per serving: Calories: 339; Fat 13.5g; Sodium 93mg; Total Carbs 11g; Net Carbs: 6.7g; Fiber 2.7g; Sugars 5.5g; Protein 42.8g

Beer Beef

Prep Time: 8-10 minutes | Cook time: 15 minutes | Serves: 4-5

1 bottle beer
2-3 cloves garlic, finely minced
1 ½ pounds short loin
2 tablespoons olive oil
2 bay leaves

1. Use the kitchen towel to pat the beef dry. 2. Thoroughly mix the beef and other ingredients in a medium-size bowl. Set aside for 60-80 minutes. 3. Coat the cooking basket of your air fryer with cooking oil or spray. 4. Place the marinated beef on the basket and arrange the basket to the air fryer. 5. Cook the marinated beef at 395 degrees F/ 200 degrees C for 7 minutes. 6. After that, turn the meat and cook for another 8 minutes. 7. Serve warm!
Per serving: Calories: 163; Fat 12g; Sodium 354mg; Total Carbs 3g; Net Carbs: 1g; Fiber 0g; Sugars 0g; Protein 6g

Delicious Pork Shoulder with Molasses Sauce

Prep Time: 2 hours 15 minutes. | Cook time: 25 Minutes | Serves: 3

1 tablespoon molasses
1 tablespoon soy sauce
2-tablespoon Shaoxing wine
2 garlic cloves, minced
1 teaspoon fresh ginger, minced
1 tablespoon cilantro stems and leaves, finely chopped
1 lb. boneless pork shoulder
1 tablespoon sesame oil

1. Thoroughly mix up the molasses, soy sauce, wine, garlic, ginger, and cilantro in a large bowl. 2. Put the pork shoulder in the spice mixture and allow it to refrigerate for 2 hours. 3. Oil the cooking basket with sesame oil, put the pork shoulder in it and reserve the marinade. 4. Cook the pork shoulder at 395 degrees F/ 200 degrees C for 14 to 17 minutes, turning them over and basting with the reserved marinade halfway through. 5. While cooking the pork should, heat a skillet and cook the marinade in it over medium heat, until thickened. 6. When the pork shoulder cooked, let it rest for 5 to 6 minutes before slicing and serving. 7. Brush the pork shoulder with the sauce and enjoy!
Per serving: Calories: 283; Fat 9.9g; Sodium 390mg; Total Carbs 6.5g; Net Carbs: 1g; Fiber 0.2g; Sugars 3.8g; Protein 40.1

Garlic Pork Roast

Cook time: 30 Minutes | Serves: 8

2 lbs. pork roast
1 ½-teaspoon garlic powder
1 ½-teaspoon coriander powder
⅓-teaspoon salt
1 ½-teaspoon black pepper
1 ½ dried thyme
1 ½-teaspoon dried oregano
1 ½-teaspoon cumin powder
3 cups water
1 lemon, halved

1. Mix up the garlic powder, coriander powder, salt, black pepper, thyme, oregano and cumin powder in a suitable bowl. 2. Dry the pork well and then poke holes all around it using a fork. 3. Smear the oregano rub thoroughly on all sides with your hands and squeeze the lemon juice all over it. Set aside for 5 minutes. 4. Cook the pork at 300 degrees F/ 150 degrees C for 10 minutes. 5. Turn the pork and increase the temperature to 350 F and continue cooking for 10 minutes. 6. Once ready, remove it and place it in on a chopping board to sit for 4 minutes before slicing. Serve the pork slices with a side of sautéed asparagus and hot sauce.
Per serving: Calories: 240; Fat 10.8g; Sodium 164mg; Total Carbs 1g; Net Carbs: 0g; Fiber 0.3g; Sugars 0.2g; Protein 32.6g

Beef Sausage with Tomato Puree

Prep Time: 15 minutes. | Cook time: 40 Minutes | Serves: 2

1 tablespoon lard, melted
1 shallot, chopped
1 bell pepper, chopped
2 red chilies, finely chopped
1 teaspoon ginger-garlic paste
Sea salt, to taste
¼-teaspoon ground black pepper
4 beef good quality sausages, thinly sliced
½ teaspoon smoked paprika
1 cup beef bone broth
½ cup tomato puree
2 handfuls spring greens, shredded

1. In a skillet, melt the lard over medium-high flame; sauté the shallots and peppers about 4 minutes or until fragrant. 2. Add the ginger-garlic paste and then cook for 1 more minute. 3. After seasoning with salt and black pepper, transfer the food to a lightly sprayed cooking basket. 4. Sauté the sausages and stir occasionally, until brown, working in batches. 5. Add the sausages, smoked paprika, broth, and tomato puree to the cooking basket. 6. Cook the beef sausage at 325 degrees F/ 160 degrees C for 30 minutes. 7. When the time is up, stir in the spring greens and cook for 5 minutes more. 8. Serve over the hot rice if desired. Bon appétit!
Per serving: Calories: 265; Fat 9.5g; Sodium 691mg; Total Carbs 5g; Net Carbs: 2g; Fiber 1.2g; Sugars 1.5g; Protein 37.9g

Liver Muffins

Prep Time: 15 minutes. | Cook time: 25 Minutes | Serves: 2

2 large eggs	1 tablespoon cream
1 tablespoon butter	Salt and black pepper
½-tablespoon black truffle oil	½ lb. beef liver, minced

1. At 320 degrees F/ 160 degrees C, heat your air fryer in advance. 2. Crack the eggs to separate the whites from the yolks, and put each yolk in a cup. 3. Cut the liver into thin slices and refrigerate for 10 minutes. 4. In a separate bowl, mix up the cream, truffle oil, salt and pepper with a fork. 5. In a small ramekin, arrange half of the mixture. 6. Equally divide the whites between ramekins after pouring in. 7. Top with the egg yolks. 8. Use each liver to surround each yolk. 9. Cook for 15 minutes at 320 degrees F/ 160 degrees C. 10. When cooled, serve and enjoy.
Per serving: Calories: 316; Fat 18.4g; Sodium 199mg; Total Carbs 1g; Net Carbs: 0g; Fiber 0g; Sugars 0.5g; Protein 34.2g

Pork Meatloaf with Onion

Prep Time: 15 minutes. | Cook time: 20 Minutes | Serves: 4

1 egg, lightly beaten	1 tablespoon almond flour
1 onion, chopped	1 lb. ground pork
½ tablespoon thyme, chopped	Pepper
1 oz. chorizo, chopped	Salt

1. In a suitable bowl, mix up all of the ingredients, then transfer the mixture to the cooking pan of your air fryer. 2. Cook at 390 degrees F/ 200 degrees C for 20 minutes. 3. When cooked, slice to serve and enjoy.
Per serving: Calories: 234; Fat 8.7g; Sodium: 250 mg; Total Carbs 3g; Net Carbs: 1g; Fiber 1g; Sugars 1.3g; Protein 33.5g

Creole Pork Chops

Prep Time: 15 minutes. | Cook time: 12 Minutes | Serves: 4

1 ½ lbs. pork chops, boneless	⅓ cup almond flour
1 teaspoon garlic powder	1 ½-teaspoon paprika
5-tablespoon parmesan cheese, grated	1 teaspoon Creole seasoning

1. Heat the air fryer to 360 degrees F/ 180 degrees C in advance. 2. In a zip-lock bag, in addition to the pork chops, mix the other ingredients well. 3. Add pork chops into the bag and coat it with the mixture well by shaking the bag. 4. Coat the basket of your air fryer with cooking spray. 5. Place pork chops into the air fryer basket and cook for 12 minutes at 360 degrees F/ 180 degrees C. 6. Serve and enjoy.
Per serving: Calories: 478; Fat 36.2g; Sodium 299mg; Total Carbs 2g; Net Carbs: 0.5g; Fiber 0.9g; Sugars 0.2g; Protein 34.5g

Garlic Beef Meatloaf

Prep Time: 15 minutes. | Cook time: 15 Minutes | Serves: 4

1 lb. ground beef	1 teaspoon cayenne
¼-teaspoon cinnamon	1 teaspoon turmeric
tablespoon ginger, minced	1 teaspoon garam masala
¼ cup fresh cilantro, chopped	1 tablespoon garlic, minced
1 cup onion, diced	1 teaspoon salt
2 eggs, lightly beaten	

1. Prepare a large bowl, mix up all of the ingredients. 2. Place the meat mixture in the cooking pan of your air fryer. 3. Arrange the pan to the air fryer and cook at 360 degrees F/ 180 degrees C for 15 minutes. 4. Slice before serving and enjoying.
Per serving: Calories: 265; Fat 9.5g; Sodium 691mg; Total Carbs 5g; Net Carbs: 2g; Fiber 1.2g; Sugars 1.5g; Protein 37.9g

Spicy Pork Belly Pieces

Prep Time: 15 minutes. | Cook time: 50 Minutes | Serves: 4

1 ½ lbs. pork belly, cut into 4 pieces	½-teaspoon turmeric powder
Kosher salt and ground black pepper, to taste	1 tablespoon oyster sauce
	1 tablespoon green onions
1 teaspoon smoked paprika	4 cloves garlic, sliced
	1 lb. new potatoes, scrubbed

1. Heat your Air Fryer to 390 degrees F/ 200 degrees C in advance. 2. Use the kitchen to pat the pork belly pieces dry and season with the remaining spices. 3. Spray the coated pieces with a non-stick spray on all sides and add the oyster sauce. 4. Cook the pork belly pieces in the preheated Air Fryer for 30 minutes. 5. Turn them over every 10 minutes. 6. When the time is over, increase the temperature to 400 degrees F/ 205 degrees C. 7. Add the green onions, garlic, and new potatoes and cook for another 15 minutes, shaking regularly. 8. When done, serve warm and enjoy.
Per serving: Calories: 581; Fat 30.7g; Sodium 1855mg; Total Carbs 13g; Net Carbs: 7g; Fiber 2.1g; Sugars 1g; Protein 53.8g

Festive Pork Fillets

Prep Time: 15 minutes. | Cook time: 20 Minutes | Serves: 3

¼ cup chickpea flour	1 teaspoon cayenne pepper
1 tablespoon Romano cheese, grated	2 pork fillets (1 lb.)
1 teaspoon onion powder	1 Granny Smiths apple, peeled and sliced
1 teaspoon garlic powder	1 tablespoon lemon juice
½-teaspoon ground cumin	1 oz. butter, cold

1. In a zip-lock bag, mix the flour, cheese, onions powder, garlic powder, cumin, and cayenne pepper well, the add the pork fillets in it and shake to coat on all sides. 2. Spray the cooking basket of your air fryer with cooking spray and then arrange the coated pork fillets to it. 3. Cook the pork fillets at 370 degrees F/ 185 degrees C for 10 minutes. 4. When the time is up, add the apples, drizzle the lemon juice and place the cold butter on the top in order. Cook for 5 minutes more. 5. Once done, serve and enjoy.
Per serving: Calories: 325; Fat 18.1g; Sodium 196mg; Total Carbs 19g; Net Carbs: 6.7g; Fiber 4.9g; Sugars 8.2g; Protein 21.4g

Country-style Pork Ribs

Prep Time: 15 minutes. | Cook time: 40 Minutes | Serves: 4

1 teaspoon salt	½-teaspoon onion powder
1 teaspoon cayenne pepper	½-teaspoon porcini powder
½-teaspoon ground black pepper	1 teaspoon mustard seeds
1 teaspoon raw honey	1 tablespoon sweet chili sauce
2 garlic cloves, minced	1 tablespoon balsamic vinegar
1 (1-inch) piece ginger, peeled and grated	1 ½ lbs. pork country-style ribs

1. Thoroughly mix up the cayenne pepper, honey, garlic, ginger, onion powder, porcini powder, mustard seeds, sweet chili sauce, balsamic vinegar, salt and black pepper in a suitable bowl. 2. Rub the pork ribs with the spice mixture. 3. Cook the ribs in your air fryer at 360 degrees F/ 180 degrees C for 15 minutes. 4. After 15 minutes, flip the ribs and cook for 20 minutes more or until they are tender inside and crisp outside. 5. Garnished with fresh chives if desired. 6. Serve and enjoy.
Per serving: Calories: 312; Fat 23.2g; Sodium 629mg; Total Carbs 2g; Net Carbs: 0.5g; Fiber 0.4g; Sugars 1.7g; Protein 21.6g

Filet Mignon with Peanut Sauce

Prep Time: 10 minutes | Cook time: 25 Minutes | Serves: 4

2 lbs. filet mignon, sliced into bite-sized strips	1 tablespoon honey
1 tablespoon oyster sauce	1 teaspoon chili powder
1 tablespoon sesame oil	¼ cup peanut butter
1 tablespoon tamari sauce	1 tablespoon lime juice
1 tablespoon ginger-garlic paste	1 teaspoon red pepper flakes
1 tablespoon mustard	1 tablespoon water

1. Prepare a large dish, add the oyster sauce, sesame oil, tamari sauce, ginger-garlic paste, mustard, honey, chili powder and beef strips, then cover and refrigerate to marinate completely. 2. Cook the beef strips at 400 degrees F/ 205 degrees C for 18 minutes, flipping them occasionally. 3. To make the sauce, mix up the peanut butter, lime juice, red pepper flakes and water. 4. Serve and enjoy the beef strips with the sauce.
Per serving: Calories: 589; Fat 29.6g; Sodium 242mg; Total Carbs 10.3g; Net Carbs: 0g; Fiber 1.7g; Sugars 6.1g; Protein 68.8g

Lamb Chops with Mustard Mixture

Prep Time: 15 minutes. | Cook time: 15 Minutes | Serves: 4

8 lamb chops	3 tablespoons Dijon mustard
1 tablespoon lemon juice	Pepper
4 teaspoons tarragon	Salt
½-teaspoon olive oil	

1. Thoroughly mix up the mustard, lemon juice, tarragon, and olive oil in a small bowl. 2. Coat the lamb chops with the mustard mixture. 3. Arrange the coated lamb chops to the air fryer basket and cook at 390 degrees F/ 200 degrees C for 15 minutes, flipping halfway through. 4. Serve and enjoy.
Per serving: Calories: 411; Fat 16.5g; Sodium 196mg; Total Carbs 0.2g; Net Carbs: 0g; Fiber 0.1g; Sugars 0.1g; Protein 61.4g

Spiced Rib Eye Steak

Prep Time: 15 minutes. | Cook time: 9 Minutes | Serves: 3

1 lb. rib eye steak	
½-teaspoon chipotle powder	¼-teaspoon black pepper
¼-teaspoon paprika	⅛ teaspoon coffee powder
¼-teaspoon onion powder	⅛-teaspoon cocoa powder
½-teaspoon garlic powder	⅛-teaspoon coriander powder
½ teaspoon chili powder	1 ½-teaspoon sea salt

1. In addition to the steak, mix the other ingredients well in a small bowl. 2. Rub the steak with the spice mixture and marinate the steak for 20 minutes. 3. Coat the cooking basket of your air fryer with cooking spray. 4. Cook the marinated steak on the basket in your air fryer at 390 degrees F/ 200 degrees C for 9 minutes. 5. Once done, serve and enjoy.
Per serving: Calories: 419; Fat 33.5g; Sodium 1032mg; Total Carbs 1g; Net Carbs: 0g; Fiber 0.5g; Sugars 0.3g; Protein 26.9g

Steak with Onion and Bell Peppers

Prep Time: 10 minutes | Cook time: 15 Minutes | Serves: 6

1 lb. steak, sliced	gluten-free
1 tablespoon olive oil	½ cup onion, sliced
1 tablespoon fajita seasoning,	3 bell peppers, sliced

1. Line up the aluminum foil on the cooking basket of your air fryer. 2. In a large bowl, mix up all of the ingredients and toss well until coated. 3. Arrange the fajita mixture to the basket and cook at 390 degrees F/ 200 degrees C for 5 minutes. 4. After 5 minutes, toss well again and cook for 5-10 minutes more. 5. Serve and enjoy.
Per serving: Calories: 199; Fat 6.3g; Sodium 123mg; Total Carbs 6g; Net Carbs: 2.5g; Fiber 1g; Sugars 3.4g; Protein 28g

Marinated Beef and Vegetable Stir Fry

Prep Time: 15 minutes | Cook time: 35 Minutes | Serves: 4

2 lbs. top round, cut into bite-sized strips	Salt and black pepper, to taste
2 garlic cloves, sliced	½ tablespoon olive oil
1 teaspoon dried marjoram	1 red onion, sliced
¼ cup red wine	2 bell peppers, sliced
1 tablespoon tamari sauce	1 carrot, sliced

1. In a suitable bowl, add the top round, marjoram, red wine, garlic, tamari sauce, salt, and pepper in a bowl; cover and marinate for 1 hour. 2. Oil the cooking tray of your air fryer. 3. Take the marinated beef out of the marinade and arrange to the tray. 4. Cook at 390 degrees F/200 degrees C for 15 minutes. 5. After that, add the garlic, onion, peppers and carrot, cook for 15 minutes more or until tender. 6. Open the Air Fryer every 5 minutes and baste the meat with the remaining marinade. 7. When done, serve and enjoy.
Per serving: Calories: 489; Fat 14.8g; Sodium 153mg; Total Carbs 9g; Net Carbs: 4.3g; Fiber 1.9g; Sugars 5.1g; Protein 73g

Roasted Garlic Ribeye with Mayo

Prep Time: 15 minutes | Cook time: 20 Minutes | Serves: 3

1 ½ lbs. ribeye, bone-in	½-teaspoon dried dill
1 tablespoon butter, room temperature	½-teaspoon cayenne pepper
Salt, to taste	½-teaspoon garlic powder
½-teaspoon crushed black pepper	½-teaspoon onion powder
	1 teaspoon ground coriander
1 tablespoon mayonnaise	1 teaspoon garlic, minced

1. Use the kitchen towel to pat the ribeye dry, then rub it with the softened butter on all sides. 2. Transfer the ribeye to the basket of your air fryer after sprinkling with the seasonings. 3. Cook the ribeye at 400 degrees F/ 205 degrees C for 15 minutes, flipping halfway through. 4. Meanwhile, mix the mayonnaise and garlic well, and refrigerate the mixture until the ribeye cooked. 5. When ready, serve and enjoy!
Per serving: Calories: 552; Fat 48.2g; Sodium 200mg; Total Carbs 2g; Net Carbs: 0.5g; Fiber 0.2g; Sugars 0.6g; Protein 24.3g

Cajun Spareribs with Coriander

Prep Time: 10 Minutes | Cook time: 30 Minutes | Serves: 4

2 slabs spareribs	1 tablespoon paprika
2 teaspoons Cajun seasoning	1 teaspoon coriander seed powder
¼ cup brown sugar	2 tablespoons onion powder
½ teaspoon lemon	1 tablespoon salt

1. After mixing well the paprika, lemon, coriander, onion, and salt, rub the spareribs with the spice mixture. 2. Cook one sparerib in your air fryer at 390 degrees F/ 200 degrees C for 20 minutes. 3. Cook another sparerib with the same steps. 4. When done, serve and enjoy.
Per serving: Calories: 490; Fat: 13.3 g; Sodium: 144 mg; Total Carbs: 3g; Net Carbs: 1g; Fiber: 0.9g; Sugar: 0.7g; Protein: 32.2g

Montreal Steak

Prep Time: 10 minutes | Cook time: 7 Minutes | Serves: 2

12 oz. steak	1 tablespoon Montreal steak seasoning
½-teaspoon liquid smoke	
1 tablespoon soy sauce	Pepper
½-tablespoon cocoa powder	Salt

1. In a large zip-lock bag, coat the steak well with the liquid smoke, soy sauce, and steak seasonings, then refrigerate the mixture for overnight. 2. Coat the cooking basket of your air fryer with cooking spray. 3. Arrange the marinated steak to the air fryer and cook at 375 degrees F/ 190 degrees C for 7 minutes. 4. After that, turn the steak and cook another side for 5 minutes more. 5. Serve and enjoy.
Per serving: Calories: 346; Fat 8.7g; Sodium 528mg; Total Carbs 1g; Net Carbs: 0g; Fiber 0.5g; Sugars 0.2g; Protein 62.2g

Pork Chops with Soy Sauce

Prep Time: 10 minutes | Cook time: 20 minutes | Serves 2

2 pork chops	1 teaspoon paprika
1 teaspoon onion powder	1 tablespoon mustard
½ teaspoon garlic powder	2 tablespoons soy sauce
1 tablespoon brown sugar	1 teaspoon dried cilantro
Salt and pepper, to taste	2 tablespoons olive oil

1. In a zip-lock bag, put the olive oil, garlic powder, onion powder, brown sugar, paprika, mustard, soy sauce, dried cilantro, salt, pepper and add the pork chops, then shake up to coat well. 2. When coated, cook the pork chops in your air fryer at 390 degrees F/ 200 degrees C for 15 minutes. 3. When the time is over, serve and enjoy.
Per serving: Calories: 438; Fat 35.7g; Sodium 961mg; Total Carbs 9g; Net Carbs: 4.3g; Fiber 1.5g; Sugars 5.7g; Protein 20.8g

Porterhouse Steak with Mustard and Butter

Prep Time: 15 minutes | Cook time: 15 Minutes | Serves: 2

1 lb. porterhouse steak, cut meat from bone in 2 pieces	½ teaspoon garlic powder
	½-teaspoon dried thyme
½-teaspoon ground black pepper	½-teaspoon dried marjoram
½ teaspoon cayenne pepper	½ teaspoon Dijon mustard
½-teaspoon salt	1 tablespoon butter, melted

1. Sprinkle all the seasonings on the top of the porterhouse steak. 2. Evenly coat the steak with the mustard and butter. 3. Cook the processed steak at 390 degrees F/ 200 degrees C for 12 to 14 minutes. 4. When done, serve and enjoy.
Per serving: Calories: 234; Fat 10.9g; Sodium 686mg; Total Carbs 2g; Net Carbs: 0.5g; Fiber 0.8g; Sugars 0.5g; Protein 30.3g

Moroccan-style Steak with Salad

Prep Time: 15 minutes. | Cook time: 20 Minutes | Serves: 4

2 lbs. flank steak
¼ cup soy sauce
1 cup dry red wine
Salt, to taste
½-teaspoon ground black pepper
2 parsnips, peeled and sliced
lengthways
1 tablespoon paprika
½ teaspoon onion powder

½ teaspoon garlic powder
½-teaspoon ground coriander
¼-teaspoon ground allspice
1 tablespoon olive oil
½ tablespoon lime juice
1 teaspoon honey
1 cup lettuce leaves, shredded
½ cup pomegranate seeds

1. In a suitable bowl, add the soy sauce, wine, salt, black pepper and flank steak, then refrigerate the mixture for 2 hours to marinate the steak completely. 2. Spray the cooking basket with cooking spray and then transfer the marinated steak on it. 3. Sprinkle the parsnips on the top, add the paprika, onion powder, garlic powder, coriander, and allspice. 4. Cook at 400 degrees F/ 205 degrees C for 7 minutes, then turn the steak over and cook for 5 minutes more. 5. To make the dressing, mix up the olive oil, lime juice and honey. In a salad bowl, add the lettuce leaves and roasted parsnip, then toss with the dressing. 6. When the steak cook, slice and place on top of the salad. 7. Sprinkle over the pomegranate seeds and serve. Enjoy!
Per serving: Calories: 558; Fat 22.7g; Sodium 1073mg; Total Carbs 19g; Net Carbs: 6.7g; Fiber 4g; Sugars 7g; Protein 65.4g

Italian-style Honey Pork

Prep Time: 10 minutes | Cook time: 50 Minutes | Serves: 3

1 teaspoon Celtic sea salt
½-teaspoon black pepper, freshly cracked
¼ cup red wine
1 tablespoon mustard

1 tablespoon honey
2 garlic cloves, minced
1 lb. pork top loin
1 tablespoon Italian herb seasoning blend

1. Prepare a suitable bowl, mix up the salt, black pepper, red wine, mustard, honey, garlic and the pork top loin, then marinate the pork top loin at least 30 minutes. 2. Spray the cooking basket of your air fryer with the non-stick cooking spray. 3. Sprinkle the Italian herb on the top of the pork top loin after transfer it to the basket. 4. Cook the pork top loin at 370 degrees F/ 185 degrees C for 10 minutes, flipping and spraying with cooking oil halfway through. 5. When cooked, serve and enjoy.
Per serving: Calories: 201; Fat 7.7g; Sodium 38mg; Total Carbs 8.5g; Net Carbs: 4g; Fiber 0.7g; Sugars 6.2g; Protein 20.3g

Beef Tenderloin Steaks with Marjoram

Prep Time: 10 minutes | Cook time: 11 minutes | Serves 4

4 beef tenderloin steaks
Salt and pepper, to your taste
1 teaspoon dried oregano
1 teaspoon dried thyme
1 teaspoon marjoram
1 teaspoon dried sage

1 teaspoon garlic powder
1 teaspoon dried coriander
2 tablespoons olive oil
2 eggs, well-whisked
½ cup seasoned breadcrumbs

1. Mix up the olive oil, salt, pepper, thyme, oregano, sage, marjoram, garlic powder, oregano, and coriander in a large-size bowl, then use the spice mixture to season the beef tenderloin steaks. 2. In a shallow bowl, add the whisked egg; in another bowl, add the breadcrumbs. 3. Coat the seasoned beef tenderloin steak with the egg mixture and breadcrumbs in order; coat the left steaks with the same steps. 4. Cook the steaks in your air fryer at 380 degrees F/ 195 degrees C for 11 minutes. 5. When done, serve and enjoy with the fresh salad and potatoes.
Per serving: Calories: 310; Fat 16.3g; Sodium 262mg; Total Carbs 9g; Net Carbs: 4.3g; Fiber 1g; Sugars 0.4g; Protein 30.3g

Garlic Lamb Rack

Prep Time: 10 minutes | Cook time: 30 Minutes | Serves: 6

1 egg, lightly beaten
½ tablespoon fresh thyme, chopped
1 ¾ lbs. rack of lamb
½ tablespoon fresh rosemary,

chopped
1 tablespoon olive oil
2 garlic cloves, chopped
Pepper
Salt

1. Mix up the oil and garlic, then brush the lamb rack with the mixture. 2. Season the lamb rack with pepper and salt. 3. After mix the thyme and rosemary well, coat the lamb rack with the egg and the herb mixture. 4. Place lamb rack in the air fryer basket and cook for at 390 degrees F/ 200 degrees C for 30 minutes. 5. After 25 minutes of cooking time, turn the lamb rack and cook for 5 minutes more. 6. Serve and enjoy.
Per serving: Calories: 225; Fat 13.2g; Sodium 91mg; Total Carbs 1g; Net Carbs: 0g; Fiber 0.4g; Sugars 0.1g; Protein 24.1g

Delicious Baby Back Ribs

Prep Time: 10 minutes | Cook time: 30 Minutes | Serves: 4

1 teaspoon cayenne pepper
1 rack baby back ribs, cut into individual pieces
1 teaspoon onion powder
1 teaspoon garlic powder

1 teaspoon pomegranate molasses
1 teaspoon dried oregano
½ cup barbecue sauce
Salt and black pepper to taste
2 scallions, chopped

1. In a bowl, mix up the smoked paprika, cayenne pepper, garlic powder, pomegranate molasses, onion powder, oregano, salt, black pepper and ribs, then toss to coat well. 2. Cover and refrigerate for 30 minutes. 3. Spray the cooking basket of your air fryer with cooking spray. 4. Transfer the marinated ribs to the basket in the air fryer and cook them for 25 minutes at 360 degrees F/ 180 degrees C, flipping halfway through. 5. While cooking the ribs, in a saucepan, sauté the vegetable broth and gravy mix for 2 minutes or until the sauce thickens. 6. When the ribs cooked, drizzle the sautéed sauce, BBQ sauce and scatter scallions on the top, serve and enjoy.
Per serving: Calories: 407; Fat 24.8g; Sodium 615mg; Total Carbs 11g; Net Carbs: 6.7g; Fiber 0.5; Sugars 6.5g; Protein 0.3g

Tender Pork Ribs with BBQ Sauce

Prep Time: 10 minutes | Cook time: 25 minutes | Serves 4

1 lb. baby back ribs
3 tablespoons olive oil
½ teaspoon pepper
½ teaspoon smoked salt

1 tablespoon Dijon mustard
⅓ cup soy sauce
2 cloves garlic, minced
½ cup BBQ sauce

1. Cut the ribs in half after removing their back membrane. 2. To marinate the ribs completely, prepare a large dish, add the olive oil, pepper, salt, Dijon mustard, soy sauce, garlic and ribs, then cover and refrigerate for 2 hours. 3. When ready, cook the pork ribs in your air fryer at 370 degrees F/ 185 degrees C for 25 minutes. 4. With the BBQ sauce on the top, serve and enjoy!
Per serving: Calories: 407; Fat 24.6g; Sodium 1673mg; Total Carbs 13g; Net Carbs: 7g; Fiber 0.6g; Sugars 8.6g; Protein 31.5g

Glazed Meatloaf

Prep Time: 10 Minutes | Cook time:45 Minutes | Serves: 8

4 cups ground lean beef
1 cup (soft and fresh) bread crumb
½ cup chopped mushrooms
cloves of minced garlic
½ cup shredded carrots
¼ cup beef broth
½ cup chopped onions
2 eggs beaten

3 tbsp. ketchup
1 tbsp. Worcestershire sauce
1 tbsp. Dijon mustard
For Glaze
¼ cup honey
half cup ketchup
2-teaspoon Dijon mustard

1. Stir well the beef broth and breadcrumbs in a large bowl. 2. Set the mixture aside in a food processor, add garlic, onions, mushrooms, and carrots, and pulse at high speed until finely chopped. 3. In a separate bowl, combine well the soaked breadcrumbs, Dijon mustard, Worcestershire sauce, eggs, lean ground beef, ketchup, and salt to make them into a meatloaf. 4. Cook the meatloaf at 390 degrees F/ 200 degrees C for 45 minutes. 5. Mix well the Dijon mustard, ketchup, and brown sugar. 6. After 40 minutes of cooking time, glaze the meatloaf with the mixture. 7. Before serving, rest the cooked meatloaf for 10 minutes.
Per serving: Calories: 244; Fat: 13.3 g; Sodium: 144 mg; Total Carbs: 3g; Net Carbs: 1g; Fiber: 0.9g; Sugar: 0.7g; Protein: 32.2g

Simple Pork Chops

Prep Time: 40 minutes | Cook time: 12 minutes | Serves 3

3 boneless pork chops	1 tablespoon honey
Salt and pepper, to taste	2 tablespoons olive oil
½ cup all-purpose flour	1 tablespoon Dijon mustard
½ cup breadcrumbs	1 tablespoon soy sauce

1. In a zip-lock bag, mix up the soy sauce, honey, olive oil, Dijon mustard and pork chops, then seal and refrigerate for 30 minutes. 2. After remove the pork chops from the marinade, season them with salt, pepper and coat them with flour and breadcrumbs. 3. Cook the pork chops in your air fryer at 370 degrees F/ 185 degrees C for 12 minutes. 4. When done, serve and enjoy.
Per serving: Calories: 548; Fat 16.8g; Sodium 512mg; Total Carbs 26g; Net Carbs: 13g; Fiber 1.2g; Sugars 5.3g; Protein 69.2g

Garlic Beef Cubes

Prep Time: 10 minutes | Cook time: 20 minutes | Serves 4

1 lb. beef sirloin steak, cut into cubes	1 teaspoon dried basil
⅓ cup sesame oil	1 tablespoon dried parsley
½ teaspoon salt	2 carrots, sliced
¼ cup soy sauce	1 large onion, sliced
½ teaspoon pepper	2 Russet potatoes, peeled and sliced
½ teaspoon garlic powder	1 ½ tablespoon fresh coriander, finely chopped
¼ teaspoon ground cumin	
¼ cup fresh lemon juice	

1. In a large bowl, put the sesame oil, lemon juice, salt, pepper, garlic powder, soy sauce, cumin, basil, and parsley, then add the beef cubes to coat well. 2. Refrigerate the coated beef cubes for 2 hours. 3. Cook the marinated beef cubes in your air fryer at 360 degrees F/ 180 degrees C for 20 minutes. 4. Once cooked, serve immediately.
Per serving: Calories: 247; Fat 7.9g; Sodium 692mg; Total Carbs 14g; Net Carbs: 9.5g; Fiber 2.3g; Sugars 6.1g; Protein 27.9g

Spiced Pork Chops

Prep Time: 10 minutes | Cook time: 20 minutes | Serves 2

1 tablespoon olive oil	6 large mushrooms, cleaned and sliced
½ lb. pork chops	1 large yellow onion, chopped
½ teaspoon dried oregano	1 ½ tablespoons soy sauce
¼ teaspoon red pepper flakes	2 tablespoons fresh parsley, finely chopped
1 teaspoon dried thyme	
½ teaspoon salt	
½ teaspoon pepper	

1. Mix the pork chops with the onion, mushrooms, pepper, red pepper flakes, thyme, oregano, olive oil, soy sauce, and olive oil in a large bowl. 2. When coated, cook the pork chops and clean mushrooms in your air fryer at 390 degrees F/ 200 degrees C for 20 minutes. 3. Sprinkle with the fresh parsley, serve and enjoy!
Per serving: Calories: 480; Fat 35.6g; Sodium 1347mg; Total Carbs 11.5g; Net Carbs: 5g; Fiber 3.1g; Sugars 4.6g; Protein 29.5g

Unique Beef Cheeseburgers

Prep Time: 10 minutes | Cook time: 15 minutes | Serves 4

½ lb. ground beef	⅓ teaspoon pepper
⅓ cup breadcrumbs	4 slices Cheddar cheese
2 tablespoons parsley, finely chopped	4 burger buns
3 tablespoons parmesan cheese, shredded	1 red onion, sliced
	4 romaine lettuce leaves
½ teaspoon salt	4 teaspoons mayonnaise
	1cup pickles, sliced

1. Mix the ground beef with breadcrumbs, parmesan cheese, parsley, salt and pepper well in a suitable dish. 2. Form 4 patties from the meat mixture. 3. Cook the patties in your air fryer at 390 degrees F/ 200 degrees C for 13 minutes. 4. After that, place the cheese slices on the top and cook for 1 minute more. 5. When cooked, top with pickles, red onion, lettuce leaves, and mayonnaise. 6. Enjoy!
Per serving: Calories: 570; Fat 22.7g; Sodium 1718mg; Total Carbs 51g; Net Carbs: 15g; Fiber 3.6g; Sugars 4.3g; Protein 39.8g

Pork Sausages with Mustard Sauce

Prep Time: 10 minutes | Cook time: 18 minutes | Serves 2

4 pork sausages	1 tablespoon mayonnaise
Non-stick cooking spray	½ cup Dijon mustard
For the Mustard sauce:	1 tablespoon honey

1. Make holes in the sausages with toothpick or fork. 2. Cook the processed sausages at 370 degrees F/ 185 degrees C for 18 minutes. 3. While cooking the sausages, mix up the mayonnaise, honey, and Dijon mustard in a sauce bowl. 4. When cooked, serve and enjoy sausages with the mustard sauce.
Per serving: Calories: 191; Fat 12.3g; Sodium 957mg; Total Carbs 13g; Net Carbs: 7g; Fiber 2.1g; Sugars 9.6g; Protein 7.9g

Tasty Spaghetti with Beef Meatballs

Prep Time: 10 minutes | Cook time: 12 minutes | Serves 3

1 ½ pound ground beef	1 ½ tablespoon fresh parsley, minced
½ yellow onion, chopped	
5 tablespoons seasoned bread-crumbs	½ teaspoon salt
	¼ teaspoon pepper
½ teaspoon cumin powder	1 package spaghetti pasta, cooked

1. Combine the ground beef with the yellow onion in a large bowl, and finely chopped parsley well, then mix with the breadcrumbs, cumin, salt, and pepper well. 2. Form small balls from the mixture. 3. Cook the meat balls in your air fryer at 370 degrees F/ 185 degrees C for about 12 minutes, flipping them once halfway through. 4. With the cooked spaghetti, serve and enjoy.
Per serving: Calories: 484; Fat: 13.6g; Sodium: 2205 mg; Total Carbs: 45.5g; Net Carbs: 3g; Fiber: 5.6g; Protein: 44.6g

Delectable Pork Chops

Prep Time: 5 minutes | Cook time: 12 Minutes | Serves: 2

½ lb. pork chops, boneless	½-teaspoon steak seasoning blend
4 tablespoons Swerve	½-tablespoon mustard

1. Mix up the Swerve, steak seasoning blend and mustard in a small bowl, then rub the steak with the spice mixture. 2. Transfer the coated steak to the cooking basket in the air fryer and cook at 350 degrees F/ 175 degrees C for 12 minutes. flipping halfway through. 3. When done, serve and enjoy.
Per serving: Calories: 244; Fat: 13.3 g; Sodium: 144 mg; Total Carbs: 3g; Net Carbs: 1g; Fiber: 0.9g; Sugar: 0.7g; Protein: 32.2g

Lemon Beef Schnitzel

Prep Time: 10 Minutes | Cook time:15 Minutes | Serves: 1

1 lean beef schnitzel	1 egg
2 tablespoon Olive oil	1 lemon, to serve
¼ cup Breadcrumbs	

1. To form a crumbly mixture, mix the oil and breadcrumbs well in a bowl. 2. Coat the beef schnitzel with the whisked egg and breadcrumb mixture in order. 3. Cook the beef schnitzel at 370 degrees F/ 185 degrees C for 15 minutes. 4. When done, serve and enjoy.
Per serving: Calories: 521; Fat 36.8g; Sodium 303mg; Total Carbs 19.8g; Net Carbs: 16.6g; Fiber 1.2g; Sugars 2g; Protein 31.4g

Paprika Pork Chops

Prep Time: 15 minutes | Cook time: 12 minutes | Serves: 6

1 ½ pounds pork chops, boneless	1 teaspoon garlic powder
1 teaspoon paprika	¼ cup parmesan cheese, grated
1 teaspoon creole seasoning	⅓ cup almond flour

1. At 360 degrees F/ 180 degrees C, preheat your Air fryer. 2. Add all the recipe ingredients except pork chops in a zip-lock bag. 3. Add pork chops in the bag. Seal this bag and shake well to coat pork chops. 4. Remove pork chops from zip-lock bag and place in the air fryer basket. 5. Cook pork chops for almost 10-12 minutes. 6. Serve and enjoy.
Per serving: Calories: 237; Fat: 12.8 g; Sodium: 162 mg; Total Carbs: 3.9g; Net Carbs: 1.3g; Fiber: 0.9g; Sugar: 1.9g; Protein: 31.7g

Spice Meatloaf

Prep Time: 15 minutes | Cook time: 20 minutes | Serves: 8

1-pound ground beef
½ teaspoon dried tarragon
1 teaspoon Italian seasoning
1 tablespoon Worcestershire sauce
¼ cup ketchup
¼ cup coconut flour
½ cup almond flour
1 garlic clove, minced
¼ cup onion, chopped
2 eggs, lightly beaten
¼ teaspoon black pepper
½ teaspoon salt

1. Add all the recipe ingredients into the mixing bowl and mix until well combined. 2. Make the equal shape of patties from mixture and place on a plate. Place in refrigerator for 10 minutes. 3. Grease its air fryer basket with cooking spray. 4. At 360 degrees F/ 180 degrees C, preheat your air fryer. 5. Place prepared patties in air fryer basket and cook for 10 minutes. 6. Serve and enjoy.
Per serving: Calories: 244; Fat: 13.3 g; Sodium: 144 mg; Total Carbs: 3g; Net Carbs: 3g; Fiber: 0.9g; Sugar: 0.7g; Protein: 32.2g

Flank Steak with Honey and Paprika

Prep Time: 2 hours 10 minutes | Cook time: 15 minutes | Serves 4

1 ½ lb. flank steak
1 teaspoon salt
½ teaspoon pepper
2 tablespoons fresh thyme, chopped
2 teaspoons honey
3 garlic cloves, minced
1 ½ teaspoon paprika
1 ½ tablespoon fresh rosemary, finely chopped
4 tablespoons olive oil

1. In a sealable bag, coat the flank steak with the honey, salt, thyme, paprika, garlic, rosemary, olive oil, and pepper, then refrigerate them for at least 2 hours. 2. Cook the coated and marinated flank steak in your air fryer at 390 degrees F/ 200 degrees C for 15 minutes, flipping halfway through. 3. Serve immediately. Bon appétit!
Per serving: Calories: 475; Fat 28.6g; Sodium 679mg; Total Carbs 5g; Net Carbs: 2g; Fiber 1.5g; Sugars 3g; Protein 47.8g

Spiced Lamb Kebabs

Prep Time: 10 Minutes | Cook time: 60 Minutes | Serves: 3

1 ½ pounds lamb shoulder, bones removed and cut into pieces
2 tablespoons cumin seeds, toasted
2 teaspoons caraway seeds, toasted
1 tablespoon Sichuan peppercorns
1 teaspoon sugar
2 teaspoons crushed red pepper flakes
Salt and pepper

1. In a suitable bowl, add all of the ingredients, stir well and refrigerate for at least 2 hours to marinate the lamb shoulder pieces completely. 2. Cook the marinated pieces at 390 degrees F/ 200 degrees C for 15 minutes. 3. After 8 minutes, flip the pieces for even grilling and then cook for 7 minutes more. 4. Working in batches is suggested. 5. When done, serve warm and enjoy.
Per serving: Calories: 450; Fat 17.9g; Sodium 180mg; Total Carbs 4.5g; Net Carbs: 0.5g; Fiber 1.3g; Sugars 1.6g; Protein 64.8g

Flank Steak with Tamari Sauce

Prep Time: 20 Minutes | Cook time: 30 Minutes | Serves: 2

olive oil spray
2 pounds flank steak, cut into 6 pieces
kosher salt and black pepper
2 cloves of minced garlic
4 cups asparagus
half cup tamari sauce
3 bell peppers: sliced thinly
beef broth: ⅓ cup
1 tbsp. of unsalted butter
¼ cup balsamic vinegar

1. Rub the steak pieces with salt and pepper. 2. In a zip-lock bag, toss the steak pieces well with Tamari sauce and garlic, seal the bag and let the steak pieces marinate for overnight. 3. Top the steak pieces with the bell peppers and asparagus. 4. Roll the steak piece around the vegetables and secure with toothpick. Deal the remaining pieces with the same steps. 5. Transfer the processed steak rolls to the oiled cooking basket and cook at 400 degrees F/ 205 degrees C for 15 minutes. 6. When the time is up, remove the rolls from the air fryer and set aside for 5 minutes. 7. Meanwhile, stir fry the balsamic vinegar, butter, and broth over medium flame. 8. Mix well and reduce it by half. Add salt and pepper to taste. 9. Pour over steaks, serve and enjoy.
Per serving: Calories: 471; Fat: 13.3 g; Sodium: 144 mg; Total Carbs: 3g; Net Carbs: 1g; Fiber: 0.9g; Sugar: 0.7g; Protein: 32.2g

Simple and Tasty Hamburgers

Prep Time: 5 Minutes | Cook time:13 Minutes | Serves: 4

4 buns
4 cups lean ground beef chuck
Salt to taste
4 slices of any cheese
Black pepper, to taste

1. Mix well the lean ground beef with salt and pepper. Form patties from the mixture. 2. Cook the patties at 350 degrees F/ 175 degrees C for 6 minutes, flipping halfway through. 3. After 5 minutes of cooking time, top the cheese and cook for 1 minute more. 4. When cooked, add ketchup, any dressing to your buns, add tomatoes and lettuce and patties. 5. Enjoy.
Per serving: Calories: 520; Fat: 13.3 g; Sodium: 144 mg; Total Carbs: 3g; Net Carbs: 1g; Fiber: 0.9g; Sugar: 0.7g; Protein: 32.2g

Delicious Empanadas

Prep Time: 10 Minutes | Cook time:20 Minutes | Serves: 2

8 pieces square gyoza wrappers
1 tablespoon olive oil:
¼ cup white onion, finely diced
¼ cup mushrooms, finely diced
½ cup lean ground beef
2 teaspoons chopped garlic
¼ teaspoon paprika
¼ teaspoon ground cumin
6 green olives, diced
⅛ teaspoon ground cinnamon
½ cup diced tomatoes
1 egg, lightly beaten

1. In a skillet, sauté the oil, onions, and beef over a medium heat for 3 minutes or until beef turns brown. 2. After that, add mushrooms and cook for 6 minutes until they start to brown. 3. Add paprika, cinnamon, olives, cumin, garlic and cook for 3 minutes more. 4. Put in the chopped tomatoes and cook for 1 minute. When cooked, set aside for 5 minutes. 5. Place the gyoza wrappers on a flat surface, add 1-½ tablespoons of beef filling to each wrapper. 6. To better fold the wrappers and pinch the edges, brush the edges with water or eggs. 7. Cook 4 empanadas in your air fryer at 400 degrees F/ 205 degrees C for 7 minutes, until nicely browned. 8. Cook the left empanadas with the same steps. 9. When done, serve and enjoy.
Per serving: Calories: 343; Fat: 13.3 g; Sodium: 144 mg; Total Carbs: 3g; Net Carbs: 1g; Fiber: 0.9g; Sugar: 0.7g; Protein: 32.2g

Steak Kabobs with Vegetables

Prep Time: 30 Minutes | Cook time:10 Minutes | Serves: 4

2 tablespoons light soy sauce
4 cups lean beef chuck ribs, cut into one-inch pieces
⅓ cup low-fat: sour cream:
½ onion
8 6-inch skewers:
1 bell peppers

1. Mix well the soy sauce and sour cream in a suitable bowl, then add the lean beef chunks and coat well. 2. Marinate the chunks for 30 minutes. 3. Soak skewers for 10 minutes in boil water. 4. Cut onion and bell pepper in 1-inch pieces. 5. Add bell peppers, onions and beef chunks on skewers. You can also choose to sprinkle with black pepper. 6. Cook them in air fryer at 400 degrees F/ 205 degrees C for 10 minutes, flipping halfway through. 7. When done, serve with yogurt dipping sauce.
Per serving: Calories: 268; Fat: 13.3 g; Sodium: 144 mg; Total Carbs: 3g; Net Carbs: 1g; Fiber: 0.9g; Sugar: 0.7g; Protein: 32.2g

Cajun Pork

Prep Time: 10 Minutes | Cook time: 12 Minutes | Serves: 3

1 lb. pork loin, sliced into 1-inch cubes
2 tablespoons Cajun seasoning
3 tablespoons brown sugar
¼ cup cider vinegar

1. Coat the pork loin well with Cajun seasoning and 3 tablespoons of brown sugar in a suitable dish. Let the pork loin marinate for 3 hours. 2. To baste, mix the brown sugar and vinegar well in a bowl. 3. Thread pork pieces onto skewers, then baste with sauce. 4. Cook at 360 degrees F/ 180 degrees C for 12 minutes, flipping and basting with sauce halfway through. 5. Cooking in batches is suggested. 6. When done, serve and enjoy.
Per serving: Calories: 303; Fat 15.8g; Sodium 148mg; Total Carbs 6g; Net Carbs: 2.5g; Fiber 0g; Sugars 6.6g; Protein 31.1g

Simple Rib-Eye Steak

Prep Time: 5 Minutes | Cook time: 14 Minutes | Serves: 2

2 medium-sized rib eye steaks
Salt & freshly ground black
pepper, to taste

1. Use the kitchen towels to pat dry the steaks. 2. Season the rib eye steaks with salt and pepper well on both sides. 3. Cook the steaks at 400 degrees F/ 205 degrees C for 14 minutes, flipping halfway through. 4. Let the steaks cool for 5 minutes before serving.
Per serving: Calories: 180; Fat 9g; Sodium 980mg; Total Carbs 0g; Net Carbs: 0g; Fiber 0g; Sugars 0g; Protein 23g

Flank Steaks with Capers

Prep Time: 10 Minutes | Cook time: 45 Minutes | Serves: 4

1 anchovy fillet, minced
1 clove of garlic, minced
1 cup pitted olives
1 tablespoon capers, minced
2 tablespoons fresh oregano
2 tablespoons garlic powder
2 tablespoons onion powder
2 tablespoons smoked paprika
⅓ cup extra-virgin olive oil
2 pounds flank steak, pounded
Salt and pepper

1. Season the anchovy fillet with salt and pepper. 2. Sprinkle the steaks with onion powder, oregano, paprika, and garlic powder. 3. Cook the steaks in your air fryer at 390 degrees F/ 200 degrees C for 45 minutes, flipping every 10 minutes. 4. Meanwhile, stir well the olive oil, capers, garlic, olives, and anchovy fillets. 5. When done, serve and enjoy.
Per serving: Calories: 446; Fat 26.7g; Sodium 350mg; Total Carbs 7g; Net Carbs: 3g; Fiber 2.7g; Sugars 1.8g; Protein 43.7g

Homemade Steak

Prep Time: 70 Minutes | Cook time: 20 Minutes | Serves: 6

3 pounds steak
1 cup chimichurri
Salt and pepper

1. To better marinate, mix up the beef steak with the remaining ingredients in a sealed zip-lock bag and refrigerate for at least 60 minutes. 2. When marinated, cook the steak in your air fryer at 390 degrees F/ 200 degrees C for 20 minutes in batches, flipping halfway through. 3. When done, serve and enjoy.
Per serving: Calories: 481; Fat 14.5g; Sodium 113mg; Total Carbs 0.3g; Net Carbs: 0g; Fiber 0g; Sugars 0.1g; Protein 82g

Marinated Beef with BBQ Sauce

Prep Time: 1 hour 10 Minutes | Cook time: 20 minutes | Serves: 4

2 pounds beef steak, pounded
¼ cup bourbon
1 tablespoon Worcestershire sauce
¼ cup barbecue sauce
Salt and pepper

1. Marinate the beef steak with the remaining ingredients in a sealed zip-lock bag for at least 60 minutes. 2. When marinated, cook beef steak at 390 degrees F/ 200 degrees C for 20 minutes in batches. 3. Flip the steak halfway through for even cooking. 4. While cooking the steak, in a saucepan, simmer the marinade until the sauce starts to thicken. 5. With the bourbon sauce, serve and enjoy.
Per serving: Calories: 481; Fat 14.2g; Sodium 366mg; Total Carbs 6g; Net Carbs: 2.5g; Fiber 0.1g; Sugars 4.8g; Protein 68.8g

Garlic Beef with Sauce

Prep Time: 1 hour 10 minutes | Cook time: 1 hour | Serves: 12

1 ½ tablespoon garlic
1 cup beef stock
1 teaspoon thyme leaves, chopped
3 tablespoons butter
1 pound eye of round roast
6 tablespoons extra-virgin olive oil
1 teaspoon pepper
1 teaspoon salt

1. In a zip-lock bag, mix all of the ingredients, seal and put in the refrigerator to marinate for 60 minutes. 2. Transfer the marinated food to the cooking pan of your air fryer and cook at 400 degrees F/ 205 degrees C for 60 minutes, basting the beef with sauce halfway through. 3. When done, serve and enjoy.
Per serving: Calories: 150; Fat 11.5g; Sodium 294mg; Total Carbs 0.5g; Net Carbs: 0g; Fiber 0.1g; Sugars 0g; Protein 11.5g

Broccoli Pork Chops

Prep Time: 15 minutes | Cook time: 10 minutes | Serves: 4

2 (5-oz.) bone-in pork chops
2 garlic cloves
2 tablespoons avocado oil
½ teaspoon paprika
½ teaspoon onion powder
1 teaspoon salt
½ teaspoon garlic powder
2 cups broccoli florets

1. At 350 degrees F/ 175 degrees C, preheat your air fryer. 2. Spitz basket with cooking spray. Brush 1 tablespoon of oil per side of the ready pork chops. 3. Season the ready pork chops from per side with the paprika, onion powder, garlic powder, and ½ teaspoon of salt. 4. Put pork chops in the preheated air fryer basket and cook for 5 minutes. 5. Meanwhile pork chops are cooking put the broccoli, garlic, of the remaining salt, and the remaining oil to a bowl and toss to coat. 6. Put the broccoli to the basket and go back to the air fryer. 7. Now cook for 5 more minutes, stirring the broccoli during cooking. 8. Remove the food from the air fryer and serve.
Per serving: Calories: 379; Fat: 19g; Sodium: 184mg; Total Carbs: 12.3g; Net Carbs:5g; Fiber: 0.6g; Sugar: 2g; Protein: 37.7g

Spiced Beef Chuck Roast

Prep Time: 10 minutes | Cook time: 1 hour | Serves: 6

1 pound beef chuck roast
1 onion, chopped
2 cloves of garlic, minced
2 tablespoons olive oil
3 cups water
1 tablespoon butter
1 tablespoon Worcestershire sauce
1 teaspoon rosemary
1 teaspoon thyme
3 stalks of celery, sliced

1. Stir all of the ingredients and arrange them to the cooking pan of your air fryer. 2. Cook them at 350 degrees F/ 175 degrees C for 60 minutes, braising the meat with its sauce halfway through. 3. When done, serve and enjoy.
Per serving: Calories: 345; Fat 27.7g; Sodium 101mg; Total Carbs 3g; Net Carbs: 1g; Fiber 0.7g; Sugars 1.4g; Protein 20.2g

Pork Tenderloins

Prep Time: 5 minutes | Cook time: 30 minutes | Serves: 3

1 teaspoon salt
½ teaspoon pepper
1 lb. pork tenderloin
2 tablespoons minced fresh rosemary
2 tablespoons olive oil, divided
1 garlic cloves, minced
Apricot Glaze Ingredients:
1 cup apricot preserves
3 garlic cloves, minced
4 tablespoons lemon juice

1. After mixing the pepper, salt, garlic, oil, and rosemary well, brush the pork with them on all sides. 2. If needed, you can cut pork crosswise in half. 3. Arrange the pork to the sprayed cooking pan and cook at 390 degrees F/ 200 degrees C for 3 minutes on each side. 4. While cooking the pork, mix all of the glaze ingredients well. 5. Baste the pork every 5 minutes. 6. Cook at 330 degrees F/ 165 degrees C and cook for 20 minutes more. 7. When done, serve and enjoy.
Per serving: Calories: 569; Fat 15.4g; Sodium 910mg; Total Carbs 71g; Net Carbs: 0g; Fiber 1.5g; Sugars 46.7g; Protein 40.7g

Pork Curry

Prep Time: 15 minutes | Cook Time: 37 minutes | Servings: 8

2 lbs. pork shoulder, boneless and cut into chunks
2 garlic cloves, diced
1 onion, minced
1 cups chicken broth
1 cups of coconut milk
½ tbsp. turmeric
2 tbsps. olive oil
½ tbsp. curry
2 tbsps. fresh ginger, grated
Pepper
Salt

1. Sprinkle the Air Fryer Basket with olive oil and add the meat. 2. Season meat with pepper and salt. Air Fry the meat at 370 degrees F/ 185 degrees C for 7 minutes until golden brown, stirring occasionally in the basket. 3. Add remaining ingredients and stir everything well. Air Fry the food for 30 minutes at 350 degrees F/ 175 degrees C, stirring occasionally. 4. Stir and serve.
Per serving: Calories 216; Total Carbs 8g; Net Carbs 5g; Protein: 10 g; Fat 7g; Sugars 5 g; Fiber 2g

Teriyaki Pork

Prep Time: 15 minutes | Cook Time:45 minutes | Servings: 4

2 lb. pork loin	½ cup water
½ tbsp. onion powder	¼ cup soy sauce
1 tbsp. ground ginger	1 cup chicken stock
2 tbsps. honey	2 tsps. dry garlic

1. Put and mix all the recipe ingredients in a suitable bowl except main meat and stock. 2. Pour the stock into the Air Fryer. Place meat into the pot then pours bowl mixture over the pork. 3. Air Fry the meat at 370 degrees F/ 185 degrees C for 45 minutes. Turn the meat periodically. 4. After the beep sounds, open the cover. 5. Enjoy.
Per serving: Calories 201; Fat: 9g; Total Carbs 2.9g; Net Carbs 2g; Protein: 26.1g; Fiber: 0.1g; Sugar: 0.2g

Garlic Beef with Egg and Bell Pepper

Prep Time: 10 minutes | Cook time: 30 minutes | Serves: 4

1 pound ground beef	1 onion, chopped
6 eggs, beaten	3 cloves of garlic, minced
1 green bell pepper, seeded and chopped	3 tablespoons olive oil
	Salt and pepper

1. Stir the ground beef well with the olive oil, onion, garlic, and bell pepper in the cooking basket of your air fryer. 2. Dress with salt and pepper, then pour in the beaten eggs and mix. 3. Cook at 330 degrees F/ 165 degrees C for 30 minutes. 4. When done, serve and enjoy.
Per serving: Calories: 419; Fat 24.3g; Sodium 169mg; Total Carbs 6g; Net Carbs: 2.5g; Fiber 1g; Sugars 3.2g; Protein 43.4g

Asian Pork

Prep Time: 15 minutes | Cook Time:15 minutes | Servings: 4

1 lb. pork shoulder, boneless and cut into slices ½ inch sliced	2 tbsps. red pepper paste
	1 onion, sliced
3 tbsps. green onions, sliced	1 tbsp. sesame seeds
3 garlic cloves, diced	¾ tbsp. cayenne pepper
1 tbsp. ginger, diced	1 tbsp. sesame oil
	1 tbsp. rice wine

1. Add all the recipe ingredients into the bowl and mix well and place in the refrigerator for 1 hour. 2. Place marinated meat and onion slices into the Air Fryer Basket. Air Fry the food at 380 degrees F/ 195 degrees C for 15 min, flipping halfway through. 3. Serve with sesame seeds and green onions. 4. Enjoy.
Per serving: Calories 255; Total Carbs 18g; Net Carbs 16g; Protein 20g; Fat 11g; Sugar 3g; Fiber 2g

Great Garlicky Pork Roast

Prep Time: 15 minutes | Cook Time:35 minutes | Servings: 2

1 lb. pork roast	½ cup chicken stock
1 tbsp. basil	½ tbsp. corn-starch
1 ½ tbsp. soy sauce	½ tbsp. olive oil
2 tbsps. honey	salt, to taste
3 garlic cloves, diced	

1. Mix all the recipe ingredients into the bowl. 2. Transfer the entire contents of the bowl to the Air Fryer Basket. 3. Air Fry the food at 370 degrees F/ 185 degrees C for 35 minutes. 4. Stir the meat periodically during cooking. 5. Stir and serve.
Per serving: Calories 325; Total Carbs 20g; Net Carbs 14g; Protein 5g; Fat 26g; Sugar 10g; Fiber 6g

Bratwurst with Vegetables

Prep Time: 15 minutes | Cook Time:20 minutes | Servings: 6

1 package bratwurst, sliced into identical pieces	¼ cup onion, diced
	1 carrot, sliced
½ tbsp. red chili pepper	

1. Add all the recipe ingredients into the large mixing bowl and toss well. 2. Sprinkle the basket with oil spray. 3. Add vegetable and bratwurst mixture into the sprayed "Air Fryer Basket" and Air Fry them at 370 degrees F/ 185 degrees C for 10 min. 4. Toss well and Air Fry for 10 min more. 5. Enjoy.

Per serving: Calories 291; Total Carbs 19g; Net Carbs 15g; Protein 5g; Fat 23g; Sugar 13g; Fiber 4g

Air Fried Pork Strips

Prep Time: 15 minutes | Cook Time:30 minutes | Servings: 2

4 pork loin chops	⅛ tbsp. ground ginger
2 tbsps. honey	1 garlic clove, minced
1 tbsp. soy sauce	½ tbsp. apple sider vinegar

1. Cut pork into strips. Tenderize meat and season with pepper and salt. 2. In a suitable bowl, mix honey, soy sauce, and vinegar. Add ginger and garlic and set aside. 3. At 360 degrees F/ 180 degrees C, preheat your Air Fryer. 4. Add marinated meat into the Air Fryer Basket and Air Fry them for 15 minutes on each side. 5. Serve with Greek yogurt souse. Enjoy.
Per serving: Calories 256; Total Carbs 15g; Net Carbs 10g; Protein 9g; Fat 18g; Sugar 5g; Fiber 5g

Spicy Steak

Prep Time: 15 minutes | Cook Time:18 minutes | Servings: 4

2 tbsps. low-sodium salsa	⅛ tsp. red pepper flakes
1 tbsp. apple cider vinegar	¾ lb. sirloin tip steak, cut into
1 tsp. ground oregano	4 pieces and gently pounded to
⅛ tsp. freshly ground black pepper	about ⅓ inch thick

1. In a suitable bowl, mix up the salsa, chipotle pepper, cider vinegar, oregano, red pepper flakes and black pepper. 2. Rub this spice mixture into both sides of each steak piece. 3. Let stand for 15 minutes at room temperature. Place the steaks in the Air Fryer Basket. 4. Air Fry the steaks at 370 degrees F/ 185 degrees C, 2 at a time, for 6 to 9 minutes, or until they reach at least 145 degrees F/ 60 degrees C on a meat thermometer. 5. Cook another 2 steaks with the same steps.
Per serving: Calories 253; Total Carbs 19g; Net Carbs 13g; Protein 4g; Fat 19g sugar 9g; Fiber 6g

Greek Vegetable Mix

Prep Time: 15 minutes | Cook Time:19 minutes | Servings: 4

½ lb. 96 percent lean ground beef	2 tbsps. freshly squeezed lemon juice
2 medium tomatoes, minced	⅓ cup low-sodium beef broth
1 onion, minced	2 tbsp. crumbled low-sodium feta cheese
2 garlic cloves, diced	
2 cups fresh baby spinach	

1. Crumble the ground beef in the Air Fryer for 3 to 7 minutes at 370 degrees F/ 185 degrees C, stirring once during cooking, until browned. Drain off any fat or liquid. 2. Add the tomatoes, onion, and garlic to the basket. Air-fry for 4 to 8 minutes more, or until the onion is tender. 3. Add the spinach, lemon juice, and beef broth. Air-fry for 2 to 4 minutes more, or until the spinach is wilted. 4. Sprinkle with the feta cheese and serve immediately.
Per serving: Calories 239; Total Carbs 20g; Net Carbs 13g; Net Carbs 2g; Protein 4g; Fat 18g; Sugar 4g; Fiber 7g

Keto Crispy Pork Chops

Prep Time: 10 minutes | Cook Time: 12 minutes | Serves: 4

Salt and black pepper to taste	⅛ tsp. paprika
1 tbsp. crushed pork rinds	1 egg
¼ tsp. garlic powder	4 small slices cold butter
¼ tsp. onion powder	

1. At 390 degrees F/ 200 degrees C, preheat your Air Fryer. 2. In a suitable bowl, combine all the recipe ingredients except the pork, egg, and butter and mix well. in another bowl, whisk the egg with salt. 3. Dip the pork first in the egg and then coat with the pork rind mixture. 4. Spray with some cooking spray and place them in the "Air Fryer Basket". Air Fry them at 390 degrees F/ 200 degrees C for 12 minutes, flipping once halfway through. 5. Garnish with a slice of butter to serve.
Per serving: Calories 193; Fat 15.3 g; Total Carbs 10.9 g; Net Carbs 2g; Protein 5.2 g; Sugar 5.6 g; Fiber 2g

Beef Chops with Broccoli

Prep Time: 15 minutes	**Cook Time:30 minutes**	**Servings: 1**

8 oz. Beef chops	⅛ tbsp. kosher salt
6 oz. Broccoli	½ tbsp. black pepper
olive oil spray	1 tbsp. dried garlic
1 tbsp. olive oil	

1. Brush the beef chop with olive oil cooking spray; sprinkle with salt and ¼ tablespoon of pepper. 2. Mix beef and broccoli with spices in a suitable bowl. 3. Place the beef chops on one side of the Air Fryer Basket and the marinated Broccoli sprouts on the other. 4. Air Fry the food at 380 degrees F/ 195 degrees C for 20 minutes. Broccoli will be ready in 6 minutes. 5. Serve hot with balsamic sauce.
Per serving: Calories 200; Total Carbs 7g; Net Carbs 4g; Protein 3g; Fat 18g; Sugar 2g; Fiber 3g

Air Fried Pork Loin

Prep Time: 15 minutes	**Cook Time:40 minutes**	**Servings: 6**

3 lbs. pork loin	½ tbsp. herbs de Provence
½ tbsp. dried garlic	1 tbsp. olive oil
¼ tbsp. pepper	

1. Coat meat with olive oil, pepper, garlic salt, and herb de Provence. 2. Place the loin in the Air Fryer Basket and Air Fry at 360 degrees F/ 180 degrees C for 25 minutes. 3. Turn to another side and Air Fry for 15 minutes more. 4. Stir and serve.
Per serving: Calories 306; Total Carbs 20g; Net Carbs 15g; Protein 15g; Fat 19g; Sugar 4g; Fiber 5g

Pork Chops with Seasoning marinade

Prep Time: 15 minutes	**Cook Time:12 minutes**	**Servings: 1**

8 oz. pork chops	1 tsp. onion powder
1 tsp. olive oil	1 tsp. salt
1 tsp. paprika	1 tsp. pepper

1. At 380 degrees F/ 195 degrees C, preheat your Air fryer. 2. Brush pork chops with some olive oil. 3. Mix the pork seasonings together in a suitable bowl and apply to both sides of the pork chops. 4. Place pork chops in Air Fryer Basket and Air Fry them at 380 degrees F/ 195 degrees C for 9 to 12 minutes, turning the chop over halfway, until it reaches a minimum temp of 145 degrees F/ 60 degrees C.
Per serving: Calories 117; Total Carbs 4g; Net Carbs 0g; Protein 14g; Fat 5g; Sugar 2g; Fiber 0g

Honey Mustard Meatballs

Prep Time: 15 minutes	**Cook Time:15 minutes**	**Servings: 8**

2 onions, minced	2 tsps. honey
1 lb. ground beef	salt and black pepper, to taste
4 tsps. fresh basil, minced	2 tsps. mustard
2 tsps. chopped garlic	

1. At 385 degrees F/ 195 degrees C, preheat your Air fryer and grease an Air Fryer basket. 2. Mix all the recipe ingredients in a suitable bowl well. 3. Shape the prepared mixture into equal-sized balls gently and arrange the meatballs in the Air Fryer Basket. 4. Air Fry the food at 385 degrees F/ 195 degrees C for 15 minutes. 5. Dish out to serve warm with tomato salsa.
Per serving: Calories 320; Total Carbs: 10; Net Carbs 1.2g; Protein: 42g; Fat: 8; Sugar: 1g; Fiber: 2g

Adorable Air Fried Steak

Prep Time: 15 minutes	**Cook Time:10 minutes**	**Servings: 2**

2 sirloin steaks	pepper
2 tbsps. olive oil	salt
2 tbsps. steak seasoning	

1. At 350 degrees F/ 175 degrees C, preheat your Air Fryer F. 2. Coat sirloin steaks with olive oil and season with steak seasoning, pepper, and salt. 3. Spray "Air Fryer Basket" with some cooking spray and place steaks in it. 4. Air Fry the steaks for 10 min, turning halfway through. 5. Slice and serve with boiled white rice and tomato salsa.
Per serving: Calories 330; Total Carbs: 9g; Net Carbs 2g; Protein: 49g; Fat: 12; Sugar: 1g; Fiber: 2g

Classic Burger

Prep Time: 15 minutes	**Cook Time:12 minutes**	**Servings: 2**

1 lb. (450g) 80/20 ground chuck	4 slices tomato
¾ tsp. salt	1 cup shredded lettuce
½ tsp. ground black pepper	4 tbsps. mayonnaise
4 gluten free burger buns	4 slices cheddar cheese

1. Crumble the beef into a bowl and sprinkle over the black pepper and salt. 2. Form into 4 evenly sized burger patties by hand or with a burger press. 3. At 350 degrees F/ 175 degrees C, preheat your Air Fryer. 4. Air Fry the food at 350 degrees F/ 175 degrees C for 8-12 minutes, or until the burger patty is cooked to your liking, flip the burger over after 4 minutes of cooking. 5. If you want to add a slice of cheese, simply add it on top of each hot burger after the air fryer has switched off, if it's still on, it may blow the cheese off the burger! 6. Serve while hot and add your preferred burger toppings.
Per serving: Calories 300; Total Carbs: 4g; Net Carbs 2g; Protein: 40g; Fat: 12; Sugar: 1g; Fiber: 2g

Teriyaki Steak

Prep Time: 15 minutes	**Cook Time:10 minutes**	**Servings: 4**

1 lb. (450g) steak, cut into strips	½ tsp. onion powder
¼ cup brown sugar	½ tsp. garlic powder
¼ cup soy sauce	¼ tsp. crushed red pepper
⅛ cup teriyaki sauce	¼ tsp. pepper

1. Mix all the recipe ingredients the marinade in a suitable bowl. 2. Add steak to bowl, dip in and cover. Marinate the steak for 1 hour in the refrigerator. 3. Place the steak strips in the Air Fryer Basket and Air Fry them at 360 degrees F/ 180 degrees C for 7 minutes on one side and 3 minutes on the other.
Per serving: Calories 290; Total Carbs: 22g; Net Carbs 2g; Protein: 34g; Fat:10g; Sugar: 1g; Fiber: 2g

Tasty & Spicy Lamb

Prep Time: 15 minutes	**Cook Time:20 minutes**	**Servings: 4**

1 lb. lamb meat, cut into pieces	1 cup of coconut milk
2 tbsps. lemon juice	1 cup grape tomatoes, minced
½ cup fresh parsley, minced	½ tbsp. cumin powder
2 onions, minced	2 ½ tbsps. chili powder
2 cups chicken stock	1 tsp. salt

1. Season the lamb meat pieces with black pepper and salt. 2. Transfer the meat pieces to the "Air Fryer Basket" and Air Fry them at 370 degrees F/ 185 degrees C for 5 minutes. 3. When the time is up, add the remaining ingredients and stir, then resume cooking for 15 minutes more. 4. Serve and enjoy.
Per serving: Calories 240; Total Carbs: 9g; Net Carbs 1.2g; Protein: 35g; Fat: 10g; Sugar: 1g; Fiber: 2g

Gorgeous Lamb Meatballs

Prep Time: 15 minutes	**Cook Time:8 minutes**	**Servings: 4**

2 eggs, beaten	2 garlic cloves, diced
2 tbsps. pistachios, minced	2 tbsps. fresh lemon juice
1 lb. ground lamb	2 tsps. oregano
1 tbsp. plain flour	2 tsps. salt
2 tbsps. flat-leaf parsley, minced	olive oil
1 tsp. chili pepper	1 tsp. freshly ground black pepper

1. At 355 degrees F/ 180 degrees C, heat your air fryer in advance and grease an Air Fryer basket. 2. Mix lamb, pistachios, eggs, juice, chili, flour, oregano, parsley, salt, and black pepper in an exceedingly large bowl. 3. Form meatballs, place the meatballs in the "Air Fryer Basket" and Air Fry them for 8 minutes. 4. Enjoy.
Per serving: Calories 200; Total Carbs: 12g; Fat: 7; Net Carbs 0.5g; Protein: 41; Sugar: 1g; Fiber: 2g

Nourishing Lamb with Potatoes

Prep Time: 15 minutes | Cook Time:20 minutes | Servings: 2

½ lb. lamb meat
2 small potatoes, peeled and halved
½ small onion, peeled and halved

1 garlic clove, crushed
½ tbsp. dried rosemary, crushed
1 tsp. olive oil
salt, pepper

1. Preheat the Air Fryer to 355 degrees F/ 180 degrees C and arrange a divider in the Air Fryer Basket. 2. Rub the lamb evenly with garlic and rosemary and place on 1 side of Air Fryer Basket. 3. Cut the potatoes into desired pieces, add the onion, olive oil, black pepper and salt. Put the potato pieces on the other side of basket. 4. Air Fry the lamb meat for 20 minutes, but get the potatoes after 10 minutes of cooking time. 5. Cut meat in portions. Serve hot.
Per serving: Calories 310; Total Carbs: 20g; Sugar: 3g; Fat: 5g; Net Carbs 2g; Protein: 27g; Sugar: 1g; Fiber: 2g

Roast Lamb with Rosemary

Prep Time: 15 minutes | Cook Time:15 minutes | Servings: 2

10 oz. (280g) butterflied lamb leg roast
1 tbsp. olive oil

1 tsp. rosemary, fresh or dried
1 tsp. thyme, fresh or dried
½ tsp. black pepper

1. Preheat the Air Fryer to 360 degrees F/ 180 degrees C. 2. Add olive oil with rosemary and thyme in a plate and mix well. 3. Pat lamb roast dry and place into the herb oil mixture. 4. Place lamb in the Air Fryer Basket and Air Fry for 15 minutes at 360 degrees F/ 180 degrees C. 5. Remove roast lamb from air fryer, cover it with foil and leave to rest for 5 minutes before serving. 6. Cut against the grain to serve.
Per serving: Calories 250; Total Carbs: 5g; Sugar: 0g; Fat: 10g; Net Carbs 2g; Protein: 40g; Sugar: 1g; Fiber: 2g

Steak Bites with Mushrooms

Prep Time: 10 minutes | Cook Time: 18 minutes | Serves: 3

1 lb. steaks, cut into ½-inch cubes
½ tsp. garlic powder
1 tsp. Worcestershire sauce
2 tbsps. butter, melted

8 oz. mushrooms, sliced
Pepper
Salt

1. Add all the recipe ingredients into the large mixing bowl and toss well. 2. Spray the "Air Fryer Basket" with some cooking spray. 3. At 400 degrees F/ 205 degrees C, preheat your Air Fryer. 4. Add steak mushroom mixture into the "Air Fryer Basket" and Air Fry at 400 degrees F/ 205 degrees C for 15-18 minutes. Shake basket twice during cooking. 5. Serve and enjoy.
Per serving: Calories 347; Total Carbs 23g; Net Carbs 11g; Protein 9g; Fat 12 g; Sugar 6g; Fiber 3g

Beef with Creamed Mushroom Sauce

Prep Time: 10 minutes | Cook Time: 15 minutes | Serves: 5

2 tbsps. butter
2 lbs. sirloin, cut into 4 pieces
Salt and cracked black pepper, to taste
1 tsp. cayenne pepper
½ tsp. dried rosemary

½ tsp. dried dill
¼ tsp. dried thyme
1 lb. Cremini mushrooms, sliced
1 cup sour cream
1 tsp. mustard
½ tsp. curry powder

1. Start by preheating your Air Fryer to 395 degrees F/ 200 degrees C. Grease a baking pan with butter. 2. Add the sirloin, salt, black pepper, cayenne pepper, rosemary, dill, and thyme to the baking pan. Air Fry the food at 395 degrees F/ 200 degrees C for 9 minutes. 3. Next, stir in the mushrooms, sour cream, mustard, and curry powder. 4. Continue to cook for 5 minutes or until everything is heated through. 5. Spoon onto individual serving plates. Bon appétit!
Per serving: Calories 375; Total Carbs 14g; Net Carbs 4g; Protein 6g; Fat 13g; Sugar 7g; Fiber 2g

Simple Air Fryer Steak

Prep Time: 10 minutes | Cook Time: 18 minutes | Serves: 2

12 oz. steaks, ¾-inch thick
1 tsp. garlic powder
1 tsp. olive oil

Pepper
Salt

1. Coat steaks with oil and season with garlic powder, pepper, and salt. 2. At 400 degrees F/ 205 degrees C, preheat your Air Fryer. 3. Place the prepared steaks in "Air Fryer Basket" and Air Fry them at 400 degrees F/ 205 degrees C for 15-18 minutes, turning halfway through. 4. Serve and enjoy.
Per serving: Calories 375; Total Carbs 14g; Net Carbs 4g; Protein 6g; Fat 13g; Sugar 7g; Fiber 2g

Savoury Apple Pork Bites

Prep Time: 25 minutes | Cook Time: 25 minutes | Serves: 10

1 whole egg, beaten
3 ½ oz. onion, chopped
2 tbsps. dried sage
2 tbsps. almonds, chopped

½ tsp. pepper
3 ½ oz. apple, sliced
½ tsp. salt

1. At 350 degrees F/ 175 degrees C, preheat your Air fryer. 2. In a suitable bowl, mix onion, almonds, sliced apples, egg, pepper and salt. 3. Add the almond mixture and sausage to a Ziploc bag. 4. Mix to coat well and set aside for 15 minutes. Use the prepared mixture to form cutlets. 5. Add them to the Air Fryer Basket and Air Fry them at 350 degrees F/ 175 degrees C for 25 minutes. 6. Serve with heavy cream.
Per serving: Calories 409; Total Carbs 20g; Net Carbs 6.7g; Protein 4.3g; Fat 5g; Sugar 1.1g; Fiber 2g

Crisp Pork Chops

Prep Time: 10 minutes | Cook Time: 12 minutes | Serves: 6

1 ½ lbs. pork chops, boneless
1 tsp. paprika
1 tsp. creole seasoning

1 tsp. garlic powder
¼ cup parmesan cheese, grated
⅓ cup almond flour

1. At 360 degrees F/ 180 degrees C, preheat your Air Fryer. 2. Add all the recipe ingredients except pork chops in a zip-lock bag. 3. Add pork chops in the bag. Seal this bag and shake well to coat pork chops. 4. Remove pork chops from zip-lock bag and place them in the Air Fryer Basket. 5. Air Fry the pork chops at 360 degrees F/ 180 degrees C for 10-12 minutes. 6. Serve and enjoy.
Per serving: Calories 401; Total Carbs 21g; Net Carbs 9g; Protein 5.3g; Fat 7g; Sugar 2.1g; Fiber 2g

Easy Pork & Parmesan Meatballs

Prep Time: 10 minutes | Cook Time: 10 minutes | Serves: 3

1 lb. ground pork
2 tbsps. tamari sauce
1 tsp. garlic, minced
2 tbsps. spring onions, chopped
1 tbsp. brown sugar

1 tbsp. olive oil
½ cup breadcrumbs
2 tbsps. parmesan cheese, preferably freshly grated

1. Combine the ground pork, tamari sauce, garlic, onions, and sugar in a mixing dish. Mix until everything is well incorporated. 2. Form the prepared mixture into small meatballs. 3. In a shallow bowl, mix the olive oil, breadcrumbs, and parmesan. 4. Roll the meatballs over the parmesan mixture. 5. Air Fry the meatballs at 380 degrees F/ 195 degrees C for 3 minutes; shake the basket and cook an additional 4 minutes or until meatballs are browned on all sides. 6. Bon appétit!
Per serving: Calories 375; Total Carbs 20g; Net Carbs 11g; Protein 7.6g; Fat 11g; Sugar 5g; Fiber 1g

Classic Pork

Prep Time: 10 minutes | Cook Time: 10 minutes | Serves: 4

1 lb. pork shoulder, thinly sliced
1 tbsp. fish sauce
3 garlic cloves, minced
1 tbsp. Swerve

2 tbsps. olive oil
¼ cup onion, minced
½ tsp. pepper
1 tbsp. lemongrass paste

1. In a suitable bowl, whisk together onion, pepper, lemongrass paste, fish sauce, garlic, sweetener, and oil. 2. Add meat slices into the bowl and coat well. Place in the fridge for 1 hour. 3. Place marinated meat in the "Air Fryer Basket" and Air Fry them at 400 degrees F/ 205 degrees C for 10 minutes, turning halfway through. 4. Serve and enjoy.
Per serving: Calories 389; Total Carbs 21g; Net Carbs 9g; Protein 5.3g; Fat 7g; Sugar 2.1g; Fiber 2g

Coconut Butter Pork Chops

Prep Time: 10 minutes | Cook Time: 15 minutes | Serves: 2

4 pork chops	¼ tsp. rosemary
1 tbsp. coconut oil	3 garlic cloves, minced
1 tbsp. coconut butter	Pepper
1 tsp. dried parsley	Salt
¼ tsp. dried basil	

1. At 350 degrees F/ 175 degrees C, preheat your Air Fryer. 2. In a suitable bowl, mix garlic, coconut butter, coconut oil, parsley, basil, rosemary, pepper, and salt. 3. Rub garlic mixture over pork chops. Place in the refrigerator for 2 hours. 4. Place marinated pork chops into the "Air Fryer Basket" and Air Fry them at 350 degrees F/ 175 degrees C for 7 minutes. 5. Turn pork chops to another side and Air Fry for 8 minutes more. 6. Serve and enjoy.
Per serving: Calories 409; Total Carbs 20g; Net Carbs 6.7g; Protein 4.3g; Fat 5g; Sugar 1.1g; Fiber 2g

Mushrooms Meatballs

Prep Time: 10 minutes | Cook Time: 20 minutes | Serves: 2

½ lb. ground beef	1 tbsp. parsley, chopped
2 tbsps. onion, chopped	¼ cup almond flour
2 mushrooms, diced	½ tsp. salt
¼ tsp. pepper	

1. In a suitable mixing bowl, combine together all the recipe ingredients well. 2. Make small balls from meat mixture and place into the Air Fryer Basket. 3. Air Fry the balls at 350 degrees F/ 175 degrees C for 20 minutes. 4. Serve and enjoy.
Per serving: Calories 389; Total Carbs 21g; Net Carbs 9g; Protein 5.3g; Fat 7g; Sugar 2.1g; Fiber 2g

Mustard Pork Tenderloin

Prep Time: 10 minutes | Cook Time: 15 minutes | Serves: 2

1 pork tenderloin, cut into pieces	1 tbsp. oil
½ tbsp. mustard	2 tsps. herb de Provence
1 onion, sliced	Pepper
1 bell pepper, cut into strips	Salt

1. At 390 degrees F/ 200 degrees C, preheat your Air Fryer. 2. In a suitable bowl, mix bell pepper strips, herb de Provence, onion, pepper, and salt. Add ½ tablespoon of oil and mix well. 3. Season pork tenderloin with mustard, pepper, and salt. 4. Coat pork tenderloin with the remaining oil. 5. Place pork tenderloin pieces into the air fryer pan and top with bell pepper mixture. 6. Place pan in the air fryer and Air Fry the food for 15 minutes. Stir halfway through cooking. 7. Serve and enjoy.
Per serving: Calories 347; Total Carbs 23g; Net Carbs 11g; Protein 9g; Fat 12 g; Sugar 6g; Fiber 3g

Spanish-style Pork with Padrón Peppers

Prep Time: 10 minutes | Cook Time: 26 minutes | Serves: 4

1 tbsp. olive oil	1 tsp. paprika
8 oz. Padrón peppers	1 heaped tbsp. capers, drained
2 lbs. pork loin, sliced	8 green olives, pitted and halved
1 tsp. Celtic salt	

1. Drizzle olive oil all over the Padrón peppers; Air Fry them at 400 degrees F/ 205 degrees C for 10 minutes, turning occasionally, until well blistered all over and tender-crisp. 2. Season the pork loin slices with salt and paprika. 3. Add the capers and Air Fry them at 360 degrees F/ 180 degrees C for 16 minutes, turning them over halfway through the Cook Time. 4. Serve with olives and the reserved Padrón peppers.
Per serving: Calories 415; Total Carbs 21g; Net Carbs 10g; Protein 7g; Fat 14g; Sugar 8g; Fiber 3g

McCormick Pork Chops

Prep Time: 40 minutes | Cook Time: 15 minutes | Serves: 2

2 pork chops	2 tbsps. arrowroot flour
½ tsp. McCormick Montreal chicken seasoning	1 ½ tbsps. coconut milk
	Salt

1. Season pork chops with pepper and salt. 2. Drizzle milk over the pork chops. 3. Place pork chops in a zip-lock bag with flour and shake well to coat. 4. Marinate the pork chops for 30 minutes. 5. Place marinated pork chops into the "Air Fryer Basket" and Air Fry them at 380 degrees F/ 195 degrees C for 15 minutes, turning halfway through. 6. Serve and enjoy.
Per serving: Calories 375; Total Carbs 20g; Net Carbs 11g; Protein 7.6g; Fat 11g; Sugar 5g; Fiber 1g

Dreamy Beef Roast

Prep Time: 10 minutes | Cook Time: 50 minutes | Serves: 3

4 lb. top round roast beef	½ tsp. fresh rosemary, chopped
1 tsp. salt	3 lbs. red potatoes, halved
¼ tsp. fresh ground black pepper	Olive oil, black pepper and salt for garnish
1 tsp. dried thyme	

1. At 360 degrees F/ 180 degrees C, preheat your Air Fryer. 2. In a suitable bowl, mix rosemary, salt, pepper and thyme; rub oil onto beef. 3. Season with the spice mixture. 4. Place the prepared meat in your air fryer's "Air Fryer Basket" and Air Fry them at 360 degrees F/ 180 degrees C for 20 minutes. 5. Give the meat a turn and add potatoes, more pepper and oil. Air Fry the food for 20 minutes more. 6. Take the steak out and set aside to cool for 10 minutes. 7. Air Fry the potatoes in your air fryer for 10 more minutes at 400 degrees F/ 205 degrees C. 8. Serve hot.
Per serving: Calories 401; Total Carbs 21g; Net Carbs 9g; Protein 5.3g; Fat 7g; Sugar 2.1g; Fiber 2g

St. Louis-style Pork Ribs with Roasted Peppers

Prep Time: 10 minutes | Cook Time: 50 minutes | Serves: 2

2 lbs. St. Louis-style pork spare-ribs, individually cut	1 tbsp. sweet paprika
1 tsp. seasoned salt	½ tsp. mustard powder
½ tsp. ground black pepper	2 tbsps. sesame oil
	4 bell pepper, seeded

1. Toss and rub the spices all over the pork ribs; drizzle with 1 tablespoon of sesame oil. 2. Air Fry the pork ribs at 360 degrees F/ 180 degrees C for 15 minutes; flip the ribs and cook an additional 20 minutes or until they are tender inside and crisp on the outside. 3. Toss the peppers with the remaining 1 tablespoon of oil; season to taste and Air Fry them at 390 degrees F/ 200 degrees C for 15 minutes. 4. Serve the warm spareribs with the roasted peppers on the side. Enjoy!
Per serving: Calories 409; Total Carbs 20g; Net Carbs 6.7g; Protein 4.3g; Fat 5g; Sugar 1.1g; Fiber 2g

Hawaiian Cheesy Meatball Sliders

Prep Time: 10 minutes | Cook Time: 15 minutes | Serves: 4

1 lb. ground pork	½ cup Romano cheese, grated
2 tbsps. bacon, chopped	1 cup tortilla chips, crushed
2 garlic cloves, minced	1 ½ cups marinara sauce
2 tbsps. scallions, chopped	8 Hawaiian rolls
Salt and ground black pepper, to taste	1 cup Cheddar cheese, shredded

1. Mix the ground pork with the bacon, garlic, scallions, salt, black pepper, cheese, and tortilla chips. Shape the prepared mixture into 8 meatballs. 2. Add the meatballs to the lightly greased baking pan. 3. Pour in the marinara sauce and lower the pan onto the Air Fryer Basket. 4. Air Fry the meatballs at 380 degrees F/ 195 degrees C for 10 minutes. 5. Check the meatballs halfway through the Cook Time. 6. Place one meatball on top of the bottom half of one roll. 7. Spoon the marinara sauce on top of each meatball. 8. Top with cheese and Air Fry them at 370 degrees F/ 185 degrees C for 3 to 4 minutes. 9. Add the other half of the Hawaiian roll on top and serve immediately. Bon appétit!
Per serving: Calories 390; Total Carbs 20g; Net Carbs 6.7g; Protein 4.3g; Fat 5g; Sugar 1.1g; Fiber 2g

Chapter 7 Dessert Recipes

Yogurt Treat with Berries 81

Plum Apple Crumble with Cranberries 81

Vanilla Pineapple Cinnamon Treat 81

Pumpkin Almond Flour Muffins 81

Chocolate Cake with Raspberries 81

Chocolate Banana Brownie 81

Vanilla Banana Puffs 81

Chocolate Lava Cake 82

Easy-to-Make Almond Cookies 82

Cinnamon Butter Muffins 82

Creamy Cheesecake Bites 82

Apple Chips with Cinnamon 82

Vanilla Cheesecake 82

Blueberry Vanilla Muffins 82

Vanilla Coconut Pie 82

Spiced Apple Chips 82

Strawberry Muffins with Cinnamon 83

Almond Pecan Muffins 83

Cookies with Mashed Strawberry 83

Chocolate Peanut Butter Mug Cake 83

Almond Cherry Bars 83

Berry Pudding 83

Cheese Cake with Strawberries 83

Sweet Orange Muffins 83

Coffee Cookies 84

Yummy Apple Chips 84

Cheese Muffins with Cinnamon 84

Fluffy Cocoa Cupcakes 84

Lemon Creamy Muffins 84

Coconut Walnuts 84

Butter Cheesecake 84

Lemon Butter Bars 84

Zucchini Bars with Cream Cheese 84

Lemon Nut Bars 85

Enticing Cappuccino Muffins 85

Scones with Cream Cheese 85

Cocoa Nutmeg Cake 85

Simple Donuts 85

Lava Cakes 85

Donuts with Cardamom 85

Walnut Banana Split 85

Vanilla Bars with Sesame Seeds 86

Moist Cinnamon Muffins 86

Aromatic Cup with Blondies 86

Vanilla Spread 86

Vanilla Cookies 86

Tasty Mozzarella Balls 86

Enticing Ricotta Cheese Cake 86

Pineapple Chips with Cinnamon 86

Vanilla Cheese Custard 86

Divine Apple Pie 87

Banana Muffin 87

Dark Chocolate Lava Cakes 87

Churros 87

Almond Biscuit 87

Sweet Cinnamon Donuts 87

Cardamom Bombs 87

Vinegar Cake 87

Butter Custard 87

Lemon Peppermint Bars 88

Vinegar Cake 88

Avocado Cream Pudding 88

Delicious Walnut Bars 88

Chocolate Candies 88

Ginger Lemon Pie 88

Vanilla Yogurt Cake 88

Cobbler 88

Almond Pudding 88

Lemon Almond Biscotti 89

Plum Almond Cake 89

Cream Cheese Muffins 89

Chocolate Fudge 89

Creamy Crumble 89

Blackberries Cake 89

Turmeric Almond Pie 89

Chia Cinnamon Pudding 89

Yogurt Treat with Berries

Prep Time: 8-10 minutes | Cook time: 6 minutes | Serves: 4-5

1 teaspoon vanilla extract
2 eggs, large
2 slices sourdough bread
Butter as needed

1 to 2 teaspoon squeeze honey
Greek yogurt for serving
Your favorite choice of berries

1. On a flat kitchen surface, plug your air fryer and turn it on. 2. Gently coat your air fryer basket with cooking oil or spray. 3. Preheat your air fryer to 355 degrees F/ 180 degrees C for about 4 to 5 minutes. 4. Whisk the large eggs and vanilla extract together in a medium sized bowl. 5. Brush the both sides of the bread slices with butter. 6. Then soak the bread slices in the egg mixture. 7. Arrange the bread slices onto the air fryer basket. 8. Cook in the preheated air fryer for 3 minutes. 9. When cooked, remove from the air fryer and serve with the berries and yogurt honey on the top. 10. Enjoy!
Per serving: Calories:77 Fat:2g; Sodium: 423 mg; Total Carbs:38.7g; Net Carbs: 30g; Fiber:1.5g; Sugar: 5.6g; Protein:4g

Plum Apple Crumble with Cranberries

Prep Time: 10-15 minutes | Cook time: 25 minutes | Serves: 6-7

2 ½ ounces caster sugar
⅓ cup oats
⅔ cup flour
½ stick butter, chilled
1 tablespoon cold water
1 tablespoon honey
½ teaspoon ground mace

¼ pound plums, pitted and chopped
¼ pound apples, cored and chopped
1 tablespoon lemon juice
½ teaspoon vanilla paste
1 cup cranberries

1. On a flat kitchen surface, plug your air fryer and turn it on. 2. Gently coat your cake pan with cooking oil or spray. 3. Before cooking, heat your air fryer to 390 degrees F/ 200 degrees C for about 4 to 5 minutes. 4. Mix the lemon juice, sugar, honey, mace, apples, and plums in a medium sized bowl. 5. Place the fruits onto the cake pan. 6. In a second medium sized bowl, mix thoroughly the rest of the ingredients and add the fruit mixture on the top. Transfer to the cake pan. 7. Bake the apple crumble in the preheated air fryer for 20 minutes. 8. When cooked, remove from the air fryer and serve warm.
Per serving: Calories:188 Fat:8g; Sodium: 11 mg; Total Carbs:27.8g; Net Carbs: 0.16g; Fiber:1.8g; Sugar: 25.84g; Protein:1.6g

Vanilla Pineapple Cinnamon Treat

Prep Time: 8-10 minutes | Cook time: 8 minutes | Serves: 6

½ teaspoon baking soda
½ teaspoon ground cinnamon
¼ teaspoon ground anise star
¼ cup flaked coconut, unsweetened
1 pineapple, sliced
A pinch of kosher salt

½ cup water
⅔ cup all-purpose flour
⅓ cup rice flour
½ teaspoon baking powder
1 cup rice milk
½ teaspoon vanilla essence
4 tablespoons caster sugar

1. On a flat kitchen surface, plug your air fryer and turn it on. 2. Gently coat your air frying basket with cooking oil or spray. 3. Before cooking, hear your air fryer to 380 degrees F/ 195 degrees C for about 4 to 5 minutes. 4. Mix baking soda, ground cinnamon, ground anise star, coconut flakes, kosher salt, water, all-purpose flour, rice flour, baking powder, rice milk, vanilla essence, and caster sugar together in a medium sized bowl to make the batter. 5. Then coat the batter mixture over the pineapple slices. 6. Transfer the slices to the air frying basket. 7. Cook them in the preheated air fryer for 8 minutes. 8. When cooked, remove from the air fryer and pour the maple syrup over the pineapple slices. 9. Add vanilla ice cream on the top to garnish. 10. Serve and enjoy!
Per serving: Calories: 160; Fat 1.7g; Sodium 148mg; Total Carbs 34g; Net Carbs: 18g; Fiber 1.4g; Sugars 11g; Protein 2.3g

Pumpkin Almond Flour Muffins

Prep Time: 10 minutes | Cook time: 20 minutes | Serves: 10

4 large eggs
½ cup pumpkin puree
1 tbsp. pumpkin pie spice
1 tbsp. baking powder, gluten-free

⅔ cup erythritol
1 tsp. vanilla
⅓ cup coconut oil, melted
½ cup almond flour

½ cup coconut flour

½ tsp sea salt

1. Before cooking, heat your air fryer to 325 degrees F/ 160 degrees C. 2. Add pumpkin pie spice, erythritol, sea salt, almond flour, and coconut flour in a large bowl and stir until well combined. 3. Then combine the mixture with the whisked eggs, pumpkin puree, and coconut oil. 4. Divide the batter into the silicone muffin molds. 5. Cook in batches in your air fryer for 20 minutes. 6. Serve and enjoy!
Per serving: Calories: 84; Fat 4.5g; Sodium 125mg; Total Carbs 7g; Net Carbs: 3g; Fiber 3.3g; Sugars 0.6g; Protein 4.3g

Chocolate Cake with Raspberries

Prep Time: 10 minutes | Cook time: 3 minutes | Serves: 5-6

2 eggs
⅔ cup all-purpose flour
5 tablespoons sugar
⅔ cup unsalted butter

Salt as needed
1 cup chocolate chips, melted
⅓ cup raspberries

1. On a flat kitchen surface, plug your air fryer and turn it on. 2. Preheat your air fryer for about 4-5 minutes to 355 degrees F/ 180 degrees C. Gently grease 6 ramekins with oil and dust some sugar inside. 3. Whisk the butter and sugar in a medium sized bowl. Then beat the eggs in the mixture till fluffy. 4. Combine together with salt and flour. Then mix in the melted chocolate chips until well combined. 5. Then divide the mixture into the prepared ramekins with ¼ empty. 6. Transfer the ramekins onto the air fryer basket. 7. Cook the chocolate cake in the preheated air fryer for 3 minutes. 8. When cooked, remove from the air fryer. 9. Sprinkle the raspberries on the top and serve warm.
Per serving: Calories: 443; Fat 30.4g; Sodium 215mg; Total Carbs 38g; Net Carbs: 23.5g; Fiber 1.8g; Sugars 24.9g; Protein 5.7g

Chocolate Banana Brownie

Prep Time: 10 minutes | Cook time: 16 minutes | Serves: 4

1 cup bananas, overripe
1 scoop protein: powder
2 tablespoons unsweetened cocoa

powder
½ cup almond butter, melted

1. Before cooking, heat your air fryer to 325 degrees F/ 160 degrees C. 2. Using cooking spray, spray a baking pan that fits in your air fryer. 3. In a blender, mix the bananas, protein powder, cocoa powder, and the almond butter together until smooth. 4. Spread the better onto the baking pan. 5. Cook the brownie in the preheated air fryer for 16 minutes. 6. Serve and enjoy!
Per serving: Calories: 52; Fat 1.6g; Sodium 1mg; Total Carbs 10.4g; Net Carbs: 0g; Fiber 2.1g; Sugars 4.7g; Protein 1.4g

Vanilla Banana Puffs

Prep Time: 10-15 min. | Cook time: 10 min. | Serves: 8

4 ounces instant vanilla pudding
4 ounces cream cheese, softened
1 package (8-ounce) crescent dinner rolls, refrigerated

1 cup milk
2 bananas, sliced
1 egg, lightly beaten

1. On a flat kitchen surface, plug your air fryer and turn it on. 2. Before cooking, heat your air fryer to 355 degrees F/ 180 degrees C for about 4 to 5 minutes. 3. Make 8 squares from the crescent dinner rolls. 4. Mix thoroughly the milk and pudding in a medium sized bowl. Then whisk the cream cheese in the mixture. 5. Divide the mixture onto the squares. Add the banana slices on the top. 6. Fold the rolls over and press the edges to seal the filling inside. Brush the whisked egg over each pastry puff. 7. Transfer to the air fryer basket. 8. Cook the banana puffs in the preheated air fryer for 10 minutes. 9. When the cooking time runs out, remove from the air fryer and serve warm. 10. Enjoy!
Per serving: Calories: 307; Fat:7.2g; Sodium: 346 mg; Total Carbs:58.65g; Net Carbs: 2.1g; Fiber:4g; Sugar: 37.53g; Protein:5.6g

Chocolate Lava Cake

Prep Time: 10 minutes | Cook time: 9 minutes | Serves: 2

1 egg
½ teaspoon baking powder
1 tablespoon coconut oil, melted
1 tablespoon flax meal
2 tablespoons erythritol
2 tablespoons water
2 tablespoons unsweetened cocoa powder
Pinch of salt

1. Before cooking, heat your air fryer to 350 degrees F/ 175 degrees C. 2. In a bowl, whisk all the ingredients. Then divide the mixture into 2 ramekins. 3. Transfer the ramekins inside the air fryer basket and bake in the preheated air fryer for 8 to 9 minutes. 4. When cooked, remove from the air fryer and set aside to cool for 10 minutes. Serve and enjoy!
Per serving: Calories: 119; Fat 11g; Sodium 34mg; Total Carbs 4g; Net Carbs: 2g; Fiber 2.8g; Sugars 0.3g; Protein 4.6g

Easy-to-Make Almond Cookies

Prep Time: 5 minutes | Cook time: 15 minutes | Serves: 8

1 and ½ cups almonds, crushed
2 tablespoons Erythritol
½ teaspoon baking powder
¼ teaspoon almond extract
2 eggs, whisked

1. In a bowl, whisk all of the ingredients well. 2. Scoop 8 servings of the mixture and then arrange them to the cooking pan lined with parchment paper. 3. Cook them at 350 degrees F/ 175 degrees C for 15 minutes. 4. Serve cold.
Per serving: Calories: 89; Fat 7.3g; Sodium 16mg; Total Carbs 2g; Net Carbs: 0.5g; Fiber 1.6g; Sugars 0.6g; Protein 4g

Cinnamon Butter Muffins

Prep Time: 15 minutes | Cook time: 10 minutes | Serves: 2

1 teaspoon of cocoa powder
2 tablespoons coconut flour
2 teaspoons swerve
½ teaspoon vanilla extract
2 teaspoons almond butter, melted
¼ teaspoon baking powder
1 teaspoon apple cider vinegar
¼ teaspoon ground cinnamon

1. After adding the cocoa powder, coconut flour, swerve, vanilla extract, almond butter, baking powder, apple cider vinegar and ground cinnamon, use a spoon to stir them until smooth. 2. Pour the brownie mixture in the muffin molds and let them rest for 10 minutes. 3. Cook the muffins at 365 degrees F/ 185 degrees C for 10 minutes. 4. Cool them completely before serving.
Per serving: Calories: 135; Fat: 9.9g; Sodium: 2mg; Total Carbs: 9g; Net Carbs: 4.3g; Fiber: 5g Sugars: 0.9g; Protein 4.6g

Creamy Cheesecake Bites

Prep Time: 10 minutes | Cook time: 2 minutes | Serves: 16

8 ounces cream cheese, softened
2 tablespoons erythritol
½ cup almond flour
½ tsp vanilla
4 tablespoons heavy cream
½ cup erythritol

1. In a stand mixer, mix cream cheese, 2 tbsp. heavy cream, vanilla, and ½ cup erythritol until smooth. 2. Line a plate with parchment paper and spread the cream cheese onto the parchment. 3. Refrigerate for 1 hour. 4. Mix together 2 tbsp. Erythritol and almond flour in a small bowl. 5. Drip the remaining heavy cream over the cheesecake bites and dip in the almond flour mixture to coat. 6. Arrange evenly the cheesecake bites inside the air fryer basket and cook in the air fryer at 350 degrees F/ 175 degrees C for 2 minutes. 7. Halfway cooking, check the cheesecake bites to ensure they are still frozen. 8. Serve with chocolate syrup on the top.
Per serving: Calories: 84; Fat 8g; Sodium 45mg; Total Carbs 1g; Net Carbs: 0g; Fiber 0.4g; Sugars 0.1g; Protein 1.9g

Apple Chips with Cinnamon

Prep Time: 10 minutes | Cook time: 12 minutes | Serves: 4

1 apple, thinly slice using a mandolin slicer
1 tablespoon almond butter
¼ cup plain yogurt
2 teaspoons olive oil
1 teaspoon ground cinnamon
4 drops liquid stevia

1. In a large bowl, toss together oil, cinnamon, and the apple slices. 2. Using cooking spray, spray the air fryer basket. 3. Transfer the apple slices in the air fryer basket. 4. Set the temperature to 375 degrees F/ 190 degrees C and timer for 12 minutes. 5. Turn over the apple slices every 4 minutes. 6. Then mix together the yogurt, sweetener, and the almond butter in a small bowl. 7. When cooked, remove the apple slices from the air fryer. 8. Serve the apple slices with the yogurt dip.
Per serving: Calories: 86; Fat 4.9g; Sodium 12mg; Total Carbs 10g; Net Carbs: 6.7g; Fiber 2.1g; Sugars 7.1g; Protein 1.9g

Vanilla Cheesecake

Prep Time: 10 minutes | Cook time: 10 minutes || Serves:6

2 eggs
16 ounces cream cheese, softened
2 tablespoons sour cream
½ teaspoon fresh lemon juice
1 teaspoon vanilla
¾ cup erythritol

1. Before cooking, heat your air fryer to 350 degrees F/ 175 degrees C. 2. In a large bowl, mix the whisked eggs, vanilla, lemon juice, and sweetener together and use a hand mixer to beat until smooth. 3. Then beat in cream cheese and sour cream until fluffy. 4. Divide the batter into 2 4-inch springform pan that fits in your air fryer. 5. Cook in your air fryer at 350 degrees F/ 175 degrees C for 8 to 10 minutes. 6. When cooked, remove from the air fryer and set it aside to cool completely. 7. Transfer in the fridge to reserve. 8. Serve and enjoy!
Per serving: Calories: 296; Fat 28.7g; Sodium 247mg; Total Carbs 2g; Net Carbs: 0.5g; Fiber 0g; Sugars 0.4g; Protein 7.7g

Blueberry Vanilla Muffins

Prep Time: 10 minutes | Cook time: 20 minutes | Serves: 12

3 large eggs
⅓ cup coconut oil, melted
1 ½ teaspoons gluten-free baking powder
½ cup erythritol
2 ½ cups almond flour
¾ cup blueberries
½ teaspoon vanilla
⅓ cup unsweetened almond milk

1. Before cooking, heat your air fryer to 325 degrees F/ 160 degrees C. 2. Stir together the baking powder, erythritol, and almond flour in a large bowl. 3. Mix vanilla, almond milk, coconut oil, and the whisked eggs in the bowl. Then add in the strawberries and fold together. 4. Divide the batter into the silicone muffin molds. 5. Cook in batches in the preheated air fryer for 20 minutes. 6. Serve and enjoy!
Per serving: Calories: 77; Fat 7.4g; Sodium 23mg; Total Carbs 1.5g; Net Carbs: 0g; Fiber: 0.3g; Sugars: 1g; Protein 1.7g

Vanilla Coconut Pie

Prep Time: 10 minutes | Cook time: 12 minutes | Serves: 6

2 eggs
½ cup coconut flour
½ cup erythritol
1 cup shredded coconut
1 ½ tsp vanilla
¼ cup butter
1 ½ cups coconut milk

1. Beat the 2 eggs in a large bowl and mix them with coconut flour, erythritol, shredded coconut, vanilla, butter, and coconut milk until well combined. 2. Using cooking spray, spray a baking dish that fits in your air fryer. 3. Transfer the batter onto the greased baking dish. 4. Cook in your air fryer at 350 degrees F/ 175 degrees C for 10 to 12 minutes. 5. Before serving, slice into your desired size. 6. Serve and enjoy!
Per serving: Calories: 317; Fat 28.9g; Sodium 87mg; Total Carbs 12g; Net Carbs: 7g; Fiber 6.5g; Sugars: 3.1g; Protein 5.1g

Spiced Apple Chips

Prep Time: 10 minutes | Cook time: 10 minutes | Serves: 6

4 small apples, sliced
1 tsp apple pie spice
½ cup erythritol
2 tablespoons coconut oil, melted

1. In a mixing dish, mix the apple pie spice, coconut oil, apple slices, and coconut oil together until the apple slices are well tossed. 2. Place the apple slices inside the air fryer basket. 3. Cook in your air fryer at 350 degrees F/ 175 degrees C for 10 minutes. 4. Serve and enjoy!
Per serving: Calories: 117; Fat 4.8g; Sodium 1mg; Total Carbs 20.7g; Net Carbs: 0g; Fiber 3.6g; Sugars 15.5g; Protein 0.4g

Strawberry Muffins with Cinnamon

Prep Time: 10 minutes | Cook time: 15 minutes | Serves: 12

3 eggs
1 teaspoon ground cinnamon
2 teaspoons baking powder
2 ½ cups almond flour
⅔ cup fresh strawberries, diced
⅓ cup heavy cream
1 teaspoon vanilla
½ cup Swerve
5 tablespoons butter

1. Before cooking, heat your air fryer to 325 degrees F/ 160 degrees C. 2. In a bowl, add the sweetener and butter and use a hand mixer to beat until smooth. 3. Beat in cream, whisked eggs, and vanilla until frothy. 4. Sift the cinnamon, baking powder, salt, and almond flour together in a second bowl. 5. Mix the flour mixture together with the wet ingredients until well incorporated. 6. Then place the strawberries. Fold and press well. 7. Divide the batter into the silicone muffin molds. 8. Cook in batches in your air fryer at 325 degrees F/ 160 degrees C for 15 minutes. 9. Enjoy!
Per serving: Calories: 215; Fat 18.2g; Sodium 60mg; Total Carbs 6g; Net Carbs: 2.5g; Fiber 2.8g; Sugars 0.5g; Protein 6.6g

Almond Pecan Muffins

Prep Time: 10 minutes | Cook time: 15 minutes | Serves: 12

4 eggs
1 teaspoon vanilla
¼ cup almond milk
2 tablespoons butter, melted
½ cup swerve
1 teaspoon psyllium husk
1 tablespoon baking powder
½ cup pecans, chopped
½ teaspoon ground cinnamon
2 teaspoons allspice
1 ½ cups almond flour

1. Before cooking, heat your air fryer to 370 degrees F/ 185 degrees C. 2. In a bowl, beat the butter, sweetener, almond milk, whisked eggs, and vanilla together with a hand mixer until smooth. 3. Then mix all the remaining ingredients together until well combined. 4. Divide the batter into the silicone muffin molds. 5. Cook in batches in the pre-heated air fryer for 15 minutes. 6. Serve and enjoy!
Per serving: Calories: 142; Fat 11.6g; Sodium 43mg; Total Carbs 5g; Net Carbs: 2g; Fiber 2.5g; Sugars 0.3g; Protein 5g

Cookies with Mashed Strawberry

Prep Time: 15 minutes | Cook time: 9 minutes | Serves: 4

2 teaspoons butter, softened
1 tablespoon Splenda
1 egg yolk
½ cup almond flour
1 oz. strawberry, chopped, mashed

1. In a suitable bowl, mix the butter, Splenda, egg yolk and almond flour well. Knead the non-sticky dough. 2. Form the small balls from the dough and use your finger to make small holes in each ball. 3. Fill the balls with the mashed strawberries. 4. Arrange to the balls to the cooking pan lined with baking paper and cook them at 360 degrees F/ 180 degrees C for 9 minutes. 5. When done, serve and enjoy.
Per serving: Calories: 132; Fat 9.7g; Sodium 21mg; Total Carbs 6g; Net Carbs: 2.5g; Fiber 1.6g; Sugars: 3.4g; Protein 3.7g

Chocolate Peanut Butter Mug Cake

Prep Time: 5 minutes | Cook time: 20 minutes | Serves: 1

1 egg, lightly beaten
1 tablespoon heavy cream
¼ teaspoon baking powder
2 tablespoons unsweetened cocoa powder
2 tablespoons Erythritol
½ teaspoon vanilla
1 tablespoon peanut butter
1 teaspoon salt

1. Before cooking, heat your air fryer to 400 degrees F/ 205 degrees C. 2. Mix the beaten egg, heavy cream, baking powder, cocoa powder, Erythritol, vanilla, peanut butter, and salt together in a bowl until well incorporated. 3. Using cooking spray, spritz a mug. 4. Add the mixture into the mug. Transfer inside your air fryer. 5. Cook in the preheated air fryer at 400 degrees F/ 205 degrees C for 20 minutes. 6. When cooked, remove from the air fryer and serve.
Per serving: Calories: 241; Fat 19.5g; Sodium 2470mg; Total Carbs 10.6g; Net Carbs: 0g; Fiber 4.6g; Sugars 2.3g; Protein 12g

Almond Cherry Bars

Prep Time: 10 minutes | Cook time: 35 minutes | Serves: 12

2 eggs, lightly beaten
1 cup erythritol
½ tsp vanilla
¼ cup water
½ cup butter, softened
¾ cup cherries, pitted
1 ½ cup almond flour
1 tablespoon xanthan gum
½ teaspoon salt

1. Mix vanilla, butter, salt, almond flour, the beaten eggs, and erythritol together in a bowl to form a dough. 2. Transfer the dough to a baking dish that fits in your air fryer and press the dough to flatten the surface. 3. Bake in your air fryer at 375 degrees F/ 190 degrees C for 10 minutes. 4. While baking, stir together the xanthan gum, water, and cherries in a separate bowl. 5. When the cooking time is up, add the cherry mixture over the dough. Cook again for 25 minutes. 6. Once cooked, cut the dough into your desired size and serve.
Per serving: Calories: 206; Fat 15.1g; Sodium 174mg; Total Carbs 13.5g; Net Carbs: 6.5g; Fiber 1.7g; Sugars 0.1g; Protein 4.1g

Berry Pudding

Prep Time: 10 minutes | Cook time: 15 minutes | Serves: 6

2 cups coconut cream
1 lime zest, grated
3 tablespoons erythritol
¼ cup blueberries
⅓ cup blackberries

1. In a blender, add coconut cream, the grated lime zest, erythritol, blueberries, and blackberries and combine together. 2. Using cooking spray, spritz 6 ramekins. 3. Divide the mixture into the ramekins. 4. Transfer the ramekins inside the air fryer basket. 5. Cook in your air fryer at 340 degrees F/ 170 degrees C for 15 minutes. 6. When cooked, remove the ramekins onto a rack to cool. 7. Serve and enjoy.
Per serving: Calories: 191; Fat 19.1g; Sodium 12mg; Total Carbs 6g; Net Carbs: 2.5g; Fiber 2.3g; Sugars 3.7g; Protein 2g

Cheese Cake with Strawberries

Prep Time: 10 minutes | Cook time: 35 minutes | Serves: 6

1 cup almond flour
3 tablespoons coconut oil, melted
½ teaspoon vanilla
1 egg, lightly beaten
1 tablespoon fresh lime juice
¼ cup erythritol
1 cup cream cheese, softened
1-pound strawberries, chopped
2 teaspoons baking powder

1. Combine almond flour, the melted coconut oil, vanilla, the beaten egg, fresh lime juice, erythritol, softened cream cheese, chopped strawberries, and baking powder together in a large bowl. 2. Using cooking spray, spray an air fryer cake pan that fits in your air fryer. 3. Then pour the batter into the greased pan and evenly spread it. Transfer to your air fryer. 4. Cook in your air fryer at 350 degrees F/ 175 degrees C for 35 minutes. 5. When cooked, remove the pan onto a wire rack to cool completely. 6. Then slice the cake into your desired size and serve. 7. Enjoy!
Per serving: Calories: 345; Fat 30.1g; Sodium 134mg; Total Carbs 12g; Net Carbs: 7g; Fiber 3.6g; Sugars 4g; Protein 8.4g

Sweet Orange Muffins

Prep Time: 10 minutes | Cook time: 10 minutes | Serves: 5

5 eggs, beaten
1 tablespoon poppy seeds
1 teaspoon vanilla extract
¼ teaspoon ground nutmeg
½ teaspoon baking powder
1 teaspoon orange juice
1 teaspoon orange zest, grated
5 tablespoons coconut flour
1 tablespoon Monk fruit
2 tablespoons coconut flakes
Cooking spray

1. After adding the eggs, poppy seeds, vanilla extract, ground nutmeg, baking powder, orange juice, orange zest, coconut flour, Monk fruit and coconut flakes, mix them well until homogenous and have no clumps. 2. Spray the inside of the muffin molds. 3. Pour the mixture batter in the molds and then arrange them to the air fryer. 4. Cook them at 360 degrees F/ 180 degrees C for 10 minutes. 5. When cooked, serve and enjoy.
Per serving: Calories: 114; Fat 6.6g; Sodium 63mg; Total Carbs 6g; Net Carbs: 2.5g; Fiber 3.4g; Sugars 0.9g; Protein 7g

Coffee Cookies

Prep Time: 10 minutes | Cook time: 15 minutes | Serves: 12

1 cup almond flour	¼ cup erythritol
2 eggs, lightly beaten	¼ cup brewed espresso
2 teaspoons baking powder	½ cup ghee, melted
½ tablespoon cinnamon	

1. In a bowl, combine almond flour, the beaten eggs, baking powder, cinnamon, erythritol, brewed espresso, and the melted ghee together. 2. Then shape the mixture into small cookies. Transfer to an oven-safe cookie sheet. 3. Place the sheet onto the air fryer basket. 4. Then cook in your air fryer at 350 degrees F/ 175 degrees C for 15 minutes. 5. When cooked, remove from the air fryer and serve.
Per serving: Calories: 143; Fat 13.7g; Sodium 15mg; Total Carbs 2g; Net Carbs: 0.5g; Fiber 1.2g; Sugars 0.1g; Protein 3g

Yummy Apple Chips

Prep Time: 10 minutes | Cook time: 8 minutes | Serves: 6

3 Granny Smith apples, wash, core and thinly slice	1 teaspoon ground cinnamon
	1 pinch of salt

1. In the air fryer basket, add cinnamon, salt, and apple slices together and rub well. 2. Cook in your air fryer at 390 degrees F/ 200 degrees C for 8 minutes. Flip the apple slices halfway through cooking. 3. When cooked, remove from the air fryer and serve.
Per serving: Calories: 59; Fat 0.2g; Sodium 28mg; Total Carbs 15g; Net Carbs: 5.6g; Fiber 2.9g; Sugars 11.6g; Protein 0.3g

Cheese Muffins with Cinnamon

Prep Time: 10 minutes | Cook time: 16 minutes | Serves: 10

2 eggs	1 teaspoon ground cinnamon
½ cup erythritol	½ tsp vanilla
8 ounces cream cheese	

1. Before cooking, heat your air fryer to 325 degrees F/ 160 degrees C. 2. Mix together vanilla, erythritol, eggs, and cream cheese until smooth. 3. Divide the batter into the silicone muffin molds. Top the muffins with cinnamon. 4. In the air fryer basket, transfer the muffin molds. 5. Cook in your air fryer for 16 minutes. 6. Serve and enjoy!
Per serving: calories:93; Fat 8.8g; Sodium 79mg; Total Carbs 0.9g; Net Carbs: 0g; Fiber 0.1g; Sugars 0.2g; Protein 2.8g

Fluffy Cocoa Cupcakes

Prep Time: 5 minutes | Cook time: 25 minutes | Serves: 4

⅓ cup coconut flour	4 eggs, whisked
½ cup cocoa powder	1 teaspoon vanilla extract
3 tablespoons stevia	4 tablespoons coconut oil, melted
½ teaspoon baking soda	¼ cup almond milk
1 teaspoon baking powder	Cooking spray

1. In addition to the cooking spray, whisk the other ingredients well. 2. Spray the cooking pan of your air fryer with the cooking spray, then pour the mixture on it. 3. Cook the mixture at 350 degrees F/ 175 degrees C for 25 minutes. 4. Cool down before serving.
Per serving: Calories: 283; Fat 24g; Sodium 226mg; Total Carbs 14g; Net Carbs: 9.5g; Fiber 7.6g; Sugars 1.2g; Protein 9.2g

Lemon Creamy Muffins

Prep Time: 15 minutes | Cook time: 11 minutes | Serves: 6

1 cup almond flour	½ teaspoon baking powder
3 tablespoons Erythritol	½ teaspoon instant coffee
1 scoop protein: powder	1 teaspoon lemon juice
1 teaspoon vanilla extract	2 tablespoons heavy cream
3 tablespoons coconut oil, melted	Cooking spray
1 egg, beaten	

1. After adding the almond flour, Erythritol, protein: powder, vanilla extract, coconut oil, egg, baking powder, instant coffee, lemon juice, and heavy cream in a suitable bowl, use the immersion blender to whisk them until smooth. 2. Spray the muffin molds with cooking spray. 3. Fill half of each muffin mold with muffin batter and arrange them to the cooking basket of your air fryer. 4. Cook them at 360 degrees F/ 180 degrees C for 11

minutes. 5. When done, serve and enjoy.
Per serving: Calories: 202; Fat 18.4g; Sodium 19mg; Total Carbs: 4.5g; Net Carbs: 0.5g; Fiber: 2g; Sugars: 0.2g; Protein 5g

Coconut Walnuts

Prep Time: 5 minutes | Cook time: 40 minutes | Serves: 12

1 and ¼ cups almond flour	1 and ½ cups coconut, flaked
1 cup swerve	1 egg yolk
1 cup butter, melted	¾ cup walnuts, chopped
½ cup coconut cream	½ teaspoon vanilla extract

1. Stir the flour, half of the swerve and half of the butter well, then press the mixture on the cooking pan of your air fryer. 2. Cook the mixture at 350 degrees F/ 175 degrees C for 15 minutes. 3. While cooking the mixture, heat the rest of the ingredients in a pan for 1 to 2 minutes. 4. Arrange the heated mixture to the air fryer and continue to cook for 25 minutes more. 5. Before serving, cool the food down and cut into bars.
Per serving: Calories: 232; Fat: 24.2g; Sodium 115mg; Total Carbs 2g; Net Carbs: 0.5g; Fiber: 1.1g; Sugars: 0.9g; Protein: 3.1g

Butter Cheesecake

Prep Time: 15 minutes | Cook time: 28 minutes | Serves: 6

For crust:

2 tablespoons butter, melted	½ cup almond flour
¼ teaspoon cinnamon	Pinch of salt
1 tablespoon swerve	

For Cheesecake:

1 egg	½ cup swerve
½ teaspoon vanilla	8 oz. cream cheese

1. At 280 degrees F/ 140 degrees C, preheat your air fryer. 2. Grease its air fryer basket with cooking spray. 3. Add all crust ingredients into the bowl and mix until combined. Transfer crust mixture into the prepared baking dish and press down into the bottom of the dish. 4. Place dish in the preheated Air Fryer and cook for 12 minutes. 5. In a suitable bowl, beat cream cheese using a hand mixer until smooth. 6. Stir in vanilla, egg, and salt and stir to combine. 7. Pour cream cheese mixture over cooked crust and cook for 16 minutes. 8. Allow to cool completely. 9. Slice and serve.
Per serving: Calories: 276; Fat: 2.1 g; Sodium: 18 mg; Total Carbs: 65.9g; Net Carbs: 23g; Fiber: 4.5g; Sugar: 59g; Protein: 2.6g

Lemon Butter Bars

Prep Time: 10 minutes | Cook time: 35 minutes | Serves: 8

½ cup butter, melted	3 eggs, whisked
1 cup Erythritol	Zest of 1 lemon, grated Juice of 3
1 and ¾ cups almond flour	lemons

1. In a bowl, stir 1 cup flour, half of the Erythritol and butter well, then press the mixture into the cooking pan lined with parchment paper. 2. Cook the mixture at 350 degrees F/ 175 degrees C for 10 minutes. 3. While cooking, prepare a bowl, whisk the rest of flour, the remaining Erythritol and other ingredients well. 4. When the mixture cooked, spread the mixture over the it and cook at 350 degrees F/ 175 degrees C for 25 minutes more. 5. Cool down and cut into bars before enjoying.
Per serving: Calories: 210; Fat: 13.7g; Sodium: 15mg; Total Carbs 2g; Net Carbs: 0.5g; Fiber: 1.2g; Sugars: 0.1g; Protein: 3g

Zucchini Bars with Cream Cheese

Prep Time: 10 minutes | Cook time: 15 minutes | Serves: 12

3 tablespoons coconut oil, melted	½ teaspoon baking powder
6 eggs	4 ounces' cream cheese
3 ounces' zucchini, shredded 2 teaspoons vanilla extract	2 tablespoons erythritol

1. Whisk the coconut oil, zucchini, vanilla extract, baking powder, cream cheese, and erythritol in a bowl, then pour in the cooking pan lined with parchment paper. 2. Cook at 320 degrees F/ 160 degrees C for 15 minutes. 3. Slice and cool down. 4. Serve and enjoy.
Per serving: Calories: 211; Fat: 12.6g; Sodium: 104mg; Total Carbs: 4g; Net Carbs: 2g; Fiber: 0.5g; Sugars: 1g; Protein: 19.5g

Lemon Nut Bars

Prep Time: 15 minutes | Cook time: 30 minutes | Serves: 10

½ cup coconut oil, softened	1 teaspoon vanilla extract
1 teaspoon baking powder	2 eggs, beaten
1 teaspoon lemon juice	2 oz. hazelnuts, chopped
1 cup almond flour	1 oz. macadamia nuts, chopped
½ cup coconut flour	Cooking spray
3 tablespoons Erythritol	

1. Mix the coconut oil, baking powder, lemon juice, almond flour, coconut flour, Erythritol, vanilla extract and eggs well until smooth. 2. Continue to add the hazelnuts and macadamia nuts and stir the mixture until homogenous. 3. Transfer the nut mixture to the cooking basket and use the spatula to flatten it. 4. Cook the mixture at 325 degrees F/ 160 degrees C for 30 minutes. 5. When done, cool the mixture well and cut it into the serving bars. 6. Enjoy.
Per serving: Calories: 135; Fat: 9.9g; Sodium: 2mg; Total Carbs: 9g; Net Carbs: 4.3g; Fiber: 5g Sugars: 0.9g; Protein: 4.6g

Enticing Cappuccino Muffins

Prep Time: 10 minutes | Cook time: 20 minutes | Serves: 12

4 eggs	1 teaspoon cinnamon
2 cups almond flour	2 teaspoons baking powder
½ teaspoon vanilla	¼ cup coconut flour
1 teaspoon espresso powder	½ cup Swerve
½ cup sour cream	¼ teaspoon salt

1. Before cooking, heat your air fryer to 325 degrees F/ 160 degrees C. 2. In a blender, mix together vanilla, espresso powder, eggs, and sour cream until smooth. 3. Then blend again with cinnamon, coconut flour, baking powder, salt, and sweetener until smooth. 4. Divide the batter into the silicone muffin molds. 5. Cook in batches in the preheated air fryer for 20 minutes. 6. Serve and enjoy!
Per serving: Calories: 150; Fat: 13 g; Sodium 114mg; Total Carbs: 5.3 g; Net Crabs:3.8g; Fiber: 1g; Sugar: 0.8 g; Protein: 6 g

Scones with Cream Cheese

Prep Time: 20 minutes | Cook time: 10 minutes | Serves: 4

4 oz. almond flour	¼ cup coconut cream
½ teaspoon baking powder	1 teaspoon vanilla extract
1 teaspoon lemon juice	1 tablespoon Erythritol
¼ teaspoon salt	1 tablespoon heavy cream
2 teaspoons cream cheese	Cooking spray

1. Mix up the almond flour, baking powder, lemon juice, salt and cream cheese in a suitable bowl and stir well. 2. In another bowl, mix up the vanilla extract, coconut cream and then add this mixture in the almond flour mixture. Stir gently and then knead the dough. 3. Roll the dough up and cut it into scones. 4. Cook the scones on the oiled basket in your air fryer at 360 degrees F/ 180 degrees C for 10 minutes, or until they are light brown. 5. When cooked, cool them to the room temperature, and at the same time, mix up the heavy cream and Erythritol. 6. Brush each scone with the cream mixture, then serve and enjoy.
Per serving: Calories: 107; Fat: 9.9g; Sodium: 2mg; Total Carbs: 9g; Net Carbs: 4.3g; Fiber: 5g Sugars: 0.9g; Protein: 4.6g

Cocoa Nutmeg Cake

Prep Time: 20 minutes | Cook time: 40 minutes | Serves: 8

½ cup heavy cream	3 tablespoons Erythritol
3 eggs, beaten	1 cup almond flour
3 tablespoons cocoa powder	¼ teaspoon ground nutmeg
1 teaspoon vanilla extract	1 tablespoon avocado oil
1 teaspoon baking powder	1 teaspoon Splenda

1. In a bowl, stir the heavy cream, eggs and cocoa powder well until smooth, then add vanilla extract, baking powder, Erythritol, almond flour, ground nutmeg, avocado oil and whisk well. 2. Pour the mixture in the cake mold. 3. Use the toothpick to pierce the foil. 4. Arrange the cake mold to the cooking basket and cook in the air fryer at 360 degrees F/ 180 degrees C for 40 minutes. 5. When cooked, sprinkle the Splenda on the top after cooling completely. 6. Serve and enjoy.
Per serving: Calories: 209; Fat: 12.6g; Sodium: 104mg; Total Carbs: 4g; Net Carbs: 2g; Fiber: 0.5g; Sugars: 1g; Protein: 19.5g

Simple Donuts

Prep Time: 5 minutes | Cook time: 15 minutes | Serves: 4

8 ounces' coconut flour 2 table-	1-½ tablespoons butter, melted
spoons stevia	4 ounces' coconut milk
1 egg, whisked	1 teaspoon baking powder

1. Thoroughly mix up all of the ingredients in a bowl. 2. Form donuts from the mixture. 3. Cook the donuts in your air fryer at 370 degrees F/ 185 degrees C for 15 minutes. 4. When cooked, serve and enjoy.
Per serving: Calories: 135; Fat: 9.9g; Sodium: 2mg; Total Carbs: 9g; Net Carbs: 4.3g; Fiber: 5g Sugars: 0.9g; Protein: 4.6g

Lava Cakes

Prep Time: 15 minutes | Cook time: 9 minutes | Serves: 2

1 tablespoon cocoa powder	3 eggs, beaten
2 tablespoons coconut oil, softened	1 teaspoon spearmint, dried
2 tablespoons Erythritol	4 teaspoons almond flour
1 teaspoon peppermint	Cooking spray

1. To melt the coconut oil, microwave it for 10 seconds, then add in the cocoa powder, almond flour, Erythritol, peppermint, spearmint and eggs. 2. Whisk the mixture well until smooth. 3. Spray the ramekins with cooking spray and pour the chocolate mixture inside. 4. Cook the lava cakes in your air fryer at 375 degrees F/ 190 degrees C for 9 minutes. 5. When the cooking is finished, remove and rest for 5 minutes. 6. Serve and enjoy.
Per serving: Calories: 209; Fat: 12.6g; Sodium: 104mg; Total Carbs: 4g; Net Carbs: 2g; Fiber: 0.5g; Sugars: 1g; Protein: 19.5g

Donuts with Cardamom

Prep Time: 20 minutes | Cook time: 6 minutes | Serves: 4

1 teaspoon ground cardamom	1 egg, beaten
½ teaspoon ground cinnamon	1 tablespoon butter, softened
½ teaspoon baking powder	¼ teaspoon salt
½ cup coconut flour	Cooking spray
1 tablespoon Erythritol	

1. Thoroughly mix up the Erythritol, ground cinnamon and ground cardamom in a suitable bowl. 2. In another bowl, mix up the coconut flour, baking powder, egg, salt, and butter. Knead the non-sticky dough. 3. Roll up the dough and use the donut cutter to form 4 donuts. 4. Coat every donut with the cardamom mixture, then place the donuts in a warm place to let it rest for 10 minutes. 5. Spray the cooking basket of your air fryer with cooking spray and transfer the donuts on it. 6. Cook the donuts at 355 degrees F/ 180 degrees C for 6 minutes or until they are golden brown. 7. Sprinkle the remaining cardamom mixture on the hot donuts. 8. Enjoy!
Per serving: Calories: 114; Fat: 9.9g; Sodium: 2mg; Total Carbs: 9g; Net Carbs: 4.3g; Fiber: 5g Sugars: 0.9g; Protein: 4.6g

Walnut Banana Split

Prep Time: 15 minutes | Cook time: 15 minutes | Serves: 8

3 tablespoons coconut oil	lengthwise
1 cup panko breadcrumbs	3 tablespoons sugar
½ cup of corn flour	¼ teaspoon ground cinnamon
2 eggs	2 tablespoons walnuts, chopped
4 bananas, peeled and halved	

1. In a suitable skillet, melt the coconut oil over medium heat and cook the breadcrumbs until they are golden brown and crumbly, for about 4 minutes. Stirconstantly. 2. Transfer the breadcrumbs to a shallow bowl and set aside to cool. 3. In a second bowl, place the cornmeal. 4. In a third bowl, beat the eggs. 5. Coat the banana slices with the flour, dip them in the eggs and finally coat them evenly with the breadcrumbs. 6. In a suitable bowl, mix the sugar and cinnamon. 7. Set the cook time to 10 minutes and set the temperature to 280 degrees F/ 140 degrees C on the air fryer. 8. Arrange banana slices in Air Fry Basket and sprinkle with cinnamon sugar. 9. Transfer banana slices to plates to cool slightly. 10. Sprinkle with chopped walnuts.
Per serving: Calories: 416; Fat: 8.3 g; Sodium: 208 mg; Total Carbs: 22.9g; Net Carbs: 8g; Fiber: 0.5g; Sugar: 19g; Protein: 60.6g

Vanilla Bars with Sesame Seeds

Prep Time: 15 minutes | Cook time: 10 minutes | Serves: 6

1 cup coconut flour	1 teaspoon vanilla extract
2 tablespoons coconut flakes	1 tablespoon butter, softened
2 eggs, beaten	1 teaspoon sesame seeds
1 teaspoon baking powder	Cooking spray
¼ cup Erythritol	

1. In a suitable bowl, add the coconut flour, coconut flakes, eggs, baking powder, Erythritol, vanilla extract, and sesame seeds, then use a spoon to stir the mixture well until it is homogenous. 2. Roll up the dough into the square and cut into the bars. 3. Cook the coconut bars at 325 degrees F/ 160 degrees C for 10 minutes. 4. When done, serve and enjoy.
Per serving: Calories: 143; Fat: 0.3 g; Sodium: 3 mg; Total Carbs: 38g; Net Carbs: 23.5g; Fiber: 0.5g; Sugar: 33.9g; Protein: 0.6g

Moist Cinnamon Muffins

Prep Time: 10 minutes | Cook time: 12 minutes | Serves: 20

1 tablespoon cinnamon	½ cup coconut oil
1 teaspoon baking powder	½ cup pumpkin puree
2 scoops vanilla protein: powder	½ cup almond butter
½ cup almond flour	

1. Before cooking, heat your air fryer to 325 degrees F/ 160 degrees C. 2. Combine together cinnamon, baking powder, vanilla protein: powder, and almond flour in a large bowl. 3. Then mix the dry mixture together with the coconut oil, pumpkin puree, and almond butter until well incorporated. 4. Divide the batter into the silicone muffin molds. 5. Cook in batches in your air fryer for 12 minutes. 6. Serve and enjoy!
Per serving: Calories: 135; Fat: 9.9g; Sodium: 2mg; Total Carbs: 9g; Net Carbs: 4.3g; Fiber: 5g Sugars: 0.9g; Protein: 4.6g

Aromatic Cup with Blondies

Prep Time: 10 minutes | Cook time: 15 minutes | Serves: 1

1 egg, beaten	½ teaspoon vanilla extract
1 tablespoon peanut butter	1 teaspoon Erythritol
½ teaspoon baking powder	2 tablespoons coconut flour
1 teaspoon lemon juice	

1. In a cup, thoroughly mix up all of the ingredients until homogenous. 2. Arrange the cup with blondies to your air fryer and cook the mixture at 350 degrees F/ 175 degrees C for 15 minutes. 3. When done, serve and enjoy.
Per serving: Calories: 237; Fat: 12.6g; Sodium: 104mg; Total Carbs: 4g; Net Carbs: 2g; Fiber: 0.5g; Sugars: 1g; Protein: 19.5g

Vanilla Spread

Prep Time: 10 minutes | Cook time: 5 minutes | Serves: 4

2 oz. walnuts, chopped	1 tablespoon Erythritol
5 teaspoons coconut oil	1 teaspoon of cocoa powder
½ teaspoon vanilla extract	

1. Preheat the air fryer to 350F. 2. Put the walnuts in the mason jar, then add the coconut oil, vanilla extract, Erythritol and cocoa powder. 3. Stir the walnut mixture with a spoon until smooth. 4. Arrange the mason jar with Nutella to your air fryer and cook at 350 degrees F/ 175 degrees C for 5 minutes. 5. Before serving, stir Nutella.
Per serving: Calories: 91; Fat: 12.6g; Sodium: 104mg; Total Carbs: 4g; Net Carbs: 2g; Fiber: 0.5g; Sugars: 1g; Protein: 19.5g

Vanilla Cookies

Prep Time: 10 minutes | Cook time: 15 minutes | Serves: 12

2 cups almond flour 1 cup swerve	¼ teaspoon nutmeg, ground
¼ cup butter, melted 1 egg	¼ teaspoon cinnamon powder
2 teaspoons ginger, grated	1 teaspoon vanilla extract

1. Thoroughly mix up all of the ingredients in a bowl. 2. Form small balls from the mixture with a spoon, then arrange them to the cooking pan lined with parchment patter and flatten them. 3. Cook the balls in your air fryer at 360 degrees F/ 180 degrees C for 15 minutes. 4. Before serving, cool them.
Per serving: Calories: 200; Fat 12.6g; Sodium: 104mg; Total Carbs:

4g; Net Carbs: 2g; Fiber: 0.5g; Sugars: 1g; Protein: 19.5g

Tasty Mozzarella Balls

Prep Time: 20 minutes | Cook time: 20 minutes | Serves: 8

2 eggs, beaten	1 tablespoon butter
1 teaspoon almond butter, melted	2 tablespoons swerve
7 oz. coconut flour	1 teaspoon baking powder
2 oz. almond flour	½ teaspoon vanilla extract
5 oz. Mozzarella, shredded	Cooking spray

1. Mix up butter and Mozzarella in a suitable bowl, then microwave the mixture for 10 to 15 minutes or until it is melted. 2. Add the almond flour, coconut flour, swerve, baking powder and vanilla extract, then stir well. Knead the soft dough. 3. Microwave the mixture for 2-5 seconds more to melt better. 4. In the bowl, mix up almond butter and eggs. Form 8 balls from the mixture and coat them with the egg mixture. 5. Coat the cooking basket of your air fryer with cooking spray. 6. Cook the food at 400 degrees F/ 205 degrees C for 4 minutes. 7. Before serving, cool the food completely and sprinkle with Splenda if desired.
Per serving: Calories: 249; Fat: 9g; Sodium: 91mg; Total Carbs: 27g; Net Carbs: 19g; Fiber: 2.4g; Sugar: 15g; Protein: 1.3g

Enticing Ricotta Cheese Cake

Prep Time: 10 minutes | Cook time: 30 minutes | Serves: 8

3 eggs, lightly beaten	1 cup almond flour
1 teaspoon baking powder	⅓ cup erythritol
½ cup ghee, melted	1 cup ricotta cheese, soft

1. Combine the beaten eggs, baking powder, melted ghee, almond flour, erythritol, and soft ricotta cheese in a large mixing bowl. 2. Gently grease a baking dish that fits in your air fryer. 3. Add the mixture onto the prepared baking dish. Transfer the baking dish inside your air fryer. 4. Cook in the air fryer at 350 degrees F/ 175 degrees C for 30 minutes. 5. When cooked, remove from the air fryer and cool. 6. Then slice the cake into your desired size and serve. 7. Enjoy!
Per serving: Calories: 148; Fat: 0.3 g; Sodium: 3 mg; Total Carbs: 38g; Net Carbs: 23.5g; Fiber: 0.5g; Sugar: 33.9g; Protein: 0.6g

Pineapple Chips with Cinnamon

Prep Time: 5 minutes | Cook time: 20 minutes | Serves: 4

4 pineapple slices	2 tablespoons erythritol
1 teaspoon cinnamon	

1. In a zip-lock bag, add the cinnamon, sweetener, and pineapple slices. Seal the bag and shake. Then cool the bag in the refrigerator for 30 minutes. 2. Before cooking, heat your air fryer to 350 degrees F/ 175 degrees C. 3. In the air fryer basket, arrange the pineapple slices. 4. Cook in the preheated air fryer at 350 degrees F/ 175 degrees C for 20 minutes. Flip the slices halfway through cooking. 5. When cooked, remove from the air fryer and serve.
Per serving: Calories: 46; Fat: 9g; Sodium: 91mg; Total Carbs: 27g; Net Carbs: 19g; Fiber: 2.4g; Sugar: 15g; Protein: 1.3g

Vanilla Cheese Custard

Prep Time: 10 minutes | Cook time: 20 minutes | Serves: 2

5 eggs	½ cup unsweetened almond milk
2 tablespoons swerve	½ cup cream cheese
1 teaspoon vanilla	

1. Beat the eggs with a hand mixer in a bowl. 2. Then beat in sweetener, almond milk, vanilla, and cream cheese for 2 minutes or until beaten well. 3. Using cooking spray, spray two ramekins. 4. Divide the beaten mixture into the greased ramekins. 5. Before cooking, heat your air fryer to 350 degrees F/ 175 degrees C. 6. Transfer the ramekins inside your air fryer. 7. Then cook the ramekins at 350 degrees F/ 175 degrees C for 20 minutes. 8. When cooked, remove the ramekins onto a wire rack to cool. 9. Now it's time to treat yourself.
Per serving: Calories: 374; Fat: 25g; Sodium: 275mg; Total Carbs: 7g; Net Carbs: 3g; Fiber: 0g; Sugar: 6g; Protein: 12.3g

Divine Apple Pie

Prep Time: 15 minutes | Cook Time:30 minutes | Servings: 4

2 apples
1 tbsp. sugar
2 sheets of puff pastry

2 tbsps. of melted butter
1 egg yolk

1. Peel your apples, cut into small pieces. 2. Add your apple on the puff pastry sheets and sprinkle with sugar and cinnamon. 3. In the air fryer, Air Fry the food at 360 degrees F/ 180 degrees C for 30 minutes. 4. With 10 minutes of cooking remaining, wrap the sides and brush with egg yolk. 5. Serve!
Per serving: Calories 389; Total Carbs 21g; Net Carbs 9g; Protein 5.3g; Fat 7g; Sugar 2.1g; Fiber 2g

Banana Muffin

Prep Time: 15 minutes | Cook Time: 20 minutes | Servings: 5

1 banana
½ cup almond flour
1 egg
1 tbsp. sugar

½ tsp. salt
1 tsp. baking powder
1 tbsp. butter

1. Mash the banana well and mix all the recipe ingredients until smooth. 2. Place the dough in a silicone baking dish. 3. In the air fryer, cook the food for 20 minutes at 340 degrees F/ 170 degrees C on Bake mode. 4. Serve with chocolate if you like. Enjoy.
Per serving: Calories 375; Total Carbs 20g; Net Carbs 11g; Protein 7.6g; Fat 11g; Sugar 5g; Fiber 1g

Dark Chocolate Lava Cakes

Prep Time: 15 minutes | Cook Time:12 minutes | Servings: 4

¼ cup butter, melted
2 tbsps. sugar
¾ cup flour

¼ cup dark chocolate, melted
1 egg

1. Beats the eggs and sugar until frothy. 2. Stir in butter and chocolate; gently fold in the flour. 3. Divide the prepared mixture between the ramekins and Air Fry at 400 degrees F/ 205 degrees C for 10 min. 4. Let cool for 2 min before turning the cakes upside down onto serving plates.
Per serving: Calories 401; Total Carbs 21g; Net Carbs 9g; Protein 5.3g; Fat 7g; Sugar 2.1g; Fiber 2g

Churros

Prep Time: 15 minutes | Cook Time:10 minutes | Servings: 6

1 cup of water
½ cup butter
½ cup almond flour
2 eggs

2 tbsps. cinnamon sugar
2 tbsps. sugar
½ tsp. salt

1. In a suitable saucepan, bring the water and butter to a boil. 2. Once it is bubbling, add the 2 eggs, flour and mix to create a doughy consistency. 3. Transfer the dough into a piping bag. 4. At 380 degrees F/ 195 degrees C, preheat your Air Fryer. 5. Pipe the dough into the fryer in several 3-inch-long segments. 6. Air Fry for 10 min before removing from the fryer and coating in the cinnamon sugar. 7. Serve with chocolate sauce of your choice.
Per serving: Calories 347; Total Carbs 23g; Net Carbs 11g; Protein 9g; Fat 12 g; Sugar 6g; Fiber 3g

Almond Biscuit

Prep Time: 15 minutes | Cook Time:35 minutes | Servings: 4

½ cup almond flour
3 tbsps. flour
1 egg

⅓ cup sugar
almond nuts, as desired

1. Combine sugar, flour and almond flour. Whisk in egg and add to dry ingredients. 2. Shape into small cookies and place almonds on top. 3. Place the cookies in the "Air Fryer Basket" or special molds. 4. Air Fry the cookies for 30-35 minutes at 320 degrees F/ 160 degrees C. 5. Serve and enjoy.
Per serving: Calories 415; Total Carbs 21g; Net Carbs 10g; Protein 7g; Fat 14g; Sugar 8g; Fiber 3g

Sweet Cinnamon Donuts

Prep Time: 15 minutes | Cook Time:6 minutes | Servings:3

½ cup granulated sugar
1 tbsp. ground cinnamon
1 (16.3-oz.) can flaky large bis-

cuits
olive oil spray or coconut oil spray
4 tbsps. unsalted butter, melted

1. Line a baking pan with baking paper. 2. Mix cinnamon and sugar in a suitable bowl. 3. Place the biscuits on the baking pan. 4. Use a 1-inch round biscuit cutter to cut holes out of the center of each. 5. Lightly coat the Air Fryer Basket with olive or coconut oil spray. Place 3 to 4 donuts in a single layer in the basket. 6. In the air fryer, Air Fry the food at 350 degrees F/ 175 degrees C for 5 to 6 minutes, until the donuts are golden-brown. Turn the food halfway through cooking. 7. Transfer donuts place to the baking pan. Repeat with the remaining biscuits. 8. Brush the donuts with melted butter, coat in the cinnamon sugar, and flip to coat both sides. 9. Serve warm.
Per serving: Calories 375; Total Carbs 20g; Net Carbs 11g; Protein 7.6g; Fat 11g; Sugar 5g; Fiber 1g

Cardamom Bombs

Prep time: 10 minutes | Cook Time: 5 minutes | Servings: 2

2 oz. avocado, peeled
1 egg, beaten
½ tsp. ground cardamom

1 tbsp. Erythritol
2 tbsps. coconut flour
1 tsp. butter, softened

1. Set the avocado in the bowl and mash it with the help of the fork. 2. Add egg and stir the prepared mixture until it is smooth. 3. Then add ground cardamom, Erythritol, and coconut flour. 4. After this, add butter and stir the prepared mixture well. 5. Make the balls from the avocado mixture and press them gently. 6. At 400 degrees F/ 205 degrees C, preheat your Air Fryer. 7. Put the avocado bombs in the air fryer and Air Fry them at 400 degrees F/ 205 degrees C for 5 minutes.
Per serving: Calories 143; Total Carbs 7.5g; Net Carbs 2g; Protein 4.9g; Fat 10.9g; Sugar 2g; Fiber 5g

Vinegar Cake

Prep time: 25 minutes | Cook Time: 30 minutes | Servings: 4

2 tsps. cream cheese
1 tsp. Truvia
1 tsp. vanilla extract
½ cup heavy cream
1 egg, beaten

1 tsp. baking powder
1 tsp. apple cider vinegar
1 ½ cups coconut flour
2 tbsps. butter, softened
Cooking spray

1. Pour heavy cream in the bowl. 2. Add vanilla extract, egg, baking powder, apple cider vinegar, and butter. 3. Stir the liquid until homogenous. Then add coconut flour. 4. Whisk the liquid until smooth. Grease the pound cake mold with some cooking spray. 5. Pour the pound cake batter in the mold. Flatten its surface with the help of the spatula. 6. At 365 degrees F/ 185 degrees C, preheat your Air Fryer. 7. Put the mold with the pound cake in the air fryer and Air Fry it for 30 minutes. 8. When the cake is cooked, cool it to the room temperature. 9. Meanwhile, in the shallow bowl whisk together cream cheese and Truvia. 10. Then spread the surface of the pound cake with sweet cream cheese. 11. Slice the dessert on the servings.
Per serving: Calories 339; Total Carbs 28.7g; Net Carbs 2g; Protein 10.9g; Fat 20.5g; Sugar 2g; Fiber 18g

Butter Custard

Prep time: 15 minutes | Cook Time: 35 minutes | Servings: 2

¼ cup heavy cream
1 tbsp. Erythritol
1 tsp. coconut flour

3 egg yolks
1 tsp. butter

1. Whip the heavy cream and them mix it up with Erythritol and coconut flour. 2. Whisk the egg yolks and add them in the whipped cream mixture. 3. Then grease 2 ramekins with butter and transfer the whipped cream mixture in the ramekins. 4. At 300 degrees F/ 150 degrees C, preheat your Air Fryer. 5. Put the ramekins with custard in the air fryer and Air Fry them at 300 degrees F/ 150 degrees C for 35 minutes.
Per serving: Calories 155; Total Carbs 2.1g; Net Carbs 2g; Protein 4.6g; Fat 14.4g; Sugar 2g; Fiber 0.5g

Lemon Peppermint Bars

Prep time: 15 minutes | Cook Time: 16 minutes | Servings: 8

1 tsp. peppermint	½ tsp. baking powder
1 cup almond flour	1 tsp. lemon juice
⅓ cup peanut butter	½ tsp. orange zest, grated

1. In the bowl, mix up almond flour, peppermint, baking powder, and orange zest. 2. Then add peanut butter and lemon juice. Knead the non-sticky dough. 3. Cut the dough on 8 pieces and roll the balls. Press them gently to get the shape of the bars. 4. At 365 degrees F/ 185 degrees C, preheat your Air Fryer. Layer the "Air Fryer Basket" with baking paper. 5. Put 4 cookies in the basket in one layer. Air Fry them at 365 degrees F/ 185 degrees C for 8 minutes. 6. Remove the cooked bars from the air fryer. Repeat the same steps with uncooked bars.
Per serving: Calories 84; Total Carbs 3.1g; Net Carbs 2g; Protein 3.5g; Fat 7.2g; Sugar 2g; Fiber 1.1g

Vinegar Cake

Prep time: 25 minutes | Cook Time: 30 minutes | Servings: 4

2 tsps. cream cheese	1 tsp. baking powder
1 tsp. Truvia	1 tsp. apple cider vinegar
1 tsp. vanilla extract	1 ½ cups coconut flour
½ cup heavy cream	2 tbsps. butter, softened
1 egg, beaten	Cooking spray

1. Pour heavy cream in the bowl. 2. Add vanilla extract, egg, baking powder, apple cider vinegar, and butter. 3. Stir the liquid until homogenous. Then add coconut flour. 4. Whisk the liquid until smooth. Grease the pound cake mold with some cooking spray. 5. Pour the pound cake batter in the mold. Flatten its surface with the help of the spatula. 6. At 365 degrees F/ 185 degrees C, preheat your Air Fryer. 7. Put the mold with the pound cake in the air fryer and Air Fry it for 30 minutes. 8. When the cake is cooked, cool it to the room temperature. 9. Meanwhile, in the shallow bowl whisk together cream cheese and Truvia. 10. Then spread the surface of the pound cake with sweet cream cheese. 11. Slice the dessert on the servings.
Per serving: Calories 339; Total Carbs 28.7g; Net Carbs 2g; Protein 10.9g; Fat 20.5g; Sugar 2g; Fiber 18g

Avocado Cream Pudding

Prep time: m5inutes Cook Time: 25 minutes | Servings: 6

4 small avocados, peeled, pitted	¾ cup swerve
and mashed	½ tsp. cinnamon powder
2 eggs, whisked	½ tsp. ginger powder
1 cup coconut milk	

1. In a suitable bowl, mix all the recipe ingredients and whisk well. 2. Pour the mixture into a pudding mold, put it in the air fryer and Air Fry at 350 degrees F/ 175 degrees C for 25 minutes. 3. Serve warm.
Per serving: Calories 192; Total Carbs 5g; Net Carbs 2g; Protein 4g; Fat 8g; Sugar 2g; Fiber 2g

Delicious Walnut Bars

Prep Time: 5 minutes | Cook time: 16 minutes | Serves: 4

1 egg	teaspoon vanilla extract
⅓ cup cocoa powder 3 tablespoons	¼ cup almond flour
swerve	¼ cup walnuts, chopped
7 tablespoons ghee, melted 1	½ teaspoon baking soda

1. Thoroughly mix up all of the ingredients in a bowl. 2. Arrange the mixture to the cooking pan lined with parchment paper. 3. Cook at 330 degrees F/ 165 degrees C for 16 minutes. 4. Cool the bars before serving.
Per serving: Calories: 182; Fat: 9g; Sodium: 91mg; Total Carbs: 27g; Net Carbs: 19g; Fiber: 2.4g; Sugar: 15g; Protein: 1.3g

Chocolate Candies

Prep time: 15 minutes | Cook Time: 2 minutes | Servings: 4

1 oz. almonds, crushed	2 tbsps. peanut butter
1 oz. dark chocolate	2 tbsps. heavy cream

1. At 390 degrees F/ 200 degrees C, preheat your Air Fryer. 2. Chop the dark chocolate and put it in the air fryer mold. 3. Add peanut butter and heavy cream. Stir the prepared mixture and transfer in the air fryer. 4. Air Fry the food at 390 degrees F/ 200 degrees C for 2 minutes or until it starts to be melt. Then layer the air tray with parchment. 5. Put the crushed almonds on the tray in one layer. 6. Then pour the cooked chocolate mixture over the almonds. 7. Flatten gently if needed and let it cool. 8. Crack the cooked chocolate layer into the candies.
Per serving: Calories 154; Total Carbs 7.4g; Net Carbs 2g; Protein 3.9g; Fat 12.9g; Sugar 2g; Fiber 1.9g

Ginger Lemon Pie

Prep time: 15 minutes | Cook Time: 30 minutes | Servings: 6

2 eggs	1 tsp. lemon juice
6 tbsps. coconut flour	½ tsp. ground ginger
½ tsp. vanilla extract	3 tbsps. Erythritol
6 tbsps. ricotta cheese	1 tbsp. butter, melted
½ tsp. baking powder	

1. Crack the eggs and separate them on the egg whites and egg yolks. 2. Then whisk the egg yolks with Erythritol until you get the lemon color mixture. 3. Then whisk the egg whites to the soft peaks. Add egg whites in the egg yolk mixture. 4. Then add ricotta cheese, baking powder, lemon juice, ground ginger, vanilla extract, Erythritol. 5. Then add butter and coconut flour and stir the pie butter until smooth. 6. Layer the "Air Fryer Basket" with the baking paper. Pour the pie batter inside. 7. At 330 degrees F/ 165 degrees C, preheat your Air Fryer. 8. Put the baking pan with pie in the air fryer and Air Fry the food at 330 degrees F/ 165 degrees C for 30 minutes.
Per serving: Calories 97; Total Carbs 5.8g; Net Carbs 2g; Protein 5.2g; Fat 5.9g; Sugar 2g; Fiber 3g

Vanilla Yogurt Cake

Prep Time: 5 minutes | Cook Time: 30 minutes | Servings: 12

6 eggs, whisked	9 oz. coconut flour
1 tsp. vanilla extract	4 tbsps. stevia
1 tsp. baking powder	8 oz. Greek yogurt

1. In a suitable bowl, mix all the recipe ingredients and whisk well. 2. Add this prepared batter into a cake pan that fits the air fryer lined with baking paper 3. Put this pan in the air fryer and Air Fry the food at 330 degrees F/ 165 degrees C for 30 minutes.
Per serving: Calories 181; Total Carbs 4g; Net Carbs 2g; Protein 5g; Fat 13g; Sugar 2g; Fiber 2g

Cobbler

Prep time: 15 minutes | Cook Time: 30 minutes | Servings: 4

¼ cup heavy cream	1 tsp. vanilla extract
1 egg, beaten	2 tbsps. butter, softened
½ cup almond flour	¼ cup hazelnuts, chopped

1. Mix up heavy cream, egg, almond flour, vanilla extract, and butter. 2. Then whisk the prepared mixture gently. 3. At 325 degrees F/ 160 degrees C, preheat your Air Fryer. 4. Layer the suitable cooking pan with baking paper. 5. Pour ½ part of the batter in the baking pan, flatten it gently and top with hazelnuts. 6. Then pour the remaining batter over the hazelnuts and place the pan in the air fryer. 7. Air Fry the cobbler at 325 degrees F/ 160 degrees C for 30 minutes.
Per serving: Calories 145; Total Carbs 2g; Net Carbs 2g; Protein 3g; Fat 14.2g; Sugar 2g; Fiber 0.8g

Almond Pudding

Prep Time: 10 minutes | Cook Time: 20 minutes | Servings: 6

24 oz. cream cheese, soft	3 eggs, whisked
2 tbsps. almond meal	1 tbsp. vanilla extract
¼ cup erythritol	½ cup heavy cream
12 oz. dark chocolate, melted	

1. In a suitable bowl mix all the recipe ingredients and whisk well. 2. Divide this into 6 ramekins, put them in your air fryer and Air Fry them at 320 degrees F/ 160 degrees C for 20 minutes. 3. Keep in the fridge for 1 hour before serving.
Per serving: Calories 200; Total Carbs 4g; Net Carbs 2g; Protein 6g; Fat 7g; Sugar 2g; Fiber 2g

Lemon Almond Biscotti

Prep time: 15 minutes | Cook Time: 40 minutes | Servings: 6

¼ cup almond, crushed	1 tsp. lemon zest, grated
¼ cup butter, softened	½ tsp. baking powder
2 eggs, beaten	1 tsp. lemon juice
1 tsp. of cocoa powder	¼ cup heavy cream
1 tsp. vanilla extract	1 tsp. avocado oil
1 cup almond flour	3 tbsps. Erythritol

1. In the mixing bowl mix up butter, eggs, cocoa powder, vanilla extract, almond flour, lemon zest, baking powder, lemon juice, heavy cream, and Erythritol. 2. Then add almonds and knead the smooth dough. 3. Brush the "Air Fryer Basket" with avocado oil and put the dough inside. 4. Flatten it well. At 365 degrees F/ 185 degrees C, preheat your Air Fryer. 5. Put this pan with dough inside and Air Fry the food at 365 degrees F/ 185 degrees C for 25 minutes. 6. Then slice the cooked dough on the pieces (biscotti). 7. Place the biscotti in the "Air Fryer Basket" and Air Fry them for 15 minutes at 350 degrees F/ 175 degrees C or until they are light brown.
Per serving: Calories 160; Total Carbs 2.7g; Net Carbs 2g; Protein 4g; Fat 15.4g; Sugar 2g; Fiber 1.2g

Plum Almond Cake

Prep Time: 10 minutes | Cook Time: 30 minutes | Servings: 8

½ cup butter, soft	1 and ½ cups almond flour
3 eggs	½ cup coconut flour
½ cup swerve	2 tsp. baking powder
¼ tsp. almond extract	¾ cup almond milk
1 tbsp. vanilla extract	4 plums, pitted and chopped

1. In a suitable bowl, mix all the recipe ingredients and whisk well. 2. Add this prepared mixture into a cake pan that fits the air fryer after you've lined it with baking paper. 3. Put this pan in the air fryer and Air Fry the food at 370 degrees F/ 185 degrees C for 30 minutes. 4. Cool the cake down, slice and serve.
Per serving: Calories 183; Total Carbs 4g; Net Carbs 2g; Protein 7g; Fat 4g; Sugar 2g; Fiber 3g

Cream Cheese Muffins

Prep time: 15 minutes | Cook Time: 11 minutes | Servings: 4

4 tsps. cream cheese	4 tsps. coconut flour
1 egg, beaten	2 tbsps. heavy cream
½ tsp. baking powder	2 tsps. Erythritol
1 tsp. vanilla extract	Cooking spray
4 tsps. almond flour	

1. Mix up cream cheese, egg, baking powder, vanilla extract, almond flour, coconut flour, heavy cream, and Erythritol. 2. Grease the air fryer muffin molds with some cooking spray. 3. Add the prepared batter in the muffin molds (fill ½ part of every mold). 4. At 365 degrees F/ 185 degrees C, preheat your Air Fryer. 5. Insert the muffin molds in the air fryer and Air Fry the food at 365 degrees F/ 185 degrees C for 11 minutes. 6. Cool the cooked muffins and remove them from the molds.
Per serving: Calories 229; Total Carbs 8.3g; Net Carbs 2g; Protein 8.3g; Fat 19.5g; Sugar 2g; Fiber 4g

Chocolate Fudge

Prep time: 15 minutes | Cook Time: 30 minutes | Servings:8

½ cup butter, melted	1 tsp. vanilla extract
1 oz. dark chocolate, chopped, melted	2 eggs, beaten
2 tbsp. cocoa powder	3 tbsp. Splenda
3 tbsp. coconut flour	Cooking spray

1. In the bowl mix up melted butter and dark chocolate. 2. Then add vanilla extract, eggs, and cocoa powder. 3. Stir the prepared mixture until smooth and add Splenda, and coconut flour. Stir it again until smooth. 4. At 325 degrees F/ 160 degrees C, preheat your Air Fryer. 5. Layer the "Air Fryer Basket" with baking paper and spray it with some cooking spray. 6. Pour the fudge mixture in the basket, flatten it gently with the help of the spatula. 7. Air Fry the fudge at 325 degrees F/ 160 degrees C for 30 minutes. 8. Then cut it on the serving squares

and cool the fudge completely.
Per serving: Calories 177; Total Carbs 8.3g; Net Carbs 2g; Protein 2.6g; Fat 14.8g; Sugar 2g; Fiber 1.6g

Creamy Crumble

Prep time: 15 minutes | Cook Time: 20 minutes | Servings: 4

4 oz. rhubarb, chopped	1 cup almond flour
¼ cup heavy cream	1 egg, beaten
1 tsp. ground cinnamon	1 tsp. avocado oil
¼ cup Erythritol	4 tsp. butter, softened

1. In the bowl mix up heavy cream, ground cinnamon, almond flour, egg, and butter. 2. Stir the prepared mixture until you get the crumbly texture. Then mix up rhubarb and Erythritol. 3. Brush the air fryer mold with avocado oil. 4. Separate the crumbled dough on 4 parts. Put 1 part of the dough in the air fryer mold. 5. Then sprinkle it with a small amount rhubarb. 6. Repeat the same steps till you use all the recipe ingredients. Put the crumble in the air fryer. 7. Air Fry the food at 375 degrees F/ 190 degrees C for 20 minutes.
Per serving: Calories 124; Total Carbs 4.1g; Net Carbs 2g; Protein 3.4g; Fat 11.4g; Sugar 2g; Fiber 1.9g

Blackberries Cake

Prep time: 10 minutes | Cook Time: 25 minutes | Servings: 4

2 eggs, whisked	1 cup blackberries, chopped
4 tbsp. swerve	½ tsp. baking powder
2 tbsp. ghee, melted	1 tsp. lemon zest, grated
¼ cup almond milk	1 tsp. lemon juice
1 and ½ cups almond flour	

1. In a suitable bowl, mix all the recipe ingredients and whisk well until smooth. 2. Add this prepared mixture into a cake pan that fits the air fryer lined with baking paper. 3. Put this pan in your air fryer and Air Fry the cake at 340 degrees F/ 170 degrees C for 25 minutes. 4. Cool the cake down, slice and serve.
Per serving: Calories 193; Total Carbs 4g; Net Carbs 2g; Protein 4g; Fat 5g; Sugar 2g; Fiber 1g

Turmeric Almond Pie

Prep time: 20 minutes | Cook Time: 35 minutes | Servings: 4

4 eggs, beaten	1 tsp. lemon juice
1 tbsp. poppy seeds	1 cup almond flour
1 tsp. ground turmeric	2 tbsp. heavy cream
1 tsp. vanilla extract	¼ cup Erythritol
1 tsp. baking powder	1 tsp. avocado oil

1. Put the eggs in the bowl. Add vanilla extract, baking powder, lemon juice, almond flour, heavy cream, and Erythritol. 2. Then add avocado oil and poppy seeds. Add turmeric. 3. With the help of the immersion blender, blend the pie batter until it is smooth. 4. Layer the air fryer cake mold with baking paper. Pour the pie batter in the cake mold. 5. Flatten the pie surface with the help of the spatula if needed. 6. At 365 degrees F/ 185 degrees C, preheat your Air Fryer. 7. Put the cake mold in the air fryer and Air Fry the pie at 365 degrees F/ 185 degrees C for 35 minutes. 8. When the pie is cooked, cool it completely and remove it from the cake mold. 9. Cut the cooked pie into the servings.
Per serving: Calories 149; Total Carbs 3.8g; Net Carbs 2g; Protein 7.7g; Fat 11.9g; Sugar 2g; Fiber 1.2g

Chia Cinnamon Pudding

Prep Time: 10 minutes | Cook Time: 25 minutes | Servings: 6

2 cups coconut cream	¼ cup chia seeds
6 egg yolks, whisked	2 tsp. cinnamon powder
2 tbsp. stevia	1 tbsp. ghee, melted

1. In a suitable bowl, mix all the recipe ingredients. Whisk, divide into 6 ramekins. 2. Place them all in your air fryer and Air Fry at 340 degrees F/ 170 degrees C for 25 minutes. 3. Cool the puddings down and serve.
Per serving: Calories 180; Total Carbs 5g; Net Carbs 2g; Protein 7g; Fat 4g; Sugar 2g; Fiber 2g

Conclusion

The Air fryer is an advanced cooking appliance. It has many useful cooking programs, and it takes less space in your kitchen. It comes with useful accessories that you need in cooking every meal. I recommend this appliance because it cooks food in very little time. The cleaning process is very simple. This unit is safe to use. My cookbook has delicious air frying recipes. You can choose recipes for the whole day and prepare food for your friends and family. Place food in the basket, adjust temperature and cooking time, and enjoy your time with your family. I hope you love this cookbook. Thank you for your love and appreciation.

Appendix 1 Measurement Conversion Chart

WEIGHT EQUIVALENTS

US STANDARD	METRIC (APPROXINATE)
1 ounce	28 g
2 ounces	57 g
5 ounces	142 g
10 ounces	284 g
15 ounces	425 g
16 ounces (1 pound)	455 g
1.5pounds	680 g
2pounds	907 g

VOLUME EQUIVALENTS (LIQUID)

US STANDARD	US STANDARD (OUNCES)	METRIC (APPROXIMATE)
2 tablespoons	1 fl.oz	30 mL
¼ cup	2 fl.oz	60 mL
½ cup	4 fl.oz	120 mL
1 cup	8 fl.oz	240 mL
1½ cup	12 fl.oz	355 mL
2 cups or 1 pint	16 fl.oz	475 mL
4 cups or 1 quart	32 fl.oz	1 L
1 gallon	128 fl.oz	4 L

VOLUME EQUIVALENTS (DRY)

US STANDARD	METRIC (APPROXIMATE)
⅛ teaspoon	0.5 mL
¼ teaspoon	1 mL
½ teaspoon	2 mL
¾ teaspoon	4 mL
1 teaspoon	5 mL
1 tablespoon	15 mL
¼ cup	59 mL
½ cup	118 mL
¾ cup	177 mL
1 cup	235 mL
2 cups	475 mL
3 cups	700 mL
4 cups	1 L

TEMPERATURES EQUIVALENTS

FAHRENHEIT(F)	CELSIUS(C) (APPROXIMATE)
225 ℉	107 ℃
250 ℉	120 ℃
275 ℉	135 ℃
300 ℉	150 ℃
325 ℉	160 ℃
350 ℉	180 ℃
375 ℉	190 ℃
400 ℉	205 ℃
425 ℉	220 ℃
450 ℉	235 ℃
475 ℉	245 ℃
500 ℉	260 ℃

Appendix 2 Air Fryer Cooking Chart

Beef	Temp(℉)	Time (min)
Burgers (1/4 Pound)	350	8-12
Filet Mignon (4 oz.)	370	15-20
Flank Steak (1.5 lbs)	400	10-14
Meatballs (1 inch)	380	7-10
London Broil (2.5 lbs.)	400	22-28
Round Roast (4 lbs)	390	45-55
Sirloin Steak (12oz)	390	9-14

Chicken	Temp(℉)	Time(min)
Chicken Whole (3.5 lbs)	350	45-60
Chicken Breast (boneless)	380	12-15
Chicken Breast (bone-in)	350	22-25
Chicken Drumsticks	380	23-25
Chicken Thighs (bone-in)	380	23-25
Chicken Tenders	350	8-12
Chicken Wings	380	22-25

Fish & Seafood	Temp(℉)	Time
Calamari	400	4-5
Fish Fillets	400	10-12
Salmon Fillets	350	8-12
Scallops	400	5-7
Shrimp	370	5-7
Lobster Tails	370	5-7
Tuna Steaks	400	7-10

Pork & Lamb	Temp(℉)	Time
Bacon	350	8-12
Lamb Chops	400	8-12
Pork Chops (1" boneless)	400	8-10
Pork Loin (2 lbs.)	360	18-21
Rack of Lamb (24-32 oz.)	375	22-25
Ribs	400	10-15
Sausages	380	10-15

Frozen Foods	Temp(℉)	Time
Breaded Shrimp	400	8-9
Chicken Burger	360	12
Chicken Nuggets	370	10-12
Chicken Strips	380	12-15
Corn Dogs	400	7-9
Fish Fillets (1-2 lbs.)	400	10-12
Fish Sticks	390	12-15
French Fries	380	12-17
Hash Brown Patties	380	10-12
Meatballs (1-inch)	350	10-12
Mozzarella Sticks (11 oz.)	400	8
Meat Pies (1-2 pies)	370	23-25
Mozzarella Sticks	390	7-9
Onion Rings	400	10-12
Pizza	390	5-10
Tater Tots	380	15-17

Vegetables	Temp(℉)	Time
Asparagus (1" slices)	400	5
Beets (whole)	400	40
Broccoli Florets	400	6
Brussel Sprouts (halved)	380	12-15
Carrots (1/2" slices)	360	12-15
Cauliflower Florets	400	10-12
Corn on the Cob	390	6-7
Eggplant (1 1/2" cubes)	400	12-15
Green Beans	400	4-6
Kale Leaves	250	12
Mushrooms (1/4" slices)	400	4-5
Onions (pearl)	400	10
Peppers (1" chunks)	380	8-15
Potatoes (whole)	400	30-40
Potatoes (wedges)	390	15-18
Potatoes (1" cubes)	390	12-15
Potatoes (baby, 1.5 lbs.)	400	15
Squash (1" cubes)	390	15
Sweet Potato (whole)	380	30-35
Tomatoes (cherry)	400	5
Zucchini (1/2" sticks)	400	10-12

Appendix 3 Recipes Index

A

Adorable Air Fried Steak 77
Air Fried Artichokes 37
Air Fried Catfish 49
Air Fried Cheese Sticks 26
Air Fried Pork Loin 77
Air Fried Pork Strips 76
Air Fried Pork with Fennel 22
Air Fried Prawns 49
Air Fried Scallops 48
Air Fried Shrimp & Bacon 19
Air Fried Turkey Wings 63
Air Fryer Chicken Breasts 63
Air Fryer Chicken Wings 62
Air Fryer Cornish Hen 63
Air Fryer Turkey Breast 64
Air-Fried Eggplant 36
Air-fried Pork with Wine Sauce 69
Air-fried Sweet Potato Bites 24
Air-fried Whole Chicken 56
Alfredo Chicken with Mushrooms 58
Almond Biscuit 87
Almond Cherry Bars 83
Almond Pecan Muffins 83
Almond Pudding 88
Almond Shrimp 50
Apple Brussel Sprout Salad 30
Apple Chips with Cinnamon 82
Aromatic Cup with Blondies 86
Artichoke Dip 26
Asian Chicken Filets with Cheese 66
Asian Pork 76
Asparagus Arugula Salad 13
Asparagus Egg Strata 15
Asparagus Pork Fries 27
Asparagus with Almonds 36
Avocado Balls 20
Avocado Cabbage Salad 16
Avocado Cream Pudding 88
Avocado Parsley Omelet 11
Awesome Chicken with Mustard Rosemary Sauce 57
Awesome Duck with Potato Rösti 54
Awesome Mushroom Tots 30

B

Bacon Lovers' Stuffed Chicken 63
Bacon Muffins 11
Bacon Pickle Spear Rolls 20
Bacon Poppers 25
Bacon Shrimp 49
Bacon Smokies with Tomato Sauce 22
Bacon with Chocolate Coating 21
Bacon Wrapped Eggs 12

Baguette Bread 27
Baked Chicken with Parmesan Cheese 60
Baked Eggs 9
Baked Eggs with Mascarpone 9
Baked Parmesan Eggs with Kielbasa 10
Baked Sardines 45
Baked Yams 37
Balsamic Brussels Sprouts 29
Balsamic Chicken Drumsticks 58
Balsamic Kale 38
Balsamic Sautéed Greens 29
Balsamic Tomatoes with Garlic 31
Balsamic Turkey in Hoisin Sauce 56
Banana Cinnamon Bread 17
Banana Muffin 87
Banana-Pecan French Toast 7
Barbecued Chicken Skewers 58
Basic BBQ Chicken 54
Basil Parmesan Shrimp 49
Basil Potatoes 39
Basil Turkey with Chili Mayo 54
BBQ Chicken Breasts 61
BBQ Chicken Wings 25
BBQ Pork Chops with Vegetables 68
Bean Burritos with Cheddar Cheese 43
Beans and Sweet Potato Boats 30
Beef Chops with Broccoli 77
Beef Cubes with Vegetables 68
Beef Meatballs with Chives 21
Beef Sausage with Tomato Puree 69
Beef Tenderloin Steaks with Marjoram 72
Beef with Creamed Mushroom Sauce 78
Beer Beef 69
Beer Squid 42
Berry Pudding 83
Blackberries Cake 89
Blueberry Vanilla Muffins 82
Bratwurst with Vegetables 76
Breaded Chicken without Flour 64
Breaded Salmon Patties 51
Broccoli and Asparagus 38
Broccoli Mix 38
Broccoli Nuggets 26
Broccoli Pop-corn 27
Broccoli Pork Chops 75
Broccoli Quiche 17
Broccoli Salad 38
Broccoli Tots 25
Brussels Sprouts and Mushrooms 32
Brussels Sprouts Tomatoes Mix 38
Buffalo Cauliflower Bites 33
Buffalo Chicken Tenders 62
Buffalo Crusted Cauliflower 29

Butter Cheesecake 84
Butter Custard 87
Buttered Shrimp Fry 45

C

Cabbage Crackers 25
Cajun Cheese Shrimp 49
Cajun Fish Cakes 46
Cajun Lemon Branzino 45
Cajun Peppers 39
Cajun Pork 74
Cajun Shrimp with Veggie 47
Cajun Spareribs with Coriander 71
Canadian Bacon English Muffin 15
Caraway Bread 24
Cardamom Bombs 87
Carrots with Honey Glaze 36
Catfish Fillets with Tortilla Chips 43
Cauliflower Bake with Basil Pesto 31
Cauliflower Bites 24
Cauliflower Hash 36
Cauliflower Rice 17
Cheddar Bacon Frittata 7
Cheddar Hash Brown 16
Cheddar Peppers 12
Cheddar Tomatillos with Lettuce 31
Cheese Artichoke Dip 27
Cheese Broccoli with Basil 32
Cheese Cake with Strawberries 83
Cheese Cauliflower Tots 29
Cheese Muffins with Cinnamon 84
Cheese Salmon 49
Cheese Sticks with Coconut 20
Cheese Taquitos with Cilantro 12
Cheesy Brussels sprouts 27
Cheesy Chicken Tenders 63
Cheesy Dip 50
Cheesy Zucchini Tots 34
Chia Cinnamon Pudding 89
Chicken and Carrot 54
Chicken and Onion Sausages 60
Chicken and Veggies Salad 55
Chicken Bites with Coconut 21
Chicken Bowls with Berries 24
Chicken Breast 64
Chicken Dip 26
Chicken Fillet 65
Chicken Fillets, Brie & Ham 63
Chicken in Beer 64
Chicken in Soy Sauce 56
Chicken Jalapeno Poppers 26
Chicken Meatballs 65
Chicken Parmesan Wings 61
Chicken Quesadillas with Ricotta Cheese 57

Chicken Vegetable Omelet 12
Chicken Wings with Garlic Butter Sauce 56
Chicken with Lemon and Bahian Seasoning 65
Chili Broccoli 38
Chili Shrimp 50
Chinese Cabbage with Bacon 30
Chinese-Style Sticky Turkey Thighs 66
Chip-crusted Tilapia with Parmesan Cheese 42
Chocolate Banana Brownie 81
Chocolate Bread 17
Chocolate Cake with Raspberries 81
Chocolate Candies 88
Chocolate Fudge 89
Chocolate Lava Cake 82
Chocolate Peanut Butter Mug Cake 83
Chunky Fish with Mustard 44
Churros 87
Cinnamon Almonds 24
Cinnamon Butter Muffins 82
Cinnamon French Toast 10
Cinnamon Pudding 14
Clams with Spring Onions 45
Classic Burger 77
Classic No Frills Turkey Breast 66
Classic Pork 78
Classical Buffalo Wings 55
Classical Eggs Ramekins 9
Classical French Frittata 11
Classical Greek Keftedes 60
Coated Cauliflower 23
Cobbler 88
Cocoa Nutmeg Cake 85
Coconut Brussels Sprouts 32
Coconut Butter Pork Chops 79
Coconut Granola with Almond 21
Coconut Muffins with Cinnamon 10
Coconut Veggie and Eggs Bake 7
Coconut Walnuts 84
Coffee Cookies 84
Cojita Chicken Taquitos 56
Cookies with Mashed Strawberry 83
Country-style Pork Ribs 70
Coxinha Fit 64
Crab Mushrooms 26
Crab Patties 49
Cream Cheese Muffins 89
Creamy Baked Sausage 8
Creamy Bread 17
Creamy Broccoli Casserole 8
Creamy Broccoli Florets with Eggs 10
Creamy Broccoli Omelet 7
Creamy Cauliflower Mash 34
Creamy Cauliflower Puree 34
Creamy Cheesecake Bites 82
Creamy Cilantro Peppers Mix 33
Creamy Coconut Chicken 62
Creamy Crumble 89
Creamy Eggs and Leeks 12
Creamy Garlic Bread 32
Creamy Shrimp 49

Creamy Spinach with Nutmeg 35
Creamy Turkey Sausage Cups 55
Creole Pork Chops 70
Crisp Kale 39
Crisp Pork Chops 78
Crispy Air Fryer Butter Chicken 63
Crispy Cauliflower Florets 24
Crispy Chicken Nuggets 57
Crispy Chicken Nuggets with Turnip 59
Crispy Fish Sticks 8
Crispy Kale Chips 23
Crispy Mustard Fried Leek 23
Crispy Paprika Chips 22
Crispy Pickles with Parmesan 36
Crispy Spiced Asparagus 35
Crispy Tofu with Soy Sauce 30
Crumbed Fish Fillets with Parmesan
Cheese 43
Crunchy Chicken Bites 57
Crunchy Chicken Tenders with Peanuts 66
Crusted Chicken Tenders 54
Crusted Onion Rings 27
Crusty Catfish with Parmesan Cheese 42
Cube Steak 68
D
Dark Chocolate Lava Cakes 87
Delectable Beef with Kale Pieces 68
Delectable Chaffles 22
Delectable Fish Nuggets 23
Delectable Pork Chops 73
Delicious Baby Back Ribs 72
Delicious Empanadas 74
Delicious Fillets with Avocado Sauce 42
Delicious Grouper Filets 48
Delicious Mushroom Pizzas 21
Delicious Pork Shoulder with Molasses
Sauce 69
Delicious Walnut Bars 88
Delicious Zucchini Crackers 21
Dijon Chicken 12
Dijon Turkey with Gravy 59
Divine Apple Pie 87
Donuts with Cardamom 85
Dreamy Beef Roast 79
Duck Fillet Wraps 19
E
Easy Hot Chicken Drumsticks 66
Easy Pork & Parmesan Meatballs 78
Easy-to-Make Almond Cookies 82
Easy-to-make Cheese Rounds 20
Egg Cheese Roll Ups 14
Egg Peppers Cups 11
Eggplant Chips 21
Enticing Cappuccino Muffins 85
Enticing Cauliflower Tots 29
Enticing Jalapeno Poppers 24
Enticing Ricotta Cheese Cake 86
Enticing Scotch Eggs 11
F
Fava Beans and Bacon Medley 29

Festive Pork Fillets 70
Filet Mignon with Peanut Sauce 70
Fish Fillets with Tarragon 51
Fish Mania with Mustard 42
Fish Packets 48
Fish Tacos 12
Fish with Chips 51
Flank Steak with Honey and Paprika 74
Flank Steak with Tamari Sauce 74
Flank Steaks with Capers 75
Flavor Beef Ribs 68
Flavor Calamari with Mediterranean Sauce 47
Flavor Moroccan Harissa Shrimp 47
Flavored Salmon Grill with Oregano &
Cumin 45
Flavorful Cheesy Frittata 9
Flavorful Chicken with Bacon 53
Flavorful Cornstarch Chicken 59
Flavorful Radish Salad 33
Flounder Filets with Parmesan Cheese 48
Flounder Fillets with Coconut Aminos 41
Fluffy Cocoa Cupcakes 84
Fresh Shrimp Balls 20
Fried Bacon with Pork Rinds 9
Fried Brussel Sprouts 36
Fried Leeks 38
G
Garlic Beef Cubes 73
Garlic Beef Meatloaf 70
Garlic Beef with Egg and Bell Pepper 76
Garlic Beef with Sauce 75
Garlic Brussel Sprouts with Celery 33
Garlic Butter Scallops with Lemon Zest 47
Garlic Chicken Strips 12
Garlic Chicken with Bacon 58
Garlic Lamb Rack 72
Garlic Mushroom Bites 20
Garlic Pork Roast 69
Garlic Provolone Asparagus 33
Garlic Scallops with Parsley 46
Garlic Tilapia Fillets 46
Garlic-Basil Turkey Breast 55
Garlicky Mushrooms with Parsley 29
Garlicky Rosemary Lamb Chops 68
Ginger Lemon Pie 88
Ginger-garlic Swordfish 45
Glazed Fillets 41
Glazed Meatloaf 72
Gorgeous Lamb Meatballs 77
Great Garlicky Pork Roast 76
Greek Sardines with Sauce 46
Greek Vegetable Mix 76
Green Bean Casserole 39
Green Beans with Parsley 33
Grilled Butter Sandwich 12
Grilled Cajun Chicken 57
Grilled Chicken Legs with Coconut Cream 55
Grilled Curried Chicken Wings 56
Grouper with Miso-Honey Sauce 46
H

Haddock Cakes 48
Halibut Soy Treat with Rice 41
Ham Cup 16
Ham Egg Cups 14
Ham Omelet 15
Hard-Boiled Eggs 13
Hawaiian Cheesy Meatball Sliders 79
Healthy Hot Salmon 46
Herb Air Fried Chicken Thighs 64
Herbed and Garlic Salmon Fillets 45
Herbed Chicken and Broccoli 60
Herbed Cornish Game Hens 61
Herbed Mushroom Pilau 33
Herbed Omelet 10
Herbed Potatoes Medley 31
Herbed Potatoes with Bacon 13
Herbs Chicken Drumsticks with Tamari
Sauce 55
Homemade Breaded Nugget in Doritos 64
Homemade Lobster Tails Ever 44
Homemade Steak 75
Honey Duck Breasts 62
Honey Mustard Meatballs 77
Honey Onions 37
Honey Turkey Tenderloin 59
Honey-Mustard Chicken Breasts 61
Honey-Mustard Duck Breasts 53
Hot Egg Cups 9
Hot Sauce Crab Dip 48

I
Indian Fish Fingers 51
Italian-style Honey Pork 72

J
Juicy Beef Meatballs 25

K
Kale and Eggplant Omelet 8
Kale Mushrooms Mix 38
Kale Olives Salad 38
Keto Crispy Pork Chops 76

L
Lamb Chops with Mustard Mixture 71
Lava Cakes 85
Lemon Almond Biscotti 89
Lemon Beef Schnitzel 73
Lemon Broccoli 36
Lemon Butter Bars 84
Lemon Butter Salmon 50
Lemon Cabbage with Cilantro 35
Lemon Cajun Cod 50
Lemon Chicken Drumsticks 62
Lemon Creamy Muffins 84
Lemon Fennel with Sunflower Seeds 33
Lemon Jumbo Scallops 47
Lemon Nut Bars 85
Lemon Peppermint Bars 88
Lemon Salmon Fillet 44
Lemon Tofu 25
Lemony Cabbage Slaw 33
Light and Airy Breaded Chicken Breasts 62
Liver Muffins 70

M
Maple Glazed Parsnips 36
Marinated Beef and Vegetable Stir Fry 71
Marinated Beef with BBQ Sauce 75
Marinated Chicken with Peppercorns 54
Marjoram Butter Chicken 58
Marjoram Chicken Drumsticks 56
Mashed Yams 39
Mayo Shrimp 48
Mayo Tortellini 19
Mayonnaise Chicken Drumettes with
Peppers 58
Mayonnaise Taco Chicken 55
McCormick Pork Chops 79
Meat Burger with Salad 68
Mediterranean Chicken Breasts with Roasted
Tomatoes 66
Mediterranean Fried Chicken 60
Mexican Beef Muffins with Tomato Sauce 22
Mild Shishito Peppers 25
Moist Cinnamon Muffins 86
Monkey Bread with Cinnamon 16
Montreal Steak 71
Morning Frittata 13
Moroccan-style Steak with Salad 72
Mouthwatering Squash Bites 19
Mozzarella Broccoli and Cauliflower 34
Mozzarella Chicken and Pork Muffins 10
Mozzarella Eggplant Gratin 35
Mozzarella Eggs with Basil Pesto 7
Mozzarella Rolls 11
Mozzarella Spinach Mash 35
Mushroom Mozzarella Risotto 31
Mushroom Risotto Croquettes 30
Mushroom Salad 13
Mushrooms Meatballs 79
Mushrooms Spread 14
Mushrooms with Sauce 27
Mustard Chicken Tenders 64
Mustard Pork Tenderloin 79

N
Nourishing Lamb with Potatoes 78

O
Old Bay Cod Fish Fillets 46
Olives and Eggs Medley 9
Olives Avocado Mix 39
Olives Fritters with Zucchinis 20
Olives Kale Salad 14
Olives, Green beans and Bacon 39
Onion Omelet 16
Open-faced Sandwich 34
Oregano Kale 39

P
Pancetta-Wrapped Scallops with Pancetta
Slices 47
Paprika Baked Tilapia 51
Paprika Pork Chops 73
Paprika Zucchini Spread 8
Parmesan Brussel Sprouts 39
Parmesan Cauliflower Dip 23

Parmesan Chicken Tenders 62
Parmesan Spinach Muffins 11
Parmesan Steak Nuggets 23
Parmesan Turkey Meatballs 58
Parmesan Zucchini Bites 26
Parmesan Zucchini Gratin 35
Parsley Cabbage 32
Pasta Shrimp 43
Peanut Butter Turkey Wings 53
Perfect Chicken Thighs 65
Perfectly Spiced Chicken Tenders 65
Pesto Gnocchi 16
Pickles with Egg Wash 21
Pineapple Chips with Cinnamon 86
Plum Almond Cake 89
Plum Apple Crumble with Cranberries 81
Pollock Fillets with Rosemary & Oregano 42
Pork Chops with Seasoning marinade 77
Pork Chops with Soy Sauce 71
Pork Curry 75
Pork Cutlets 69
Pork Meatballs 27
Pork Meatloaf with Onion 70
Pork Rinds with Keto Tomato Sauce 20
Pork Sausages with Mustard Sauce 73
Pork Tenderloin with Bell Pepper 69
Pork Tenderloins 75
Pork Tenderloins with Soy Sauce 68
Porterhouse Steak with Mustard and Butter 71
Potato Pastries 19
Potatoes with Bacon 23
Pretzel Crusted Chicken with Spicy Mustard
Sauce 65
Provolone Zucchini Balls 34
Pumpkin Almond Flour Muffins 81
Pungent Mushroom Pizza 30

Q
Quiche Cups 15

R
Radish Hash 38
Raspberries Bowls 13
Raspberries Cinnamon Oatmeal 14
Red Snapper with Hot Chili Paste 45
Roast Lamb with Rosemary 78
Roasted Bell Peppers 29
Roasted Chicken Thighs 64
Roasted Garlic Head 36
Roasted Garlic Ribeye with Mayo 71
Roasted Garlic Slices 37
Roasted Mushrooms 37
Roasted Nut Mixture 24
Roasted Pepper Salad with Pine Nuts 31
Roasted Turkey Thighs and Cauliflower 53
Roasted Turkey with Veggies 60
Rolled Turkey Breast 65
Rosemary Beans 27
Rosemary Chicken with Sweet Potatoes 57
Rosemary Salmon 44
Rutabaga Fries 35

S

Salmon Bites with Coconut 20
Salmon Bowl with Lime Drizzle 42
Salmon Burgers 44
Salmon Fillets 47
Salmon with Sweet Potato 41
Sausage and Potato Frittata 9
Savory Breaded Shrimp 50
Savoury Apple Pork Bites 78
Scones with Cream Cheese 85
Scotch Eggs 14
Scrambled Eggs 13
Scrambled Eggs with Spinach 7
Sea Bream Fillet with Tomato Sauce 43
Seasoned Cheese Sticks 16
Shirred Eggs 16
Shredded Cabbage 38
Shrimp Kabobs 25
Shrimp Rice Frittata 15
Shrimp with Parsley 44
Simple & Delicious Chicken Wings 59
Simple Air Fryer Steak 78
Simple and Tasty Hamburgers 74
Simple Apple Chips 22
Simple Cherry Tarts 10
Simple Chicken Burgers 54
Simple Donuts 85
Simple Eggplant Spread 9
Simple Fish Sticks 45
Simple Grilled Chicken 59
Simple Lemon Chicken Thighs 63
Simple Marinated Chicken Wings 65
Simple Meatballs 59
Simple Pizza Bites 22
Simple Pork Chops 73
Simple Rib-Eye Steak 75
Simple Strawberry Toast 15
Simple Tomato Cheese Sandwich 8
Smoked Almonds 26
Smoked White Fish 51
Southern Fried Chicken 61
Southwestern Prawns with Asparagus 48
Spanish-style Pork with Padrón Peppers 79
Spice Meatloaf 74
Spiced Apple Chips 82
Spiced Beef Chuck Roast 75
Spiced Cauliflower Medley 34
Spiced Chicken with Pork Rind 60
Spiced Duck Legs 58
Spiced Lamb Kebabs 74
Spiced Pork Chops 73
Spiced Rib Eye Steak 71
Spicy and Crispy Duck 55
Spicy Cocktail Wieners 23
Spicy Eggplant 37
Spicy Jumbo Shrimps 44
Spicy Pork Belly Pieces 70
Spicy Prawns 49
Spicy Salmon and Fennel Salad 43

Spicy Shrimp 49
Spicy Shrimp Kebab 51
Spicy Steak 76
Spinach Bacon Spread 11
Sprouts Wraps Appetizer 23
Squash Chips with Parmesan 22
Squash Chips with Sauce 19
Squash Fritters 13
Sriracha Chicken Thighs 61
St. Louis-style Pork Ribs with Roasted
Peppers 79
Steak Bites with Mushrooms 78
Steak Kabobs with Vegetables 74
Steak with Onion and Bell Peppers 71
Steamed Salmon with Sauce 50
Strawberries Coconut Oatmeal 13
Strawberry Muffins with Cinnamon 83
Stuffed Peppers 35
Stuffed Poblanos 15
Sunflower Bread 16
Sweet and Spicy Tofu 32
Sweet Cinnamon Donuts 87
Sweet Marinated Chicken Wings 53
Sweet Orange Muffins 83
Sweet Potato Fries 39
Sweet Potato Onion Mix 37
Sweet-Potato Chips 15
T
Tangy Cod Fillets 51
Tarragon Turkey Tenderloins with Baby
Potatoes 66
Tasty & Spicy Lamb 77
Tasty Anchovies and Cheese Wontons 46
Tasty Chicken Fajitas 57
Tasty Coconut Prawns 41
Tasty Juicy Salmon 44
Tasty Mozzarella Balls 86
Tasty Pasta Chicken 53
Tasty Shrimp Bacon Wraps 19
Tasty Spaghetti with Beef Meatballs 73
Tasty Spiced Tofu 34
Tasty Spinach Frittata 11
Tasty Sweet Potato Wedges 29
Tender Chicken with Parmesan Cheese 59
Tender Pork Ribs with BBQ Sauce 72
Teriyaki Pork 76
Teriyaki Steak 77
Teriyaki Wings 62
Thai Chicken Wings 25
Thai Coconut Fish 43
Thai Shrimp 50
Tilapia Fillets with Mayonnaise 41
Tofu Steaks 26
Tomato Rolls 34
Tomatoes Chard Salad 14
Tomatoes Hash with Cheddar Cheese 10
Trimmed Mackerel with Spring Onions 44
Tuna Onions Salad 14

Tuna Steak with Niçoise Salad 41
Turkey Breast with Fresh Herbs 61
Turkey Breasts 61
Turkey Casserole with Cheddar Cheese 8
Turkey Sausage Casserole 56
Turmeric Almond Pie 89
Turmeric Cauliflower Patties 32
Turmeric Cauliflower with Cilantro 32
Turmeric Chicken Cubes with Coriander 21
Turmeric Chicken Sticks 53
Turmeric Tofu Cubes 31
Typical Cod Nuggets 43
Typical Crab Cakes with Lemon Wedges 47
U
Unique Beef Cheeseburgers 73
V
Vanilla Banana Puffs 81
Vanilla Bars with Sesame Seeds 86
Vanilla Cheese Custard 86
Vanilla Cheesecake 82
Vanilla Coconut Pie 82
Vanilla Cookies 86
Vanilla Pineapple Cinnamon Treat 81
Vanilla Spread 86
Vanilla Yogurt Cake 88
Vegetable Kabobs 25
Vinegar Cake 87
Vinegar Cake 88
W
Walnut Banana Bread 17
Walnut Banana Split 85
Walnut Zucchini Bread 17
Week 1 4
Week 2 4
Week 3 5
Week 4 5
Western Chicken Wings 65
Whole Chicken 62
Wrapped Asparagus 37
Y
Yogurt Bread 22
Yogurt Eggs with Chives 7
Yogurt Treat with Berries 81
Yummy Apple Chips 84
Yummy Bagel Breakfast 8
Z
Za'atar Chives Chicken with Lemon Zest 61
Zucchini and Potato Polenta 31
Zucchini Bars with Cream Cheese 84
Zucchini Chips with Cheese 20
Zucchini Cubes 37
Zucchini Fritters 7
Zucchini Mix 13
Zucchini Tots with Mozzarella 30
Zucchini with Parmesan Cheese 24
Zucchinis and Arugula Salad 35